PRIMARY SOURCEBOOK SERIES

THE
HOLOCAUST

PRIMARY SOURCEBOOK SERIES

THE HOLOCAUST

Jeff Hill

Foreword by
Stephen C. Feinstein, Director
Center for Holocaust and Genocide Studies

Omnigraphics

615 Griswold, Detroit MI 48226

Omnigraphics, Inc.

Kevin Hillstrom, *Series Editor*
Cherie D. Abbey, *Managing Editor*

Peter E. Ruffner, *Publisher*
Frederick G. Ruffner, Jr., *Chairman*
Matthew P. Barbour, *Senior Vice President*

Kay Gill, *Vice President – Directories*
Elizabeth Barbour, *Research and Permissions Coordinator*
David P. Bianco, *Marketing Director*
Kevin Hayes, *Operations Manager*

Barry Puckett, *Librarian*
Cherry Stockdale, *Permissions Assistant*
Shirley Amore, Kevin Glover, Martha Johns, Kirk Kauffman, Angelesia Thorington, *Administrative Staff*

Copyright © 2006 Omnigraphics, Inc.
ISBN 0-7808-0935-1

Library of Congress Cataloging-in-Publication Data

Hill, Jeff.
  The Holocaust / Jeff Hill; foreword by Stephen C. Feinstein. — 1st ed.
     p. cm. — (Primary sourcebook series)
  Includes bibliographical references and index.
  ISBN 0-7808-0935-1 (hardcover : alk. paper) 1. Holocaust, Jewish (1939-1945) — Sources. I. Title.
  D804.19H55 2006
  940.53'18--dc22

                                                                        2006024128

The information in this publication was compiled from the sources cited and from other sources considered reliable. Additional copyright information can be found on the photograph credits page of this book. While every possible effort has been made to ensure reliability, the publisher will not assume liability for damages caused by inaccuracies in the data, and makes no warranty, express or implied, on the accuracy of the information contained herein.

This book is printed on acid-free paper meeting the ANSI Z39.48 Standard. The infinity symbol that appears above indicates that the paper in this book meets that standard.

Printed in the United States

TABLE OF CONTENTS

FOREWORD

Where did the idea for the mass murder of the Jews of Europe—what we now call the Holocaust—originate? Another puzzle is how Germany, one of the most technologically modern and culturally advanced countries in the world, could become the author of such a sustained campaign of mass murder—especially since Europe had experienced significant growth in social democratic principles and liberal institutions as recently as the end of the nineteenth century. The answers to these questions about the Holocaust are complex and troubling, even more than sixty years after the end of World War II. However, as the intelligently selected and arranged articles and documents of this volume illustrate, most of the elements that led to the Holocaust were in place by the end of the nineteenth century; they only needed someone to step forth and mold them together into a weapon of annihilation. That "someone" was Adolf Hitler, who perfected a vitriolic brand of political leadership based on hatred and racism. Supported by a compliant group of bureaucrats and functionaries, it was Hitler who breathed life into the Third Reich and transformed it into a machine of genocidal destruction.

Another question warrants consideration when one studies the Holocaust: how may one situate the mass murders of the Jews in relation to other events of mass violence and genocide in world history? While not the first genocide of the twentieth century, it was of such a great scale that Winston Churchill termed it "a crime without a name" as it was still unfolding. It was Raphael Lemkin, a legal scholar and refugee from Poland who eventually escaped to the United States, who invented the word "genocide," meaning "the killing of peoples," in 1943. But while Hitler's plan to exterminate the Jews was a genocidal campaign, a consensus emerged that a stronger word was necessary to describe the event. For better or worse, "Holocaust" ("Shoah" in Hebrew) became the designation of choice. There are indications that the term "Holocaust" (meaning "an offering totally burnt," as in sacrifices of ancient religions) may have been used as early as 1942, and today it is the most frequently employed term used to refer specifically to the Nazi extermination of the Jews.

Primary documents from the Holocaust are critical to any study of that dark era in world history. These documents provide us with greater understanding of this event because they give us the voices of both the victims and the perpetrators. Many voices of the victims of the Holocaust can be found in this collection of primary documents. Some of the most powerful can be found in the testimonials and reflections provided by Holocaust survivors and witnesses at the Nuremberg war crimes tribunal. While the memoirs of survivors were sometimes recorded long after the end of the Holocaust, the uniformity and precision of their stories underscores the wide scope of Nazi persecution. Survivors from far-flung lands who speak diverse languages—from those speaking English in the Channel Islands of the North Sea to the Russian Jews near the Volga River in the East—have produced an unsettling historical record of what the Nazis called the "final solution." The record is one of persecution on a country by country basis, and also one by one.

The voices of the perpetrators of the Holocaust are also well represented in this collection. The millions of pages of documents left by the Nazi bureaucracy provide what might be called the "smoking gun" for proving the intent of genocide. Many of the most damning of these documents are included in this volume, including several of Hitler's speeches and Hermann Göring's July 31, 1941, letter to Reinhold Heydrich authorizing the "complete solution" to the "Jewish question." Why did the Nazis produce so many documents of this sort? An answer probably lies in German bureaucratic traditions that go back to the eighteenth century. A structure was created where obedience to authority was instilled into the population from an early age. This environment proved fertile ground for the policies that the Nazis sought to institute across the Third Reich. The Nazi laws added intense negative propaganda that made immoral and illegal acts—now called crimes against humanity—the law of the land. Thus, we may ask, were those who carried out some of the most heinous crimes just following orders, or were they willing executioners? And does the distinction even matter, given the blood on their hands? When it came time for the post-war trials, the defense offered by those accused of war crimes and crimes against humanity was that no crime had been committed, since they were following orders based on German law. The legitimacy of that defense is still being debated by historians.

As the compendium of documents in this volume also indicates, the Holocaust was a secular event that happened in Christian Europe. Prior to the emancipation of the Jews that began at the end of the eighteenth century, the Jews were looked upon by European rulers and religious leaders as a people with a fallen faith that had yet to see the importance of Christ's message. Yet the European doctrine preached "tolerance," which meant a conditional acceptance of Jews in the hope that they might eventually undergo religious conversion. Thus, students of history are forced to confront the intolerance of a great religious leader like Martin Luther who first pointed to the Jews as a persecuted people. But later, when religious conversion failed, Luther published a polemic—"On Jews and Their Lies"—that appears, in light of the Holocaust, as a document that advocates genocide. It is indeed a troubling document, written in a tone that suggests the later writings of Nazi propagandists.

But National Socialism (the Nazi Party) was hardly Christian in its orientation, although its leaders appropriated some of the language of Christianity in their speeches and references. Rather, the philosophical underpinnings of National Socialism were based on race theory, which developed at the end of the nineteenth century partially as a replacement for the class-based concept of aristocracy that had been shaken by the French Revolution. Indeed, the racial theories espoused by writers like Joseph Arthur Comte de Gobineau and Houston Stewart Chamberlain can be seen as a means to create a new aristocracy based on race and managed through biological identification and segregation.

In looking at these documents, the Nazis' struggles to implement this system become clear. First one must recognize that the notion of racial purity embraced by the Nazis was a construction—and a fiction from a biological point of view. The Aryan laws passed by the Nazis in 1933 created discriminatory laws against Jews; however, the precise definition of a Jew was not even codified in the Third Reich until the passage of the Nuremberg Laws of 1935. Since the Nuremberg Laws defined Jews by race, even people of Jewish background who had earnestly accepted Christianity were still viewed by the Nazis as Jews, not Christians. Even then, with grandparentage being a critical element of racial identity, the Germans were still not certain about how to classify the half-Jews, or *Mishlinge*. Still, the Nazis forged ahead with their efforts to separate Jews from the other alleged dominant race, the Aryans, and before long the Yellow Star of David was a common sight on streets all across Germany.

The documents contained in this volume also help one understand the ways in which the anti-Semitism that existed in Germany during the first half of the twentieth century was different from other forms of anti-Semitism that had existed in Europe over the previous two thousand years. These earlier forms of bigotry had produced outbreaks of violence, but never the massive scale of murder that occurred at the hands of Nazi Germany and its collaborators. How did anti-Semitism in the Third Reich move beyond this familiar level of anti-Semitism to become a genocidal conflagration? The enclosed documents suggest that in the Third Reich during the period 1933-1945, the devil really was in the details.

Some writers and historians date the Holocaust as a general period of persecution from January 1933 until the end of the war in May 1945, but it seems reasonably clear that the Nazis themselves viewed forced emigration of Jews to other countries as a viable solution to the "Jewish question" until 1939. The major roadblock to this solution, which would have saved most of the Jews lost in the Holocaust from annihilation, was the failure of the outside world to effectively confront the anti-Semitic actions of the Nazis, either through diplomatic means, military force, or liberalized immigration policies. As a result, nations around the world deprived themselves of Jewish immigrants who could have made lasting contributions to their cultures in the spheres of science, business, and the arts (as Jewish people who managed to emigrate to the United States were able to do). Students might ponder these facts as they study current immigration issues facing the United States.

A question that often comes up in teaching about the Holocaust is "why didn't the victims resist more?" It's an understandable question, but it reflects an underappreciation of the totality of the Nazi "final solution" and the brutality with which it was implemented. As readers review this collection's contents, they might ponder the following questions: How could Jews and other victims of the Nazis' homicidal policies have understood in advance that the same Germans who had been viewed as a "civilized people"—and liberators during World War I campaigns in Eastern Europe—were turning into mass killers? How could the affected Jewish population, rounded up primarily in families and other small groups, have mounted significant violent resistance? How does one resist when the men, women, and children at your shoulder are among the frailest and most vulnerable members of your community? Finally, suggestions that Jews went meekly to their doom ignore events such as the Warsaw Ghetto uprising of 1943, wherein Jewish fighters held out against German forces for nearly a month—roughly the same span of time that Poland's army held out before surrendering to German invaders four years earlier.

Holocaust survivor and Nobel Peace Prize winner Elie Wiesel has said that "the study of the Holocaust provides questions, but no answers." We hope that he is wrong in this instance, and that this volume will provide many questions and answers for those who study this difficult subject.

Stephen C. Feinstein
Director, Center for Holocaust and Genocide Studies
University of Minnesota

PREFACE

The *Primary Sourcebook* Series has been created to provide students and other users with an overview of the most important and influential eras, events, and movements of the modern world. The *Series* seeks to meet this goal by assembling a wide cross-section of the most historic and illuminating primary documents on these subjects. Primary source materials featured in each volume of the *Series* include treaties, speeches, legislation, diplomatic dispatches, journalism, editorials, personal correspondence, government reports, memoirs, and oral histories.

The documents featured in each volume of *Primary Sourcebook Series* are supplemented by narrative features—chapter overviews and document-specific introductory pieces—that place each document within its historical context. This context is essential for readers to understand the full significance of these documents and competently interpret for themselves the meaning of the eras and events that shaped the world they live in today.

Arrangement of the Work

Primary Sourcebook Series: The Holocaust assembles 100 primary documents to help users gain a greater understanding of this terrible event in world history. These primary source materials are distributed among fifteen chapters, arranged roughly in chronological order. Each of these chapters, beginning with "The Roots of Anti-Semitism" and concluding with "Reflection and Remembrance," focuses on a specific topic or event within the larger historical period under discussion.

Each of these chapters begins with an introductory overview that provides readers with the background information they need to understand the significance of the documents selected for inclusion. In essence, these chapter overviews introduce the main players, events, and themes that will be illuminated in the documents to come.

Each chapter then moves on to the documents themselves. Every document featured in *The Holocaust* is preceded by a brief introduction that provides additional background on the origins and significance of that particular document. The documents themselves include source materials that are universally recognized as essential to any meaningful study of the Holocaust, as well as works that provide insight into the thoughts and emotions of Jewish people and others who became caught in the maelstrom of Nazi terror. For example, the volume's second chapter covers the rise of the Nazi Party in Germany in the 1930s; it includes both an excerpt from Adolf Hitler's *Mein Kampf* and a Holocaust survivor's recollection of a childhood darkened by the presence of Nazi "Brown Shirts" in his neighborhood.

Since each of the enclosed chapters focuses on a significant topic in its own right, the chapters have a user-friendly, stand-alone quality to them. Taken together, however, the chapters tell a much larger, but thoroughly coherent story. Strung together like historical beads, they can guide readers through the world's most momentous historical events.

Other valuable features included in *Primary Sourcebook Series: The Holocaust* include:

- Glossary of important Holocaust figures and terms.

- Detailed Chronology of events with a *see reference* feature. Under this arrangement, events listed in the chronology include page references to relevant primary documents featured in the book.

- Extensive bibliography of works consulted in the creation of this book, including books, periodicals, Internet sites, and videotape materials.

- A Subject Index.

Document Selection

In approaching historical subjects of great size and scope, it is impossible to assemble a truly comprehensive selection of primary documents in a single book. Inevitably, some worthwhile material is left out due to space constraints. What we set out to do, then, was to bring together a representative sampling of primary source materials that provides a framework for understanding the major political, social, and economic currents that shaped the era being studied. These source materials run the gamut from what might be termed "official views"—treaties, speeches, legislation, diplomatic dispatches, newspaper coverage, and doctrinal pronouncements—to documents that bring the "human" side of history to life, such as personal correspondence, memoirs, and oral histories. Blended together, these disparate materials form a fascinating narrative that can provide the basis for both lively, informed debate and somber reflection.

Similarly, excerpting a document is a delicate undertaking, for one never wishes to alter the meaning of the original source. In instances where we have chosen to publish excerpts instead of the full text of documents, we have taken care to excerpt representative sections of the featured document and to focus on the portions of text that are most relevant to Holocaust studies. All excerpts are clearly labeled as such.

In closing, we believe that the *Primary Sourcebook Series* will give readers a greater appreciation for the importance of history and its impact on their lives. It will also sharpen their capacity to analyze and interpret materials that often provide conflicting perspectives on major historical events, causes, and individuals. Finally, we hope that the series will motivate users to seek out even more information on the rich and fascinating tapestry of people, places, and events that have brought us to this point in our collective history.

Editor's Note: This volume includes quoted material containing deeply racist and offensive language and epithets. It also contains harrowing accounts of conditions in Nazi Germany and inside the Nazi death camps. We regret any pain or discomfort created by the inclusion of this material. We feel, however, that the inclusion of these documents will help users more fully understand the environment in which the Holocaust took place.

Acknowledgements

The editors would like to thank Holocaust scholar Stephen Feinstein for providing the foreword for this volume. Mr. Feinstein is Director of the Center for Holocaust and Genocide Studies at the University of Minnesota, Minneapolis.

This series was developed in consultation with a distinguished Advisory Board comprised of public librarians, school librarians, and educators. The editors would like to extend their appreciation to the following Board members:

Melissa C. Bergin, L.M.S., NBCT
Library Media Specialist
Niskayuna High School
Niskayuna, NY

Linda Garrett, M.L.I.S.
Librarian
Crestwood High School
Dearborn Heights, MI

Nancy Larsen, M.L.S., M.S. Ed.
Library Media Specialist
Clarkston High School
Clarkston, MI

Rosemary Orlando, M.L.I.S.
Library Director
St. Clair Shores Public Library
St. Clair Shores, MI

Comments and Suggestions

We welcome your comments on the *Primary Sourcebook Series,* including suggestions for topics that you would like to see covered in future volumes. Correspondence should be addressed to:

Editor, *Primary Sourcebook Series*
Omnigraphics, Inc.
615 Griswold
Detroit, MI 48226
E-mail: editorial@omnigraphics.com

THE
HOLOCAUST

THE HOLOCAUST

*Perhaps one cannot, what is more, one must not, understand what happened, because
to understand is almost to justify … "understanding" a proposal or human behavior
means to "contain" it, contain its author, put oneself in his place, identify with him.…
But there is no rationality in the Nazi hatred: it is a hate that is not in us; it is outside
man, it is a poison fruit sprung from the deadly trunk of Fascism, but it is outside and
beyond Fascism itself. We cannot understand it, but we can and must understand
from where it springs, and we must be on our guard. If understanding is impossible,
knowing is imperative, because what happened could happen again.*

—Primo Levi

When considering the Holocaust—the mass killing of Jews and
other groups in Europe by German leaders and their allies in the
late 1930s and early 1940s—most people express amazement
and incomprehension. How could the German government have
carried out the systematic murder of nearly six million people simply because of
their ethnic, cultural, and religious beliefs? How could such an atrocity have
unfolded in an era otherwise known for great worldwide advances in science, technology, and art? Why did it occur in one of the most technologically advanced
regions of the world?

The reality is that the Holocaust was caused by a collision of elements old and
new. It was in part a product of the two world wars that erupted in the twentieth
century—enormous conflicts fought with sophisticated technology that carried
wartime death and destruction to levels never before experienced. It also was nur-

1

tured by cultural and economic problems that buffeted German society in the late nineteenth and early twentieth centuries. The ideology that justified the murder of the Jews, though, can be traced much farther back in history. Anti-Semitism—hostility and discrimination against Jews—had been widespread in Europe since the Middle Ages, and it had migrated to most other parts of the world since that time.

While the term "Holocaust" is most commonly used to refer to the Nazi genocide against the Jews, some historians also apply it to Nazi attacks on other groups who were singled out because of their ethnic heritage, religious beliefs, nationality, sexual behavior, or disabilities. These included the Poles and other Slavic peoples, the Roma or Gypsies, Jehovah's Witnesses, homosexuals, and Germans suffering from mental or physical impairments.

The misfortune suffered by these groups at the hands of the Nazis was in no way insignificant. As many as three million Polish civilians (Jews and non-Jews combined) perished during the war, and the death toll for the Roma is estimated at between 220,000 and 500,000. The number of physically or mentally handicapped people who were murdered in the Third Reich's euthanasia programs, meanwhile, has been estimated at 200,000 or more. As Nazi forces spread across Europe, millions of other lives were destroyed as well. For example, an estimated three million Soviet prisoners of war died at the hands of the Nazis, either by execution, starvation, or other forms of maltreatment.

But the sheer number of Jews slain during the Nazis' genocidal reign—almost two-thirds of the estimated nine million Jews who lived in Europe in 1933—make them the focus of most Holocaust studies. In addition, the Nazi preoccupation with issues of race, heritage, and religion was focused on the Jewish population more strongly than any other group. The Nazis consciously pursued a policy of genocide against people of Jewish faith; their behavior toward other groups, by contrast, seemed to be less focused on total annihilation. For example, the Nazi leaders murdered many non-Jewish Poles, especially those that might serve as resistance leaders, but they did not attempt to destroy the entire Polish population. These considerations have led many historians to use the term "Holocaust" strictly in reference to the attempted Nazi extermination of Europe's Jewish population.

1

THE ROOTS OF ANTI-SEMITISM

Anti-Jewish pograms were commonplace in eastern Europe in the nineteenth century.
This painting portrays a Jewish family being expelled from eastern Roumelia,
a province in the Ottoman Empire that was annexed to Bulgaria in 1885.

INTRODUCTION

To understand the extreme anti-Jewish actions that took place in Germany in the 1930s and 1940s, one first needs to look at the prejudice that had been directed toward the followers of Judaism in previous centuries. For a large part of their history, the Jewish people have been dispersed among various kingdoms and nations (the term "Diaspora" is commonly used to refer to the spread of the Jewish people outside of Palestine and modern Israel). The Jews often came in conflict with the other inhabitants in the areas where they settled because they were a minority group with their own distinctive identity and religious beliefs. This was especially true after the rise of Christianity, which became the dominant religion in Europe beginning in the fourth century A.D.

The Jewish and Christian faiths have much in common. For instance, early Christians adopted the scriptures of the Torah or Hebrew Bible as their Old Testament. But historically, a great deal of animosity has existed between the faiths. The discord stems in large part from differences in core religious beliefs: Christians believe Jesus Christ to be the son of God and the Messiah foretold in the Old Testament; Jews do not. Other differences in religious teachings and doctrine also contributed to Christian hostility toward Jews. Anti-Semitic Christians had labeled Jews as "Christ-killers" because the Jewish population of Jerusalem plays a role in the biblical account of Jesus' final days. In the Middle Ages, some Christians even believed that Jews were in league with the devil. Sensational tales of Jews committing ritual murder and drinking the blood of non-Jewish children originated in this period. Calamities such as the Black Death were also blamed on the Judaic community.

Issues of economics played a part in the anti-Jewish attitudes of the Middle Ages as well. Some Jews became traders and merchants because they retained strong links to Jews in other cities and other kingdoms. Those Jewish business owners who prospered often earned the scorn of less affluent gentiles (non-Jews). Jews also worked as farmers and craftspeople, but over time prejudicial rules were adopted that prevented Jews from pursuing some of these jobs. Jews were barred from membership in craft guilds in many regions, for instance. Since some occupations were closed to them, European Jews turned to other career paths. For example, church decrees prevented Christians from charging interest on loans—what was often termed usury—but Jews faced no such religious prohibitions. As feudalism waned and early capitalism took root, financing became increasingly important in community development. Gentile resentment of Jewish moneylenders rose during this period, and the stereotype of the greedy, heartless banker was added to the other negative images of the Jew.

Anti-Jewish feelings often boiled over into violence. In 1096, when the first European crusaders set out to conquer the Christian holy sites in the Middle East, they began by targeting Jews who were living in Europe. Other pogroms (massacres of Jews) took place periodically throughout Europe in the Middle Ages. They were sometimes urged on by rulers who distrusted the Jews or who wished to vent public displeasure in a way that wouldn't threaten their power. A less deadly but more sweeping means of persecution against people of the Jewish faith occurred in 1290, when all of the Jews in England were expelled from the country. Other kingdoms followed suit, including France in 1306 and Spain in 1492. Prominent Christian religious leaders such as Martin Luther, the influential Protestant religious reformer from Germany, were among those at the forefront of anti-Jewish movements.

Though the violent pogroms were sporadic, Europe's Jews were nearly always treated as a people apart. Christians generally embraced a "Contra-Judeaos" tradition which did not urge *acceptance* of Jews, but rather *tolerance* of Jews until they might be redeemed through conversion to Christianity. Jews were not considered citizens of the countries where they lived, even if their families had resided there for many generations. Often they were forced to live in special Jewish areas known as ghettos and were not allowed to venture out of their neighborhoods after nightfall. In some places they were forced to wear the Star of David or some other form of badge that identified them as Jews. These forms of identification made it easier for non-Jews to spot and persecute Jews. These repressive measures kept many Jewish families mired in poverty, even though the stereotype of the rich Jew remained widespread.

The closed world of Europe's Jews began to open during the Enlightenment of the late 1700s and early 1800s. This was particularly true after the French Revolution, when liberal reforms were adopted in many parts of the continent. Restrictions on Jewish movement and activities were eased, and in certain areas Jews achieved legal equality with other citizens. They began to blend in with the wider society in which they lived, in some cases joining the middle class and moving out of ghetto areas where they had long been forced to reside. Some Jews became prosperous owners of large companies and others made their mark in the arts and in medicine.

Anti-Semitism in the Nineteenth Century

But prejudice against Jews persisted, even in this more enlightened environment. Pogroms remained common in Russia and other parts of eastern Europe until the early 1900s. In addition, the philosophy of Social Darwinism became prominent in the second half of the 1800s, and this concept would have an enormous influence on the people who would carry out the Holocaust a century later. According to this philosophy, some humans were more highly evolved and better adapted for survival than others. Some people embraced this theory of evolution to argue that entire races were genetically superior to others. Sometimes known as racialism or eugenics, this school of thought generally held that the "white" (European) race was superior to those who were of "yellow" (Asian) or "black" (African) descent. Among those promoting racialism was French writer Joseph Arthur Comte de Gobineau, who argued that a particular subgroup of whites—the so-called Aryan race—was the most highly developed of all.

Gobineau's ideas were later echoed by Houston Stewart Chamberlain, who applied the theory of racialism specifically to Germany in his book *The Foundations of the Nineteenth Century,* first published in 1899. In addition to praising the superior qualities of the Germanic or Teutonic people, Chamberlain decried the dangerous influence of the Jews, calling them an "alien race" that should take no role in the country's future. To many thinkers the idea of a separate Aryan race was absurd, but the concept had many supporters. For some, heredity or "blood" became an obsession, a pivotal factor in determining who was superior and desirable and who was inferior and dangerous.

A term for this virulent hatred of all Jews—"anti-Semitism"—was coined and popularized by German journalist Wilhelm Marr in 1879, when he published *The Way to Victory of Germanicism over Judaism.* In this work, Marr argued that the Germanic and Judaic peoples were locked in a struggle for survival that only one side could win. Using the term "anti-Semitism" as a euphemism for "Jew hate," he urged all Germans to become anti-Semites and forcibly remove all Jews from German territory.

7

In this poisonous atmosphere, the ancient characterization of the Jew as a devious figure plotting evil against the rest of humankind was given new life. One of the most sensational charges against the Judaic community involved a document entitled *Protocols of the Elders of Zion,* which surfaced in Russia in 1903 and was widely distributed throughout Europe and other parts of the world. In the United States, for example, automaker Henry Ford, who harbored strong anti-Semitic beliefs, published the document in both his Dearborn, Michigan, newspaper and in book form.

The *Protocols* were allegedly the minutes of a secret meeting in which Jews discussed an intricate and diabolical plan to "conquer the world for Zion." In reality, the document was a forgery. An unknown anti-Semitic author had created it by rewriting a nineteenth-century French political essay and inventing details of a sinister and secretive Jewish conspiracy. Nonetheless, many people accepted *Protocols of the Elders of Zion* as truth. It became well known in Germany during World War I, was later used by the Nazi leadership as "proof" of the Jewish threat, and continues to be cited by anti-Semitic groups as evidence of Jewish treachery.

DOCUMENTS

1.1
Anti-Semitism from a Christian Religious Leader—1543
Excerpt from "On Jews and Their Lies" by Martin Luther

A leader in the Protestant revolt against Roman Catholic authority, Martin Luther proved to be one of the most revolutionary Christian religious figures of the Middle Ages. Early in his career, Luther urged Christians to "deal gently" with their fellow Jewish citizens. But in the ensuing years his attitude changed considerably, eventually resulting in his 1543 work "On Jews and Their Lies." In this vicious polemic, Luther recites a long list of complaints against the Jewish people in a tone of bitter condemnation. In the process, he repeatedly characterizes people of the Jewish faith in stereotypical, hateful terms.

The Jews' most grievous sin, in Luther's opinion, is their refusal to accept Christ as the messiah and convert to the Christian cause he champions. Luther's proposed solution for Jewish "treachery" is to drive them out of the country through violence and ruthless anti-Semitic legislation. His call to burn homes and synagogues and to drive Jews from the land were not adopted in his German homeland during the 1500s. But it certainly reflected and furthered the discord between the followers of Christianity and Judaism in Europe—and much of his rhetoric was echoed four centuries later in Nazi Germany. Following are excerpts from Luther's pamphlet.

What shall we Christians do with this rejected and condemned people, the Jews? Since they live among us, we dare not tolerate their conduct, now that we are aware of their lying and reviling and blaspheming. If we do, we become sharers in their lies, cursing and blasphemy. Thus we cannot extinguish the unquenchable fire of divine wrath, of which the prophets speak, nor can we convert the Jews. With prayer and the fear of God we must practice a sharp mercy to see whether we might save at least a few from the glowing flames. We dare not avenge ourselves. Vengeance a thousand times worse than we could wish them already has them by the throat. I shall give you my sincere advice:

First, to set fire to their synagogues or schools and to bury and cover with dirt whatever will not burn, so that no man will ever again see a stone or cinder of them. This is to be done in honor of our Lord and of Christendom, so that God

From Luther's Works vol. 47, edited by Franklin Sherman © 1971 Fortress Press. Used by permission.

might see that we are Christians, and do not condone or knowingly tolerate such public lying, cursing, and blaspheming of his Son and of his Christians. For whatever we tolerated in the past unknowingly—and I myself was unaware of it—will be pardoned by God. But if we, now that we are informed, were to protect and shield such a house for the Jews, existing right before our very nose, in which they lie about, blaspheme, curse, vilify, and defame Christ and us (as was heard above), it would be the same as if we were doing all this and even worse ourselves, as we very well know.

> *"I advise that their houses also be razed and destroyed. For they pursue in them the same aims as in their synagogues.... I advise that their rabbis be forbidden to teach henceforth on pain of loss of life and limb."*

In Deuteronomy 13:12 Moses writes that any city that is given to idolatry shall be totally destroyed by fire, and nothing of it shall be preserved. If he were alive today, he would be the first to set fire to the synagogues and houses of the Jews. For in Deuteronomy 4:2 and 12:32 he commanded very explicitly that nothing is to be added to or subtracted from his law. And Samuel says in I Samuel 15:23 that disobedience to God is idolatry. Now the Jews' doctrine at present is nothing but the additions of the rabbis and the idolatry of disobedience, so that Moses has become entirely unknown among them (as we said before), just as the Bible became unknown under the papacy in our day. So also, for Moses' sake, their schools cannot be tolerated; they defame him just as much as they do us. It is not necessary that they have their own free churches for such idolatry.

Second, I advise that their houses also be razed and destroyed. For they pursue in them the same aims as in their synagogues. Instead they might be lodged under a roof or in a barn, like the gypsies. This will bring home to them the fact that they are not masters in our country, as they boast, but that they are living in exile and in captivity, as they incessantly wail and lament about us before God.

Third, I advise that all their prayer books and Talmudic writings, in which such idolatry, lies, cursing, and blasphemy are taught, be taken from them.

Fourth, I advise that their rabbis be forbidden to teach henceforth on pain of loss of life and limb. For they have justly forfeited the right to such an office by holding the poor Jews captive with the saying of Moses (Deuteronomy 17:10) in which he commands them to obey their teachers on penalty of death, although Moses clearly adds: "what they teach you in accord with the law of the Lord." Those villains ignore that. They wantonly employ the poor people's obedience contrary to the law of the Lord and infuse them with this poison, cursing, and blasphemy. In the same way the pope also held us captive with the declaration in Matthew 16:18, "You are Peter," etc., inducing us to believe all the lies and deceptions that issued from his devilish mind. He did not teach in accord with the word of God, and therefore he forfeited the right to teach.

Fifth, I advise that safe-conduct on the highways be abolished completely for the Jews. For they have no business in the countryside, since they are not lords, officials, tradesmen, or the like. Let them stay at home. I have heard it said that a rich Jew is now traveling across the country with twelve horses—his ambition is to become a Kokhba—devouring princes, lords, lands, and people with his usury, so that the great lords view it with jealous eyes. If you great lords and princes will not forbid such usurers the highway legally, some day a troop may gather against them, having learned from this booklet the true nature of the Jews and how one should deal with them and not protect their activities. For you, too, must not and cannot protect them unless you wish to become participants in their abominations in the sight of God. Consider carefully what good could come from this, and prevent it.

Sixth, I advise that usury be prohibited to them, and that all cash and treasure of silver and gold be taken from them and put aside for safekeeping. The reason for such a measure is that, as said above, they have no other means of earning a livelihood than usury, and by it they have stolen and robbed from us all they possess. Such money should now be used in no other way than the following: Whenever a Jew is sincerely converted, he should be handed one hundred, two hundred, or three hundred florins, as personal circumstances may suggest. With this he could set himself up in some occupation for the support of his poor wife and children, and the maintenance of the old or feeble. For such evil gains are cursed if they are not put to use with God's blessing in a good and worthy cause.

But when they boast that Moses allowed or commanded them to exact usury from strangers, citing Deuteronomy 23:20—apart from this they cannot adduce as much as a letter in their support—we must tell them that there are two classes of Jews or Israelites. The first comprises those whom Moses, in compliance with God's command, led from Egypt into the land of Canaan. To them he issued his law, which they were to keep in that country and not beyond it, and then only until the advent of the Messiah. The other Jews are those of the emperor and not of Moses. These date back to the time of Pilate, the procurator of the land of Judah. For when the latter asked them before the judgment seat, "Then what shall I do with Jesus who is called Christ?" they all said, "Crucify him, crucify him!" He said to them, "Shall I crucify your King?" They shouted in reply, "We have no king but Caesar!" (Matt. 27:22; John 19:15). God had not commanded of them such submission to the emperor; they gave it voluntarily....

Seventh, I recommend putting a flail, an ax, a hoe, a spade, a distaff, or a spindle into the hands of young, strong Jews and Jewesses and letting them earn their bread in the sweat of their brow, as was imposed on the children of Adam (Gen. 3:19). For it is not fitting that they should let us accursed Goyim toil in the sweat of our faces while they, the holy people, idle away their time behind the stove, feasting and farting, and on top of all, boasting blasphemously of their lordship over the Christians by means of our sweat. No, one should toss out these lazy rogues by the seat of their pants.

But if we are afraid that they might harm us or our wives, children, servants, cattle, etc., if they had to serve and work for us—for it is reasonable to assume that such noble lords of the world and venomous, bitter worms are not accustomed to working and would be very reluctant to humble themselves so deeply before the accursed Goyim—then let us emulate the common sense of other nations such as France, Spain, Bohemia, etc., compute with them how much their usury has extorted from us, divide, divide this amicably, but then eject them forever from the country. For, as we have heard, God's anger with them is so intense that gentle mercy will only tend to make them worse and worse, while sharp mercy will reform them but little. Therefore, in any case, away with them!

I hear it said that the Jews donate large sums of money and thus prove beneficial to governments. Yes, but where does this money come from? Not from their own possessions but from that of the lords and subjects whom they plunder and rob by means of usury. Thus the lords are taking from their subjects what they receive from the Jews, i.e., the subjects are obliged to pay additional taxes and let themselves be ground into the dust for the Jews, so that they may remain in the country, lie boldly and freely, blaspheme, curse, and steal. Shouldn't the impious Jews laugh up their sleeves because we let them make such fools of us and because we spend our money to enable them to remain in the country and to practice every malice? Over and above that we let them get rich on our sweat and blood, while we remain poor and they suck the marrow from our bones. If it is right for a servant to give his master or for a guest to give his host ten florins annually and, in return, to steal one thousand florins from him, then the servant or the guest will very quickly and easily get rich and the master or the host will soon become a beggar.

And even if the Jews could give the government such sums of money from their own property, which is not possible, and thereby buy protection from us, and the privilege publicly and freely to slander, blaspheme, villify, and curse our Lord Jesus Christ so shamefully in their synagogues, and in addition to wish us every misfortune, namely, that we might all be stabbed to death and perish with our Haman, emperor, princes, lords, wife, and children—this would really be selling Christ our Lord, the whole of Christendom together with the whole empire, and ourselves, with wife and children, cheaply and shamefully. What a great saint the traitor Judas would be in comparison with us! Indeed, if each Jew, as many as there are of them, could give one hundred thousand florins annually, we should nevertheless not yield them for this the right so freely to malign, curse, defame, impoverish by usury a single Christian. That would still be far too cheap a price. How much more intolerable is it that we permit the Jews to purchase with our money such license to slander and curse the whole Christ and all of us and, furthermore, reward them for this with riches and make them our lords, while they ridicule us and gloat in their malice. That would prove a delightful spectacle for the devil and his angels, over which they could secretly grin like a sow grins at her litter, but which would indeed merit God's great wrath.

In brief, dear princes and lords, those of you who have Jews under your rule: if my counsel does not please you, find better advice, so that you and we all can be rid of the unbearable, devilish burden of the Jews. Lest we become guilty sharers before God in the lies, the blasphemy, the defamation, and the curses which the mad Jews indulge in so freely and wantonly against the person of our Lord Jesus Christ, his dear mother, all Christians, all authority, and ourselves. Do not grant them protection, safe-conduct, or communion with us. Do not aid and abet them in acquiring your money or your subjects' money and property by means of usury. We have enough sin of our own without this, dating back to the papacy, and we add to it daily with our ingratitude and our contempt of God's word and all his grace; so it is not necessary to burden ourselves also with these alien, shameful vices of the Jews and over and above it all, to pay them for it with money and property. Let us consider that we are now daily struggling with the Turks, which surely calls for a lessening of our sins and a reformation of our life. With this faithful counsel and warning I wish to cleanse and exonerate my conscience.

And you, my dear gentlemen and friends who are pastors and preachers, I wish to remind very faithfully of your official duty, so that you too may warn your parishioners concerning their eternal harm, as you know how to do, namely, that they be on their guard against the Jews and avoid them so far as possible. They should not curse them or harm their persons, however. For the Jews have cursed and harmed themselves more than enough by cursing the Man Jesus of Nazareth, Mary's son, which they unfortunately have been doing for over fourteen hundred years. Let the government deal with them in this respect, as I have suggested. But whether the government acts or not, let everyone at least be guided by his own conscience and form for himself a definition or image of a Jew.

When you lay eyes on or think of a Jew you must say to your self: Alas, that mouth which I there behold has cursed and execrated and maligned every Saturday my dear Lord Jesus Christ, who has redeemed me with his precious blood; in addition, it prayed and pleaded before God that I, my wife and children, and all Christians might be stabbed to death and perish miserably. And he himself would gladly do this if he were able, in order to appropriate our goods. Perhaps he has spat on the ground many times this very day over the name of Jesus, as is their custom, so that the spittle still clings to his mouth and beard, if he had a chance to spit. If I were to eat, drink or talk with such a devilish mouth, I would eat or drink myself full of devils by the dish or cupful just as I surely make myself a cohort of all the devils that dwell in the Jews and that deride the precious blood of Christ. May God preserve me from this!

We cannot help it that they do not share our belief. It is impossible to force anyone to believe. However, we must avoid confirming them in their wanton lying, slandering, cursing, and defaming. Nor dare we make ourselves partners in their devilish ranting and raving by shielding and protecting them, by giving them food, drink, and shelter, or by other neighborly acts, especially since they boast so proudly and despicably when we do help and serve them that God has ordained them as lords and us as servants. For instance, when a Christian kindles their fire for them on a Sabbath, or cooks for them in an inn whatever they want, they curse and defame and revile us for it, supposing this to be something praiseworthy, and yet they live on our wealth, which they have stolen from us. Such a desperate, thoroughly evil, poisonous, and devilish lot are these Jews, who for these fourteen hundred years have been and still are our plague, our pestilence, and our misfortune....

But what will happen even if we do burn down the Jews' synagogues and forbid them publicly to praise God, to pray, to teach, to utter God's name? They will still keep doing it in secret. If we know that they are doing this in secret, it is the same as if they were doing it publicly. For our knowledge of their secret doings and our toleration of them implies that they are not secret after all, and thus our conscience is encumbered with it before God. So let us beware. In my opinion the problem must be resolved thus: If we wish to wash our hands of the Jews' blasphemy and not share in their guilt, we have to part company with them. They must be driven from our country. Let them think of their fatherland; then they need no longer wail and lie before God against us that we are holding them captive, nor need we then any longer complain that they are burdening us with their blasphemy and their usury. This is the most natural and the best course of action, which will safe guard the interest of both parties....

If I had power over the Jews, as our princes and cities have, I would deal severely with their lying mouth. They have one lie with which they work great harm among their children and their common folk and with which they slander our faith so shamefully: namely, they accuse us and slander us among their people, declaring that we Christians worship more than one God. Here they vaunt and pride themselves without measure. They beguile their people with the claim that they are the only people, in contrast to the Gentiles, who worship no more than one God. Oh, how cocksure they are about this!

Even though they are aware that they are doing us an injustice and are lying on this point as malicious and wicked scoundrels, even though they have heard for fifteen hundred years, and still hear, that any of us Christians disavow this, they still stuff their ears shut like serpents and deliberately refuse to hear us, but rather insist that their venomous lies about us must be accepted by their people as the truth. This they do even though they read in our writings that we agree with Moses' words in Deuteronomy 6:4: "Hear, O Israel, the Lord our God is one God," and that we confess, publicly and privately, with our hearts, tongues and writings, our life and our death, that there is but one God, of whom Moses writes here and whom the Jews themselves call upon. I say, even if they know this and have heard and read it about us for almost fifteen hundred years, it is of no avail; their lies must still stand, and we Christians have to tolerate their slander that we worship many gods....

I wish and I ask that our rulers who have Jewish subjects exercise a sharp mercy toward these wretched people, as suggested above, to see whether this might not help (though it is doubtful). They must act like a good physician who, when gangrene has set proceeds without mercy to cut, saw, and burn flesh, veins, bone, and marrow. Such a procedure must also be followed in this instance. Burn down their synagogues, forbid all that I enumerated earlier, force them to work, and deal harshly with them, as Moses did in the wilderness, slaying three thousand lest the whole people perish. They surely do not know what they are doing; moreover, as people possessed, they do not wish to know it, hear it, or learn it. Therefore it would be wrong to be merciful and confirm them in their conduct. If this does not help we must drive them out like mad dogs, so that we do not become partakers of their abominable blasphemy and all their other vices and thus merit God's wrath and be damned with them. I have done my duty. Now let everyone see to his. I am exonerated.

Source: Luther, Martin. "On Jews and Their Lies." Reprinted in *Luther's Works.* Vol. 47: *The Christian in Society IV.* Edited by Franklin Sherman. Translated by Martin H. Bertram. Philadelphia: Fortress Press, 1971.

1.2
Arguing the Superiority of the "Aryan" Race – 1853
Excerpt from The Moral and Intellectual Diversity of Races *by Joseph Arthur Comte de Gobineau*

Joseph Arthur Comte de Gobineau, the scion of a wealthy French family that opposed the liberal reforms of the French Revolution, was one of the most influential figures of the nineteenth century to argue that race is the basis of human culture and society. In the following passage he touches on several points that were key to his theory of racialism. First, he asserts that there are three "primary" groups that compose the human population—"white," "black," and "yellow"—and that the whites are genetically superior to the others. In addition, Gobineau argues that civilizations decline when racial groups mix with one another, especially when whites have children with members of the other groups. Finally, he claims that a particular segment of the white population—the so-called Arian or Aryan race—is the source of mankind's highest cultural accomplishments and most advanced civilizations.

All of these ideas would later be adopted by Adolf Hitler and other Nazi leaders. The Third Reich also embraced another of Gobineau's theories— that the Jews were among the lowest members of the human family because they were created by intermixing all three primary groups. It should be remembered that Gobineau's ideas were essentially a quasi-scientific means of promoting white supremacy and that his theories were dismissed by other ethnologists in his day and by a long line of anthropologists in later decades. Nonetheless, theories of this kind would attract many followers in the late nineteenth and early twentieth centuries and they persist among racist individuals and groups today.

In the preceding pages, I have endeavored to show that, though there are both scientific and religious reasons for not believing in a plurality of origins of our species, the various branches of the human family are distinguished by permanent and irradicable differences, both mentally and physically. They are unequal in intellectual capacity, in personal beauty, and in physical strength. Again I repeat, that in coming to this conclusion, I have totally eschewed the method which is, unfortunately for the cause of science, too often resorted to by ethnologists, and by which, to say the least of it, is simply ridiculous. The discussion has not rested upon the moral and intellectual worth of isolated individuals.

With regard to moral worth, I have proved that all men, to whatever race they may belong, are capable of receiving the lights of true religion, and of sufficiently appreciating that blessing to work out their own salvation. With regard to intellectual capacity, I must emphatically protest against that mode of arguing which consists in saying, "every negro is a dunce;" because, by the same logic, I should be compelled to admit that "every white man is intelligent;" and I shall take good care to commit no such absurdity.

I shall not even wait for the vindicators of the absolute equality of all races, to adduce to me such and such passage in some missionary's or navigator's journal, wherefrom it appears that some Yolof has become a skilled carpenter, that some Hottentot has made an excellent domestic, that some Caffre plays well on the violin, or that some Bambarra has made very respectable progress in arithmetic.

I am prepared to admit—and to admit without proof—anything of that sort, however remarkable, that may be related of the most degraded savages. I have already denied the excessive stupidity, the incurable idiocy of even the lowest on the scale of humanity. Nay I go further than my opponents, and am not in the least disposed to doubt that, among the chiefs of the rude negroes of Africa, there could be found a considerable number of active and vigorous minds, greatly surpassing in fertility of ideas and mental resources, the average of our peasantry, and even of some of our middle class. But the unfairness of deductions based upon a comparison of the most intelligent blacks and the least intelligent whites, must be obvious to every candid mind....

After having mentioned the facts which prove the inequality of various branches of the human family, and having laid down the method by which that proof should be established, I arrived at the conclusion that the whole of our species is divisible into three great groups, which I call primary varieties, in order to distinguish them from others formed by intermixture. It now remains for me to assign each of these groups the principal characteristics by which it is distinguished from the others.

The dark races are the lowest on the scale. The shape of the pelvis has a character of animalism, which is imprinted on the individuals of that race ere their birth, and seems to portend their destiny. The circle of intellectual development of that group is more contracted than that of either of the two others.

If the negro's narrow and receding forehead seems to mark him as inferior in reasoning capacity, other portions of his cranium as decidedly point to faculties of an humbler, but not the less powerful character. He has energies of a not despicable order, and which sometimes display themselves with an intensity truly formidable. He is capable of violent passions, and passionate attachments. Some of his senses have an acuteness unknown to the other races: the sense of taste, and that of smell, for instance.

But it is precisely this development of the animal faculties that stamps the negro with the mark of inferiority to other races. I said that his sense of taste was acute; it is by no means fastidious. Every sort of food is welcome to his palate; none disgusts him; there is no flesh nor fowl too vile to find a place in his stomach. So it is with regard to odor. His sense of smell might rather be called greedy than acute. He easily accommodates himself to the most repulsive.

To these traits he joins a childish instability of humor. His feelings are intense, but not enduring. His grief is as transitory as it is poignant, and he rapidly passes from it to extreme gayety. He is seldom vindictive—his anger is violent, but soon appeased. It might almost be said that this variability of sentiments annihilates for him the existence of both virtue and vice. The very ardency with which his sensibilities are aroused, implies a speedy subsidence; the intensity of his desire, a prompt gratification, easily forgotten. He does not cling to life with the tenacity of the whites. But moderately careful of his own, he easily sacrifices that of others, and kills, though not absolutely bloodthirsty, without much provocation or subsequent remorse. Under intense suffering he exhibits a moral cowardice which readily seeks refuge in death, or in a sort of monstrous impassivity.

With regard to his moral capacities, it may be stated that he is susceptible, in an eminent degree, of religious emotions; but unless assisted by the light of the Gospel, his religious sentiments are of a decidedly sensual character.

Having demonstrated the little intellectual and strongly sensual character of the black variety, as the type of which I have taken the negro of Western Africa, I shall now proceed to examine the moral and intellectual characteristics of the second in the scale—the yellow.

This seems to form the complete antithesis to the former. In them, the skull, instead of being thrown backward, projects. The forehead is large, often jutting out, and of respectable height. The facial conformation is somewhat triangular, but neither the chin nor nose has the rude, animalish development that characterizes the negro. A tendency to obesity is not precisely a specific feature, but it is more often met with among the yellow races than among any others. In muscular vigor, in intensity of feelings and desires, they are greatly inferior to the black. They are supple and agile, but not strong. They have decided taste for sensual pleasures, but their sensuality is less violent, and, if I may so call it, more vicious than the negro's, and less quickly appeased. They place a somewhat greater value on human life than the negro does, but they are more cruel for the sake of cruelty. They are as gluttonous as the negro, but more fastidious in their choice of viands, as is proved by the immoderate attention bestowed on the culinary art among the more civilized of these races. In other words, the yellow races are less impulsive than the black. Their will is characterized by obstinacy rather than energetic violence; their anger is vindictive rather than clamorous; their cruelty more studied than passionate; their sensuality more refinedly vicious than absorbing. They are, therefore, seldom prone to extremes. In morals, as in intellect, they display a mediocrity: they are given to groveling vices rather than to dark crimes; when virtuous, they are so oftener from a sense of practical usefulness than from exalted sentiments. In regard to intellectual capacity, they easily understand whatever is not very profound, nor very sublime; they have a keen appreciation of the useful and practical, a great love of quiet and order, and even a certain conception of a slight modicum of personal or municipal liberty. The yellow races are practical people in the narrowest sense of the word. They have little scope of imagination, and therefore invent but little: for great inventions, even the most exclusively utilitarian, require a high degree of the imaginative faculty. But they easily understand and adopt whatever is of practical utility. The *summum bonum* of their desires and aspiration is to pass smoothly and quietly through life.

It is apparent from this sketch that they are superior to the blacks in aptitude and intellectual capacity. A theorist who would form some model society, might wish such a population to form the substratum upon which to erect his structure; but a society, composed entirely of such elements, would display neither great stamina not capacity or anything great and exalted.

We are now arrived at the third and last of the "primary" varieties—the white. Among them we find great physical vigor and capacity of endurance; an intensity of will and desire, but which is balanced and governed by the intellectual faculties. Great things are undertaken, but not blindly, not without a full appreciation of the obstacles to be overcome, and with a systematic effort to overcome them. The utilitarian tendency is strong, but is united with a powerful imaginative faculty, which elevates, ennobles, idealizes it. Hence, the power of invention; while the negro can merely imitate, the Chinese only utilize, to a certain extent, the practical results attained by the white, the latter is continually adding new ones to those already gained. His capacity for the combination of ideas leads him perpetually to construct new facts from fragments of the old; hurries him along through a series of unceasing modifications and changes. He has as keen a sense of order as the man of the yellow race, but not, like him, from love of repose and inertia, but from a desire to protect and preserve his acquisitions. At the same time, he has an ardent love of liberty, which is often carried to an extreme; an instinctive aversion to the trammels of that rigidly formalistic organization under which the Chinese vegetates with luxurious ease; and he as indignantly rejects the haughty despotism which alone proves a sufficient restraint for the black races.

The white man is also characterized by a singular love of life. Perhaps it is because he knows better how to make use of it than other races, that he attaches to it greater value and spares it more both in himself and in others. In the extreme of his cruelty, he is conscious of his excesses; a sentiment which it may well be doubted whether it exists among the blacks. Yet though he loves life better than other races, he has discovered a number of reasons for sacrificing it or laying it down without murmur. His valor, his bravery, are not brute, unthinking passions, not the result of callousness or impassivity: they spring from exalted, though often erroneous, sentiments, the principal of which is expressed by the word "honor." This feeling, under a variety of names and applications, has formed the mainspring of action of most of the white races since the beginning of historical times. It accommodates itself to every mode of existence, every walk of life. It is as puissant in the pulpit and at the martyr's stake, as on the field of battle; in the most peaceful and humble pursuits of life as in the highest and most stirring. It were impossible to define all the ideas this word comprises; they are better felt than expressed. But this feeling—we might call it instinctive—is unknown to the yellow, and unknown to the black races: while in the white it quickens every noble sentiment—the sense of justice, liberty, patriotism, love, religion—it has no name in the language, no place in the hearts, of other races. This I consider as the principal reason of the superiority of our branch of the human family over all others; because even in the lowest, the most debased of our race, we generally find some spark of this redeeming trait, and however misapplied it may often be, and certainly is, it prevents us, even in our deepest errors, from falling so fearfully low as the others. The extent of moral abasement in which we find so many of the yellow and black races is absolutely impossible even to the very refuse of our society. The latter may equal, nay, surpass them in crime; but even they would shudder at that hideous abyss of corrosive vices, which opens before the friend of humanity on a closer study of these races.

Before concluding this picture, I would add that the immense superiority of the white races in all that regards the intellectual faculties, is joined to an inferiority as strikingly marked, in the intensity of sensations. Though his whole structure is more vigorous, the white man is less gifted in regard to the perfection of the senses than either the black or the yellow, and therefore less solicited and less absorbed animal gratifications.

I have now arrived at the historical portion of my subject. There I shall place the truths enounced in this volume in a clearer light, and furnish irrefragable proofs of the fact, which forms the basis of my theory, that nations degenerate only in consequence and in proportion to their admixture with an inferior race—that a society receives its death-blow when, from the number of diverse ethnical elements which it comprises, a number of diverse modes of thinking and interests contend for predominance; when these modes of thinking, and these interests have arisen in such multiplicity that every effort to harmonize them, to make them subservient to some great purpose, is in vain; when, therefore, the only natural ties that can bind large masses of men, homogeneity of thoughts and feelings, are severed, the only solid foundation of a social structure sapped and rotten.

To furnish the necessary details for this assertion, to remove the possibility of even the slightest doubt, I shall take up separately, every great and independent civilization that the world has seen flourish…. Here, then, is the proper test of my theory; here we can see the laws that govern ethical relations in full force on a magnificent scale;….

We shall find every civilization owes its origin, its development, its splendors to the agency of the white races. In China and in India, in the vast continent of the West, centuries ere Columbus found it—it was one of the group of white races that gave the impetus, and, so long as it lasted, sustained it…. Everywhere the white races have taken the initiative, everywhere they have *brought* civilization to others—everywhere they have sown the seed: the vigor and beauty of the plant depended on whether the soil found it was congenial or not….

Source: De Gobineau, A. *The Moral and Intellectual Diversity of Races, with Particular Reference to Their Respective Influence in the Civil and Political History of Mankind.* Philadelphia: J. B. Lippincott, 1856.

1.3
Racist Theory on Aryans and Jews – 1899
Excerpt from The Foundations of the Nineteenth Century *by Houston Stewart Chamberlain*

Houston Stewart Chamberlain was a British-born historian and race theorist who later emigrated to Germany. Building upon the theories of Joseph Arthur Comte de Gobineau, Chamberlain wrote The Foundations of the Nineteenth Century (1899), *which proclaimed the superiority of the Aryan people and criticized the Jews as a negative force in the development of Europe. These ideas, combined with the fact that Chamberlain focused specifically on Germany, made his book a touchstone for those who would take charge of the Nazi Party. (Before his death, Chamberlain became a supporter of Hitler and the National Socialist Party.) Widely read in Germany, the book helped to popularize the ideas of nationalism and racialism among the German public, especially in the years leading up to World War I. In the following excerpt from his study, Chamberlain discusses the Jews as a separate and "alien" force in Europe. He is careful to define the Jews as a "nation" in addition to being a religious group. This idea was seized on by Hitler to support the idea that Jews in German territory were hostile foreigners that must be banished.*

THE JEWISH QUESTION

Had I been writing a hundred years ago, I should hardly have felt compelled at this point to devote a special chapter to the entrance of the Jews into Western history. Of course the share they had in the rise of Christianity, on account of the peculiar and absolutely un-Aryan spirit which they instilled into it, would have deserved our full attention, as well as also the economic part which they played in all Christian countries; but an occasional mention of these things would have sufficed; anything more would have been superfluous. [Johann Gottfried von] Herder wrote at that time [in *Von den deutsch-orientalischen Dichtern*, Div. 2]: "Jewish history takes up more room in our history and more attention than it probably deserves in itself." In the meantime, however, a great change has taken place: the Jews play in Europe, and wherever European influence extends, a different part to-day from that which they played a hundred years ago; as Viktor Hehn expresses it [in *Gedanken über Goethe*, 3rd ed. p. 40], we live to-day in a "Jewish age"; we may think what we like about the past history of the Jews, their present history actually takes up so much room in our own history that we cannot possibly refuse to notice them. Herder in spite of his outspoken humanism had expressed the opinion [in *Bekehrung der Juden.* Abschnitt 7 of the *Untersuchungen des vergangenen Jahrhunderts zur Beförderung eines geistigen Reiches*] that "the Jewish people is and remains in Europe an Asiatic people alien to our part of the world, bound to that old law which it received in a distant climate, and which according to its own confession it cannot do away with." Quite correct. But this alien people, everlastingly alien, because—as Herder well remarks—it is indissolubly bound to an alien law that is hostile to all other peoples—this alien people has become precisely in the course of the nineteenth century a disproportionately important and in many spheres actually dominant constituent of our life. Even a hundred years ago that same witness had sadly to confess that the "ruder nations of Europe" were "willing slaves of Jewish usury"; to-day he could say the same of by far the greatest part of the civilised world. The possession of money in itself is, however, of least account; our governments, our law, our science, our commerce, our literature, our art … practically all branches of our life have become more or less willing slaves of the Jews, and drag the feudal fetter if not yet on two, at least on one leg. In the meantime the "alien" element emphasised by Herder has become more and more prominent; a hundred years ago it was rather indistinctly and vaguely felt; now it has asserted and proved itself, and so forced itself on the attention of even the most inattentive. The Indo-European, moved by ideal motives, opened the gates in friendship: the Jew rushed in like an enemy, stormed all positions and planted the flag of his, to us, alien nature—I will not say on the ruins, but on the breaches of our genuine individuality.

> *"The Indo-European …opened the gates in friendship: the Jew rushed in like an enemy, stormed all positions and planted the flag of his, to us, alien nature—I will not say on the ruins, but on the breaches of our genuine individuality."*

Are we for that reason to revile the Jews? That would be as ignoble as it is unworthy and senseless. The Jews deserve admiration, for they have acted with absolute consistency according to the logic and truth of their own individuality, and never for a moment have they allowed themselves to forget the sacredness of physical laws because of foolish humanitarian day-dreams which they shared only when such a policy was to their advantage. Consider with what mastery they use the law of blood to extend their power: the principal stem remains spotless, not a drop of strange blood comes in; as it stands in the *Thora,* "A bastard shall not enter into the congregation of the Lord; even to his tenth generation shall he not enter into the congregation of the Lord" (*Deuteronomy* xxiii. 2); in the meantime, however, thousands of side branches are cut off and employed to infect the Indo-Europeans with Jewish blood. If that were to go on for a few centuries, there would be in Europe only one single people of pure race, that of the Jews, all the rest would be a herd of pseudo-Hebraic mestizos, a people beyond all doubt degenerate physically, mentally and morally…. That mixture then undoubtedly signifies a degeneration: degeneration of the Jew, whose character is much too alien, firm and strong to be quickened and ennobled by Teutonic blood, degeneration of the European who can naturally only lose by crossing with an "inferior type"—or, as I should prefer to say, with so different a type. While the mixture is taking place, the great chief stem of the pure unmixed Jews remains unimpaired. When Napoleon, at the beginning of the nineteenth century, dissatisfied that the Jews, in spite of their emancipation, should remain in proud isolation, angry with them for continuing to devour with their shameful usury the whole of his Alsace, although every career was now open to them, sent an ultimatum to the council of their elders demanding the unreserved fusion of the Jews with the rest of the nation—the delegates of the French Jews adopted all the articles prescribed but one, namely, that which aimed at absolute freedom of marriage with Christians. Their daughters might marry outside the Israelite people, but not their sons; the dictator of Europe had to yield. This is the admirable law by which real Judaism was founded. Indeed, the law in its strictest form forbids marriage altogether between Jews and non-Jews; in *Deuteronomy* vii. 3, we read, "Thy daughter thou shalt not give unto his son nor his daughter shalt thou take unto thy son"; but, as a rule, emphasis is laid only on the last clause; for example, in *Exodus* xxxiv. 16, the sons alone are forbidden to take strange daughters, not the daughters to take strange sons, and in *Nehemiah* xiii., after both sides have been forbidden to marry outside the race, only the marriage of a son with a foreign wife is described as a "sin against God." That is also a perfectly correct view. By the marriage of a daughter with a Goy, the purity of the Jewish stem is in no way altered, while this stem thereby gets a footing in the strange camp; on the other hand, the marriage of a son with a Goya "makes the holy seed common" as the book of *Ezra* ix. 2, drastically expresses it. The possible conversion of the Goya to Judaism would not help matters: the idea of such a conversion was rightly quite strange to the older law—for the question is one of physical conditions of descent—but the newer law [cited in the *Talmud*] says, with enviable discernment: "Proselytes are as injurious to Judaism as ulcers to a sound body." Thus was the Jewish race kept pure in the past and it is still kept so: daughters of the house of Rothschild have married barons, counts, dukes, princes, they submit to baptism without demur; no son has ever married a European; if he did so he would have to leave the house of his fathers and the community of his people.

These details are somewhat premature; they really belong to a later portion of the book; but my object has been at once and by the shortest way to meet the objection—which unfortunately is still to be expected from many sides—that there is no "Jewish question," from which would follow that the entrance of the Jews into our history had no significance. Others, again, talk of religion: it is a question, they say, of religious differences only. Whoever says this overlooks the fact that there would be no Jewish religion if there were no Jewish nation. But there is one. The Jewish nomocracy (that is, rule of the law) unites the Jews, no matter how scattered they may be over all the lands of the world, into a firm, uniform and absolutely political organism, in which community of blood testifies to a common past and gives a guarantee for a common future. Though it has many elements not purely Jewish in the narrower sense of the word, yet the power of this blood, united with the incomparable power of the Jewish idea, is so great that these alien elements have long ago been assimilated; for nearly two thousand years have passed since the time when the Jews gave up their temporary inclination to proselytising. Of course, I must, as I showed in the preceding chapter, distinguish between Jews of noble and of less noble birth; but what binds together the incompatible parts is (apart from gradual fusing) the tenacity of life which their national idea possesses. This national idea culminates in the unshakable confidence in the universal empire of the Jews, which Jehovah promised. "Simple people who have been born Christians" (as Auerbach expresses it in his sketch of Spinoza's life) fancy that the Jews have given up that hope, but they are very wrong; for "the existence of Judaism depends upon the clinging to the Messianic hope," as one of the very moderate and liberal Jews [Skreinka] lately wrote [in *Entwickelungsgeschichte der jüdischen Dogmen*, p. 75]. The whole Jewish religion is in fact founded on this hope. The Jewish faith in God, that which can and may be called "religion" in their case, for it has become since the source of a fine morality, is a part of this national idea, not *vice versa*. To assert that there is a Jewish religion but no Jewish nation is simply nonsense.

The entry of the Jews into the history of the West signifies therefore beyond doubt the entrance of a definite element, quite different from and in a way opposed to all European races, an element which remained essentially the same, while the nations of Europe went through the most various phases; in the course of a hard and often cruel history it never had the weakness to entertain proposals of fraternity, but, possessed as it was of its national idea, its national past, and its national future, felt and still feels all contact with others as a pollution; thanks also to the certainty of its instinct, which springs from strict uniformity of national feeling, it has always been able to exercise a powerful influence upon others, while the Jews themselves have been influenced but skin-deep by our intellectual and cultural development. To characterise this most peculiar situation from the standpoint of the European, we must repeat the words of Herder: the Jewish people is and remains alien to our part of the world; from the standpoint of the Jew the same fact is formulated somewhat differently; we know from a former chapter how the great free-thinking philosopher Philo put it: "only the Israelites are men in the true sense of the word." What the Jew here says in the intolerant tone of racial pride was more politely expressed by Goethe [in *Conversations with Eckermann*, October 7, 1828], when he disputed the community of descent of Jews and Indo-Europeans, no matter how far back the origin was put: "We will not dispute with the chosen people the honour of its descent from Adam. We others, however, have certainly had other ancestors as well."

THE "ALIEN PEOPLE"

These considerations make it our right and our duty to look upon the Jew in our midst as a peculiar and, in fact, alien element. Outwardly his inheritance was the same as ours; inwardly it was not so: he inherited quite a different spirit. One single trait is all that is necessary to reveal in an almost alarming manner to our consciousness the yawning gulf which here separates soul from soul: the revelation of Christ has no significance for the Jew! ... And while we find even in Mohammed's *Koran* at least a vague conception of the importance of Christ and profound reverence for His personality, a cultured, leading Jew of the nineteenth century calls Christ "the new birth with the deathmask," [Graetz, from *Volkstüm-*

liche Geschichte der Juden, i, 591] which inflicted new and painful wounds upon the Jewish people; he cannot see anything else in Him. In view of the cross he assures us that "the Jews do not require this convulsive emotion for their spiritual improvement," and adds, "particularly not among the middle classes of the inhabitants of the cities." His comprehension goes no further. In a book, republished in 1880, by a Spanish Jew (Mose de Leon) Jesus Christ is called a "dead dog" that lies "buried in a dunghill." Besides, the Jews have taken care to issue in the latter part of the nineteenth century several editions (naturally in Hebrew) of the so-called "censured passages" from the *Talmud,* those passages usually omitted in which Christ is exposed to our scorn and hatred as a "fool," "sorcerer," "profane person," "idolater," "dog," "bastard," "child of lust," etc.; so, too, his sublime mother [Laible: *Jesus Christus im Talmud,* p. 2 ff, *Schriften des Institutum Judaicum in Berlin,* No. 10]. We certainly do the Jews no injustice when we say that the revelation of Christ is simply something incomprehensible and hateful to them. Although he apparently sprang from their midst, he embodies nevertheless the negation of their whole nature—a matter in which the Jews are far more sensitive than we. This clear demonstration of the deep cleft that separates us Europeans from the Jew is by no means given in order to let religious prejudice with its dangerous bias settle the matter, but because I think that the perception of two so fundamentally different natures reveals a real gulf; it is well to look once into this gulf, so that on other occasions, where the two sides seem likely to unite each other, we may not be blind to the deep abyss which separates them.

When we understand what a chasm there is between us we are forced to a further conclusion. The Jew does not understand us, that is certain; can we hope to understand him, to do him justice? Perhaps, if we are really intellectually and morally superior to him, as Renan insisted in the passage quoted above, and as other perhaps more reliable scholars have likewise said. But we should then have to judge him from the lofty heights of our superiority, not from the low depths of hatred and superstition, and still less from the swampy shallows of misunderstanding in which our religious teachers have been wading for the last two thousand years. It is surely an evident injustice to ascribe to the Jew thoughts which he never had, to glorify him as the possessor of the most sublime religious intuitions, which were perhaps more alien to him than to any one else in the world, and at best are to be found only in the hearts of a few scattered individuals as a cry of revolt against the special hardness of heart of this people—and then to condemn him for being to-day quite different from what he should be according to such fictitious conceptions. It is not only unfair, but as regards public feeling, regrettably misleading; for through his connection with our religious life—a connection which is entirely fictitious—his head seems enveloped in a kind of nimbus, and then we are greatly incensed when we find no holy person under this sham halo. We expect more of the Jews than of ourselves, who are merely the children of the heathen. But the Jewish testimony is very different and more correct; it leads us to expect so little that every noble trait discovered later and every explanation found for Jewish failings gives us genuine pleasure. Jehovah, for instance, is never tired of explaining, "I have seen this people and behold it is a stiff-necked people" [*Exodus* xxxii. 9, xxxiv. 9; *Deuteronomy* ix. 13,etc.], and Jeremiah gives such a characterisation of the moral constitution of the Jews that Monsieur Edouard Drumont could not wish it to be more richly coloured, "And they will deceive every one his neighbour, and will not speak the truth: they have taught their tongue to speak lies, and weary themselves to commit iniquity." Little wonder, after this description, that Jeremiah calls the Jews "an assembly of treacherous men," and knows only one desire, "Oh that I had in the wilderness a lodging-place of wayfaring men; that I might leave my people and go from them." For our incredible ignorance of the Jewish nature we are ourselves solely to blame; never did a people give so comprehensive and honest a picture of its own personality as the Hebrew has done in his Bible, a picture which (so far as I can judge from fragments) is made more complete by the *Talmud,* though in faded colours. Without, therefore, denying that it must be very difficult for us who are "descended from other ancestors" to form a correct judgment of the "alien Asiatic people," we must clearly see that the Jews from time immemorial have done their best to inform the unprejudiced about themselves, a circumstance which entitles us to hope that we may gain a thorough knowledge of their nature. As a matter of fact, the events which take place before our eyes should be sufficient for that. Is it possible to read the daily papers without becoming acquainted with Jewish ways of thinking, Jewish taste, Jewish morals, Jewish aims? A few annual volumes of the *Archives israélites* teach us in fact more than a whole anti-Semitic library, and indeed not only about the less admirable, but also about the excellent qualities of the Jewish character. But here, in this chapter, I shall leave the present out of account. If we are to form a practical and true judgment concerning the significance of the Jew as joint-heir and fellow-worker in the nineteenth century, we must above all become clear as to what he is. From what a man is by nature follows of strict necessity what he will do under certain conditions; the philosopher says: *operari sequitur esse;* an old German proverb expresses the same thing in a more homely way, "Only what a man is, can one get out of him."

Source: Chamberlain, Houston Stewart. *The Foundations of the Nineteenth Century.* Vol. 1. London: John Lane the Bodley Head, 1910.

1.4
The Myth of a Jewish Conspiracy – 1903
Excerpt from Protocols of the Meetings of the Zionist Men of Wisdom

Anti-Semitism was aided by a misguided belief that all Jews were engaged in an elaborate conspiracy to rule the world. The document most responsible for this misconception was Protocols of the Meetings of the Zionist Men of Wisdom *(also known as* Protocols of the Elders of Zion*), which appeared in Russia in 1903 and quickly spread throughout Europe and the rest of the world. The document was said to be the text of a secret Jewish plan to dominate all governments, but it was actually a forgery designed to whip up anti-Jewish hatred. The plan worked surprisingly well: both before and after World War I,* Protocols *was held up as proof that Jews were a dangerous threat to civilized nations. The Nazis frequently referred to the document to justify their anti-Semitic policies, even after* Protocols *was revealed as a fraud in the mid-1920s. The following excerpt from an English translation of* Protocols *depicts the Jewish elders as using liberal political reforms and capitalistic economics to control the "Goys" (non-Jews).*

PROTOCOL NO. V

What form of government can be given to societies in which bribery has penetrated everywhere, where riches are obtained only by clever tricks and semi-fraudulent means, where corruption reigns, where morality is sustained by punitive measures and strict laws and not by voluntary acceptance of moral principles, where cosmopolitan convictions have eliminated patriotic feelings and religion? What form of government can be given to such societies other than despotism such as I shall describe?

We will create a strong centralized government, so as to gather the social forces into our power. We will mechanically regulate all the functions of political life of our subjects by new laws. These laws will gradually eliminate all concessions and liberties permitted by the GOYS. Our kingdom will be crowned by such a majestic despotism that it will be able, at all times and in all places, to crush both antagonistic and discontented GOYS.

We may be told that the despotism outlined by me is inconsistent with modern progress, but I will prove to you that the contrary is the case.

At the time when people considered rulers as an incarnation of the will of God, they subjected themselves without murmur to the autocracy of the sovereigns; but as soon as we inspired them with the thought of their personal rights, they began to regard the rulers as ordinary mortals. The holy anointment fell from the heads of the sovereigns in the opinion of the people; and when we deprived them of their belief in God, then authority was thrown into the street, where it became public property and was seized by us. Moreover, the art of governing the masses and individuals by means of cunningly constructed theories and phraseology, by rulers of social life, and other devices not understood by the GOYS, belongs, among other faculties, to our administrative mind, which is educated in analysis and observation, and is also based upon skillful reasoning in which we have no competitors, just as we have none in the preparation of plans for political action and solidarity. Only the Jesuits could be compared to us in this; but we were able to discredit them in the mind of the senseless mob as a visible organization, whereas we, with our secret organization, remained in the dark. After all, is it not the same to the world who will be its master—whether it be the head of Catholicism or our despot of Zionist blood? To us, however, the Chosen People, it is by no means a matter of indifference.

Temporarily, a world coalition of the GOYS would be able to hold us in check, but are insured against this by roots of dissension so deep among them that they cannot now be extracted. We have set at variance the personal and national interests of the GOYS; we have incited religious and race hatred, nurtured by us in their hearts for twenty centuries. Owing to all this, no state will obtain the help it asks for from any side because each of them will think that a coalition against us will be disadvantageous to it. We are too powerful—*we must be taken into consideration. No country can reach even an insignificant private understanding without our being secret parties to it.*

Per me reges regnant—"Through me the sovereigns reign." The prophets have told us we were chosen by God himself to reign over the world. God endowed us with genius to enable us to cope with the problem. Were there a genius in the opposing camp, he would struggle against us, but a newcomer is not equal to the old inhabitant. The struggle between us would be of such a merciless nature as the world has never seen before; moreover their genius would be too late.

All the wheels of government mechanism move by the action of the motor which is in our hands, and *that motor is gold.* The science of political economy, invented by our wise men, has long ago demonstrated the royal prestige of capital.

To attain freedom of action, capital must obtain freedom to monopolize industry and trade; this is already being done by an unseen hand in all parts of the world. Such liberty will give political power to traders, and will aid in subjugating the people. At present it is more important to disarm peoples than to lead them to war; it is more important to utilize flaming passions for our purposes than to extinguish them; more important to grasp and interpret the thoughts of others in our own way than to discard them.

The most important problem of our government is to weaken the popular mind by criticism; to disaccustom it to thought, which creates opposition; to deflect the power of thought into empty eloquence.

At all times both peoples and individuals have mistaken words for deeds, as they are satisfied with the visible, rarely noticing whether the promise is performed in the fields of social life.

Therefore, we will organize ostensible institutions which will prove eloquently their good work in the direction of "progress."

We will appropriate to ourselves the liberal aspect of all parties, of all shades of opinion, and we will provide our *orators with the same aspect, and they will talk so much that they will exhaust the people by their speeches and cause them to turn away from orators in disgust.*

To control public opinion it is necessary to perplex it by the expression of numerous contradictory opinions until the GOYS get lost in the labyrinth, and come to understand that it is best to have no opinion on political opinions.

Such questions are not intended to be understood by the people, since only he who rules knows them. This is the first secret.

The second secret necessary for the success of governing consists in so multiplying the popular failings, habits, passions, and conventional laws that no one will be able to disentangle himself in the chaos, and consequently, people will cease to understand each other. This measure would help us to sow dissension within all parties, to disintegrate all those collective forces which still do not wish to subjugate themselves to us; to discourage all individual initiative which might in any degree hamper our work.

There is nothing more dangerous than individual initiative; if it has a touch of genius it can accomplish more than a million people among whom we have sown dissensions. We must direct the education of the GOY societies so that their arms will drop helplessly when they face every task where initiative is required. The intensity of action resulting from individual freedom of action dissipates its force when it encounters another person's freedom. This results in heavy blows at morale, disappointments and failures.

We will so tire the GOYS by all this that we will force them to offer us an international power, which by its position will enable us conveniently to absorb, without destroying, all governmental forces of the world and thus to form a super-government. In lieu of modern rulers, we will place a monster which will be called the Super-Governmental Administration. Its hands will be stretched out like pincers in every direction so that this colossal organization cannot fail to conquer all the peoples.

Source: *The Protocols and World Revolution, including a Translation and Analysis of the "Protocols of the Meetings of the Zionist Men of Wisdom."* Boston: Small, Maynard & Company, 1920.

2

WORLD WAR I AND THE RISE OF THE NAZI PARTY

Adolf Hitler salutes passing SS troops at the third Nazi Party Congress in Nuremberg, Germany, in 1927. Infamous Nazi propagandist Julius Streicher (hatless, with hands clasped together) can be seen standing to the left of Hitler's car.

INTRODUCTION

Fought between 1914 and 1918, World War I proved a key factor in Adolf Hitler's rise to power. Because it was the leading nation among the Central Powers who lost the war, Germany was stripped of its colonies and most of its military and forced to give up territory to neighboring countries. Germany also had to pay reparations to its enemies, and this added to the extreme economic difficulties the country faced following the war. Finally, Germany's defeat in World War I brought about the overthrow of the German emperor, Kaiser Wilhelm II. His removal triggered even greater political uncertainty and societal unrest across the country.

In 1919 Germany adopted a new republican form of government—known as the Weimar Republic—in which the people elected their political leaders. But the democratic tradition was very weak in Germany, and the coalition of socialists and centrist politicians who took power was challenged by radical leftists on one end of the political spectrum and by conservative, nationalistic, and militaristic groups on the other.

One of the conservative parties was a small group originally known as the German Workers' Party and later the National Socialist German Workers' Party. In German, its name was *Nationalsozialistische Deutsche Arbeiterpartei,* and it was often known as the NSDAP or the Nazi Party. (Despite the "Socialist" and "Workers' Party" labels, the Nazis were far more conservative than leftist in their early years, and they moved farther to the right as time passed.) In 1919 thirty-year-old Adolf Hitler, then a corporal about to be discharged from the German Army, became a member of the party after attending one of the group's meetings in Munich.

Hitler had been born in Austria, but he had come to think of himself as a German during the war, and he was crushed by the nation's defeat. Like many other

Germans, he was convinced that the country's surrender had occurred not because it had been defeated on the battlefield but because it had been "stabbed in the back" by some of its own citizens. This conviction was based on the fact that citizens and military units had rebelled against the German emperor in the closing months of the war, after the war's momentum turned decisively against Germany.

Hitler joined the Nazi party in large measure because it shared his belief that the two groups most responsible for Germany's defeat were Jews and Communists. In fact, Hitler saw little difference between the two, believing that Communism was one part of a vast Jewish conspiracy. In the coming years, Hitler and other members of the Nazi Party would allege that the Jews were the cause for almost every misfortune experienced by the German people (this in spite of the fact that the Judaic community totaled only about 1 percent of the country's population). For example, Hitler later stated that the Jews had not only caused the German defeat in World War I but had also brought about the war in the first place. He would make a similar claim in the lead up to World War II, accusing Jews of "inciting ... the nations into a conflict which is utterly senseless and only serves Jewish interests." At its core, the rabid racism of Hitler and his Nazi allies rested on the genetic theories of Houston Stewart Chamberlain, Joseph Arthur Comte de Gobineau, and others. The National Socialists promoted the idea of a supreme Aryan race and feared that marriages and sexual relations between Jews and gentiles would pollute the "purity" of German blood. When the Nazis issued their political platform in 1920, they made little attempt to mask their anti-Semitic orientation.

The Nazi Formula—Intimidation and Violence

Hitler assumed the title of *führer* (leader) soon after joining the Nazi Party, and he began attracting converts with his rousing public speeches. In fact, Hitler's charisma and the Nazis' paranoid anti-Semitic platform proved to be a potent recruiting combination. Membership in the party soared from 50 in 1919 to 15,000 by 1923. As their numbers grew, Hitler and the Nazis increasingly relied on intimidation and force to advance their message. In 1921 they formed a militaristic squad, the *Sturmabteilung* (Storm Troopers), also known as the S.A. or the Brown Shirts. These members willingly battled political opponents in violent street clashes and marched through towns singing pro-Nazi anthems and harassing Jewish shop owners. One of their favorite chants was "*Deutschland erwache, Juda verrecke!*"—"Germany awake, death to the Jews!"

Meanwhile, the country continued to struggle with a variety of problems. One of the most serious was the hyperinflation that took place in 1922 and 1923, when German currency lost much of its value and prices skyrocketed to astonishing levels. Hitler claimed that the inflation was "instigated and carried through by the Jews," and the chaotic conditions inspired him to declare an armed rebellion against the Weimar government in November 1923. The Munich-based uprising failed miserably, however. Hitler and other Nazi leaders were arrested and tried for treason. Hitler was found guilty, but he received just a five-year sentence—and he only spent about eight months behind bars.

When Hitler emerged from prison, he found that his stature had actually been dramatically enhanced by his arrest, trial, and prison term. Many Germans had been impressed by his efforts to portray himself as a German patriot. In addition, he had written an autobiography and political manifesto called *Mein Kampf* (*My Struggle*) during his incarceration. This work, which was heavily laced with anti-Semitic declarations, brought him even greater fame when it was published in 1926.

After Hitler was freed, the Nazis attempted to use the ballot box to gain power, but even though the party continued to grow in the late 1920s, their candidates received little support from the public at large. It took another and more drastic crisis—the Great Depression that began in late 1929—to change the fortunes of the Nazi Party. The economic slump hit Germany particularly hard. Within a year unemployment doubled across the country, and by 1933 six million people—one of every three German workers—had lost their jobs.

In a country desperate to find a solution to their woes—and someone to blame for the nation's difficulties—the Nazi message suddenly had more appeal than ever before. This became clear in September 1930, when the party suddenly won 107 seats in the German parliament (up from just 12 in the previous parliament). Two years later they claimed 230 seats, becoming the most powerful party in the country, and Hitler finished second in the presidential election. The growing political power of the Nazis was further underscored by the increasing visibility of their Storm Troopers. By 1932, approximately 400,000 Brown Shirts were roaming through Germany's cities—four times the number of troops in the entire German army.

Hitler Consolidates Power

Armed with greater political clout than ever before, Hitler undertook several shrewd moves that made him the absolute ruler of Germany. He urged powerful conservative politicians to name him chancellor—the head of the government (the office of the German presidency, by comparison, had fewer powers). The politicians agreed, believing they could control Hitler, but they were badly mistaken.

35

Hitler was named chancellor on January 30, 1933. A month later, with the approval of President Paul von Hindenburg, Hitler assumed special "emergency" powers that allowed him to suspend many key civil rights guaranteed under the national constitution. The excuse for this decree was a fire that had been set at the Reichstag (the German parliament building). Hitler blamed it on Communist revolutionaries, but there has always been strong suspicion that Nazis set the fire themselves as a pretext for consolidating control over the nation. Under the emergency decree, 10,000 people were arrested, most of them Communists or other rivals of the Nazis. Newspapers unfriendly to Hitler were shut down. Meetings of opposition political parties were banned.

Under these conditions another election was held in early March 1933. The results allowed the Nazis to strengthen their hold on parliament. With these additions, and with many of the Communist and Socialist members of parliament in jail or in hiding, the Nazis pushed through the decisive Law to Remove the Distress of People and State (also known as the Enabling Law) in late March 1933. It gave Hitler the power to issue laws without the approval of the German parliament. (The initial law had a four-year time limit, but its provisions were later extended.) Once enacted, Germany became a dictatorship—a state ruled by a single, all-powerful leader. In the following months all political parties except the Nazis were abolished.

Some Germans spoke out against the Enabling Law, but many citizens reasoned that this drastic measure would give Hitler the necessary authority to decisively address the country's problems. Weary after years of political deadlock between rival parties, many Germans hoped that Hitler could use his increased power to put the country back on the path to prosperity. Improving the economy and restoring Germany's stature may have been the primary aim of many of the non-Nazis who supported Hitler, but only the most oblivious could have been unaware of his anti-Semitism. Some may have assumed that the more extreme views of the Nazis would moderate in time, but they did not. Instead, Hitler's government immediately launched a series of legal maneuvers that brought great hardship to Germany's Jewish population.

2.1
The Treaty of Versailles – 1919
Text of the Treaty of Peace Between the Allied and Associated Powers and Germany

The impact of World War I on the German nation was immense. Prior to the war, Germany had become one of the most powerful nations in Europe. Nationalistic fervor and a belief in the country's military might led many Germans to expect a quick victory in the conflict. Instead they became immersed in what was, at that time, the most deadly war ever fought. After more than four years of battle, Germany and the other nations of the Central Powers were forced to surrender to the combined forces of Great Britain, France, and the United States. The Treaty of Versailles, which specified the terms of peace, went into effect in June 1919. Its harsh terms were bitterly condemned by the German population, which saw them as humiliating and vindictive.

As the following excerpts indicate, Germany was forced to accept responsibility for the war, give up territory to neighboring countries, relinquish its foreign colonies, reduce the size of its military, and pay reparations to its enemies. There was widespread opposition to the treaty among the Germans, but the country's postwar leaders signed the agreement, not wishing to risk a resumption of hostilities. The stiff terms of the treaty contributed to the economic problems that plagued Germany in the early 1920s, which in turn helped fuel the growth of extreme groups such as the National Socialist German Workers' Party (the Nazis). The specter of the war defeat and the terms of the Versailles Agreement were raised again and again by the Nazis as they sought to draw supporters to their cause. In addition, Nazi arguments that the Jews were responsible for the country's defeat resonated with many Germans who were seeking someone to blame for their nation's struggles.

PART III

POLITICAL CLAUSES FOR EUROPE

SECTION I

BELGIUM

Article 31

Germany, recognizing that the Treaties of 19 April 1839, which established the status of Belgium before the war, no longer conform to the requirements of the situation, consents to the abrogation of the said Treaties and undertakes immediately to recognize and to observe whatever conventions may be entered into by the Principal Allied and Associated Powers, or by any of them, in concert with the Governments of Belgium and of the Netherlands, to replace the said Treaties of 1839. If her formal adhesion should be required to such conventions or to any of their stipulations, Germany undertakes immediately to give it.

Article 32

Germany recognizes the full sovereignty of Belgium over the whole of the contested territory of Moresnet (called *Moresnet neutre*).

Article 33

Germany renounces in favour of Belgium all rights and title over the territory of Prussian Moresnet situated on the west of the road from Liège to Aix-la-Chapelle; the road will belong to Belgium where it bounds this territory.

Article 34

Germany renounces in favour of Belgium all rights and title over the territory comprising the whole of the *Kreise* of Eupen and of Malmédy....

SECTION II

LUXEMBURG

Article 40

With regard to the Grand Duchy of Luxemburg, Germany renounces the benefit of all the provisions inserted in her favour in the Treaties of 8 February 1842, 2 April 1847, 20-25 October 1865, 18 August 1866, 21 February and 11 May 1867, 10 May 1871, 11 June 1872 and 11 November 1902, and in all Conventions consequent upon such Treaties.

Germany recognizes that the Grand Duchy of Luxemburg ceased to form part of the German Zollverein as from 1 January 1919, renounces all rights to the exploitation of the railways, adheres to the termination of the regime of neutrality of the Grand Duchy, and accepts in advance all international arrangements which may be concluded by the Allied and Associated Powers relating to the Grand Duchy.

Article 41

Germany undertakes to grant to the Grand Duchy of Luxemburg, when a demand to that effect is made to her by the Principal Allied and Associated Powers, the rights and advantages stipulated in favour of such Powers or their nationals in the present Treaty with regard to economic questions, to questions relative to transport and to aerial navigation.

SECTION III

LEFT BANK OF THE RHINE

Article 42

Germany is forbidden to maintain or construct any fortifications either on the left bank of the Rhine or on the right bank to the west of a line drawn 50 kilometres to the east of the Rhine.

Article 43

In the area defined above the maintenance and the assembly of armed forces, either permanently or temporarily, and military manoeuvres of any kind, as well as the upkeep of all permanent works for mobilization, are in the same way forbidden.

Article 44

In case Germany violates in any manner whatever the provisions of Articles 42 and 43, she shall be regarded as committing a hostile act against the Powers signatory of the present Treaty and as calculated to disturb the peace of the world.

SECTION IV

SAAR BASIN

Article 45

As compensation for the destruction of the coal mines in the north of France and as part payment towards the total reparation due from Germany for the damage resulting from the war, Germany cedes to France in full and absolute possession, with exclusive rights of exploitation, unencumbered and free from all debts and charges of any kind, the coal mines situated in the Saar Basin as defined in Article 48.

Article 46

In order to assure the rights and welfare of the population and to guarantee to France complete freedom in working the mines, Germany agrees to the provisions of Chapters I and II of the Annex hereto....

SECTION V

ALSACE-LORRAINE

THE HIGH CONTRACTING PARTIES, recognizing the moral obligation to redress the wrong done by Germany in 1871 both to the rights of France and to the wishes of the population of Alsace and Lorraine, which were separated from their country in spite of the solemn protest of their representatives at the Assembly of Bordeaux, AGREE upon the following Articles:

Article 51

The territories which were ceded to Germany in accordance with the Preliminaries of Peace signed at Versailles on 26 February 1871 and the Treaty of Frankfort of 10 May 1871 are restored to French sovereignty as from the date of the Armistice of 11 November 1918.

The provisions of the Treaties establishing the delimitation of the frontiers before 1871 shall be restored....

SECTION VI
AUSTRIA

Article 80

Germany acknowledges and will respect strictly the independence of Austria, within the frontiers which may be fixed in a Treaty between that State and the Principal Allied and Associated Powers; she agrees that this independence shall be inalienable, except with the consent of the Council of the League of Nations.

SECTION VII
CZECHO-SLOVAK STATE

Article 81

Germany, in conformity with the action already taken by the Allied and Associated Powers, recognizes the complete independence of the Czecho-Slovak State which will include the autonomous territory of the Ruthenians to the south of the Carpathians. Germany hereby recognizes the frontiers of this State as determined by the Principal Allied and Associated Powers and the other interested States.

Article 82

The old frontier as it existed on 3 August 1914 between Austria-Hungary and the German Empire will constitute the frontier between Germany and the Czecho-Slovak State....

SECTION VIII
POLAND

Article 87

Germany, in conformity with the action already taken by the Allied and Associated Powers, recognizes the complete independence of Poland, and renounces in her favour all rights and title over the territory bounded by the Baltic Sea, the eastern frontier of Germany as laid down in Article 27 of Part II (Boundaries of Germany) of the present Treaty up to a point situated about 2 kilometres to the east of Lorzendorf, then a line to the acute angle which the northern boundary of Upper Silesia makes about 3 kilometres north-west of Simmenau, then the boundary of Upper Silesia to its meeting point with the old frontier between Germany and Russia, then this frontier to the point where it crosses the course of the Niemen, and then the northern frontier of East Prussia as laid down in Article 28 of Part II aforesaid.

The provisions of this Article do not, however, apply to the territories of East Prussia and the Free City of Danzig, as defined in Article 28 of Part II (Boundaries of Germany) and in Article 100 of Section XI (Danzig) of this Part.

The boundaries of Poland not laid down in the present Treaty will be subsequently determined by the Principal Allied and Associated Powers.

A Commission consisting of seven members, five of whom shall be nominated by the Principal Allied and Associated Powers, one by Germany and one by Poland, shall be constituted fifteen days after the coming into force of the present Treaty to delimit on the spot the frontier line between Poland and Germany.

The decisions of the Commission will be taken by a majority of votes and shall be binding upon the parties concerned....

PART IV
GERMAN RIGHTS AND INTERESTS OUTSIDE GERMANY

Article 118

In territory outside her European frontiers as fixed by the present Treaty, Germany renounces all rights, titles and privileges whatever in or over territory which belonged to her or to her allies, and all rights, titles and privileges whatever their origin which she held as against the Allied and Associated Powers.

Germany hereby undertakes to recognize and to conform to the measures which may be taken now or in the future by the Principal Allied and Associated Powers, in agreement where necessary with third Powers, in order to carry the above stipulation into effect.

In particular Germany declares her acceptance of the following Articles relating to certain special subjects.

SECTION I
GERMAN COLONIES

Article 119

Germany renounces in favour of the Principal Allied and Associated Powers all her rights and titles over her overseas possessions.

Article 120

All movable and immovable property in such territories belonging to the German Empire or to any German State shall pass to the Government exercising authority over such territories, on the terms laid down in Article 257 of Part IX (Financial Clauses) of the present Treaty. The decision of the local courts in any dispute as to the nature of such property shall be final....

PART V

MILITARY, NAVAL AND AIR CLAUSES

In order to render possible the initiation of a general limitation of the armaments of all nations, Germany undertakes strictly to observe the military, naval and air clauses which follow.

SECTION I

MILITARY CLAUSES

Chapter I

Effectives and cadres of the German Army

Article 159

The German military forces shall be demobilized and reduced as prescribed hereinafter.

Article 160

1. By a date which must not be later than 31 March 1920, the German Army must not comprise more than seven divisions of infantry and three divisions of cavalry.

After that date the total number of effectives in the Army of the States constituting Germany must not exceed one hundred thousand men, including officers and establishments of depots. The Army shall be devoted exclusively to the maintenance of order within the territory and to the control of the frontiers....

PART VIII

REPARATION

SECTION I

GENERAL PROVISIONS

Article 231

The Allied and Associated Governments affirm and Germany accepts the responsibility of Germany and her allies for causing all the loss and damage to which the Allied and Associated Governments and their nationals have been subjected as a consequence of the war imposed upon them by the aggression of Germany and her allies.

Article 232

The Allied and Associated Governments recognize that the resources of Germany are not adequate, after taking into account permanent diminutions of such resources which will result from other provisions of the present Treaty, to make complete reparation for all such loss and damage.

The Allied and Associated Governments, however, require, and Germany undertakes, that she will make compensation for all damage done to the civilian population of the Allied and Associated Powers and to their property during the period of the belligerency of each as an Allied or Associated Power against Germany by such aggression by land, by sea and from the air, and in general all damage as defined in Annex I hereto....

Article 235

In order to enable the Allied and Associated Powers to proceed at once to the restoration of their industrial and economic life, pending the full determination of their claims, Germany shall pay in such installments and in such manner (whether in gold, commodities, ships, securities or otherwise) as the Reparation Commission may fix, during 1919, 1920 and the first four months of 1921, the equivalent of 20,000,000,000 gold marks. Out of this sum the expenses of the armies of occupation subsequent to the Armistice of 11 November 1918 shall first be met, and such supplies of food and raw materials as may be judged by the Governments of the Principal Allied and Associated Powers to be essential to enable Germany to meet her obligations for reparation may also, with the approval of the said Governments, be paid for out of the above sum. The balance shall be reckoned towards liquidation of the amounts due for reparation. Germany shall further deposit bonds as prescribed in paragraph 12(c) of Annex II hereto.

Source: *Treaty of Peace with Germany.* Washington, D.C.: Government Printing Office, 1919.

2.2
The Nazis Spell Out Their Political Goals – 1920
Program of the National Socialist German Workers' Party

In 1919 Adolf Hitler joined the German Workers' Party, soon to become the National Socialist German Workers' Party with Hitler as its leader. On February 24, 1920, the National Socialists issued the following twenty-five-point plan that outlined the party's political aims. Their anti-Semitic beliefs inform several of the points, specifically numbers 4 through 8, 23, and 24, most of which would later be addressed in the policies of the Nazi government. The version that follows is a reprint of the original program and was published in the National Socialistic Yearbook in 1941. Though the points remain unaltered from those originally published in 1920, this document includes an additional explanatory note that was issued in 1928.

The program of the NSDAP

The program is the political foundation of the NSDAP and accordingly the primary political law of the State. It has been made brief and clear intentionally.

All legal precepts must be applied in the spirit of the party program.

Since the taking over of control, the Fuehrer has succeeded in the realization of essential portions of the Party program from the fundamentals of the detail.

The Party Program of the NSDAP was proclaimed on the 24 February 1920 by Adolf Hitler at the first large Party gathering in Munich and since that day has remained unaltered. Within the national socialist philosophy is summarized in 25 points:

1. We demand the unification of all Germans in the Greater Germany on the basis of the right of self-determination of peoples.

2. We demand equality of rights for the German people in respect to the other nations; abrogation of the peace treaties of Versailles and St. Germain.

3. We demand land and territory (colonies) for the sustenance of our people, and colonization for our surplus population.

4. Only a member of the race can be a citizen. A member of the race can only be one who is of German blood, without consideration of creed. Consequently no Jew can be a member of the race.

5. Whoever has no citizenship is to be able to live in Germany only as a guest, and must be under the authority of legislation for foreigners.

6. The right to determine matters concerning administration and law belongs only to the citizen. Therefore we demand that every public office, of any sort whatsoever, whether in the Reich, the county or municipality, be filled only by citizens. We combat the corrupting parliamentary economy, office-holding only according to party inclinations without consideration of character or abilities.

7. We demand that the state be charged first with providing the opportunity for a livelihood and way of life for the citizens. If it is impossible to sustain the total population of the State, then the members of foreign nations (non-citizens) are to be expelled from the Reich.

8. Any further immigration of non-citizens is to be prevented. We demand that all non-Germans, who have immigrated to Germany since the 2 August 1914, be forced immediately to leave the Reich.

9. All citizens must have equal rights and obligations.

10. The first obligation of every citizen must be to work both spiritually and physically. The activity of individuals is not to counteract the interests of the universality, but must have its result within the framework of the whole for the benefit of all.

Consequently we demand:

11. Abolition of unearned (work and labour) incomes. Breaking of rent-slavery.

12. In consideration of the monstrous sacrifice in property and blood that each war demands of the people personal enrichment through a war must be designated as a crime against the people. Therefore we demand the total confiscation of all war profits.

13. We demand the nationalization of all (previous) associated industries (trusts).

14. We demand a division of profits of all heavy industries.

15. We demand an expansion on a large scale of old age welfare.

16. We demand the creation of a healthy middle class and its conservation, immediate communalization of the great warehouses and their being leased at low cost to small firms, the utmost consideration of all small firms in contracts with the State, county or municipality.

17. We demand a land reform suitable to our needs, provision of a law for the free expropriation of land for the purposes of public utility, abolition of taxes on land and prevention of all speculation on land.

18. We demand struggle without consideration against those whose activity is injurious to the general interest. Common national criminals, usurers, Schieber and so forth are to be punished with death, without consideration of confession or race.

19. We demand substitution of a German common law in place of the Roman Law serving a materialistic world-order.

20. The state is to be responsible for a fundamental reconstruction of our whole national education program, to enable every capable and industrious German to obtain higher education and subsequently introduction into leading positions. The plans of instruction of all educational institutions are to conform with the experiences of practical life. The comprehension of the concept of the State must be striven for by the school [Staatsbuergerkunde] as early as the beginning of understanding. We demand the education at the expense of the State of outstanding intellectually gifted children of poor parents without consideration of position or profession.

21. The State is to care for the elevating national health by protecting the mother and child, by outlawing child-labor, by the encouragement of physical fitness, by means of the legal establishment of a gymnastic and sport obligation, by the utmost support of all organizations concerned with the physical instruction of the young.

22. We demand abolition of the mercenary troops and formation of a national army.

23. We demand legal opposition to known lies and their promulgation through the press. In order to enable the provision of a German press, we demand

that: a. All writers and employees of the newspapers appearing in the German language be members of the race; b. Non-German newspapers be required to have the express permission of the State to be published. They may not be printed in the German language; c. Non-Germans are forbidden by law any financial interest in German publications, or any influence on them, and as punishment for violations the closing of such a publication as well as the immediate expulsion from the Reich of the non-German concerned. Publications which are counter to the general good are to be forbidden. We demand legal prosecution of artistic and literary forms which exert a destructive influence on our national life, and the closure of organizations opposing the above made demands.

24. We demand freedom of religion for all religious denominations within the state so long as they do not endanger its existence or oppose the moral senses of the Germanic race. The Party as such advocates the standpoint of a positive Christianity without binding itself confessionally to any one denomination. It combats the Jewish-materialistic spirit within and around us, and is convinced that a lasting recovery of our nation can only succeed from within on the framework: common utility precedes individual utility.

25. For the execution of all of this we demand the formation of a strong central power in the Reich. Unlimited authority of the central parliament over the whole Reich and its organizations in general. The forming of state and profession chambers for the execution of the laws made by the Reich within the various states of the confederation. The leaders of the Party promise, if necessary by sacrificing their own lives, to support by the execution of the points set forth above without consideration.

Adolf Hitler proclaimed the following explanation for this program on the 13 April 1928:

Explanation

Regarding the false interpretations of Point 17 of the program of the NSDAP on the part of our opponents, the following definition is necessary:

Since the NSDAP stands on the platform of private ownership[,] it happens that the passage [on] gratuitous expropriation concerns only the creation of legal opportunities to expropriate[,] if necessary, land which has been illegally acquired or is not administered from the view-point of the national welfare. This is directed primarily against the Jewish land-speculation companies.

Source: National Socialist German Workers' Party. "Program of the NSDAP." February 24, 1920. Reprinted as Document 1708-PS in *Nazi Conspiracy and Aggression*. Vol. 4. Washington, DC: United States Government Printing Office, 1946.

2.3
Social and Economic Upheaval in Postwar Germany – 1920s
Excerpt from The World of Yesterday *by Stefan Zweig*

Stefan Zweig was an Austrian Jew who became a well-known author of short stories and biographies that reflected his liberal views and belief in pacifism. In the following excerpt from his autobiographical memoir, he discusses the social and economic upheaval that existed in Germany in the five years that followed the end of World War I and how those conditions contributed to Hitler's rise to power. Zweig focuses on the hyperinflation that saw the value of German currency plummet and also discusses the 1922 assassination of Walter Rathenau—the German Foreign Minister under the Weimar Republic—by right-wing extremists. This murder was another sign of the unstable political atmosphere that existed in Germany in the early 1920s.

How wild, anarchic and unreal were those years, years in which, with the dwindling value of money all other values in Austria and Germany began to slip! It was an epoch of high ecstasy and ugly scheming, a singular mixture of unrest and fanaticism. Every extravagant idea that was not subject to regulation reaped a golden harvest: theosophy, occultism, spiritualism, somnambulism, anthroposophy, palm-reading, graphology, yoga and Paracelsism. Anything that gave hope of newer and greater thrills, anything in the way of narcotics, morphine, cocaine, heroin found a tremendous market; on the stage, incest and parricide, in politics, communism and fascism, constituted the most favored themes; unconditionally proscribed, however, was any representation of normality and moderation. But I would not for anything wipe out that era of chaos, neither from my own life nor from art in its onward movement. Thrusting forward in the orgy of its first impulse it had, like every spiritual revolution, swept the air clean of all stuffy tradition, and relieved the strains of many years; for all that may be said its daring experiments have left a residuum of valuable stimuli. Much as some of its excesses amazed us, we did not feel justified in any arrogant censure or rejection for, in essence, this youth of the new day was seeking to correct (though perhaps with too great fire and impatience) what our cautious and aloof generation had failed in. Their instinct that the post-war period had to be different from the one before the war was fundamentally correct. Had not we oldsters also longed for a new and better world before and during the war?…

A certain tension, to be sure, was in the air; for the whole country was waiting to learn whether the negotiations at Genoa and Rapallo (the first at which Germany had a seat as an equal with the formerly hostile powers) would bring the hoped for alleviations of the war burdens, or at least a faint gesture of real under-

Reprinted by permission of Williams Verlag AG.

standing. The leader of these negotiations, so memorable in the history of Europe, was no other than my old friend [Walter] Rathenau. His genial instinct for organization had already proven itself excellently during the war; from the start he had recognized the weakest spot in the German economy where, later on, it also received its mortal blow: the procurement of raw materials, and early (here too anticipating time), he centralized the whole economic system. When the war was over and a German Foreign Minister was needed who could meet the shrewdest and most experienced diplomats among the former opponents on their own ground, naturally the choice fell on him.

> *"The German people, a disciplined folk, did not know what to do with their freedom and already looked impatiently toward those who were to take it from them."*

Hesitatingly I telephoned him in Berlin. Why break in on a man absorbed in shaping our destiny? "Yes, it's difficult," he said to me over the telephone, "Even friendship must now be sacrificed to my duty." But with his extraordinary facility for employing every minute he immediately devised a meeting. He had to leave his card at certain embassies and as it was a half-hour's drive from Grunewald the simplest thing was for me to go there and have a chat in his car while he was on his way. It is a fact that his capacity for mental concentration, his stupendous facility for switching from one subject to another was so perfect, that he could talk at any time, in the car or on a train, as precisely and profoundly as in his own room. I did not wish to miss this opportunity and I believe that it afforded him satisfaction to talk with someone who was politically disinterested and bound to him personally by years of friendship....

That Rathenau accomplished his task at Rapallo as excellently as it was possible under the then prevailing circumstances is now a historical fact. His splendid gift of quickly grasping any favorable situation, his cosmopolitan and his personal prestige never proved themselves more brilliantly. But already there were groups strong in the land that knew that they would secure followers only by assuring the vanquished people again and again that they really were not vanquished and that negotiations or compromises were treason to the nation. Already the secret organizations—strongly under homosexual influence—were far more powerful than the then leaders of the republic suspected and the latter, in their conception of freedom gave free rein to those who sought to do away with freedom in Germany for good.

It was in the city then that I said good-by to him in front of the Ministry, without having any premonition that this would be the last good-by. And later I saw by photographs that the road through which we had driven together was the same where, shortly thereafter, the murderers waylaid the same automobile; it was not more than chance that I did not witness the historically fateful scene. Thus, I was the better able to appreciate fully, because of the lively impression on my senses, the tragic episode with which the disaster of Germany, the disaster of Europe began.

On that day, I was already in Westerland. Hundreds of vacationists were bathing gaily in the surf. Again, as on the day when the assassination of Franz Ferdinand was announced [the 1914 event that initiated World War I], a band played to carefree people when, like white petrels, the newsboys stormed over the boardwalk. "Walter Rathenau assassinated." A panic broke out and the tremor spread through the whole Reich. Abruptly the mark plunged down, never to stop until it had reached the fantastic figures of madness, the millions, the billions and trillions. Now the real witches' sabbath of inflation started, against which our Austrian inflation with its absurd enough ration of 15,000 old to 1 of new currency had been shabby child's play. To describe it in detail, with its incredibilities, would take a whole book and to readers of today it would seem like a fairy tale. I have known days when I had to pay fifty thousand marks for a newspaper in the morning and a hundred thousand in the evening; whoever had foreign currency to exchange did so from hour to hour, because at four o'clock he would get a better rate than at three, and at five o'clock he would get much more than he had got an hour earlier. For instance, I sent a manuscript to my publisher on which I had worked for a year; to be on the safe side I asked for an advance payment of royalties on ten thousand copies. By the time the check was deposited, it hardly paid the postage I had put on the parcel a week before; on street cars one paid in millions, trucks carried the paper money from the Reichsbank to the other banks, and a fortnight later one found hundred thousand mark notes in the gutter; a beggar had thrown them away contemptuously. A pair of shoe laces cost more than a shoe had once cost, no, more than a fashionable store with two thousand pairs of shoes had cost before; to repair a broken window more than the whole house had formerly cost, a book more than the printer's shop with a hundred presses. For a hundred dollars one could buy rows of six-story houses on Kurfürstendamm, and factories were to be had for the old equivalent of a wheelbarrow. Some adolescent boys who had found a case of soap forgotten in the harbor disported themselves for months in cars and lived like kings, selling a cake every day, while their parents, formerly well-to-do, slunk about like beggars. Messenger boys established foreign exchange businesses and speculated in currencies of all lands. Towering over all of them was the gigantic figure of the superprofiteer [Hugo] Stinnes. Expanding his credit and in thus exploiting the mark he bought whatever was for sale, coal mines and ships, factories and stocks, castles and country estates, actually for nothing because every payment, every promise became equal to naught. Soon a quarter of Germany was in his hands and, perversely, the masses, who in Germany always became intoxicated at a success that they can see with their eyes, cheered him as a genius. The unemployed stood around by the thousands and shook their fists at the profiteers and foreigners in their luxurious cars who bought whole rows of streets like a box of matches; everyone who could read and write traded, speculated and profited and had a secret sense that they were deceiving themselves and were being deceived by a hidden force which brought about this chaos deliberately in order to liberate the State from its debts and obligations. I have a pretty thorough knowledge of history, but never, to my recollection, has it produced such madness in such gigantic proportions. All values were changed, and not only material ones; the laws of the State were flouted, no tradition, no moral code was respected, Berlin was transformed into the Babylon of the world. Bars, amusement parks, honky-tonks sprang up like mushrooms. What we had seen in Austria proved to be just a mild and shy prologue to this witches' sabbath; for the Germans introduced all their vehemence and methodical organization into the perversion. Along the entire Kurfürstendamm powdered and rouged young men sauntered and they were not all professionals; every high school boy wanted to earn some money and in the dimly lit bars one might see government officials and men of the world of finance tenderly courting drunken sailors without any shame. Even the Rome of Suetonius had never known such orgies as the pervert balls of Berlin, where hundreds of men costumed as women and hundreds of women as men danced under the benevolent eyes of the police. In the collapse of all values a kind of madness gained hold particularly in the bourgeois circles which until then had been unshakeable in their probity. Young girls bragged proudly of their perversion, to be sixteen and still under suspicion of virginity would have been considered a disgrace in any school of Berlin at that time, every girl wanted to be able to tell of her adventure and the more exotic, the better. But the most revolting thing about this pathetic eroticism was its spuriousness. At bottom the orgiastic period which broke out in Germany simultaneously with the inflation was nothing more than feverish imitation; one could see that these girls of the decent middle class families much rather would have worn their hair in a simple arrangement than in a sleek man's haircut, that they would much rather have eaten apple pie with whipped cream than drink strong liquor; everywhere it was unmistakable that this over-excitation was unbearable for the people, this being stretched daily on the rack of inflation and that the whole nation, tired of war, actually only longed for order, quiet, and a little security and bourgeois life. And, secretly it hated the republic, not because it suppressed this wild freedom, but on the contrary, because it held the reins too loosely.

Whoever lived through these apocalyptic months, these years, disgusted and embittered, sensed the coming of a counterblow, a horrible reaction. And behind the scenes, smiling, there waited, watch in hand, those same people who had driven the German nation into the chaos: "The worse it is for the country, the better for us." They knew that their hour was at hand. Around [Erich] Ludendorff, more than around the then still powerless Hitler, the counterrevolution was already crystallizing openly; the officers whose epaulettes had been torn off their shoulders organized in secret, the small tradesmen who had been cheated out of their savings silently closed ranks and aligned themselves in readiness for any slogan that promised order. Nothing was as fateful to the German Republic as the idealistic attempt to give liberty not only to the people but even to its enemies. For the German people, a disciplined folk, did not know what to do with their freedom and already looked impatiently toward those who were to take it from them.

———

The day the German inflation ended (1924) could have become a turning point in history. When, as if at the sound of a gong, each billion of artificially inflated marks was exchanged for a single new mark, a norm had been created. And, truly, the muddy tide with all its filth and slime flowed back soon, the bars, the honky-tonks disappeared, conditions became normal again, everybody could now figure clearly how much he had won, how much he had lost. The great majority, the mighty masses, had lost. But the blame was laid not on those who had caused the war but on those who with sacrifice and without thanks had undertaken the burden of reconstruction. Nothing ever embittered the German people so much—it is important to remember this—nothing made them so furious with hate and so ripe for Hitler as the inflation. For the war, murderous as it was, had yet yielded hours of jubilation, with ringing of bells and fanfares of victory. And, being an incurably militaristic nation, Germany felt lifted in her pride by her temporary victories; while the inflation served only to make it feel soiled, cheated, and humiliated; a whole generation never forgot or forgave the German Republic for those years and preferred to reinstate its butchers.

Source: Zweig, Stefan. *The World of Yesterday*. New York: Viking, 1943.

2.4
Hitler Casts Himself as a Patriot – 1923
Excerpts from Adolf Hitler's Trial Address after the Beer Hall Putsch

In November 1923, hoping to capitalize on the public discontent with the country's hyperinflation, Adolf Hitler and the Nazi Party attempted to overthrow the German government by launching an insurrection in Munich that became known as the Beer Hall Putsch. They had the support of many conservative figures in the state of Bavaria, but the state ruler, Gustav von Kahr, ordered police to stop the rebels. Nineteen people were killed in the process, most of them Nazis. Hitler was wounded, as was the prominent World War I general Erich Ludendorff, who had supported the rebellion. Charged with treason, Hitler presented himself at the trial as a patriotic figure determined to save Germany from Communists and other disloyal citizens who, he charged, were the real culprits in Germany's defeat in World War I. The following passage also recounts his version of the insurrection. Though he was found guilty—a judgment that could have resulted in a death sentence—

Hitler's close ties with the conservative Bavarians resulted in a relatively light sentence of five years. He then served only eight months in prison before being released.

May it please the Court! …

Replacing the person by the cipher, energy by volume, the Marxist movement is destroying the foundation of all human cultural life. Wherever this movement breaks through, it must destroy human culture. The future of Germany means: destruction of Marxism. Either Marxism poisons the people, their Germany is ruined or the poison is going to be eliminated, then Germany can recover again, not before that. For us, Germany will be saved on that day on which the last Marxist has either been converted or broken.…

We will fight spiritually for one who is willing to fight with the weapons of the spirit; we have the fist for the one who is willing to fight with the fist.…

When we recognized that the territory of the Ruhr would be lost, our movement arrived at a big point of discord with the Bourgeois world. The National Socialist movement recognized clearly that the territory of the Ruhr would be lost if the people would not wake up from its lethargy. World politics are not made with the palm branch, but with the sword. But the Reich too must be governed by National Socialists.

A few weeks later, there was the Ruhr uprising and with that German unity broke down. Since then I did not go to Corps Area Headquarters [Wehr-Kreis-Kommando] anymore because I regarded all other discussions as completely useless.

But our movement has not been founded to gain seats in parliament and daily attendance fees; our movement was founded to turn Germany's fate in her twelfth hour.…

As we had declared at numerous public meetings, that our leaders would not, like those of the Communists did, stand in the rear in the critical hours, our leaders marched in front. On Ludendorff's right side Dr. Weber marched, on his left, I and Scheubner-Richter and the other gentlemen. We were permitted to pass by the cordon of troops blocking the Ludwig Bridge, who wept bitter tears, were deeply moved and all gone to pieces. People who had attached themselves to the columns, yelled from the rear, that the guys should be knocked down. We yelled that there was no reason to harm these people. We marched on to the Marienplatz. The rifles were not loaded. The enthusiasm was indescribable. I had to tell myself: The people are behind us, they no longer can be consoled by ridiculous resolutions. The people want a reckoning with the November criminals, as far as it still has a sense of honor and human dignity and not for slavery. In front of the Royal Residence a weak police cordon let us pass through. Then there was a short hesitation in front, and a shot was fired. I had the impression that it was no pistol shot but a rifle or carbine bullet. Shortly afterwards a volley was fired. I had the feeling that a bullet struck in my left side. Scheubner-Richter fell, I with him. At this occasion my arm was dislocated and I suffered another injury while falling.

I only was down for a few seconds and tried at once to get up. Another shot was fired, out of the little street to the rear of the Preysing Palace. Around me there were bodies. In front of us were State Police, rifles cocked. Farther in the rear there were armored cars. My men were 70 to 80 meters in back of me. A big gentleman in a black overcoat was laying half covered on the ground, soiled with blood. I was convinced that he was Ludendorff. There were a few more shots fired from inside the Royal Residence and from the little street near the Preysing Palace, and maybe also a few wild shots fired by our men. From the circle near the Rentamt, I drove out of town. I intended to be driven back the same night....

A few days later, at Uffing, we found out that I had suffered a fracture of the joint and a fracture of the collarbone.... I did not enter this court to deny anything or to reject my responsibility. I protest against the attempt that Herr von Kriebel tries to assume the responsibility, be it only for the military preparations. I bear the responsibility all alone, but I declare one thing: I am no criminal because of that and I do not feel as if I would be a criminal. I cannot plead guilty, but I do confess the act. There is no such thing as high treason against the traitors of 1918. It is impossible that I should have committed high treason, for this cannot be implicit in the action of November 8th and 9th, but only in the intentions and the actions during all the previous months. But if I really should have committed high treason, then I am surprised not to see those gentlemen here at my side, against whom the prosecutor would be obliged to file indictments; those who willed together with us the same action, discussed and prepared things down to the smallest detail, things which may be described in particular at a closed session later. I do not consider myself as a man who committed high treason, but as a German, who wanted the best for his people.

Source: Hitler, Adolf. Trial Address, November 1923. Reprinted as Document 2404-PS in *Nazi Conspiracy and Aggression*. Vol. 5. Washington, DC: United States Government Printing Office, 1946.

2.5
Hitler Rages against the Jews – 1923
Excerpt from Mein Kampf *by Adolf Hitler*

In his book Mein Kampf (My Struggle), *which was written during his jail term in 1923, Adolf Hitler outlined his theories of society and government. Though dismissed by many readers as exaggerated propaganda, the book provided an accurate window into Hitler's state of mind and the governing philosophy that he would adopt after he became leader of Germany in 1933. In the following excerpt, taken from the chapter "Nation and Race," Hitler's irrational and feverish anti-Semitism is on full display. He echoes the racist views of Joseph Arthur Comte de Gobineau and Houston Stewart Chamberlain, proclaiming the need for racial purity and the superiority of what he terms the Aryan race. He also denounces the Jewish people as an inferior, parasitic race that cause harm in all the lands where they live.*

Any crossing of two beings not at exactly the same level produces a medium between the level of the two parents. This means: the offspring will probably stand higher than the racially lower parent, but not as high as the higher one. Consequently, it will later succumb in the struggle against the higher level. Such mating is contrary to the will of Nature for a higher breeding of all life. The precondition for this does not lie in associating superior and inferior, but in the total victory of the former. The stronger must dominate and not blend with the weaker, thus sacrificing his own greatness. Only the born weakling can view this as cruel, but he after all is only a weak and limited man; for if this law did not prevail, any conceivable higher development of organic living beings would be unthinkable....

No more than Nature desires the mating of weaker with stronger individuals, even less does she desire the blending of a higher with a lower race, since, if she did, her whole work of higher breeding, over perhaps hundreds of thousands of years, might be ruined with one blow.

Historical experience offers countless proofs of this. It shows with terrifying clarity that in every mingling of Aryan blood with that of lower peoples the result was the end of the cultured people. North America, whose population consists in by far the largest part of Germanic elements who mixed but little with the lower colored peoples, shows a different humanity and culture from Central and South America, where the predominantly Latin immigrants often mixed with the aborigines on a large scale. By this one example, we can clearly and distinctly recognize the effect of racial mixture. The Germanic inhabitant of the American continent, who has remained racially pure and unmixed, rose to be master of the continent; he will remain the master as long as he does not fall a victim to defilement of the blood.

The result of all racial crossing is therefore in brief always the following:

(a) Lowering of the level of the higher race,

(b) Physical and intellectual regression and hence the beginning of a slowly but surely progressing sickness.

To bring about such a development is, then, nothing else but to sin against the will of the eternal creator.

And as a sin this act is rewarded....

All great cultures of the past perished only because the originally creative race died out from blood poisoning.

The ultimate cause of such a decline was their forgetting that all culture depends on men and not conversely; hence that to preserve a certain culture the man who creates it must be preserved. This preservation is bound up with the rigid law of necessity and the right to victory of the best and stronger in this world.

Those who want to live, let them fight, and those who do not want to fight in this world of eternal struggle do not deserve to live.

Even if this were hard—that is how it is! Assuredly, however, by far the harder fate is that which strikes the man who thinks he can overcome Nature, but in the last analysis only mocks her. Distress, misfortune, and diseases are her answer.

The man who misjudges and disregards the racial laws actually forfeits the happiness that seems destined to be his. He thwarts the triumphal march of the best race and hence also the precondition for all human progress, and remains, in consequence burdened with all the sensibility of man, in the animal realm of helpless misery.

* * *

It is idle to argue which race or races were the original representative of human culture and hence the real founders of all that we sum up under the word 'humanity.' It is simpler to raise this question with regard to the present, and here an easy, clear answer results. All the human culture, all the results of art, science, and technology that we see before us today, are almost exclusively the creative product of the Aryan. This very fact admits of the not unfounded inference that he alone was the founder of all higher humanity, therefore representing the prototype of all that we understand by the word 'man.' He is the Prometheus of mankind from whose bright forehead the divine spark of genius has sprung at all times, forever kindling anew that fire of knowledge which illumined the night of silent mysteries and thus caused man to climb the path to mastery over the other beings of this earth. Exclude him—and perhaps after a few thousand years darkness will again descend on the earth, human culture will pass, and the world turn to a desert.

If we were to divide mankind into three groups, the founders of culture, the bearers of culture, the destroyers of culture, only the Aryan could be considered as the representative of the first group. From him originate the foundations and walls of all human creation, and only the outward form and color are determined by the changing traits of character of the various peoples. He provides the mightiest building stones and plans for all human progress and only the execution corresponds to the nature of the varying men and races....

The question of the inner causes of the Aryan's importance can be answered to the effect that they are to be sought less in a natural instinct of self-preservation than in the special type of its expression....

Not in his intellectual gifts lies the source of the Aryan's capacity for creating and building culture. If he had just this alone, he could only act destructively, in no case could he organize; for the innermost essence of all organization requires that the individual renounce putting forward his personal opinion and interests and sacrifice both in favor of a larger group. Only by way of this general community does he again recover his share. Now, for example, he no longer works directly for himself, but with his activity articulates himself with the community, not only for his own advantage, but for the advantage of all. The most wonderful elucidation of this attitude is provided by his word 'work,' by which he does not mean an activity for maintaining life in itself, but exclusively a creative effort that does not conflict with the interests of the community. Otherwise he designates human activity, in so far as it serves the instinct of self-preservation without consideration for his fellow men, as theft, usury, robbery, burglary, etc.

This state of mind, which subordinates the interests of the ego to the conservation of the community, is really the first premise for every truly human culture. From it alone can arise all the great works of mankind, which bring the founder little reward, but the richest blessings to posterity. Yes from it alone can we understand how so many are able to bear up faithfully under a scanty life which imposes on them nothing but poverty and frugality, but gives the community the foundations of its existence. Every worker, every peasant, every inventor, official, etc., who works without ever being able to achieve any happiness or prosperity for himself, is a representative of this lofty idea, even if the deeper meaning of his activity remains hidden in him....

* * *

The mightiest counterpart to the Aryan is represented by the Jew. In hardly any people in the world is the instinct of self-preservation developed more strongly than in the so-called 'chosen.' Of this, the mere fact of the survival of this race may be considered the best proof. Where is the people which in the last two thousand years has been exposed to so slight changes of inner disposition, character, etc., as the Jewish people? What people, finally, has gone through greater upheavals than this one—and nevertheless issued from the mightiest catastrophes of mankind unchanged? What an infinitely tough will to live and preserve the species speaks from these facts!

The mental qualities of the Jew have been schooled in the course of many centuries. Today he passes as 'smart,' and this in a certain sense he has been at all times. But his intelligence is not the result of his own development, but of visual instruction through foreigners. For the human mind cannot climb to the top without steps; for every step upward he needs the foundation of the past, and this in the comprehensive sense in which it can be revealed only in general culture. All thinking is based only in small part on man's own knowledge, and mostly on the

56

experience of the time that has preceded. The general cultural level provides the individual man, without his noticing it as a rule, with such a profusion of preliminary knowledge that, thus armed, he can more easily take further steps of his own. The boy of today, for example, grows up among a truly vast number of technical acquisitions of the last centuries, so that he takes for granted and no longer pays attention to much that a hundred years ago was a riddle to even the greatest minds, although for following and understanding our progress in the field in question it is of decisive importance to him. If a very genius from the twenties of the past century should suddenly leave his grave today, it would be harder for him even intellectually to find his way in the present era than for an average boy of fifteen today. For he would lack all the infinite preliminary education which our present contemporary unconsciously, so to speak, assimilates while growing up amidst the manifestations of our present general civilization.

"[The Aryan] is the Prometheus of mankind from whose bright forehead the divine spark of genius has sprung at all times, forever kindling anew that fire of knowledge which illumined the night of silent mysteries."

Since the Jew—for reasons which will at once become apparent—was never in possession of a culture of his own, the foundations of his intellectual work were always provided by others. His intellect at all times developed through the cultural world surrounding him. The reverse process never took place.

For if the Jewish people's instinct of self-preservation is not smaller but larger than that of other peoples, if his intellectual faculties can easily arouse the impression that they are equal to the intellectual gifts of other races, he lacks completely the most essential requirement for a cultured people, the idealistic attitude.

In the Jewish people the will to self-sacrifice does not go beyond the individual's naked instinct of self-preservation. Their apparently great sense of solidarity is based on the very primitive herd instinct that is seen in many other living creatures in this world. It is a noteworthy fact that the herd instinct leads to mutual support only as long as a common danger makes this seem useful or inevitable. The same pack of wolves which has just fallen on its prey together disintegrates when hunger abates into its individual beasts. The same is true of horses which try to defend themselves against an assailant in a body, but scatter again as soon as the danger is past.

It is similar with the Jew. His sense of sacrifice is only apparent. It exists only as long as the existence of the individual makes it absolutely necessary. However, as soon as the common enemy is conquered, the danger threatening all averted and the booty hidden, the apparent harmony of the Jews among themselves ceases, again making way for their old causal tendencies. The Jew is only united when a common danger forces him to be or a common booty entices him; if these two grounds are lacking, the qualities of the crassest egoism come into their own, and in the twinkling of an eye the united people turns into a horde of rats, fighting bloodily among themselves.

If the Jews were alone in this world, they would stifle in filth and offal; they would try to get ahead of one another in hate-filled struggle and exterminate one another, in so far as the absolute absence of all sense of self-sacrifice, expressing itself in their cowardice, did not turn battle into comedy here too.

So it is absolutely wrong to infer any ideal sense of sacrifice in the Jews from the fact that they stand together in struggle, or, better expressed, in the plundering of their fellow men. Here again the Jew is led by nothing but the naked egoism of the individual.

That is why the Jewish state—which should be the living organism for preserving and increasing a race—is completely unlimited as to territory. For a state formation to have a definite spatial setting always presupposes an idealistic attitude on the part of the state-race, and especially a correct interpretation of the concept of work. In the exact measure in which this attitude is lacking, any attempt at forming, even of preserving, a spatially delimited state fails. And thus the basis on which alone culture can arise is lacking.

Hence the Jewish people, despite all apparent intellectual qualities, is without any true culture, and especially without any culture of its own. For what sham culture the Jew today possesses is the property of other peoples, and for the most part it is ruined in his hands.

In judging the Jewish people's attitude on the question of human culture, the most essential characteristic we must always bear in mind is that there has never been a Jewish art and accordingly there is none today either; that above all the two queens of all the arts, architecture and music, owe nothing original to the Jews. What they do accomplish in the field of art is either patchwork or intellectual theft. Thus, the Jew lacks those qualities which distinguish the races that are creative and hence culturally blessed.

To what an extent the Jew takes over foreign culture, imitating or rather ruining it, can be seen from the fact that he is mostly found in the art which seems to require least original invention, the art of acting. But even here, in reality, he is only a ' juggler,' or rather an ape; for even here he lacks the last touch that is required for real greatness; even here he is not the creative genius, but a superficial imitator, and all the twists and tricks that he uses are powerless to conceal the inner lifelessness of his creative gift. Here the Jewish press most lovingly helps him along by raising such a roar of hosannahs about even the most mediocre bungler, just so long as he is a Jew, that the rest of the world actually ends up by thinking that they have an artist before them, while in truth it is only a pitiful comedian.

No, the Jew possesses no culture-creating force of any sort, since the idealism, without which there is no true higher development of man, is not present in him and never was present. Hence his intellect will never have a constructive effect, but will be destructive, and in very rare cases perhaps will at most be stimulating, but then as the prototype of the 'force which always wants evil and nevertheless creates good.' Not through him does any progress of mankind occur, but in spite of him.

Since the Jew never possessed a state with definite territorial limits and there-fore never called a culture his own, the conception arose that this was a people which should be reckoned among the ranks of the nomads. This is a fallacy as great as it is dangerous. The nomad does possess a definitely limited living space, only he does not cultivate it like a sedentary peasant, but lives from the yield of his herds with which he wanders about in his territory. The outward reason for this is to be found in the small fertility of a soil which simply does not permit of settlement. The deeper cause, however, lies in the disparity between the technical culture of an age or people and the natural poverty of a living space. There are territories in which even the Aryan is enabled only by his technology, developed in the course of more than a thousand years, to live in regular settlements, to master broad stretches of soil and obtain from it the requirements of life. If he did not possess this technology, either he would have to avoid these territories or likewise have to struggle along as a nomad in perpetual wandering, provided that his thousand-year-old education and habit of settled residence did not make this seem simply unbearable to him. We must bear in mind that in the time when the American continent was being opened up, numerous Aryans fought for their livelihood as trappers, hunters, etc., and often in larger troops with wife and children, always on the move, so that their existence was completely like that of the nomads. But as soon as their increasing number and better implements permitted them to clear the wild soil and make a stand against the natives, more and more settlements sprang up in the land.

Probably the Aryan was also first a nomad, settling in the course of time, but for that very reason he was never a Jew! No, the Jew is no nomad; for the nomad had also a definite attitude toward the concept of work which could serve as a basis for his later development in so far as the necessary intellectual premises were present. In him the basic idealistic view is present, even if in infinite dilution, hence in his whole being he may seem strange to the Aryan peoples, but not unat-tractive. In the Jew, however, this attitude is not at all present; for that reason he was never a nomad, but only and always a parasite in the body of other peoples. That he sometimes left his previous living space has nothing to do with his own purpose, but results from the fact that from time to time he was thrown out by the host nations he had misused. His spreading is a typical phenomenon for all para-sites; he always seeks a new feeding ground for his race.

59

This, however, has nothing to do with nomadism, for the reason that a Jew never thinks of leaving a territory that he has occupied, but remains where he is, and he sits so fast that even by force it is very hard to drive him out. His extension to ever-new countries occurs only in the moment in which certain conditions for his existence are there present, without which—unlike the nomad—he would not change his residence. He is and remains the typical parasite, a sponger who like a noxious bacillus keeps spreading as soon as a favorable medium invites him. And the effect of his existence is also like that of spongers: wherever he appears, the host people dies out after a shorter or longer period.

Thus, the Jew of all times has lived in the states of other peoples, and there formed his own state, which, to be sure, habitually sailed under the disguise of 'religious community' as long as outward circumstances made a complete revelation of his nature seem inadvisable. But as soon as he felt strong enough to do without the protective cloak, he always dropped the veil and suddenly became what so many of the others previously did not want to believe and see: the Jew.

The Jew's life as a parasite in the body of other nations and states explains a characteristic which once caused [Arthur] Schopenhauer, as has already been mentioned, to call him the 'great master in lying.' Existence impels the Jew to lies and to lie perpetually, just as it compels the inhabitants of the northern countries to wear warm clothing.

His life within other peoples can only endure for any length of time if he succeeds in arousing the opinion that he is not a people but a 'religious community,' though of a special sort.

And this is the first great lie.

In order to carry on his existence as a parasite on other peoples, he is forced to deny his inner nature. The more intelligent the individual Jew is, the more he will succeed in this deception. Indeed, things can go so far that large parts of the host people will end by seriously believing that the Jew is really a Frenchman or an Englishman, a German or an Italian, though of a special religious faith. Especially state authorities, which always seem animated by the historical fraction of wisdom, most easily fall a victim to this infinite deception. Independent thinking sometimes seems to these circles a true sin against holy advancement, so that we may not be surprised if even today a Bavarian state ministry, for example, still has not the faintest idea that the Jews are members of a people and not of a ' religion' though a glance at the Jew's own newspapers should indicate this even to the most modest mind. The Jewish Echo is not yet an official organ, of course, and consequently is unauthoritative as far as the intelligence of one of these government potentates is concerned.

The Jew has always been a people with definite racial characteristics and never a religion; only in order to get ahead he early sought for a means which could distract unpleasant attention from his person. And what would have been more expedient and at the same time more innocent than the 'embezzled' concept of a religious community? For here, too, everything is borrowed or rather stolen. Due to his own original special nature, the Jew cannot possess a religious institution, if for no other reason because he lacks idealism in any form, and hence belief in a hereafter is absolutely foreign to him. And a religion in the Aryan sense cannot be imagined which lacks the conviction of survival after death in some form. Indeed, the Talmud is not a book to prepare a man for the hereafter, but only for a practical and profitable life in this world.

The Jewish religious doctrine consists primarily in prescriptions for keeping the blood of Jewry pure and for regulating the relation of Jews among themselves, but even more with the rest of the world; in other words, with non-Jews. But even here it is by no means ethical problems that are involved, but extremely modest economic ones. Concerning the moral value of Jewish religious instruction, there are today and have been at all times rather exhaustive studies (not by Jews; the drivel of the Jews themselves on the subject is, of course, adapted to its purpose) which make this kind of religion seem positively monstrous according to Aryan conceptions. The best characterization is provided by the product of this religious education, the Jew himself. His life is only of this world, and his spirit is inwardly as alien to true Christianity as his nature two thousand years previous was to the great founder of the new doctrine. Of course, the latter made no secret of his attitude toward the Jewish people, and when necessary he even took to the whip to drive from the temple of the Lord this adversary of all humanity, who then as always saw in religion nothing but an instrument for his business existence. In return, Christ was nailed to the cross, while our present-day party Christians debase themselves to begging for Jewish votes at elections and later try to arrange political swindles with atheistic Jewish parties—and this against their own nation.

On this first and greatest lie, that the Jews are not a race but a religion, more and more lies are based in necessary consequence. Among them is the lie with regard to the language of the Jew. For him it is not a means for expressing his thoughts, but a means for concealing them. When he speaks French, he thinks Jewish, and while he turns out German verses, in his life he only expresses the nature of his nationality. As long as the Jew has not become the master of the other peoples, he must speak their languages whether he likes it or not, but as soon as they became his slaves, they would all have to learn a universal language (Esperanto, for instance!), so that by this additional means the Jews could more easily dominate them!

To what an extent the whole existence of this people is based on a continuous lie is shown incomparably by the Protocols of the Wise Men of Zion, so infinitely hated by the Jews. They are based on a forgery, the Frankfurter Zeitung moans and screams once every week: the best proof that they are authentic. What many Jews may do unconsciously is here consciously exposed. And that is what matters. It is completely indifferent from what Jewish brain these disclosures originate; the important thing is that with positively terrifying certainty they reveal the nature and activity of the Jewish people and expose their inner contexts as well as their ultimate final aims. The best criticism applied to them, however, is reality. Anyone who examines the historical development of the last hundred years from the standpoint of this book will at once understand the screaming of the Jewish press. For once this book has become the common property of a people, the Jewish menace may be considered as broken.

Source: Hitler, Adolf. *Mein Kampf.* Translated by Ralph Manheim. Boston: Houghton Mifflin, 1999.

2.6
A Childhood Shadowed by Anti-Semitism – 1920s
Holocaust Survivor Henry Oertelt Remembers the Brown Shirts

> *Born in Berlin in 1921, Henry Oertelt's childhood was marked by the social and economic upheaval of the 1920s and growing persecution of German Jews. In the following excerpt from an interview conducted with the Shoah Visual History Foundation, he remembers two encounters with the so-called Brown Shirts—the* Sturmabteilung *(Storm Troopers) of the Nazi Party, who were also known as the S. A. Even before Hitler took power, these uniformed troops frequently initiated street brawls with political rivals and carried out unprovoked attacks on Jews and Jewish property.*

I remember a very vivid scene…. I don't know exactly how old I was—five, six, or seven years old—when I was of the age that I was fully aware of the fact that I am a Jewish child. My mother and I walked down the street somewhere, and these brown-shirted characters, a big hoard of those characters came down the street in marching formation with a little band in front of them. And singing a constantly repeating refrain to a regular song.

That refrain would come up again and again until finally it even landed into my little child's ear. I'll recite it in exact translation…. It goes, "Once the blood of the Jews squirts off our knives everything will go twice as well." . . .

I remember very vividly, when I turned to my mother I said, "Mom, what do they mean, what do they mean? 'Blood of the Jews, off of their knives'—what do they mean? Do they want to kill us all, what is this?"

I still feel my mother's hand on my head when she says, "listen honey, don't worry about it. These are a bunch of loudmouths. They like to do that. It doesn't mean anything. Just forget it."

Henry A. Oertelt, Videotaped Interview conducted by Solomon Awend, 21 November 1995. Survivors of the Shoah Visual History Foundation. Beverly Hills, CA, USA.

But you couldn't forget it because you could hear this—and other songs of that nature, by the way—constantly, whenever these hoodlums marched by.

Oertelt later found that the violent threats of the Brown Shirts were very real. In the following passage, he recounts an attack he witnessed in Berlin.

A Jewish couple had been standing outside of their shop, and these brown-shirted hoodlums … came marching by and started to holler and yell at them and spit at them. And so maybe these people answered something—I don't know, I wasn't that close to it at that moment—but before you knew it the brown shirts would beat up on them.

And people started to mill around. Some of them would holler encouraging words [to the Brown Shirts]. There were also some people who stood on the side-lines shaking their heads in disbelief. Sometimes when it happened again [these people] would sometimes mutter, "well this isn't right. We know that Hitler doesn't like the Jews, but he always said he's a man of law and order. Just give it some time until he's more in the saddle"—he was [then] just starting out in his new regime.… And so the police would never step in [to prevent the violence], and this appeared to happen more and more often.

Source: Oertelt, Henry. Videotaped interview conducted by Solomon Awend, 21 November 1995. Survivors of the Shoah Visual History Foundation Testimony 7069.

2.7
Germany's "Enabling Law" – 1933
Text of the Law for Removing the Distress of the People and State

After being named Germany's chancellor on January 30, 1933, Adolf Hitler invoked emergency powers to suppress political opposition and consolidate his position. The parliamentary election held in March allowed the Nazis to gain more seats. This set the stage for passage of the following piece of legislation—the so-called Enabling Law—which gave Hitler the power to rule by decree for four years. It undid the system of parliamentary rule by elected representatives that had been in place in Germany since World War I.

1933 REICHSGESETZBLATT, PART I, PAGE 141
Law for Removing the Distress of the People and State

24 March 1933

The Reichstag has resolved upon the following law which is promulgated herewith with approval of the Reichsrat after it has been established that all the requirements of legislation for changing the constitution have been complied with.

Section 1

Laws for the Reich can be resolved upon also by the Reich Cabinet besides the procedure provided by the constitution of the Reich. This also applies to the laws pursuant to sections 85 subsection 2 and 87 of the Reich-Constitution.

Section 2

The laws for the Reich resolved upon by the Reich Cabinet may deviate from the Reich-Constitution so far as they do not deal with the institution of the Reichstag or the Reichsrat as such. The powers of the Reich-President will remain intact.

Section 3

The laws for the Reich resolved upon by the Reich-Cabinet are issued by the Reich-Chancellor and promulgated in the Reichsgesetzblatt. They will become effective, so far as they do not determine otherwise on the day following their promulgation. Section 68 to 77 of the Reich-Constitution are not applicable to the laws resolved upon by the Reich-Cabinet.

Section 4

Treaties of the Reich with foreign countries relating to matters of the legislation of the Reich do not require the approval of the bodies participating in the legislation. The Reich-Cabinet issues the rules necessary for the execution of such treaties.

Section 5

This law will become effective on the day of its promulgation. It becomes ineffective on 1 April 1937. Moreover it becomes ineffective if the present Reich-Cabinet should be replaced by another.

Source: "Law for Removing the Distress of the People and State." March 1933. Reprinted as Document 2001-PS in *Nazi Conspiracy and Aggression*. Vol. 4. Washington, DC: United States Government Printing Office, 1946.

3

PERSECUTION BY LAW

Adolf Hitler (right) and Heinrich Himmler (left) review SS troops during a ceremony at the seventh *Reichsparteitag* (Reich Party Day), held in September 1935 in Nuremberg.

INTRODUCTION

The earliest of Adolf Hitler's anti-Semitic decrees were issued just weeks after the March 1933 Enabling Law was passed, giving him virtually unlimited powers over the Third Reich. The Law for the Reestablishment of the Professional Civil Service, for example, was handed down on April 7, 1933. This decree, which prohibited those of "non-Aryan descent" from working for the government, eliminated all Jewish teachers from the nation's public schools. Another law handed down by Hitler limited people of Jewish heritage to 1.5 percent of a school's population (roughly equaling the percentage of Jews in the German population). More decrees followed that expelled Jews from a variety of occupations, including journalism, acting, and the military.

In 1935 the Nazis handed down an even more repressive set of laws. These statutes, collectively known as the Nuremberg Laws, included the Reich Citizenship Law. This law explicitly stated that only those of "German or kindred blood" could be citizens of the country, and it further declared that Jews were "guests" of the nation rather than Germans with full rights. The Reich Citizenship Law became the basis for later decrees that eliminated Jews from a long list of occupations: retail trade, banking, law, medicine, and more. Clearly, the Nazis were intent on isolating Germany's Judaic community, stripping them of their jobs and property, and making their lives as miserable as possible.

In addition, Jews and other targets of the Nazi leadership were victimized in a more secretive—though technically legal—manner: the concentration camp. Almost as soon as Hitler took power, his government began constructing special prisons. Many of those sent to the camps in the beginning had been singled out because the Nazis considered them political enemies, but homosexuals and members of the Jehovah's Witness faith were also arrested.

In 1938, Hitler and the Nazi leadership began packing growing numbers of Jews off to these prisons, usually for little or no reason. These jails were operated by the elite military troops of the S.S. (for *Schutzstaffel,* which means "defense corps"), which was commanded by Heinrich Himmler. This corps would later be the primary instrument used by the Nazis in carrying out the Holocaust. The S.S. treated the concentration camp inmates brutally, and many prisoners died while in custody. Thousands of inmates were held in the camps indefinitely without ever facing trial—or even hearing formal charges.

In many ways, these early concentration camps served as a sort of grim dress rehearsal for the extermination camps that would be used in the Holocaust. They also enabled the Nazi Party to further tighten its grip on Germany. As rumors about the conditions in these camps filtered down through German society, they served to frighten German citizens into obedience to Nazi law. It became widely understood that to defend Jews from the state or to otherwise oppose the Nazis was to risk arrest, torture, imprisonment, and death.

3.1
"Aryan Heritage" Enters the German Legal System – 1933
Text of the Law for the Reestablishment of the Professional Civil Service

The following law, passed on April 7, 1933, was the first proclamation by German Chancellor Adolf Hitler to insert the concept of heritage into German law. It declared that those government employees of "non-Aryan descent" must retire—language that was primarily aimed at eliminating Jews from the civil service. The law also struck out at those who had belonged to political organizations disliked by the Nazis. Though this nakedly discriminatory law was a severe blow to those affected by it, it did make some exceptions for Jews who had served in the German army in World War I or who held their government positions prior to the war. In addition, those dismissed from the German civil service were allowed to keep their pension benefits if they had been employed for ten years or more.

1933 REICHSGESETZBLATT, PAGE 175, Art 1-18, 7 April 1933.
Law for the Reestablishment of the Professional Civil Service

7 April 1933

The Reichsgovernment has enacted the following law, which is hereby proclaimed:

Art. 1

1. For the reestablishment of a national professional civil service and for the simplification of administration, officials may be discharged from office according to the following regulations, even when the necessary conditions according to the appropriate law do not exist.

2. Officials, as used in this law, means immediate [unmittelbare] and mediate [mittlebare] officials of the Reich, immediate and mediate officials of the federal states [Laender], officials of communes [Gemeinde] and communal associations, officials of public legal corporations as well as institutions and undertakings placed upon the same status as these public legal corporations (Third decree of the Reichspresident for the safeguarding of business and finance of 6 October 1931—

RGBl. I P. 537, 3rd part, Chapter V, Section I, Art. 15, subparagraph 1). The stipulations apply also to employees of agencies supplying social insurance, who have the rights and duties of officials.

3. Officials as used in this law also includes officials in temporary retirement.

4. The Reichsbank and the German State Railway Co. are empowered to make corresponding regulations.

Art. 2

1. Officials who since 9 November 1918 have attained the status of officials without possessing the required or usual preparation or other qualifications are to be dismissed from service. Their former salaries will be accorded them for a period of 3 months after their dismissal.

2. A right to waiting allowances, pensions, or survivors pension and to the continuance of the official designation, the title, the official uniform and the official insignia is not possessed by them.

3. In case of need a pension, revocable at any time, equivalent to a third of the usual base pay of the last position held by them may be granted them, especially when they are caring for dependent relatives; reinsurance according to the provisions of the Reich's social insurance law will not take place.

4. The stipulations of Section 2 and 3 will receive corresponding application in the case of persons of the type designated in Sec. 1, who already before this law became effective had been retired.

Art. 3

1. Officials, who are of non-aryan descent, are to be retired; insofar as honorary officials are concerned, they are to be removed from official status.

2. Section 1 is not in effect for officials who were already officials since 1 August 1914, or who fought during the World War at the front for the German Reichs or who fought for its allies or whose fathers or sons were killed in the World War. The Reichsminister of the Interior can permit further exceptions in understanding with the appropriate special minister or the highest authorities of the federal states in the case of officials abroad.

Art. 4

Officials whose former political activity does not offer a guarantee that they at all times without reservation act in the interest of the national state can be dismissed from service. For a period of 3 months after dismissal they are accorded their former salary. From this time on they receive 3/4 of their pension and corresponding survivor's benefits.

Art. 5

1. Every official must allow himself to be transferred to another office of the same or equivalent career, even into such a one having less rank or regular salary—reimbursement for the prescribed costs of transfer taking place, if the needs of the service require it. In case of transferment to an office of lower rank and regular salary the official retains his previous official title and the official income of his former position.

2. The official can, in place of transfer to an office of lesser rank and regular income (section 11) demand to be retired.

Art. 6

For the simplification of administration officials can be retired, even if they are not yet unfit for service. If officials are retired for this reason, their places may not be filled again.

Art. 7

1. Dismissal from office, transfer to another office and retirement will be ordered by the highest Reichs or federal state agency which will render final decision without right of appeal.

2. The dispositions according to Art 2 to 6 must be made known at the latest by 30 Sept 1933 to those affected. The time can be shortened by agreement with the Reichsminister of the Interior, if the appropriate Reichs or federal state agency declares that the measures authorized in this law have been carried out.

Art. 8

A pension will not be granted to the officials dismissed or retired in accordance with Art 3 and 4, if they have not completed a term of service of at least 10 years; this applies also in the cases in which according to the existing stipulation a pension is already accorded after a shorter term of service. Articles 36, 47 and 49 of the Reichs officials' law, the law of 4 July 1921 on increased computation of time in service accomplished during the war (RGB1 p. 825) and the corresponding provisions of federal state laws remained unchanged....

Source: "Law for the Reestablishment of the Professional Civil Service." April 7, 1933. Reprinted as Document 1397-PS in *Nazi Conspiracy and Aggression.* Vol. 3. Washington, DC: United States Government Printing Office, 1946.

3.2

Hitler Blocks "Non-Aryans" from the German Government – 1933
Text of the Law Changing the Regulations in Regard to Public Officers

Less than two months after engineering the passage of the Law for the Reestablishment of the Professional Civil Service, Adolf Hitler handed down the Law Changing the Regulations in Regard to Public Officers. This measure prevented "non-Aryans" from being newly appointed to official government positions and also prohibited those who were married to non-Aryans from holding public positions. It also instituted strong limitations against women holding official offices. Because the Nazi leadership believed that a woman's most important function was to bear and raise children, it prevented females below age thirty-five from assuming government jobs.

1933 REICHSGESETZBLATT, PART I, PAGE 433
Law Changing the Regulations in regard to Public Officers,

June 30, 1933

Chapter 2

Article 1a

1. Only such persons may be appointed Reich officials who possess for their career the prescribed education or customary training or who have special qualifications for the office about to be given, and who guarantee that they will support the Reich at all times without reservation.

2. Women may only be appointed Reich officials for life when they have completed the 35th year.

3. Anyone of non-Aryan descent, or married to a person of non-Aryan descent, may not be appointed a Reich official. Reich officials of Aryan descent who marry a person of non-Aryan descent are to be discharged. The question of who is of non-Aryan descent is to be decided by regulations decreed by the Reich Minister of the Interior.

4. If urgent requirements of the administration so necessitate, the highest Reich officials may make exceptions in individual cases—exceptions from the provisions of (2) with the approval of the Reich Minister of Finance, exceptions from the provisions of (3) with the approval of the Reich Minister of the Interior.

****

Article 6

1. The provisions are also to be applied to the civil service regulations of the states, local communities, and of the other bodies, institutions, and foundations of public law.

2. The German State Railways, the Reichsbank, the public-legal religious societies, and the confederations are empowered to issue similar regulations.

Chapter 3

******

Article 7

2. When the economic status of a female official appears to be permanently secured because of a family income, the officials … may order a dismissal. The conditions for dismissal are always present when the husband is a permanent official not subject to dismissal….

Source: "Law Changing the Regulations in Regards to Public Officers." June 30, 1933. Reprinted as Document 1400-PS in *Nazi Conspiracy and Aggression.* Vol. 3. Washington, DC: United States Government Printing Office, 1946.

3.3
Annihilating the Adversaries – 1933-34
Statement about Nazi Persecution by Rudolf Diels

Adolf Hitler established a large network of concentration camps shortly after taking power. These camps became a key element of Nazi rule, serving as a means of silencing, punishing, and in some cases murdering those deemed to be enemies of the Third Reich. This included everyone from leftists to homosexuals to Jews. Just as importantly, the camps served as a threat to the population at large, discouraging opposition to Nazi rule. In the following sworn statement used at the Nuremberg war crimes trials, Diels, a Prussian police official, testifies about the Nazis' ruthless attacks on anyone that they considered a threat. The "blood purge" he mentions refers to the so-called Night of the Long Knives (June 30-July 1, 1934), when hundreds of Nazi Party members were murdered because they were considered a potential threat to Hitler's power.

I, Rudolf Diels, 45 years of age, testify under oath as follows: When Hitler became Chancellor of the Reich on January 30th 1933, I was a Superior Government Councillor [Oberregierungsrat] in the police section of the Prussian Ministry of Interior. There I was in the section: Political Police. Therefore I know the happenings within the police, as they occurred during the time after Hitler's seizure of power, from my own experience.

When Hitler became Chancellor of the Reich, Hermann Goering became provisional [Kommissarischer] Prussian Minister of the Interior and thereby my superior. As such he was the head of the centralized Prussian police administration. This organization constituted the strongest power [Machtfaktor] aside from the army.

The perfectly primitive Nazi conception of the conduct of a state was, that one had to annihilate or render harmless all adversaries or suspected adversaries. The inferiority complex of the Nazis towards everything they did not know, e.g. legal institution, experts and so on has much to do with that. As for that, it was a natural matter for the new Nazi government and the party, which had come into power, to annihilate their adversaries by all possible means. These actions started after the Reichstag fire. They were executed by various party groups, especially by the SA; for such criminal purposes the government also tried to make the most of certain official government agencies. The methods applied were as follows: Human beings, who deprived of their freedom subjected to severe bodily mistreatment or killed. These illegal detentions [Freiheitsberaubungen] took place in camps, often old military barracks, stormtroop quarters or fortresses. Later on these places became known as concentration camps, such as Oranienburg, near Berlin, Lichtenburg, Papenburg, Dachau in Bavaria, Columbiahouse Berlin, etc.

During this period of time, numerous politicians, deputies, writers, doctors, lawyers and other personalities of leading circles were arrested illegally, tortured and killed. Among the killed, there were the Social Democrat Stelling, Ernst Heilmann, the former Police President of Altona Otto Eggerstedt, the communist Schehr from the Ruhr territory, and numerous parties and denominations, amongst them Conservatives, Democrats, Catholics, Jews, Communists and Pacifists.

These murders were camouflaged by the expression: "shot while trying to escape" or "resisting arrest" or similar things. Approximately 5-700 people perished during this first wave of terror (from March until October 1933 approximately).

I myself and my co-workers, old civil servants Not-Nazis, tried to resist this wave of terror.

There was no legal possibility left any more, to undertake anything in order to stop these illegal arrests, because the Reich Cabinet had suspended Civil Rights by decree of February 28th 1933. On account of this fact, it was also impossible for the inmates of the concentration camps to appeal to any court. Such a state of affairs had never existed before, not even during extraordinary times. The word "protective custody" was used at that time for concentration camps etc. was an irony. There were a few cases of real protective custody, in which I put people behind safe walls, in order to protect them against terrible excesses.

The number of illegal cases attained an ever-increasing extent. When Heinrich Himmler took over the reins of power as the highest Chief of police in Prussia under Goering, these actions were really organized by the State proper. The first, great, state-organized terror project under his leadership was the blood purge of June 30th, 1934, at that time SA leaders, Generals, leading Catholics and others were murdered. He also arrested people again, who had been released from concentration camps before that time. This at a time, when actually a certain tranquility in the country had set in already.

Read by myself, approved, signed and sworn to:

[signed]

RUDOLF DIELS

Source: Nuremberg Testimony of Rudolf Diels. Reprinted as Document 2544-PS in *Nazi Conspiracy and Aggression*. Vol. 5. Washington, D.C.: United States Government Printing Office, 1946.

3.4
The Nuremberg Laws – 1935
Text of the Reich Citizenship Law

The primary legal justification for the anti-Semitic actions undertaken in Nazi Germany came with the enactment of the so-called Nuremberg Laws, which were named for the German city where a special session of the Reichstag was held. The Reich Citizenship Law was the foundation of these measures. It limited German citizenship to those who possessed "German or kindred blood." Thus, Jews were ruled to be non-citizens, and—as would soon be demonstrated—non-citizens could be legally subjected to many different forms of harassment by the Nazi government.

1935 REICHSGESETZBLATT, PART I, PAGE 1146

The Reich Citizenship Law of 15 Sept 1935

The Reichstag has adopted unanimously, the following law, which is herewith promulgated.

Article 1

1. A subject of the State is a person, who belongs to the protective union of the German Reich, and who, therefore, has particular obligations towards the Reich.

2. The status of the subject is acquired in accordance with the provisions of the Reich and State Law of Citizenship.

Article 2

1. A citizen of the Reich is only that subject, who is of German or kindred blood and who, through his conduct, shows that he is both desirous and fit to serve faithfully the German people and Reich.

2. The right to citizenship is acquired by the granting of Reich citizenship papers.

3. Only the citizen of the Reich enjoys full political rights in accordance with the provision of the laws.

Article 3

The Reich Minister of the Interior in conjunction with the Deputy of the Fuehrer will issue the necessary legal and administrative decree for the carrying out and supplementing of this law.

Source: "The Reich Citizenship Law." September 15, 1935. Reprinted as Document 1416-PS in *Nazi Conspiracy and Aggression*. Vol. 4. Washington, DC: United States Government Printing Office, 1946.

3.5
The Nazis Define Jewishness – 1935
Text of the First Regulation to the Reich Citizenship Law

Two months after the Reich Citizenship Law was handed down, German leader Adolf Hitler and his inner circle issued the following regulation. This set out specific criteria for Nazi officials to consider in deciding who should be legally classified as a Jew.

1935 REICHSGESETZBLATT, PART I, PAGE 1333

First Regulation to the Reichs Citizenship Law of 14 Nov. 1935

On the basis of Article 3, Reichs Citizenship Law, of 15 Sept. 1935 (RGB1 I, page 146) the following is ordered:

Article 1

1. Until further issue of regulations regarding citizenship papers, all subjects of German or kindred blood, who possessed the right to vote in the Reichstag elections, at the time the Citizenship Law came into effect, shall, for the time being, possess the rights of Reich citizens. The same shall be true of those whom the Reich Minister of the Interior, in conjunction with the Deputy of the Fuehrer, has given the preliminary citizenship.

2. The Reich Minister of the Interior, in conjunction with the Deputy of the Fuehrer, can withdraw the preliminary citizenship.

Article 2

1. The regulations in Article 1 are also valid for Reichs subjects of mixed, Jewish blood.

2. An individual of mixed Jewish blood, is one who descended from one or two grandparents who were racially full Jews, insofar as does not count as a Jew according to Article 5, paragraph 2. One grandparent shall be considered as full-blooded if he or she belonged to the Jewish religious community.

Article 3

Only the Reich citizen, as bearer of full political rights, exercises the right to vote in political affairs, and can hold a public office. The Reich Minister of the Interior, or any agency empowered by him, can make exceptions during the transition period, with regard to occupying public offices. The affairs of religious organizations will not be touched upon.

Article 4

1. A Jew cannot be a citizen of the Reich. He has no right to vote in political affairs, he cannot occupy a public office.

2. Jewish officials will retire as of 31 December 1935. If these officials served at the front in the World War, either for Germany or her allies, they will receive in full, until they reach the age limit, the pension to which they were entitled according to last received wages; they will, however, not advance in seniority. After reaching the age limit, their pension will be calculated anew, according to the last received salary, on the basis of which their pension was computed.

3. The affairs of religious organizations will not be touched upon.

4. The conditions of service of teachers in Jewish public schools remain unchanged, until new regulations of the Jewish school systems are issued.

Article 5

1. A Jew is anyone who descended from at least three grandparents who were racially full Jews. Article 2, par. 2, second sentence will apply.

2. A Jew is also one who descended from two full Jewish parents, if: (a) he belonged to the Jewish religious community at the time this law was issued, or who joined the community later; (b) he was married to a Jewish person, at the time the law was issued, or married one subsequently; (c) he is the offspring from a marriage with a Jew, in the sense of Section 1, which was contracted after the Law for the protection of German blood and German honor became effective (RGB1. I, page 1146 of 15 Sept 1935); (d) he is the offspring of an extramarital

relationship, with a Jew, according to Section 1, and will be born out of wedlock after July 31, 1936.

Article 6

1. As far as demands are concerned for the pureness of blood as laid down in Reichs law or in orders of the NSDAP and its echelons—not covered in Article 5—they will not be touched upon.

2. Any other demands on pureness of blood, not covered in Article 5, can only be made with permission from the Reich Minister of the Interior and the Deputy of the Fuehrer. If any such demands have been made, they will be void as of 1 Jan 1936, if they have not been requested from the Reich Minister of the Interior in agreement with the Deputy of the Fuehrer. These requests must be made from the Reich Minister of the Interior.

Article 7

The Fuehrer and Reichs Chancellor can grant exemptions from the regulations laid down in the law.

Source: "First Regulation to the Reich Citizenship Law." November 14, 1935. Reprinted as Document 1417-PS in *Nazi Conspiracy and Aggression*. Vol. 4. Washington, DC: United States Government Printing Office, 1946.

3.6

Hitler Outlaws Sexual Relations between Jews and Citizens of "German Blood" – 1935

Text of the Law for the Protection of the German Blood and of the German Honor

The following measure signed by Adolf Hitler was yet another of the Nuremberg Laws; it outlawed marriage and sexual relations between Jews and citizens of German blood. It also contained a handful of other decrees designed to further marginalize German Jews from mainstream German society.

1935 REICHGESETZBLATT, PART I, PAGE 1146

Law for the Protection of the German Blood
and of the German Honor of 15 September, 1935

Permeated by the knowledge that the purity of the German blood is the hypothesis for the permanence of the German people and animated by the inflexible determination to safeguard the German nation for all time, the Reichstag has unanimously decreed the following law which is hereby published:

1.

(1) Marriages between Jews and citizens of German or similar blood are forbidden. Contracted marriages are invalid even if they are contracted abroad within the scope of this law.

(2) The proceedings for annulment can only be brought by the Public Prosecutors.

2.

Extra marital intercourse between Jews and citizens of German and similar blood is forbidden.

3.

Jews may not employ female citizens of German and similar blood under 45 years of age in their households.

4.

(1) Jews are forbidden to hoist the Reich and national flag and to display the colors of the Reich.

(2) On the other hand, the display of the Jewish colors is permissible. The practice of this authorization is under State protection.

5.

(1) Whoever acts contrary to the prohibition of 1 will be punished by penitentiary.

(2) The man who acts contrary to the prohibition of 2 will be punished by imprisonment or penitentiary.

(3) Whoever acts contrary to the terms of 3 or 4 will be punished by imprisonment up to 1 year and by fine or by one of these penalties.

6

The Reich Minister of the Interior issues in agreement with the Fuehrer's Deputy and the Reich Minister of Justice the legal and administrative regulations necessary for the execution and supplementing of the law.

7.

The law comes into force on the day of publication.

"3" however only on 1 January 1936.

Source: "Law for the Protection of the German Blood and of the German Honor." September 15, 1935. Reprinted as Document 3179-PS in *Nazi Conspiracy and Aggression*. Vol. 5. Washington, DC: United States Government Printing Office, 1946.

3.7

The Third Reich Inventories Jewish Wealth - 1938
Text of the Decree for the Reporting of Jewish Owned Property

In 1938 Nazi Germany passed a measure that required all Jews living in Germany to supply the government with a detailed list of all their property in excess of a certain amount. Among its other consequences, the Decree for the Reporting of Jewish Owned Property forced Jewish business owners to declare their financial worth. To no one's surprise, this information was quickly used by the Nazis against the nation's Jewish population. Later in 1938, German Chancellor Adolf Hitler decreed that all Jewish business owners had to sell their assets to non-Jews. Nazi officials consulted these inventories to ensure that Hitler's directive was carried out.

1938 REICHSGESETZBLATT, PART I, PAGE 414

Decree for the Reporting of Jewish Owned Property of 26 April 1938

On the basis of the Decree for the Execution of the Four Year Plan of 18 October 1936 (RGB1 I, 887) the following is hereby decreed:

Article 1

1. Every Jew (Article 5 of the First Regulation under the Reich Citizenship Law of 14 November 1935 (RGB1 I, 1333)) shall report and evaluate in accordance with the following instructions his entire domestic and foreign property and estate on the day when this decree goes into force. Jews of foreign citizenship shall report and evaluate only their domestic property.

2. The duty to report holds likewise for the non-Jewish marital partner of a Jew.

3. Every reporting person's property must be given separately.

Article 2

1. Property in the sense of this law includes the total property of the person required to report, irrespective of whether it is exempt from any form of taxation or not.

2. It does not include movable objects used by the individual or house furnishings as far as the latter are not classed as luxury objects.

Article 3

1. Every part of the property shall be valued according to the usual value it has on the effective date of this regulation.

2. No report is necessary when the total worth of the property to be reported does not exceed 5000 marks.

Article 4

The report is to be presented on an official form by 30 June 1938, to the administrative official responsible at the place of residence of the reporting individual. When such a report is not possible by this date the responsible office can extend the period. In such case, however, an estimate is to be presented by 30 June 1938, together with a statement of the grounds of delay.

Article 5

1. The reporting individual must report, after this decree goes into force, to the responsible office, every change of said individual's total property as far as it exceeds a proper standard of living or normal business transactions.

2. The reporting requirement applies also to those Jews who were not required to report on the effective date of this regulation, but who have acquired property exceeding 5000 Reichsmarks in value, after this date. Article 1 (1) clause 2, shall apply respectively.

Article 6

1. The administrative offices responsible under this regulation are in Prussia—Highest Administrative Officer [Regierungspraesident] (in Berlin the Police President); Bavaria—Highest Administrative Officer [Regierungspraesident]; Saxony—The District Head [Kreishauptmann]; Wurtemberg—The Minister of the Interior; Baden—The Minister of the Interior; Thueringen—Reich Governor [Reichsstatthalter]; Hessen—Reich Governor; Hamburg—Reich Governor; Mecklenburg—Ministry of the State, Interior Department; Oldenburg—Minister of Interior; Braunschweig—Ministry of Interior; Bremen—Senator for Administration of Interior; Anhalt—Ministry of State Interior Department; Lippe—Reich Governor (Land Government); Schaumburg-Lippe—Land Government; Saarland—The Reich Commissioner for the Saar.

2. Austria—The Reich Governor has jurisdiction. He may transfer his authority to another board.

Article 7

The Deputy for the Four Year Plan is empowered to take such necessary measures as may be necessary to guarantee the use of the reported property in accord with the necessities of German economy.

Article 8

1. Whoever wilfully or negligently fails to comply with this reporting requirement, either by omitting it, or making it incorrectly, or not within the time speci-

fied, or whoever acts contrary to any instruction issued pursuant to Article 7 by the Deputy of the Four Year Plan shall be punishable by imprisonment and by a fine or by both of these penalties, in particularly flagrant cases of wilful violation the offender may be condemned to hard labor up to ten years. The offender is punishable notwithstanding that the action was in a foreign country.

2. Any attempt to commit such actions is punishable.

3. In addition to the imposition of the penalties under (1), the property may be confiscated, insofar as it was involved in the criminal action. In addition to hard labor confiscation may be made. Where no specific individual can be prosecuted or convicted, confiscation may be decreed independently, where the prerequisites for confiscation warrant it.

Source: "Decree for the Reporting of Jewish Owned Property." April 26, 1938. Reprinted as Document 1406-PS in *Nazi Conspiracy and Aggression*. Vol. 3. Washington, DC: United States Government Printing Office, 1946.

3.8

Nazi Decrees on Jewish Names – 1938
Text of the Second Decree on the Change of First and Family Names

Some of the anti-Semitic measures instituted by the Nazis approached surreal absurdity, such as this decree, which mandated that Jews adopt specific names. But this law had a serious purpose; it showed that the government had power over essential elements of a person's identity and further reinforced the inferior status of the Judaic community.

1938 REICHSGESETZBLATT, PART I, PAGE 1044
Second Decree

Allotting to the implementation of the law on the change of first and family names.
(Does not concern the country of Austria)

17 August 1938

Section I

(1) Jews must only be given first names which are enumerated in the directives issued by the Reich Minister of the Interior, concerning the bearing of first names.

(2) Section 1 does not apply to Jews of foreign nationality.

Section II

(1) If Jews bear other first names as such authorized for Jews by virtue of Section 1, they must—starting on January 1, 1939—adopt another additional first name, namely "Israel" for men and "Sara" for women.

Source: "Second Decree Allotting to the Implementation of the Law on the Change of First and Family Names." August 17, 1938. Reprinted as Document 2873-PS in *Nazi Conspiracy and Aggression*. Vol. 5. Washington, DC: United States Government Printing Office, 1946.

3.9
The "Marking" of the Jews – 1941
Reinhard Heydrich Mandates that Jews Wear Star of David Badges

The requirement that Jews wear a distinguishing badge on their clothing is one of the most potent symbols of anti-Semitism, and early examples of such measures date back as far as the Middle Ages. The Nazis resurrected this scheme, though the requirement was put in place at different times in different areas controlled by Germany during World War II. The following 1941 decree applied to the Protectorate of Bohemia and Moravia—an area of Czechoslovakia taken over by the Germans in 1939. Jews within Germany faced this mandate at about the same time, while those in Poland were forced to don the Star of David soon after the German invasion of 1939. The author of the decree affecting Bohemia and Moravia was Reinhard Heydrich, a central figure in the Nazi persecution of the Jews. He headed the Sicherheitsdienst (S.D.), *the security police or intelligence unit of the S.S., and later the* Reichssicherheitshauptamt (RSHA) *or Reich Chief Security Office, which played a key role in the Holocaust. Heydrich was also appointed Protector of Bohemia and Moravia in 1941.*

1941 REICHSGESETZBLATT, PART I, NO. 100, PAGE 547

Police decree concerning the "marking" of the Jews of September 1, 1941.

Based upon the decree relating to the police decrees of the Reich minister of November 1938 (Reichsgesetzblatt I S 1582) and the decree concerning the legislative power in the Protectorate Bohemia and Moravia of June 7, 1939 (Reichsgesetzblatt I S 1039) it is ordered hereby in agreement with the "Reichsprotektor" in Bohemia and Moravia as follows:

Section 1

1. Jews (Section 5 of the first decree to the Reich citizen law of November 1935—Reichsgesetzblatt I, S 1333) who finished the sixth year of their age are prohibited to appear in public without a Jewish star.

2. The Jewish star consists of a "Six Star" with black contours in the size of the palm of the hand of yellow material with the black inscription "Jew". It has to be worn on the left side of the chest of the clothing tightly sewed on.

83

Section 2

Jews are forbidden

a. to leave the boundary of their residential district without carrying a written permission of the local police authority.

b. to wear medals, decorations, and other badges.

Section 3

The sections 1 and 2 will not apply

a. to the Jewish spouse living in a mixed marriage, as far as descendants of the marriage are existent and these are not considered as Jews, and even then, if the marriage does not exist anymore or the only son has been killed in the present war.

b. to the Jewish wife of a childless mixed marriage for the duration of the marriage.

Section 4

1. Who contravenes against the prohibition of Sections 1 and 2, deliberately or carelessly, will be punished with a penalty up to 150 Reichsmark or with imprisonment up to six weeks.

2. Further reaching police security measures and also penal provisions, according to which a higher penalty is incurred, remain effective.

Section 5

The police decree is also effective in the Protectorate Bohemia and Moravia with the provision that the Reichsprotektor in Bohemia and Moravia may adopt the instruction of section 2 to the local conditions in the Protectorate Bohemia and Moravia.

Section 6

The police decree will be effective 14 days after its promulgation.

Source: "Police. Decree Concerning the 'Marking' of the Jews." September 1, 1941. Reprinted as Document 2877-PS in *Nazi Conspiracy and Aggression*. Vol. 5. Washington, DC: United States Government Printing Office, 1946.

4

PRESSURE AND PROPAGANDA

Nazi "Brown Shirts" armed with boycott signs block the entrance to a Jewish-owned shop in Berlin in 1933. The signs read: "Germans, defend yourselves against the Jewish atrocity propaganda, buy only at German shops!" and "Germans, defend yourselves, buy only at German shops!"

INTRODUCTION

In addition to the Nuremberg Laws and other anti-Semitic legislation, the Nazis persecuted the Jews by a wide array of other means during the 1930s. Within weeks of passage of the March 1933 Enabling Law, which gave German Chancellor Adolf Hitler dictator-like powers, the Nazi Party organized a nationwide boycott of Jewish businesses. The Star of David and anti-Semitic slogans were painted on Jewish-owned stores, and Nazi storm troopers were posted at the entrances of these establishments to discourage customers from entering. The boycott was masterminded by Joseph Goebbels, Hitler's Reichsminister of Propaganda.

Goebbels carried out many other actions to further the Nazi hold over Germany. He pioneered new methods of shaping and controlling public opinion in the process. One of his favorite tactics was to communicate a specific message repeatedly until it became accepted by a large portion of the public as an indisputable truth. This form of propaganda, which could easily be achieved because the Nazis controlled all of the country's radio stations and newspapers, was often used to generate support for Hitler's anti-Semitic policies.

One of the most infamous outlets in this regard was *Der Stürmer,* a newspaper edited by Nazi leader Julius Streicher. It specialized in publishing outrageous charges against the Jews, perpetuating longstanding myths about ritual murder and portraying Jewish men as sexual predators intent on defiling gentile women. Patriotic pageantry was yet another important tool in building support for Hitler's government. Massive Nazi rallies were staged through the late 1930s, employing elaborate ceremonies that showcased Hitler as an all-powerful ruler. Again, Goebbels was a central figure in these carefully calculated exercises in image building.

The Nazi Party considered youth education to be another extremely important tool in shaping public opinion. Schools began promoting a pro-Nazi agenda, which included class instruction on the treacherous nature of the Jewish people. These lesson plans convinced many Jewish parents to move their children to Judaic schools. Those Jews that remained in the public schools received poor and sometimes humiliating treatment from their teachers. The Nazis also extended their influence over the young through youth groups similar to the Boy Scouts and Girl Scouts. The Hitler Youth was the male organization, and its female counterpart was the League of German Girls. Membership was originally voluntary, but in 1938 all children who were considered German citizens were required to join. In these Nazi-directed organizations, character-building activities included lessons in anti-Semitism and, for boys, military drills to prepare them for their future roles as defenders of the "Third Reich." (The Nazis used this term as a synonym for the government of Nazi Germany; it conveyed the Nazi belief that they were erecting the third great German *reich,* or empire, of world history—the first two being the Holy Roman Empire and the German Empire of 1871-1918.)

DOCUMENTS

4.1
The Practice of "Jew Baiting" – 1933
Text of a Memorandum from the Third Reich's Propaganda Department

Proof of the continuing economic harassment of the Jews is found in the following July 7, 1933, memo. This memo orders party officials to publicize the names of those Germans who frequent Jewish businesses, using covert surveillance to determine who those customers are. Similar pressure is also advocated against those non-Jews who have personal contact with the members of the Judaic community.

To all Kreis directorates

Subject: List M. 18, Jew baiting Nr 2

You will receive in the next few days a list of the communities of your districts in which you will find the Jewish firms and businesses of your district. You will immediately check in your whole district whether the addresses given are correct or whether some have been forgotten. The highest importance is to be placed on accuracy since the list is to be printed.

Subject: Jew baiting

The district directorate will set up a committee which has the task of directing and supervising the communities in the whole district. The strength of this committee will be determined by the district directed. You are to inform the Gau propaganda directorate at once of the committees named. The Gau propaganda directorate will then set itself in coordinating with these committees through you.

Present tasks of the committees.

The committee will form in all the local groups and support localities such committees whose names shall be known only to the district committee. The members of the sub-committees shall report to the district committee the names of those Party members and other Germans who buy from Jews. The district committee will publish articles whose content is such that it will point out to the miscreant members of the nation the shamefulness of their deed, and will make them aware of the shame to which they would be subjected if they were proceeded against publicly. This article must be arranged so that only the addresses of those involved, the business and the time in which he made the purchase will be given. The article should bear no signature and will be posted on various posting spots. Further the committees have to secure female clerks from Jewish stores, who can then very easily name those who purchase in Jewish shops. This demands some caution and has to be done with the greatest secrecy. The names of these clerks shall in no case be mentioned. Negotiations are to be undertaken with the association for the employed middle class so that it will prepare the means for this action and will assume the responsibility of finding a new job in another shop of equal importance in case the clerk loses her job. Her name must not be given, only the number.

The district directorate will point out in all gatherings of members or in all public gatherings that the Jew in all countries is again carrying on a low attack which is greatly harmful to Germany. It must be made clear to the masses that no German may buy from a Jew. It is also to be demanded of the Party membership that it constantly bring this to the attention of its friends and acquaintances. The Party membership must go so far in the interest of the nation that it cease friendship with best acquaintances if the latter continue to purchase from Jews. It must go so far that no German will speak to a Jew if it is not absolutely necessary, and this must be particularly pointed out.

German girls who go with Jews are to be made cognizant of the shamefulness of their actions. A member of our party must, in no way, have anything to do with such a person.

Source: "Nazi Memorandum on 'Jew Baiting.'" July 7, 1933. Reprinted as Document 374-PS in *Nazi Conspiracy and Aggression*. Vol. 3. Washington, DC: United States Government Printing Office, 1946.

4.2
"Cluster Round the Swastika Banner" – 1933
Songs of the Hitler Youth

The Nazi Party was fond of public spectacles, expressed in everything from massive rallies to simple marches. Music and singing often played a role in these exhibitions. The following lyrics are taken from a 1933 collection of songs intended for use by the Hitler Youth. Militaristic patriotism figures prominently in the verses, as does violent anti-Semitism. The title of the first song, "Can You See Dawn in the East" even employs a veiled reference to German ambitions of conquest in eastern Europe.

Can You See the Dawn in the East?

1. Can you see the dawn in the East? A sigh of freedom and sun.

   We will keep together, whether living or dead, come what may.

Why do you still doubt, stop all this quarrelling, German blood still flows
   in our veins. People to Arms.

2. For many years the people was enslaved and misguided.
   Traitors and Jews had the upper hand, they demanded the sacrifice of legions.
   Born of our nation a Fuehrer arose, gave Germany faith and hope again.
   People to Arms.

3. Germans awake and get into line, we march towards victory.
   Labour shall be free, we will be free, and valiantly and defiantly daring.
   We clench our fists we will not be faint hearted, there is no going back, we
   will risk it.
   People to arms.

4. Young and old—man for man cluster round the Swastika banner.
   Whether a townsman, a farmer or a worker, they will wield the sword and
   hammer for Hitler, for Freedom, for work and bread.
   Germany awake, death to Jewry,
   People to arms....

Drums Sound Throughout the Land

Verse 1. Drums sound throughout the Land, the drums of the Hitler Youth,
   The flag waves in our hand, the flag is our Fatherland,
   Our enemies must go to the scaffold, the enemy must go to the scaffold.
   Chorus: Hitler Youth marches, Hitler Youth marches.

Verse 2. We firmly believe in our destiny,
   Heil Adolf Hitler,
   And though we are given the death blow,
   We will nevertheless make Germany great,
   We comrades, we comrades.

Chorus.

Verse 3. As Hitler Youth the best of the nation were killed,
   We are the last levy and carry blood red banners
   For Germany's greatest son, for Germany's greatest son.

Chorus.

Source: Pardun, A., "Can You See the Dawn in the East?" and Blumensaat, George, "Drums Sound
   Throughout the Land." Reprinted as Document 3764-PS in *Nazi Conspiracy and Aggression*. Supplement A. Washington, D.C.: United States Government Printing Office, 1946.

4.3
Witness to a Nazi Party Rally – 1934
Excerpt from Berlin Diary *by William L. Shirer*

An American radio journalist, William L. Shirer was sent to Berlin in 1934 as a correspondent for the news service Universal. He remained in the German capital until 1941 and later used his experiences there to write The Rise and Fall of the Third Reich, *one of the classic historical works on Nazi Germany. In the following passage from his memoir* Berlin Diary, *he relates events at a Nazi Party rally in Nuremberg in 1934 and offers his impressions of Adolf Hitler's command over the party faithful. The "blood flag" referred to by Shirer is a Nazi swastika flag used during the attempted Nazi Beer Hall Putsch of 1923. The "bloody purge" mentioned by Shirer is a reference to the so-called Night of the Long Knives, which took place on June 29, 1934, when certain members of the Nazi Party were murdered because they were perceived as a threat to Hitler's leadership. Foremost among the victims was Ernst Röhm, who had commanded the S.A. Storm Troopers. Several non-Nazi politicians and other potential enemies of Hitler were also targeted in these attacks.*

NUREMBERG, *September 4*

Like a Roman emperor Hitler rode into this medieval town at sundown today past solid phalanxes of wildly cheering Nazis who packed the narrow streets that once saw Hans Sachs and the *Meistersinger.* Tens of thousands of Swastika flags blot out the Gothic beauties of the place, the façades of the old houses, the gabled roofs. The streets, hardly wider than alleys, are a sea of brown and black uniforms. I got my first glimpse of Hitler as he drove by our hotel, the Württemberger Hof, to his headquarters down the street at the Deutscher Hof, a favourite old hotel of his, which has been remodelled for him. He fumbled his cap with his left hand as he stood in his car acknowledging the delirious welcome with somewhat feeble Nazi salutes from his right arm. He was clad in a rather worn gaberdine trench-coat, his face had no particular expression at all—I expected it to be stronger—and for the life of me I could not quite comprehend what hidden springs he undoubtedly unloosed in the hysterical mob which was greeting him so wildly. He does not stand before the crowd with that theatrical imperiousness which I have seen [Italian dictator Benito] Mussolini use. I was glad to see that he did not poke out his chin and throw his head back as does the *Duce* nor make his eyes glassy—though there is something glassy in his eyes, the strongest thing in his face. He almost seemed to be affecting a modesty in his bearing. I doubt if it's genuine.

This evening at the beautiful old Rathaus Hitler formally opened this, the fourth party rally. He spoke for only three minutes, probably thinking to save his voice for the six big speeches he is scheduled to make during the next five days. Putzi Hanfstängl, an immense, high-strung, incoherent clown who does not often fail to remind us that he is part American and graduated from Harvard, made the main speech of the day in his capacity of foreign press chief of the party. Obviously trying to please his boss, he had the crust to ask us to "report on affairs in Germany without attempting to interpret them." "History alone," Putzi shouted, "can evaluate the events now taking place under Hitler." What he meant, and what Goebbels and Rosenberg mean, is that we should jump on the bandwagon of Nazi propaganda. I fear Putzi's words fell on deaf, if good-humoured, ears among the American and British correspondents, who rather like him despite his clownish stupidity.

About ten o'clock tonight I got caught in a mob of ten thousand hysterics who jammed the moat in front of Hitler's hotel, shouting: "We want our Führer." I was a little shocked at the faces, especially those of the women, when Hitler finally appeared on the balcony for a moment. They reminded me of the crazed expressions I saw once in the back country of Louisiana on the faces of some Holy Rollers who were about to hit the trail. They looked up at him as if he were a Messiah, their faces transformed into something positively inhuman. If he had remained in sight for more than a few moments, I think many of the women would have swooned from excitement.

Later I pushed my way into the lobby of the Deutscher Hof. I recognized Julius Streicher, whom they call here the Uncrowned Czar of Franconia. In Berlin he is known more as the number-one Jew-baiter and editor of the vulgar and pornographic anti-Semitic sheet the *Stürmer*. His head was shaved, and this seemed to augment the sadism of his face. As he walked about, he brandished a short whip. Knick arrived today. He will cover for INS and I for Universal.

"…the little men of Germany who have made Nazism possible achieved the highest state of being the Germanic man knows: the shedding of their individual souls and minds—with the personal responsibilities and doubts and problems— until …they were merged completely in the Germanic herd."

NUREMBERG, *September 5*

I'm beginning to comprehend, I think, some of the reasons for Hitler's astounding success. Borrowing a chapter from the Roman church, he is restoring pageantry and colour and mysticism to the drab lives of twentieth-century Germans. This morning's opening meeting in the Luitpold Hall on the outskirts of

93

Nuremberg was more than a gorgeous show; it also had something of the mysticism and religious fervour of an Easter or Christmas Mass in a great Gothic cathedral. The hall was a sea of brightly coloured flags. Even Hitler's arrival was made dramatic. The band stopped playing. There was a hush over the thirty thousand people packed in the hall. Then the band struck up the *Badenweiler March,* a very catchy tune, and used only, I'm told, when Hitler makes his big entries. Hitler appeared in the back of the auditorium, and followed by his aides, Göring, Goebbels, Hess, Himmler, and the others, he strode slowly down the long centre aisle while thirty thousand hands were raised in salute. It is a ritual, the old-timers say, which is always followed. Then an immense symphony orchestra played Beethoven's *Egmont* Overture. Great Klieg lights played on the stage, where Hitler sat surrounded by a hundred party officials and officers of the army and navy. Behind them the "blood flag," the one carried down the streets of Munich in the ill-fated putsch. Behind this, four or five hundred S.A. standards. When the music was over, Rudolf Hess, Hitler's closest confidant, rose and slowly read the names of the Nazi "martyrs"—brown-shirts who had been killed in the struggle for power— a roll-call of the dead, and the thirty thousand seemed very moved.

In such an atmosphere no wonder, then, that every word dropped by Hitler seemed like an inspired Word from on high. Man's—or at least the German's—critical faculty is swept away at such moments, and every lie pronounced is accepted as high truth itself. It was while the crowd—all Nazi officials—were in this mood that the Fuhrer's proclamation was sprung on them. He did not read it himself. It was read by *Gauleiter* Wagner of Bavaria, who, curiously, has a voice and manner of speaking so like Hitler's that some of the correspondents who were listening back at the hotel on the radio thought it was Hitler. As to the proclamation, it contained such statements as these, all wildly applauded as if they were new truths: "The German form of life is definitely determined for the next thousand years. For us, the nervous nineteenth century has finally ended. There will be no revolution in Germany for the next one thousand years!" Or: "Germany has done everything possible to assure world peace. If war comes to Europe it will come only because of Communist chaos." Later before a "*Kultur*" meeting he added: "Only brainless dwarfs cannot realize that Germany has been the breakwater against Communist floods which would have drowned Europe and its culture."

Hitler also referred to the fight now going on against his attempt to Nazify the Protestant church. "I am striving to unify it. I am convinced that Luther would have done the same and would have thought of unified Germany first and last."

NUREMBERG, *September 6*

Hitler sprang his *Arbeitsdiest,* his Labour Service Corps, on the public for the first time today and it turned out to be a highly trained, semi-military group of fanatical Nazi youths. Standing there in the early morning sunlight which sparkled on their shiny spades, fifty thousand of them, with the first thousand bared above the waist, suddenly made the German spectators go mad with joy when, without warning, they broke into a perfect goose-step. Now, the goose-step has always seemed to me to be an outlandish exhibition of the human being in his most undignified and stupid state, but I felt for the first time this morning what an inner chord it strikes in the strange soul of the German people. Spontaneously they jumped up and shouted their applause. There was a ritual even for the Labour Service boys. They formed an immense *Sprechchor*—a chanting chorus—and with one voice intoned such words as these: "We want one Leader! Nothing for us! Everything for Germany! *Heil Hitler!*"

Curious that none of the relatives or friends of the S.A. leaders or, say, of General von Schleicher have tried to get Hitler or Göring or Himmler this week. Though Hitler is certainly closely guarded by the S.S., it is nonsense to hold that he cannot be killed. Yesterday we speculated on the matter, Pat Murphy of the *Daily Express,* a burly but very funny and amusing Irishman, Christopher Holmes of Reuter's, who looks like a poet and perhaps is, Knick, and I. We were in Pat's room, overlooking the moat. Hitler drove by, returning from some meeting. And we all agreed how easy it would be for someone in a room like this to toss a bomb on his car, rush down to the street, and escape in the crowd. But there has been no sign of an attempt yet, though some of the Nazis are slightly worried about Sunday, when he reviews the S.A.

NUREMBERG, *September 7*

Another great pageant tonight. Two hundred thousand party officials packed in the Zeppelin Wiese with their twenty-one thousand flags unfurled in the search-lights like a forest of weird trees. "We are strong and will get stronger," Hitler shouted at them through the microphone, his words echoing across the hushed field from the loud-speakers. And there, in the flood-lit night, jammed together like sardines, in one mass formation, the little men of Germany who have made Nazism possible achieved the highest state of being the Germanic man knows: the shedding of their individual souls and minds—with the personal responsibilities and doubts and problems—until under the mystic lights and at the sound of the magic words of the Austrian they were merged completely in the Germanic herd. Later they recovered enough—fifteen thousand of them—to stage a torchlight parade through Nuremberg's ancient streets, Hitler taking the salute in front of the station across from our hotel. Von Papen arrived today and stood alone in a car behind Hitler tonight, the first public appearance he has made, I think, since he narrowly escaped being murdered by Göring on June 30. He did not look happy.

NUREMBERG, *September 9*

Hitler faced his S.A. storm troopers today for the first time since the bloody purge. In a harangue to fifty thousand of them he "absolved" them from blame for the Röhm "revolt." There was considerable tension in the stadium and I noticed

95

that Hitler's own S.S. bodyguard was drawn up in force in front of him, separating him from the mass of the brown-shirts. We wondered if just one of those fifty thousand brown-shirts wouldn't pull a revolver, but not one did. Viktor Lutze, Röhm's successor as chief of the S.A., also spoke. He has a shrill, unpleasant voice, and the S.A. boys received him coolly, I thought. Hitler had in a few of the foreign correspondents for breakfast this morning, but I was not invited.

NUREMBERG, *September 10*

Today the army had its day, fighting a very realistic sham battle in the Zeppelin Meadow. It is difficult to exaggerate the frenzy of the three hundred thousand German spectators when they saw their soldiers go into action, heard the thunder of the guns, and smelt the powder. I feel that all those Americans and English (among others) who thought that German militarism was merely a product of the Hohenzollerns—from Frederick the Great to Kaiser Wilhelm II—made a mistake. It is rather something deeply ingrained in all Germans. They acted today like children playing with tin soldiers. The Reichswehr "fought" today only with the "defensive" weapons allowed them by Versailles, but everybody knows they've got the rest—tanks, heavy artillery, and probably airplanes.

LATER.—After seven days of almost ceaseless goose-stepping, speech-making, and pageantry, the party rally came to an end tonight. And though dead tired and rapidly developing a bad case of crowd-phobia, I'm glad I came. You have to go through one of these to understand Hitler's hold on the people, to feel the dynamic in the movement he's unleashed and the sheer, disciplined strength the Germans possess. And now—as Hitler told the correspondents yesterday in explaining his technique—the half-million men who've been here during the week will go back to their towns and villages and preach the new gospel with new fanaticism. Shall sleep late tomorrow and take the night train back to Berlin.

Source: Shirer, William L. *Berlin Diary: The Journal of a Foreign Correspondent 1934-1941.* New York: Popular Library, 1961.

4.4
The S.S. Calls You – 1930s
Text of an S.S. Recruitment Pamphlet

As noted in William Shirer's diary, the Nazis created an elite military corps—the S.S. (for Schutzstaffel or "defense corps")—upon taking power. The following recruitment pamphlet was issued to attract enlistees to the Waffen S.S.—one of the branches of the corps. The murders of the Holocaust were largely committed by S.S. personnel.

German Youth!

With this pamphlet the SS turns to you, our young comrades of the Front of tomorrow. You should be made even more familiar than before with the spirit that animates the Waffen SS, with the leadership, organization, equipment, and arms of these troops who are so especially close to the Fuehrer and who have taken such a proud part in the German victories in the West and East, in the North and South.

You know it is the duty of every German to be and prove himself to be a soldier. Those young Germans, however, who stand out in character and mien, desire to be more than soldiers! They will not want to wait until they are drafted, they will want to fight as volunteers.

The special missions of the SS require that unchangeable laws of selection be applied and thus gain the most valuable forces for the SS. The young German shall undergo the qualifying examination in confidence, to determine whether he is fit for the SS and physically qualified for the Waffen SS. In case of rejection, there still remain many possibilities to make oneself useful to the nation in the most worthy manner.

It is often said that the men of the Waffen SS are great "daredevils". That is true, but never to the extent that the Waffen SS would be committed without preparatory planning and considered leadership. The leaders of the Waffen SS are throughout, in a hundred ways, proven, experienced, schooled men. The losses of the Waffen SS indicate the difficulties of its mission, but in percentage are neither higher nor lower than those of the other branches of the army.

If you answer the call of the Waffen SS and volunteer to join the ranks of the great Front of SS Divisions, you will belong to a corps which has from the very beginning been directed toward outstanding achievements, and, because of this fact, has developed an especially deep feeling of comradeship. You will be bearing arms with a corps that embraces the most valuable elements of the young German generation. Over and above that you will be especially bound to the National Socialist ideology. Your comrades come from all districts of Germany and from the racially German regions. In its ideological expansion, the Waffen SS also includes volunteers from the Germanic lands. This community-in-arms with SS comrades from Norway, Denmark, Holland, and Flanders, and the volunteers from Finland is a significant contribution to the realization of the new, destined community of Europe into whose spearhead, standard-bearer, and elite troop the SS has made itself.

The youth of the National Socialist Reich knows that he must himself initiate proceedings in order to be able to complete his military service in the Waffen SS. That so many young Germans have volunteered for the Waffen SS is a living testimonial to the confidence of today's young generation in the Waffen SS, its spirit, and, above all, its leadership. It is also, however, a proud demonstration of the ideologically sure attitude of this German youth that it has understood the import of the SS struggle and knows exactly why the Waffen SS is a community under special oath to the Fuehrer. So will be emblazoned on your belt-buckle, too, the motto that the Fuehrer himself on the 1st of April 1931 granted to his SS—"Loyalty is my Honor".

****

The Oath of the SS Man:

I swear to you, Adolf Hitler, as Fuehrer and Reichs Chancellor, loyalty, and bravery. I vow to you, and to those you have named to command me, obedience unto death, so help me God.

****

The SS man is not only a soldier, he is the exemplary bearer of the idea of Adolf Hitler. He is characterized by experience in war, hardness, pride in the share of many victories, the consciousness of hardships and dangers endured, as well as the great legacy that the National Socialist idea has imposed upon him, since he has been fighting in the ranks of the SS.

Source: S.S. Recruitment Pamphlet. Reprinted as Document 3429-PS in *Nazi Conspiracy and Aggression.* Vol. 6. Washington, DC: United States Government Printing Office, 1946.

4.5

Anti-Jewish Propaganda at the Local Level – 1935
Text of a Nazi Memorandum on Anti-Jewish Posters

The Nazis organized a range of anti-Semitic activities, large and small, all across Germany. The following memo penned by H. Huxhagen, a district propaganda organizer of the South Hanover Chapter of National Socialist German Workers' Party, instructs all villages in the district to build large anti-Jewish signs and organize accompanying ceremonies. As with many of the larger anti-Semitic campaigns undertaken by the Nazis, these activities included carefully choreographed events that were designed to appear "spontaneous."

To all district propaganda organisers and group propaganda organisers.

The behaviour of Jews in our district, as in the whole Reich, has recently become extremely offensive. In his impertinence the Jew seems to have forgotten that he is a guest in Germany and should conduct himself accordingly. Further leniency in such matters would be treason to the People and the State. We are accordingly obliged to instruct all district propaganda organisers and local group propaganda organisers as follows:

On the 10th August in all villages of this district posters will be set up inscribed as follows: (See enclosure, i.e.: "Jews not welcome.") The minimum size for these posters is to be 30 ft. by 5 ft. The poster is to be fixed on two supports at least 7 ft.

high. As colour contrast has been selected black block lettering (both for capital and small letters) on a white background. The word "Jew" shall be underlined in red and must be conspicuous. When possible the poster is to be framed with a black margin. The posters are to be set up on all roads leading in and out of each village. The cost of the posters is to be met by agreement between the local party organisation, women's organisation, peasant union, S.A., etc., whereby each of these bodies shall undertake to provide for a poster and see that it is set up on 10th August.

Further financial support is to be canvassed from all local organisations. If insurmountable financial difficulties should arise, the district treasurer has agreed to supplement the cost of delivery and erection of one poster from the funds of the local group.

The erection of the posters on 10th August is to be accompanied by a ceremony, which shall be attended by the entire population of each village. The proceedings should include a short impressive speech by a German Comrade, and at the conclusion songs such as "We Storm Troopers Young and Old" or of similar character are to spring up spontaneously in the crowd. The Press must make no mention of this beforehand, but must deal all the more fully with it subsequently.

Finally, we attach a circular which, in the Göttingen district, has been pasted by night to the windows and doors of all persons noticed to have purchased in Jewish shops. The posters can be obtained from *The Göttinger Nachtrichten*, Göttingen, at the price of 5 marks per 1,000.

Heil Hitler !

[The following list of preferred slogans for the posters was included in an attachment:]

"Jews not welcome"; "Jews enter here at their own risk"; "Any dealings with a Jew—and out you go"; "The inhabitants of this village want nothing to do with Jews"; "No Jews wanted in this village. Signed: The inhabitants"; "The Jews are our misfortune"; "No profit for Jews here"; "We don't want to see any Jews."

Source: Huxhagen, H. Nazi Memorandum on Anti-Jewish Posters, 1935. Reprinted in *The Yellow Spot: The Outlawing of Half a Million Human Beings*, edited by Hensley Henson. London: Victor Gollancz, 1936.

4.6
Nazi Propaganda at Its Crudest – 1935
Text of an Anti-Semitic Leaflet

As Nazi Germany intensified its rhetorical and legal warfare against Jewish people, it often resorted to simplistic anti-Jewish propaganda that had no factual basis. But in many cases, these baseless charges served their purpose—to further ostracize Jews from the rest of German society. The following anti-Semitic leaflet was published in the Basler Nationalzeitung, *a German publication, on September 25, 1935.*

Fellow German,

do you know:

that the *Jew*

ravishes	your child
defiles	your wife
defiles	your sister
defiles	your sweetheart
murders	your parents
steals	your goods
insults	your honour
ridicules	your customs
ruins	your church
corrupts	your culture
contaminates	your race

that the *Jew*

slanders	you
cheats	you
robs	you
regards	you as cattle

that *Jewish*

doctors murder you slowly
lawyers never try to get you your rights
provision shops sell you rotten foodstuffs
butchers' shops are filthier than pigsties

that the *Jew*

has to act as above said in accordance with the laws of his Talmud, for to do so is a "deed good in the sight of God."

FELLOW GERMANS, DEMAND THEREFORE:

For Germans who have sexual relations with non-Aryans, penal servitude, deprivation of citizenship rights, forfeiture of property, and expulsion. For recidivists, the death penalty. The issue to be sterilised and incapable of citizenship, in addition to be expelled. Women and girls who voluntarily associate with Jews to be in no circumstances entitled to the protection of the law.

For seduction, long terms of penal servitude.

THE JEW LIVES ON LIES AND DIES OF THE TRUTH

Source: Anti-Semitic Leaflet, *Basler Nationalzeitung*, September 25, 1935. Reprinted in *The Yellow Spot: The Outlawing of Half a Million Human Beings*, edited by Hensley Henson. London: Victor Gollancz, 1936.

4.7
Poisoning the Minds of Children – 1935
Text of "The Cuckoo and the Jew" by Helga Gerbling

The Nazi Party's hateful rhetoric toward Jews became part of classroom instruction in German schools. Such lessons and other forms of propaganda turned a large number of German children into enthusiastic anti-Semites, as is shown in the following essay reprinted in the pro-Nazi newspaper Der Stürmer *in 1935. Attributed to a nine-year-old girl named Helga Gerbling, this essay was praised by the newspaper's editor as a clear indication that the girl was receiving proper classroom instruction.*

In school the other day we were talking about the Cuckoo. He is the Jew among birds; for in looks, deeds and behaviour he resembles him very much. His curved beak reminds us of the Jew's hooked nose. His feet are small, that's why he can't run very well. This is very much like the Jew, who also can't walk gracefully. When we call "Cuckoo, Cuckoo" he also scrapes and bows like the Jew merchant who always tries to be polite so that we Germans should buy from him. Both Jews, the one among the birds and the one among the humans, are parasites, which means to say that they want to become rich and fat at the expense of others. The female Cuckoo lays her eggs in the nests of other birds such as hedgesparrows and robin redbreasts and she wants them to brood them and bring up the little ones. (It's funny that the Jew does not ask us to do that too.) As soon as the Cuckoo comes out of the egg he gets impudent. He snaps for the best morsels and always wants to have everything. He squeezes back the genuine little birds as soon as the parents come with dinner. He is envious and greedy. His motto is: self-interest before common weal! Just like the Jew who too thinks only of himself and his pocket. Only for his purse to be filled and himself to have a good time! When there is no longer enough room in the bird's nest, then he tries to push the young birds out of their own home. He very often does throw a little one out. Just like the Jew wanted to do with us Germans. He came, an alien, into our "nest" and tried to drive us out. But we humans are not as stupid as the birds. We don't let him do that to us and we throw the cheeky "Cuckoo" out of our land. We children in Roth do our bit too. Some of our class often stand in front of Baer's shop and when people want to go in, we shout: "You ought to be ashamed, shopping at a Jew's; fie be upon you!" Then the women blush crimson and go away. Well *Stürmer,* you like that, don't you?

Heil Hitler!

In the name of Girls IVth Standard,

Helga Gerbling

Source: Gerbling, Helga, "The Cuckoo and the Jew," *Der Stürmer* 32 (August 1935). Reprinted in *The Yellow Spot: The Outlawing of Half a Million Human Beings,* by Hensley Henson. London: Victor Gollancz, 1936.

4.8

Anti-Semitism in Children's Storybooks – 1938
Excerpt from The Poisonous Mushroom *by Ernst Hiemer*

> *Children's storybooks were used as another vehicle of anti-Semitic propaganda. The following excerpt is taken from a book published by* Der Stürmer, *a notorious disseminator of outrageous Nazi propaganda in Germany during the years of the Third Reich.*

Inge sits in the reception room of the Jew doctor. She has to wait a long time. She looks through the journals which are on the table. But she is [al]most too nervous to read even a few sentences. Again and again she remembers the talk with her mother. And again and again her mind reflects on the warnings of her leader of the BDM [League of German Girls]: "A German must not consult a Jew doctor! And particularly not a German girl! Many a girl that went to a Jew doctor to be cured, found disease and disgrace!"

When Inge had entered the waiting room, she experienced an extraordinary incident. From the doctor's consulting room she could hear the sound of crying. She heard the voice of a young girl: "Doctor, doctor leave me alone!"

Then she heard the scornful laughing of a man. And then all of a sudden it became absolutely silent. Inge had listened breathlessly.

"What may be the meaning of all this?" she asked herself and her heart was pounding. And again she thought of the warning of her leader in the BDM.

Inge was already waiting for an hour. Again she takes the journals in an endeavor to read. Then the door opens. Inge looks up. The Jew appears. She screams. In terror she drops the paper. Frightened she jumps up. Her eyes stare into the face of the Jewish doctor. And this face is the face of the devil. In the middle of this devil's face is a huge crooked nose. Behind the spectacles two criminal eyes. And the thick lips are grinning. A grinning that expresses: "Now I got you at last, you little German girl!"

And then the Jew approaches her. His fleshy fingers stretch out after her. But now Inge has her wits. Before the Jew can grab hold of her, she hits the fat face of the Jew doctor with her hand. Then one jump to the door. Breathlessly Inge runs down the stairs. Breathlessly she escapes the Jew house.

Source: Hiemer, Ernst. *Der Giftpilz (The Poisonous Mushroom)*. Nurnberg: Der Stürmer, 1938. Reprinted as Document 1778-PS in *Nazi Conspiracy and Aggression*. Vol. 4. Washington, D.C.: United States Government Printing Office, 1946.

4.9

Julius Streicher and the Anti-Semitic Newspaper *Der Stürmer* — 1934

Text of an Article from Der Stürmer *by Martin Froehling*

Of all the pieces that comprised the Nazis' fearsome propaganda machine, perhaps no single part was as brutally effective as Der Stürmer, *a weekly newspaper that specialized in crude and vicious condemnations of Jews. Helmed by Nazi Julius Streicher, the paper became enormously popular with young and poorly educated Germans who embraced its simple language, anti-Semitic cartoons, and lurid and hateful content. Today, it is still regarded by many as the most infamous newspaper in history. The following representative excerpt is from a 1943 issue of* Der Stürmer.

.... in all schools, in all influential offices of the Party, of the Armed Forces and of the authorities, only one sentence should be written on the walls like a Mene Tekel: Hate the Jew and his brood! But also hate everybody and everything connected and allied with the Jews—with sacred, burning hatred! And when the hour of revenge strikes, we shall not let ourselves be softened by sentimentality! Let us not forget what the Jew has done to humanity for thousands of years! Let us not forget that the Jew has to pay for all the misdeeds he has committed against humanity during thousands of years! Let us remember that the Jew himself has passed sentence upon himself in his own laws: An eye for an eye, a tooth for a tooth! Let us oppose his criminal hatred with our great, sacred hatred! Let us remember that all the victims of Jewish hatred in German towns, in the graves of Katyn and Vinniza and all those mass graves which are still unknown today, the victims of the world war launched by the Jews, are crying out for revenge. When the hour of retribution strikes, our hearts must be and remain hard and must know no other sentiment and no other emotion. Juda must feel and realize that the hour of retribution and settlement has come, and that nothing will be forgotten and forgiven. Juda will then reap the hatred it has sown for centuries. Through this hatred Juda must perish.

Source: Froehling, Martin. Anti-Semitic Article, *Der Stürmer* 33 (12 August 1943). Reprinted as Document M-142 in *Nazi Conspiracy and Aggression*. Supplement A. Washington, DC: United States Government Printing Office, 1946.

4.10

Testimony about the Corrosive Effects of Anti-Jewish Propaganda – 1930s

Excerpt from an Interview with a German Jew in the Third Reich

The anti-Semitic propaganda generated in Nazi Germany had a terrible impact on the self-image of countless Jews living in Germany. In the following passage, Suzanne Sucher recounts her struggles to achieve a positive attitude about her Judaic heritage.

Very close to our building was the main building of the *Stuermer (Der Stürmer)*, the notorious Nazi newspaper. I often had to pass this building on my way to some private lessons. Since I couldn't go to school, I had private lessons. Once, while I glanced at their windows, I could see the front page of the *Stuermer*, with a caricature of the Jews. I call it caricatures because they were. It was so bad and I saw them so often, that I later on almost felt that this must be what we are, that must be how we look, and it took me a long time to get rid of this image. Propaganda is a very terrible situation and very poisonous....

Quite some time before Kristallnacht, all our friends disappeared, our Christian friends disappeared from us. We were really just a Jewish group now. I had no contact, hardly any contact with former girlfriends or other people I knew. I remained mostly in Jewish circles and also afterwards worked in the Jewish hospital, and then worked for a Jewish doctor. But nothing was permanent at this time because the people I worked for usually left the country eventually, those who could leave the country. Those who didn't, sometimes moved away. It was very difficult to immigrate into Israel since the White Paper [the British policy restricting immigration to Palestine in 1939] unless you ... married somebody who had an Israeli permit, then you were able to get out.... My sister did not go back to school. She stayed at home and didn't want to go out because she had stones thrown at her. Ever since the Kristallnacht, which I call the overture to the extermination of the Jews, ... things worsened from day to day and became almost unliveable. I became very friendly with one of the [Jewish studies] seminary students. We were under curfew, by the way. We could not go out at night. So in the evening he came over to my place or he had a little room where he studied and I went over to him and he started to make me Jewishly conscious. He taught me Hebrew ... he taught me to be a Jew. He instilled in me a pride in being Jewish. He taught me various things and also the joy of Judaism.... He instilled in me a whole new thing, to really appreciate being a Jew, not just because a Nazi tells you that you are no good, that you are terrible. And this was the most important part, because this came at a time

Reprinted with permission from Yad Vashem Archives.

when I was mowed down. I had no feeling for myself. I actually ended up thinking that they were right, that I must look like … the caricatures in the *Stuermer.* I thought that was my image, thought we were no good, that we didn't contribute to anything, that we were inferior.

Source: Yad Vashem Archive O.3 / 5132. Available online at http://www.yadvashem.org.

4.11
Propaganda for the Rest of the World – 1938
Excerpt from "National Socialist Racial Thought," by Walter Gross

> *Members of the Nazi Party also crafted propaganda that was aimed at those outside Germany. The following essay, which appeared in 1938, was penned by Walter Gross, the head of the Third Reich's Bureau for Enlightenment on Population Policy and Racial Welfare. It attempts to put a rational face on Nazi Germany's virulent policies of racial discrimination.*

Of all the measures introduced in the new Germany those bearing on National Socialist racial policy cause the greatest stir internationally, for here was a state setting its feet upon paths hitherto almost untrodden and leading through untouched preserves, whose aims were in many respects liable to clash with established Liberal views. Relevant legislation served to corroborate and achieve these aims and it was no wonder, therefore, that—in the beginning at least—this particular phase of National Socialist reconstruction met with universal misunderstanding and prejudice. We are happy meanwhile to be able to discern that other nations have come to realise that Germany is, indeed, taking to new paths, but they are right ones and are necessary and, more than that, Germany is in many respects blazing a trail for others; mention need only be made of our laws for the prevention of the transmission of hereditary diseases (Sterilisation Law) which has been followed in Norway, Sweden, Denmark and Finland by similar laws or draft proposals. However, no one will wholly understand or sympathise with our legislation who is not wholly familiar with the fundamental change in the philosophical conception of life which has come with National Socialism in the light of history.

Whereas formerly, the more especially under the powerful influence of Marxist teachings, the development and decline of States and civilisations was attributed to economic or purely political causes, we see to-day the determining role played by the human being in sustaining and shaping economy, the State, culture, politics, art and intellectual thought. We have come to feel that the protection and preservation of the people who, after all, are originally responsible for the achievements of the State and culture, is the chief factor in retaining these achievements; for good blood and the strength that comes from good blood is given a people only once and if allowed to degenerate cannot be regenerated as one would rebuild a city or restore devastated lands. Thus, wise statesmanship will place the preservation of the biological, that is, racial energy of its people before its political and economic concerns. The endless series of past empires and civilisations which have flourished and declined forcefully remind us how inexorable are the consequences of ignoring this truth....

Most open to misinterpretation are National Socialist views on the relations between the various races of the world. It has been questioned whether the fundamental racial principles of the new world theory must not breed condescension, even contempt of people of different race. Quite the contrary; these very principles offer the very best guarantee for mutual tolerance and for the peaceful co-operation of all.

We appreciate the fact that those of another race are different from us. This scientific truth is the basis, the justification and, at the same time, the obligation of every racial policy without which a restoration of Europe in our day is no longer practicable. Whether that other race is "better" or "worse" is not possible for us to judge. For this would demand that we transcend our own racial limitations for the duration of the verdict and take on a superhuman, even divine, attitude from which alone an "impersonal" verdict could be formed on the value or lack of such of the many living forms of inexhaustible Nature. But we of all people are too conscious of the inseparable ties of the blood and our own race to attempt to aspire to such an ultra-racial standpoint, even in the abstract.

History, science and life itself tell us in a thousand ways that the human beings inhabiting the earth are anything but alike; that, moreover, the greater races are not only physically but especially spiritually and intellectually different from each other. Yesterday one passed this fact by, and in attempting to unify political, economic, cultural and religious standards for all nations of the earth, one was sinning against Nature, violating the natural attributes of various racial and national groups for the sake of a false principle. Today we bow to the racial differences existing in the world. We want every type of being to find that form of self-expression most fitted to its own particular requirements.

The racial principles of National Socialism are, therefore, the surest guarantee for respecting the integrity of other nations. It is incompatible with our ideas to think of incorporating other nationalities in a Germany built up as a result of conquests, as they would always remain, because of their alien blood and spirit, a foreign body within the German State. Such foolhardy thoughts may be indulged in by a world which has as its goal economic power or purely territorial expansion of its frontiers, but never by a statesman thinking along organic, racial lines whose main care is the preservation of the greatness and along with it the essential unity of his people held together by the ties of blood relationship.

For this reason, we have nothing in common with chauvinism and imperialism because we would extend to other races peopling the earth the same privileges we claim for ourselves: the right to fashion our lives and our own particular world according to the requirements of our own nature.

And if National Socialism would wish to see the unrestricted mixing of blood avoided for the individual, there is nothing in this to suggest contempt. After all, we Germans ourselves, viewed ethnologically, are a mixture. The National Socialist demand is only that the claims of the blood and the laws of biology should be more closely observed in the future.

Here again our standpoint is not so very far removed from that of other people with a sound mental outlook. The American Immigration Laws, for instance, are based on definite racial discrimination. The Europeans and the inhabitants of India, the Pacific Islands, and so on, have instinctively held aloof from a mingling of the blood, and both sides genuinely regard any transgression as very bad form. Nevertheless, this natural attitude in no way detracts from the possibility of close cooperation and friendly interaction. And, speaking on behalf of the new Germany, let me once more emphasize:

"We do not wish our people to intermarry with those of alien race since through such mingling of the blood the best and characteristic qualities of both races are lost."

We do not wish our people to intermarry with those of alien race since through such mingling of the blood the best and characteristic qualities of both races are lost. But we will always have a ready welcome for any guests who wish to visit us whether of kindred or foreign civilization, and our racial views only lead us to a fuller appreciation of their essential peculiarities in the same way as we would want our own peculiarities respected.

On the basis of this reasoning, the National Socialist State was bound to object to the imperialistic designs of the Jewish people on German soil. Thus it is purely an internal concern of the German people who could no longer tolerate the domination—a result of political errors of the past—of an alien race having neither sympathy nor understanding for them. During the political régimes of the past the Jews had managed to obtain an increasing hold on politics, art, culture and commerce....

This predominance of alien influence foreign to the German nature in politics, science and things cultural, provide the objective for the law for the restoration of professionalism in the Civil Service and what has since come to be known as the Nuremberg Laws. The Jews in Germany constitute a group of aliens who can expect to enjoy the hospitality of the country just like members of other races. But no Frenchman would wish to have his leading offices of State occupied by Englishmen, and no Englishman would want to see the key positions in the politics, art and culture of his country occupied by, say, Japanese. Who then can reasonably object to the Germans removing the Jews from the prominent positions in their country? … The Nuremberg Laws, therefore, exclude members of the Jewish race from obtaining Reich citizenship….

These measures were necessary because we realised that a nation or a people can only preserve its culture and its intellectual individuality by keeping the blood pure. It has been said that "every race is a divine inspiration"—a shaft incidentally aimed at the racial policy. We would rejoin, however, "just because every race is a divine inspiration, the foremost task of civilisation is to keep that inspiration pure and reject the least contribution towards detracting from its purity."

Source: Gross, Walter. "National Socialist Racial Thought." In *Germany Speaks: By 21 Leading Members of Party and State*. London: Thornton Butterworth, 1938.

5

KRISTALLNACHT

When Nazi forces unleashed the Kristallnacht pogrom on Jews living all across Germany on the
night of November 9, 1938, synagogues were among the primary targets of violence.
Here lies a pile of Hebrew prayerbooks and other Jewish religious texts that were damaged by fire
at one synagogue in central Germany.

INTRODUCTION

State-sponsored persecution of Jews reached new depths in November 1938. On November 7, a German Jew named Herschel Grynszpan entered the German embassy in Paris and shot Nazi diplomat Ernst vom Rath. Grynszpan had acted after he learned that his parents, Polish-born Jews, had been deported from Germany as part of the Nazi Party's growing persecution of the Judaic community.

When Vom Rath did not die immediately, Nazi propaganda minister Joseph Goebbels and other Nazi leaders seized on the incident as a way to advance their own anti-Semitic agenda. Word was sent to local party officials throughout the country to prepare anti-Jewish attacks upon Vom Rath's death. On November 9, the diplomat died, and Kristallnacht—the Night of Broken Glass—commenced all across Germany. Synagogues were burned to the ground. Jewish businesses were vandalized, their windows shattered and their inventories looted or destroyed. Mobs invaded Jewish homes, smashing furniture and valuables.

Afterward, the Nazis claimed that the attacks had been carried out by regular citizens outraged over the Vom Rath assassination. In reality, storm troopers dressed in civilian clothes were behind the mayhem, and evidence later revealed that the pogrom had been clearly premeditated by government officials. Approximately 100 Jews were killed in the Kristallnacht attacks, and an estimated 30,000 were arrested and sent to concentration camps.

As devastating as the Kristallnacht violence had been, it proved to be only a prelude to even greater repression and brutality. Nazi leaders used the Grynszpan attack as an excuse to institute even more severe measures against the Jews. Many of these were created by Hermann Göring, the director of the German economy and one of Hitler's most trusted aides. For example, Göring levied a fine of one billion reichsmarks on Germany's Jewish population—an estimated 20 percent of their total assets. In addition, Jews were held legally responsible for repairing the widespread damage of Kristallnacht, and any insurance payments made to them for the destruction were seized by the government. The accurately named Decree Relating to the Exclusion of Jews from the German Economic Life was issued at the same time. This law, which prohibited Jews from owning or managing businesses, led to the "Aryanization" of all Jewish enterprises. All across Germany, Jews who still owned businesses were forced to sell them to non-Jews, usually at deeply discounted prices. Strict regulations on when and where Jews were allowed to appear in public were also instituted, and Jewish children were completely banned from public schools.

DOCUMENTS

5.1
The Night of Broken Glass – 1938
Text of Kristallnacht Instructions Issued by Reinhard Heydrich

When the Kristallnacht ("Night of Broken Glass") attacks on Jewish homes, businesses, and synagogues erupted across Germany on the night of November 9-10, 1938, the state's Nazi leadership framed the violence as a spontaneous outburst by German citizens who were outraged about the assassination of German diplomat Ernst vom Rath by a German Jew. But as the following document by Reinhard Heydrich, head of the intelligence unit of the S.S., makes clear, government leaders had carefully planned the violence.

SECRET

Copy of Teletype from Munich, 10 November 1938, 1:20 A.M.

To all Headquarters and Stations of the State Police.

To all Districts and Sub-districts of the SD.

Urgent! Submit immediately to the Chief or his deputy!

Re: Measures against Jews tonight.

Because of the attempt on the life of the Secretary of the Legation vom Rath in Paris tonight, 9-10 November 1938, demonstrations against Jews are to be expected throughout the Reich. The following instructions are given on how to treat these events:

1. The Chiefs of the State Police, or their deputies, must get in telephonic contact with the political leaders [Gauleitung oder Kreisleitung] who have jurisdiction over their districts and have to arrange a joint meeting with the appropriate inspector or commander of the Order Police [Ordnungspolizei] to discuss the organization of the demonstrations. At these discussions the political leaders have to be informed that the German Police has received from the Reichsfuehrer SS and Chief of the German Police the following instructions, in accordance with which the political leaders should adjust their own measures.

a. Only such measures should be taken which do not involve danger to German life or property. (For instance synagogues are to be burned down only when there is no danger of fire to the surroundings).

b. Business and private apartments of Jews may be destroyed but not looted. The police [are] instructed to supervise the execution of this order and to arrest looters.

c. On business streets, particular care is to be taken that non-Jewish business should be protected from damage.

d. Foreigners, even Jews, are not to be molested.

2. The demonstrations which are going to take place should not be hindered by the police provided that the instructions quoted above in section 1 are carried out. The police [have] only to supervise compliance with the instructions.

3. Upon receipt of this telegram, in all synagogues and offices of the Jewish communities the available archives should be seized by the police, to forestall destruction during the demonstrations. This refers only to valuable historical material, not to new lists of taxes, etc. The archives are to be turned over to the competent SS offices.

4. The direction of the measures of the Security Police concerning the demonstrations against Jews is vested with the organs of the State Police, inasmuch as the inspectors of the Security Police are not issuing their own orders. In order to carry out the measures of the Security Police, officials of the Criminal Police as well as members of the SD of the "Verfuegungstruppe" and the allgemeinen SS may be used.

5. Inasmuch as in the course of the events of this night the employment of officials used for this purpose would be possible, in all districts as many Jews, especially rich ones, are to be arrested as can be accommodated in the existing prisons [Haftraeumen]. For the time being only healthy men not too old are to be arrested. Upon their arrest, the appropriate concentration camps should be contacted immediately, in order to confine them in these camps as fast as possible. Special care should be taken that the Jews arrested in accordance with these instructions are not mistreated.

6. The contents of this order are to be forwarded to the appropriate inspectors and commanders of the Ordnungspolizei and to the districts of the SD [SD-Oberabschnitte und SD-Unterabschnitte], adding that the Reichsfuehrer SS and Chief of the German Police ordered this police measure. The Chief of the Ordnungspolizei, has given the necessary instructions to the Ordnungspolizei, including the fire brigade. In carrying out the ordered measures, the closest harmony should be assured between the Sicherheitspolizei and the Ordnungspolizei.

The receipt of this telegram is to be confirmed by the Chiefs of the State Police or their deputies by telegram to the Gestapo, care of SS Standartenfuehrer Mueller.

Source: Heydrich, Reinhard. Kristallnacht Instructions. November 1938. Reprinted as Document 3051-PS in *Nazi Conspiracy and Aggression.* Vol. 5. Washington, DC: United States Government Printing Office, 1946.

5.2

Waiting for Kristallnacht to Arrive – 1938

Excerpt from an Interview with Henry Oertelt, a Jewish Witness of Kristallnacht in Berlin

In the following interview, a Jewish resident of Berlin named Henry Oertelt recalls the tension that preceded Kristallnacht. Oertelt's recollection that Adolf Hitler himself had warned of the attack may be incorrect, though the Nazi-controlled media certainly did threaten reprisals for the assassination of German diplomat Ernst vom Rath at the hands of a Jewish attacker. He also discusses walking past a burned-out synagogue in his neighborhood—one of more than 1,500 synagogues across Germany that were attacked by the Nazis on the Night of Broken Glass. Oertelt was eventually sent to the Auschwitz death camp, but he survived the Holocaust and after the war he wrote a memoir called An Unbroken Chain: My Journey Through the Nazi Holocaust.

The next morning [November 8] … Hitler announced that if this man Vom Rath will die, there will be something happening to the Jews which they have never experienced. And so, frankly, it turned out that, just imagine, that Jews started praying for the well-being of a super Nazi…. It made us feel a little frightened. And while we in a way were happy that somebody did something—you know, stood up [to Nazi anti-Semitism]—on the other hand we were a little frightened of what would happen because by now so many bad things had happened to the Jews. Jews had lost their jobs. Jews were beaten up wherever you saw—up and down the streets….

The reports came constantly on this guy's condition, which was deteriorating very fast…. We were afraid if this guy dies there might really be something. We couldn't figure out what. On the afternoon of the 9th it had been announced that this man had succumbed to his wounds and died. And nothing much took place really, but among the Jews came the warning, don't go on the streets if you don't absolutely have to. Stay at home. Do nothing. And so we were waiting for what happened, you know, like the second shoe to fall. And we went to bed probably something like elevenish or so. My mother draws the curtains for the night. "My gosh," she says, "look guys," to my brother and me. "The sky looks really red out there. I wonder what's going on. There must be a fire somewhere." But we didn't hear any sirens or nothing, and so, you know, every once in a while somebody has a fire in the big city. And so we didn't think much. We went to bed.

Until the next morning when I was on my way to work, to my apprenticeship [as a furniture designer and builder], I had my bicycle, and all of a sudden, a street

Henry A. Oertelt, Videotaped Interview conducted by Solomon Awend, 21 November 1995. Survivors of the Shoah Visual History Foundation. Beverly Hills, CA, USA.

115

away, there were a couple of Jewish stores, and all of a sudden I noticed that all of their window glass was broken out on the street, and some of the items were still scattered out on the street from the ransacking. Then I came by, on my bicycle, also, the synagogue in the neighborhood, and that was burnt down. And at the moment I couldn't figure out what has happened. I had to carry my bike, there was so much glass on the streets. Not to talk about riding, to push it even with the glass [was impossible], so I had to carry my bike for a block or two or something like that in order not to cut the tires....

Hitler in the headlines claimed "*spontaneous* reaction by our German population against the dastardly crime committed by the organized Jewry of the world." They pushed this kind of thing—propaganda was always the big thing, of course. And so then I found out that during that night, also, about 35 Jewish men were killed, among them rabbis that tried to defend their synagogues, as well as about 30,000 Jewish men were rounded up during that night....

Well at that moment, I went on into my workplace, of course, and there we talked a little bit.... There were another couple of Jewish apprentices where I was, too. And we talked about that, and well, we were wondering what happened. We couldn't put together at this point, then later on, of course, next day or so, then we knew what happened all over the place....

Kristallnacht is considered to be the beginning of the Holocaust, the prelude, as it were, of the Holocaust. From that time on out of Germany, regularly, Jews were picked up during the night and were sent to the concentration camps. You see, Hitler built already the first concentration camp only two months after he was in power, at Dachau, near Munich. And from then on they grew up like mushrooms all over the place....

Pretty soon friends disappeared, family members disappeared, neighbors disappeared. And it was interesting, in our building that we lived in were a couple other Jewish families. Nobody ever asked what happened to these or what happened to those. And so people sort of accepted it or didn't dare to ask or talk about it.

Source: Oertelt, Henry. Videotaped interview conducted by Solomon Awend, 21 November 1995. Survivors of the Shoah Visual History Foundation Testimony 7069.

5.3

A Jewish Orphanage Under Attack – 1938
Excerpt from an Account of Kristallnacht Violence by a Jewish Orphanage Director

The following account by Y.S. Herz, the director of a Jewish orphanage in the town of Dinslaken, details some of the destruction and terror unleashed during the Kristallnacht attacks. In this incident, members of the city police carefully follow Nazi instructions: most make no effort to protect the Jewish residents of the orphanage, and other townspeople stand silently by as the destruction takes place. Herz's story begins when an unknown man knocks on the door of the orphanage.

I recognized a Jewish face. In a few words the stranger explained to me: "I am the president of the Jewish community of Duesseldorf. I spent the night in the waiting-room of the Gelsenkirchen Railway Station. I have only one request—let me take refuge in the orphanage for a short while. While I was traveling to Dinslaken I heard in the train that anti-Semitic riots had broken out everywhere, and that many Jews had been arrested. Synagogues everywhere are burning!"

With anxiety I listened to the man's story; suddenly he said with a trembling voice: "No, I won't come in! I can't be safe in your house! We are all lost!" With these words he disappeared into the dark fog which cast a veil over the morning. I never saw him again.

In spite of this Job's message I forced myself not to show any sign of emotion. Only thus could I avoid a state of panic among the children and tutors. Nonetheless I was of the opinion that the young students should be prepared to brave the storm of the approaching catastrophe. About 7:30 A.M. I ordered 46 people, among them 32 children, into the dining hall of the institution and told them the following in a simple and brief address:

"As you know, last night a Herr vom Rath, a member of the German Embassy in Paris, was assassinated. The Jews are held responsible for this murder. The high tension in the political field is now being directed against the Jews, and during the next few hours there will certainly be anti-Semitic excesses. This will happen even in our town. It is my feeling and my impression that we German Jews have never experienced such calamities since the Middle Ages. Be strong! Trust in God! I am sure we will withstand even these hard times. Nobody will remain in the rooms of the upper floor of the building. The exit door to the street will be opened only by myself! From this moment on everyone is to heed my orders only!"

After breakfast the pupils were sent to the large study-hall of the institution. The teacher in charge tried to keep them busy.

At 9:30 A.M. the bell at the main gate rang persistently. I opened the door: about 50 men stormed into the house, many of them with their coat- or jacket collars turned up. At first they rushed into the dining room, which fortunately was empty, and there they began their work of destruction, which was carried out with the utmost precision. The frightened and fearful cries of the children resounded through the building. In a stentorian voice I shouted: "Children, go out into the

---

Reprinted with permission from Yad Vashem Archives.

street immediately!" This advice was certainly contrary to the orders of the Gestapo. I thought, however, that in the street, in a public place, we might be in less danger than inside the house. The children immediately ran down a small staircase at the back, most of them without hat or coat despite the cold and wet weather. We tried to reach the next street crossing, which was close to Dinslakens Town Hall, where I intended to ask for police protection. About ten policemen were stationed here, reason enough for a sensation-seeking mob to await the next development. This was not very long in coming; the senior police officer, Freihahn, shouted at us: "Jews do not get protection from us! Vacate the area together with your children as quickly as possible!" Freihahn then chased us back to a side street in the direction of the backyard of the orphanage. As I was unable to hand over the key of the back gate, the policeman drew his bayonet and forced open the door. I then said to Freihahn: "The best thing is to kill me and the children, then our ordeal will be over quickly!" The officer responded to my "suggestion" merely with cynical laughter. Freihahn then drove all of us to the wet lawn of the orphanage garden. He gave us strict orders not to leave the place under any circumstances.

> "I recognized some familiar faces, suppliers of the orphanage or tradespeople, who only a day or a week earlier had been happy to deal with us as customers. This time they were passive, watching the destruction [of the orphanage] without much emotion."

Facing the back of the building, we were able to watch how everything in the house was being systematically destroyed under the supervision of the men of law and order, the police. At short intervals we could hear the crunching of glass or the hammering against wood as windows and doors were broken. Books, chairs, beds, tables, linen, chests, parts of a piano, a radiogram, and maps were thrown through apertures in the wall, which a short while ago had been windows or doors. In the meantime the mob standing around the building had grown to several hundred. Among these people I recognized some familiar faces, suppliers of the orphanage or tradespeople, who only a day or a week earlier had been happy to deal with us as customers. This time they were passive, watching the destruction without much emotion.

At 10:15 A.M. we heard the wailing of sirens! We noticed a heavy cloud of smoke billowing upward. It was obvious from the direction it was coming from that the Nazis had set the synagogue on fire. Very soon we saw smokeclouds rising up, mixed with sparks of fire. Later I noticed that some Jewish houses, close to the synagogue, had also been set alight under the expert guidance of the fire-brigade. Its presence was a necessity, since the firemen had to save the homes of the non-Jewish neighborhood....

In the schoolyard we had to wait for some time. Several Jews, who had escaped the previous arrest and deportation to concentration camps, joined our gathering. Many of them, mostly women, were shabbily dressed. They told me that the brown hordes had driven them out of their homes, ordered them to leave everything behind and come at once, under Nazi guard, to the schoolyard. A stormtrooper in charge commanded some bystanders to leave the schoolyard "since there is no point in even looking at such scum!"

In the meantime our "family" had increased to 90, all of whom were placed in a small hall in the school. Nobody was allowed to leave the place. Men considered physically fit were called for duty. Only those over 60, among them people of 75 years of age, were allowed to stay. Very soon we learned that the entire Jewish male population under 60 had already been transferred to the concentration camp at Dachau. During their initial waiting period, while still under police custody, the Jewish men had been allowed to buy their own food. This state of affairs, however, only lasted for a few hours.

I learned very soon from a policeman, who in his heart was still an anti-Nazi, that most of the Jewish men had been beaten up by members of the SA before being transported to Dachau. They were kicked, slapped in the face, and subjected to all sorts of humiliation. Many of those exposed to this type of ill-treatment had served in the German army during World War I. One of them, a Mr. Hugo B.C., had once worn with pride the Iron Cross First Class (the German equivalent of the Victoria Cross), which he had been awarded for bravery.

Source: Y.S. Herz. "*Kristallnacht* at the Dinslaken Orphanage." *Yad Vashem Studies* 11 (1976). Reprinted in *Documents on the Holocaust: Selected Sources on the Destruction of the Jews of Germany and Austria, Poland and the Soviet Union.* Edited by Yitzhak Arad, Yisrael Gutman, and Abraham Margaliot. Translations by Lea Ben Dor. Jerusalem: Yad Vashem, 1981.

5.4
The Nazis Seize Jewish Assets – 1938
Decree Relating to the Payment of a Fine by the Jews of German Nationality by Hermann Göring

Among the rash of government decrees that followed in the wake of the Vom Rath assassination and the Kristallnacht attacks was this November 12, 1938, mandate that the Jews of Germany each pay a fine of one billion Reichsmarks to the state. This fine was levied on them solely to punish them for their ethnic heritage. This decree became the basis for the Third Reich's later seizure of all Jewish assets and property.

1938 REICHSGESETZBLATT, PART I, PAGE 1579

Decree relating to the payment of a fine by the
Jews of German nationality of 12 Nov. 1938.

The hostile attitude of the Jewry towards the German people and Reich, which does not even shrink back from committing cowardly murder, makes a decisive defense and a harsh punishment (expiation) necessary. I order, therefore, by virtue of the decree concerning the execution of the 4-year Plan of 18 Oct. 1936 (RGB1. I, page 887) as follows:

Section 1

On the Jews of German nationality as a whole has been imposed the payment of a contribution of 1,000,000,000 Reichsmark to the German Reich.

Section 2

Provisions for the implementation are issued by the Reich-Minister of Finance in agreement with the Reich-Ministers concerned.

Source: "Decree Relating to the Payment of a Fine by the Jews of German Nationality," November 12, 1938. Reprinted as Document 1412-PS in *Nazi Conspiracy and Aggression.* Vol. 4. Washington, D.C.: United States Government Printing Office, 1946.

5.5

Göring Crushes Jewish Businesses and Livelihoods – 1938
Text of the Decree Relating to the Exclusion of Jews from the German Economic Life

> *On November 12, 1938, a mere two days after Kristallnacht, Nazi General Hermann Göring announced a sweeping ban on Jewish-owned businesses and the employment of Jewish managers and executives throughout Germany. Though various measures had been instituted previously to prevent Jews from practicing specific occupations, this decree affected virtually the entire Jewish population, and it created widespread financial difficulties for Germany's already oppressed Judaic community.*

1938 REICHSGESETZBLATT, PART I, PAGE 1580

Decree Relating to the Exclusion of Jews from the
German Economic Life of November 12, 1938

Pursuant to the decree for the execution of the four year plan of 18 October 1936 (Reichsgesetzblatt I, p. 887), the following is being decreed:

Section 1

(1) Jews (sec. 5 of the first decree relating to the Reich citizenship law of 17 November 1935—Reichsgesetzbl. I, p. 1333) are excluded from the operation of individual retail shops, exporting firms, sales agencies [Bestell Kontoren], as well as the independent operation of a trade, effective 1 January.

(2) Furthermore, effective the same day, they are prohibited to offer merchandise or business services on markets of all types, fairs or exhibitions, to advertise for such or accept orders for such.

(3) Jewish business establishments (third decree pursuant to the Reich citizenship law of 14 June 1938, Reichsgesetzbl. I, p. 627) which are being operated in violation of this decree are to be closed down by the police.

Section 2

(1) Effective 1 January 1939, a Jew can no longer be manager of an establishment as defined by the law relating to the organization of national labor of 20 January 1934 (Reichsgesetzbl. I, p. 45).

(2) If a Jew is employed as an executive in a business enterprise, he may be dismissed with 6 weeks' notice. After the expiration of this notice, all claims of the employee derived from the denounced contract become invalid, especially claims for retirement or dismissal pay.

Section 3

(1) No Jew may be a member of a cooperative [Genossenschaft].

(2) Jewish members of cooperatives will be separated effective 31 December 1938. No special notice is required.

Section 4

The minister of economics is empowered to issue regulations necessary for the implementation of this decree with the approval of the Reich ministers concerned. He may allow exceptions where, due to the transfer of Jewish business establishments into non-Jewish hands or due to the liquidation of Jewish business establishments or in special cases, this is required in order to safeguard the requirements of the public.

Source: "Decree Relating to the Exclusion of Jews from the German Economic Life," November 12, 1938. Reprinted as Document 2875-PS in *Nazi Conspiracy and Aggression*. Vol. 5. Washington, DC: United States Government Printing Office, 1946.

5.6

The Nazis Force Jews to Pay for Kristallnacht Damages – 1938
Text of the Decree for the Restoration of the Appearance of the Streets in the Case of Jewish Business Enterprises

> *Another of the decrees that followed Kristallnacht, this mandate issued by Hermann Göring on November 12, 1938, stated that Jews would be held responsible for repairing the damage caused to their property during Kristallnacht. It further stipulated that any insurance payments made to them to offset these costs would be confiscated by the government. (This version of the decree was translated by the United States Embassy in Berlin for transmission to the U.S. Secretary of State.)*

Section 1.

All damages which were caused to Jewish business houses and dwellings by the revolt of the people against the agitation of international Jewry, against National Socialist Germany on November 8, 9 and 10, must be remedied immediately by the Jewish owners or Jewish business people.

Section 2.

The costs of repairs must be borne by the owners of the Jewish business houses and dwellings.

Insurance claims of Jews of German nationality will be confiscated in favor of the Reich.

Section 3.

The Reich Minister of Economics is authorized to issue executory regulations in agreement with the Reich Ministers concerned.

Source: "Decree for the Restoration of the Appearance of the Streets in the Case of Jewish Business Enterprises," November 12, 1938. Reprinted in *The Holocaust* Vol. 1: *Legalizing the Holocaust: The Early Phase, 1933-1939.* Edited by John Mendelsohn. New York: Garland: 1982.

5.7

The Nazis Act to Curb Jewish Freedom of Movement – 1938
Text of Police Regulation of the Appearance of Jews in Public

> *Further restriction of Jewish freedom of movement was also undertaken in November 1938. The following regulation issued by S.S. Official Reinhard Heydrich, who later became one of the leading architects of the Holocaust,*

gave regional authorities permission to prevent the Jewish members of their population from leaving their homes at certain times or from entering certain off-limits areas at any time. These measures were reminiscent of those that existed in Europe in the Middle Ages, when Jews were confined to ghettos and subject to strict curfews.

1938 REICHSGESETZBLATT, PART I, PAGE 1676

Police Regulation of the Appearance of Jews in Public of 28 November 1938

On the basis of the Decree of 14 November 1938 Regarding the Police Decrees of the Reich Ministers (Reichsgesetzblatt I, P. 1582), the following is decreed:

ARTICLE 1

The Government Presidents in Prussia, Bavaria, and the Sudeten German areas, the proper authorities in the remaining provinces of the old Reich, the district captains (the Mayor in Vienna) in Austria and the Reich Commissar of the Saar district may impose upon Jews, both subjects of the German State and stateless Jews (Article 5 of the First Decree of 14 November 1935, Regarding the Reich Citizen Law, Reichsgesetzblatt I, p. 1333), restrictions as to place and time to the effect that they may not enter certain districts or may not appear in public at certain times.

ARTICLE 2

Whoever wilfully or negligently violates the regulations of Article I is to be fined up to 150 Reichsmarks or punished with imprisonment up to six weeks.

ARTICLE 3

The police decree goes into effect the day after its promulgation.

Source: "Police Regulation of the Appearance of Jews in Public," November 28, 1938. Reprinted as Document 1415-PS in *Nazi Conspiracy and Aggression*. Vol. 4. Washington, DC: United States Government Printing Office, 1946.

6

VOLUNTARY EMIGRATION
BEFORE THE WAR

Jewish refugees look out from the deck of the *SS Serpa Pinto*
before its September 1941 departure from the port of Lisbon.

INTRODUCTION

By the end of 1938, the Nazis had left little doubt that they wanted to stamp out all vestiges of Jewish culture and society in Germany. This recognition increased the pace at which Jews fled the country. The Jewish exodus from Germany actually began when Adolf Hitler first took power. Between 20,000 and 40,000 Jews emigrated each year from 1933 through 1938. In 1939, however—the first full year after Kristallnacht—the number jumped to 68,000.

The rate of Jewish emigration would have been far higher if not for the many obstacles that confronted those trying to flee. Most foreign nations had reacted to the economic turmoil of the Great Depression by imposing immigration quotas. These restrictions made it difficult for Jewish emigrants to find a country willing to accept them. Money was also a factor: the costs of travel and beginning a new life in a foreign country were considerable, and foreign nations were more accepting of immigrants who showed they had enough funds to support themselves. In addition, the Nazis instituted what became known as the "Reich Flight Tax," which required Jews who left Germany to hand over 25 percent of their property to the government. Some didn't want to pay such a high fee to their persecutors; some simply couldn't do so and still afford to leave.

Nonetheless, more than 230,000 Jews did get out before the beginning of World War II. Some of these emigrants relied on aid from family members in other countries, while others were helped by assistance groups and special programs such as Kindertransport, which relocated Jewish children to England even as their parents remained in Germany.

Heartbreaking tales became commonplace during the late 1930s, when Jewish efforts to flee their nightmarish surroundings became more desperate. In May

1939, for example, more than 900 Jews boarded the passenger ship *St. Louis,* which sailed from Germany to the Americas. Many of them held visas for the United States, but because U.S. immigration quotas had already been filled, they were denied entry. Other countries such as Cuba also refused to accept the shipload of emigrants, forcing them to return to sea. The ship waited off the coast of the United States while an emergency request was sent to President Franklin D. Roosevelt, but the plea went unanswered, and the refugees were returned to Europe. They were taken in by countries other than Germany, but many of them soon found themselves back under Hitler's rule following Nazi military victories in the early years of World War II. Two-thirds of them ended up dying in the Holocaust. Similar misfortune was experienced by thousands of other Jewish men, women, and children who fled to various parts of Europe to escape the Nazi menace, only to find themselves back under its shadow during the war.

6.1
Jewish Emigration to England – 1933
Excerpt from a Speech by Adolf Hitler

On October 24, 1933, German Chancellor Adolf Hitler delivered a speech at the Sportpalast in Berlin in which he commented directly on the subject of Jewish emigration from Germany. In the course of this address he acknowledged that he was glad to be rid of some of the Jews who had departed the country. But he falsely claimed that most Jews fled Germany because they were criminals, not because they were threatened with "atrocities" or political persecution. Following is an excerpt from that speech.

In England people assert that their arms are open to welcome all the oppressed, especially the Jews who have left Germany. England can do this! England is big, England possesses vast territories. England is rich. We are small and over populated, we are poor and without any possibility for living. But it would be still finer if England did not make her great gesture dependent on the possession of £1,000—if England should say: Anyone can enter—as we unfortunately have done for thirty or forty years. If we too had declared that no one could enter Germany save under the condition of bringing with him £1,000 or paying more, then to-day we should have no Jewish question at all. So we wild folk have once more proved ourselves better humans—less perhaps in external protestations, but at least in our actions! And now we are still as generous and give to the Jewish people a far higher percentage as their share in possibility for living than we ourselves possess.

It is true that together with the rights of the chosen people we defend the rights of the oppressed people, the German people, for in the last resort that is the reason for our being here at all! But that does not mean atrocities.... It must be admitted [that the] emigrants do not share this view. It is naturally very agreeable for knaves and usurers to travel around in world-history with a political banner to serve as a robe. It is a fine thing to be able to go abroad with the nimbus and the halo of one threatened with death, while in reality in Germany it is only the Public Prosecutor who is after you. And as for the small part of the emigrants which is really out of the country for political reasons I must confess that we are glad to be

Reprinted by permission of the Royal Institute of International Affairs (Chatham House), London.

rid of them. We do not say: Give them back to us! On the contrary we say only: Keep them and the longer the better.

Source: Hitler, Adolf. *The Speeches of Adolf Hitler April 1922-August 1939*. Vol. 1. An English translation of representative passages arranged under subjects and edited by Norman H. Baynes. London: Oxford University Press for the Royal Institute of International Affairs, 1942.

6.2
Plotting to Push Jews out of Germany – 1939
German Foreign Ministry Memorandum on Policy Regarding Jews in 1938

As this January 1939 memo makes clear, an initial goal of the Nazi government was to force the nation's Jewish population out of Germany. This document produced by the Reich Foreign Ministry boasts about the impact of anti-Semitic decrees on Jewish lives and livelihoods up to that point in time, and urges further efforts to blot out any Jewish presence in Germany. The author of the document believes that a successful operation in this regard would not only remove a "corrupting" influence from German society, but also trigger an increase in global anti-Semitism because the countries where the Jews settled would soon come to resent their presence.

Ministry for Foreign Affairs. Berlin, 25th January 1939.

83-26 19/1

Contents:

The Jewish Question as a factor in German Foreign Policy in the year 1938.

1. The German Jewish Policy as basis and consequence of the decisions for the foreign policy of the year 1938.

2. Aim of German Jewish Policy: Emigration.

3. Means, ways and aim of the Jewish Emigration.

4. The emigrated Jew as the best propaganda for the German Jewish Policy.

It is certainly no co-incidence that the fateful year 1938 has brought nearer the solution of the Jewish question simultaneously with the realization of the "idea of Greater Germany", since the Jewish policy was both the basis and consequence of the events of the year 1938. The advance made by Jewish influence and the destructive Jewish spirit in politics, economy and culture paralyzed the power and will of the German people to rise again more perhaps even than the power-policy opposition of the former enemy allied powers of the World War. The healing of this sickness among the people was therefore certainly one of the most important requirements for exerting the force which in the year 1938 resulted in the joining together of Greater Germany, in defiance of the world....

The necessity for a radical solution of the Jewish question arose however also as a consequence of the foreign political development, which resulted in a further 200,000 Jews in Austria in addition to the 500,000 of the Jewish Faith living in the Old Reich. The influence of Jewry on Austrian economy which had grown to enormous proportions under the Schuschnigg Regime, made immediate measures necessary, with the aim of excluding Jewry from German economy and utilizing Jewish property in the interests of the community. The action carried out as reprisal for the murder of Legation Councillor vom Rath accelerated this process to such an extent that Jewish shops—till then with the exception of foreign business—disappeared from the streets completely. The liquidation of the Jewish wholesale trade, manufacturing trade, and of houses and real estate in the hands of Jews, will gradually reach a point where in a conceivable time there will no longer be any talk of Jewish property in Germany. Nevertheless it must be emphasized that this is no seizure of Jewish property without compensation, as for instance the confiscation of Church Property during the French revolution. On the contrary the dispossessed Jew receives Reich Bonds for his goods, and the interest is credited to him.

The final goal of German Jewish Policy is the emigration of all the Jews living in Reich territory. It is foreseen that already the thorough measures in the economic sphere, which have prevented the Jew from earning and made him live on his dividends, will further the desire to emigrate....

The Jew was excluded from politics and culture. But until 1938 his powerful economic position in Germany was unbroken, and thereby his obstinate resolve to hold out until "better times" came. Indicative of the tactics of this "delaying" resistance is the programme of a Jewish Party recently formed in Poland, to fight against all Polish measures aimed at Jewish emigration. As long as the Jew can earn money in Germany, then in the opinion of World Jewry the Jewish bastion in Germany need not be given up.

But the Jew has underestimated the consequences and the strength of the National Socialist purpose. The powerful Jewish positions in Vienna and Prague collapsed in 1938 at the same time as the system of states in Central Europe created at Versailles to keep Germany down. Italy stood at Germany's side, with her racial Laws in the fight against Jewry. An expert on the Jewish question, Prof. Goga took over the Government in Bukarest with a programme aimed against Jewry, without however being able to carry it out because of overwhelming international pressure from Paris and London. Jewry in Hungary and Poland was subjected to special laws. Everywhere the success of German foreign policy now begins to shake Jewish strongholds which have been established for hundreds of years from Munich and in far off States, like the tremors of an earthquake.

It is also understandable that World Jewry, "which has selected America as its Headquarters" regards as its own downfall the Munich Agreement, which in American opinion signifies the collapse of the democratic front in Europe. For the system of parliamentary democracy has always, as experience proves, helped the Jews to wealth and political power at the expense of the people in whose country they live. It is certainly the first time in history that Jewry must evacuate a secure position.

This resolution was first formed in 1938. It showed itself in the efforts of the western democracies particularly those of the United States of America, to put the now finally determined Jewish withdrawal from Germany, in other words Jewish emigration, under international control and protection. The American President Roosevelt "who it is well known is surrounded by a whole row of exponents of Jewry among his closest confidants" called a State Conference as early as the middle of 1938 to discuss the refugee questions, which was held in Evian [France] without any particular results. Both of the questions, the answering of which is the first essential for organized Jewish emigration remained unanswered: firstly the question of *how* this emigration should be organized and financed and secondly the question: emigrate *to where*?

In answer to the first question, International Jewry in particular did not appear willing to contribute. On the contrary the Conference—and later the Committee formed by it in London under the direction of Rublee, an American—regarded its main task as that of forcing Germany by international pressure to release Jewish property to the greatest possible extent. In other words Germany was to pay for the emigration of her 700,000 Jews with German national property. It is at the same time to be doubted whether International Jewry ever seriously desired the mass emigration of their fellow Jews from Germany and other states at all, unless there was an equivalent of a Jewish State. The tactics hitherto employed in Jewish proposals, were in every case aimed less at mass emigration of Jews than at the transfer of Jewish property.

It goes without saying, that the transfer of even a fraction of Jewish property, would be impossible from the point of view of foreign exchange. The financing of a mass emigration of German Jews is therefore still obscure....

The second question, to what country should an organized Jewish emigration be directed, could similarly not be answered by the Evian Conference, as each of the countries taking part having announced that they were fundamentally concerned with the refugee problem, declared that they were not in a position to take large numbers of Jewish emigrants into their territory. After over 100,000 Jews even in 1933/34 had succeeded either legally or illegally in escaping abroad and establishing themselves in someone else's country either with the help of their Jewish relatives living abroad or circles sympathetically disposed from a humanitarian point of view, almost every State in the World has in the meantime hermetically sealed its borders against these parasitical Jewish intruders. The problem of Jewish emigration is therefore for all practical purposes at a standstill. Many States have already become so cautious, that they demand a permit made out by German authorities from Jews travelling in the ordinary way with German passports, saying that there is nothing against them returning.

The emigration movement of only about 100,000 Jews has already sufficed to awaken the interest if not the understanding of many countries in the Jewish danger. We can estimate that here the Jewish question will extend to a problem of international politics when large numbers of Jews from Germany, Poland, Hungary and Rumania are put on the move as a result of increasing pressure from the people of the countries where they are living. Even for Germany the Jewish problem will not be solved when the last Jew has left German soil....

Palestine—which has already become the slogan of world opinion, as the land for the emigrants—cannot be considered as the target for Jewish emigration, because it is incapable of absorbing a mass influx of Jews. Under the pressure of Arab resistance, the British-Mandatory Government has restricted Jewish immigration into Palestine to the minimum.... Germany must regard the forming of a Jewish State, as dangerous, which even in miniature would form just such an operational base as the Vatican for political Catholicism. The realization that World Jewry will always be the irreconcilable enemy of the Third Reich, forces the decision to prevent any strengthening of the Jewish position. A Jewish State however would bring an international increase in power to World Jewry. Alfred Rosenberg expressed this idea in his speech in Detmold on 15 January this year as follows:

"Jewry is striving today for a Jewish State in Palestine. Not to give Jews all over the world a homeland but for other reasons: World Jewry must have a miniature State, from which to send exterritorial ambassadors and representatives to all countries of the world and through these be able to further their lust for power. But more than anything else they want a Jewish centre, a Jewish State in which they can house the Jewish swindlers from all parts of the world, who are hunted by the Police of other countries, issue them new passports and then send them to other parts of the world. It is to be desired, that those people who are friendly disposed to Jews, above all the Western Democracies who have so much space in all parts of the world at their disposal, place an area outside Palestine for the Jews, *of course in order to establish a Jewish Reserve and not a Jewish State.*"

That is the programme expressing the foreign policy attitude of Germany towards the Jewish question. Germany is very interested in maintaining the dispersal of Jewry. The calculation, that as a consequence boycott groups and anti-German centres would be formed all over the world, disregards the following fact which is already apparent, the influx of Jews in all parts of the world invokes the opposition of the native population and thereby forms the best propaganda for the German Jewish policy.

In North America, in South America, in France, in Holland, Scandinavia and Greece, everywhere, wherever the flood of Jewish immigrants reaches, there is today already a visible increase in anti-semitism. A task of the German foreign policy must be to further this wave of anti-semitism. This will be achieved less by German propaganda abroad, than by the propaganda which the Jew is forced to circulate in his defense. In the end, its effects will recoil on themselves....

The poorer and therefore the more burdensome the immigrant Jew is to the country absorbing him, the stronger this country will react and the more desirable is this effect in the interests of German propaganda. The object of this German action is to be the future international solution of the Jewish question, dictated not by false compassion for the "United Religious Jewish minority" but by the full consciousness of all peoples of the danger which it represents to the racial composition of the nations.

By Order

Schaumburg

Source: Ministry of Foreign Affairs. "The Jewish Question as a factor in German Foreign Policy in 1938." January 25, 1939. Reprinted as Document 3358-PS in *Nazi Conspiracy and Aggression*. Vol. 6. Washington, DC: United States Government Printing Office, 1946.

6.3
Angels of Frankfurt – 1939
Recalling Terror and Kindness in Nazi Germany

It was a common experience for Jewish families to be divided as members struggled to emigrate to countries outside Germany. For those individuals left behind in Nazi Germany, daily existence ranged from difficult to nightmarish. As Elfriede Morgenstern Zundell relates in the following remembrance, she and her sister and mother had to cope with a sudden and dramatic loss of income caused by her father's departure for the United States, as well as persecution from the Nazi government and German citizens. Their difficulties, however, were made more bearable by the kindness of chance acquaintances, many of whom risked punishment for aiding the Jews.

For the Jews of Germany, Kristallnacht (The Night of the Broken Glass) was like an earthquake. Its powerful tremors were felt all over the country. Many lost their property, their freedom, or their lives. Synagogues, schools, and stores were set ablaze. When the tremors eventually subsided, the very foundation of the Jew-

"The Angels of Frankfurt," by Elfriede Morgenstern Zundell, from HEROES OF THE HOLOCAUST by Arnold Geier, copyright © 1993 by Arnold Geier. Used by permission of Berkley Publishing Group, a division of Penguin Group (USA) Inc.

ish existence in Germany had been irreparably damaged. It was the beginning of the Nazis' "final solution" to their "Jewish problem."

Early on the morning following that infamous night of November 9, 1938, we were awakened by a loud knocking and pounding on the front door of our house, in a middle-class neighborhood of Frankfurt. We could hear talking, laughing, and cursing in the street. The pounding on the door didn't let up. My mother grabbed a robe, threw it over her shoulders and opened the door. Several toughs, dressed in brown shirts and armed with clubs, barged in.

"Where is the Jew Morgenstern?" they screamed. Mother fearfully explained that my father was out of town on business and was expected back in a few days. "You lie, you Jewish swine!" With that, the men swung their clubs, knocking over whatever was in their paths. Debris of glass, china, and furniture flew everywhere. They rushed from room to room, searching for my father—under beds, in closets, behind furniture, and any other place a human could hide—smashing things as they went along. With anger and fury in their voices, the men finally left. "We'll get him!" was their parting shot. My little sister Sylvia and I, gripped with fear and horror, had hidden in a small sewing room when the raid began. As it got louder and violent, we could no longer hear our mother. We were sure they had killed her. When we came out of hiding, there was mother, holding herself up against a wall, pale with fright. We began to shake and cry. This was our first experience with sheer terror.

The toughs, accompanied by a small mob, ran to the house next to ours and banged continuously on the door. In a garage apartment in the back of that house lived a woman, Frau Storch, and her 12-year-old son Walter. We hardly knew them beyond a cordial greeting when our paths occasionally crossed. She heard the racket and came along the side of the building to the front of the house to see what was going on. Confronted, she confirmed that Mr. Morgenstern often traveled and she had not seen him for several days.

As the mob moved on to make similar stops at homes on both sides of the street, my father's car pulled up in front of our house. He had heard on the radio about "the legitimate expression of outrage of the German people against the Jews" and was worried about his family. He could not have arrived at a worse moment. Suddenly, Frau Storch ran to his car. "They are looking for you, Herr Morgenstern. Get away now before it is too late," she pleaded. He thanked her warmly and drove off. He went into hiding at the home of an old German friend and customer in the outskirts of Frankfurt.

After a few days, it became known that any Jew who possessed a visa to another country would not be detained. A person with a visa was considered to already have emigrated.

Father had been in touch with a distant cousin in the Unites States and had pleaded for papers for his family. The cousin, however, would vouch only for my father. He argued that times were bad and he could not assume the financial responsibility, as required by American immigration laws, for the whole family. Let Father come to America, and work and save to bring the others later. Having no other choice, my father had obtained a visa to the U.S.

With much apprehension, he reported to the local police station, and this visa saved him from arrest or harm. He took no chances, remained in hiding and immediately booked passage on a German liner leaving Hamburg the following week. In the middle of one night just before sailing he returned home, packed a suitcase, tearfully and tenderly hugged and kissed us, and assured us that we would soon be together again. We stood at the window and watched him drive away. He left his family, his business, his town, and his country to stay alive.

"As it got colder, we wore the clothes Erika had picked out for us to keep warm.... We slept in them, played in them, cried in them. Without them we would have frozen to death."

Mother managed to keep the family together and functioning. A few months later, we were forced to leave our home and move to a "Jewish area," a ghetto with out walls. In addition, all our assets and personal belongings were confiscated. We were assigned a small room within the apartment of an older Jewish couple on the mezzanine level of a multi-story building. We continued our schooling, while Mother was assigned to work in a bookbindery. Although this gave her some income, she was unable to be with us when we needed her. Even on her day off she had to attend to the necessary duties of surviving.

One of these duties was to obtain ration books to purchase clothing. Winter was approaching and she wanted to obtain warm items for us girls. While she stood in line at the ration book office awaiting her turn, an attractive young woman approached. Erika was her name, she said, and the man who distributed the ration books was her boyfriend. For a price, she could arrange for extra books and more clothes. "Are you interested?"

Mother was thrilled for the opportunity. But she expressed fear that she might get caught or questioned about the additional books. Erika asked Mother for the approximate measurements of her 9 and 6-year-old daughters and assured her she would obtain winter clothes for us. She wrote her address on a slip of paper and told mother to send us to her the following afternoon.

The next day, after school, Sylvia and I found Erika's apartment building. It was about halfway between our school and the room where we lived. Being the older sister, I held Sylvia's hand as we climbed to the top floor of the six-story walk-up. We knocked on Erika's door. When it opened, there stood a beautiful, tall, blond lady of about 29, a big smile on her face. We took to her instantly, and the feeling seemed mutual. As soon as we entered her small one-bedroom flat, she prepared hot chocolate and cookies. It was manna from heaven. We spent more than an hour with her, trying on warm sweaters, snow suits, mittens, and similar items. Erika invited us to come again after school the next day. We were delighted.

Our visits became a weekly routine. We marveled at her comfortable lifestyle. Erika always had plenty of food, her apartment was warm, her closet was filled with silky gowns, robes, and dainty negligees. And there was that pleasant scent of musk in the air. She showed us her photo album where she appeared in glamorous poses, often with young and older men, and she allowed us to use her make-up and high heels to play "grown up." We were never concerned when, from time to time, she would send us home after one of her many boyfriends arrived. We knew we would be with her again the next week. Mother listened to our excited tales after every visit, but she never explained to us why Erika had so many wonderful things brought to her by so many male friends. At my age, I wouldn't have understood what a prostitute was, anyway.

The kids from the Hitler Youth often waited for the students of our school to leave the grounds. Then, if they could catch them, they beat them up. Sylvia and I were good runners and fled to Erika's place. Every so often, Erika came to the school to pick us up and escort us to the safety of her apartment.

Erika left our young lives as suddenly as she had entered them. The boyfriend who was in charge of ration stamp books was drafted into the Wehrmacht, and his successor at the office discovered thousands of the stamp books missing. They had been sold illegally. Erika was quickly linked to the culprit, and she was arrested. We missed her terribly.

The school closed down, winter approached, food was getting scarcer, and we had to stay in our unheated room while Mother was at work. As it got colder, we wore the clothes Erika had picked out for us to keep warm. We never took them off. We slept in them, played in them, cried in them. Without them we would have frozen to death. Yes, we missed her terribly indeed.

At that time, my sister and I were unaware of another person involved in our lives. Every so often, Mother would give us a potato or some vegetables. She would caution us not to mention these treats to anyone. Although we didn't understand why, we promised to do so. Only later did we learn the story.

One evening, long after Sylvia and I had fallen asleep, my mother heard what sounded like scratching against her window. She peered out and saw a female figure motioning for her to come out. Mother did. There, much to her amazement, was Frau Storch, the neighbor who had warned my father away during Kristallnacht.

Her son Walter was with her. Somehow she had found out where we lived. She told my mother that every weekend she went to the suburbs where she cultivated a small plot of land. There she raised potatoes and vegetables to supplement her meager food supply. She took the risk of being seen in a Jewish area at night and brought a few potatoes and greens for us. My mother was moved to tears. Frau Storch pressed her hand, wished us well, and said she or little Walter would come again, if possible, in a week. It would be very late at night and she would signal the same way. She warned my mother to be careful and not to mention this even to the Jews living in the building. They might resent her good fortune and turn her in.

Frau Storch and her son came faithfully until the night before we left Frankfurt. It would have been difficult, if not impossible, to survive without her weekly gift of sustenance.

My father, meanwhile did everything he could to get us out. He sent proper papers to the American consulate in Stuttgart, and, as a result, we were summoned there for interrogation and examination. This entailed great trouble and expense for us, but, of course, we followed through. Unfortunately, the consulate seemed to do everything in its power not to issue the needed visas. Once we were rejected because of a cavity in one of my teeth, and another because the validity of some paper had expired. In April 1941, we were finally issued our visas.

We were sent to Berlin by train. There, together with a few other emigres, we were put into a train compartment which was locked. We remained seated upright in that car for the long journey across Germany, though France, Spain, and into Portugal. At certain stops, food was passed to us through the window. We were released in Lisbon. There, with additional funds sent by my father and with the help of H.I.A.S. (Hebrew Immigrant Aid Society), we obtained passage on a ship to the United States. Within three weeks, our family was reunited. It was a joyous time.

Years later, I returned to Frankfurt to find Erika and Frau Storch and her son. There was no trace of any of them. Their memory may eventually be buried under the sands of time and history, but not as long as I am alive.

Source: Zundell, Elfriede Morgenstern, and Arnold Geier. "The Angels of Frankfurt." In *Heroes of the Holocaust*. Edited by Arnold Geier. New York: Berkley Books, 1998.

7

WAR AND
FORCED RESETTLEMENT

After conquering Poland in 1939, Germany mounted ruthless pacification and resettlement campaigns. Here, a group of SS, police, and ethnic German auxiliary personnel prepare to enter a Polish household in Bydgoszcz in late 1939.

INTRODUCTION

The flight of Jewish families from Germany in the late 1930s coincided with a swift build-up of the German military. This build-up began in earnest in 1935, when German Chancellor Adolf Hitler implemented rules to boost the nation's troop levels and began investing heavily in new weapons and machinery. Hitler's actions were a clear violation of the terms of the Treaty of Versailles. But neither England or France took action. Hitler further tested their resolve in 1936, when he sent troops into the Rhineland area that bordered France and Belgium, violating another clause in the Versailles agreement. That same year he also began sending troops and armaments to assist right-wing nationalists in the Spanish Civil War. In March 1938 Nazi Germany forcibly annexed neighboring Austria into a "Greater Germany," then turned its gaze on the Sudetenland, a strategically important region of Czechoslovakia with a large German-speaking population.

Hitler's clear lust for the Sudetenland led many observers to believe that another major European war was imminent. But the leadership of France and Britain remained unwilling to risk war, in part because they believed Hitler's false boasts about Nazi Germany's military power. In September 1938 the leaders of England, France, Germany, and Italy met in Munich to discuss the future of Czechoslovakia. They emerged with an agreement that, in essence, surrendered most of the state to the Third Reich. British Chancellor Neville Chamberlain hailed the agreement, saying that it brought "peace for our time." But the Munich Agreement further convinced Hitler that the other major powers in Europe were too weak and frightened to stop his expansionist dreams. Today, the Munich Agreement is widely regarded as a prime example of failed "appeasement"—the practice of making concessions to an aggressor, even if it requires violating moral principles, in order to keep peace.

Even after his gains in Austria and Czechoslovakia, Hitler demanded more *Lebensraum* (living space) for the German people. In 1939 he set his sights on Poland, which contained territory that had belonged to Germany prior to World War I. Many believed that Hitler wouldn't invade Poland because doing so risked war not only with Polish, French, and British forces but also with the Soviet Union, which bordered Poland to the east. But the Nazis surprised the world by striking a nonaggression pact with the Soviets in August 1939. This agreement stated that the two nations would maintain peaceful relations. It also divided eastern Europe into distinct German and Russian spheres of influence. A little more than a week later, on September 1, Hitler issued orders for the German Army to invade Poland. England and France honored their alliance with Poland and declared war on Germany, beginning World War II.

German Forces Roll Across Europe

In the first two years of the conflict, the Germans scored a string of stunning victories. The successes of Hitler's military machine brought a large portion of the European continent under his control. The outbreak of war also made conditions even more perilous for Jews living both in Germany and other nations conquered by the Nazis. Poland, for instance, was home to 3.3 million Jews, and there were millions more in the other countries that would eventually be touched by the war.

An estimated 5,000 Jews were killed in Poland in the opening weeks of World War II, many of them brutally executed. But Germany's initial policies in Poland did not call for the wholesale slaughter of the Jewish population. Instead, Hitler's regime began by "resettling" Jews—forcibly moving them from one place to another. In Poland, the area controlled by the Germans was divided into two zones. Western and northern portions were annexed by Germany—they became part of the Third Reich. An area in the central part of the country became the General Government of Poland, which was under German control but was not officially part of the German nation. A third portion of Poland was taken over by the Soviet Union—part of the nonaggression bargain that Hitler had struck with Soviet leader Joseph Stalin.

Almost immediately after the partition of Poland, the Nazis began deporting Jews from the annexed territories to the General Government—in other words, removing them from the German nation. Many non-Jewish Poles were uprooted in similar fashion by German authorities looking to repopulate the annexed area with German settlers. Resettlement also took place in regions along the French-German border in 1940. There, Jews were sent to southern France (which by that time was

142

under Nazi control) as part of a failed scheme to deport Jews to the island of Madagascar, a French colony located in the Indian Ocean off the southeast coast of Africa.

Resettlement was a brutal process wherever it was carried out. Residents were given little advance notice of their deportation—usually just a matter of hours—then were forced from their homes by soldiers brandishing guns and whips. Those who disobeyed were beaten or shot; those who cooperated usually found themselves sealed inside railroad cattle cars or freight cars rather than passenger coaches. Given little or no food or water for journeys that could last for days, many died en route. These cruel tactics were pioneered in the early years of the war in order to clear Jews out of specific areas, but they would later be applied to another kind of transport— the herding of Jews and other targeted groups to Nazi extermination camps.

7.1
Hitler Defends the Invasion of Poland – 1939
Adolf Hitler's September 1, 1939, Speech before the Reichstag

*After gaining control of Austria and Czechoslovakia in 1938 and 1939, Ger-
man Chancellor Adolf Hitler set his sights on Poland. After months of
increasing tension and international negotiations, he made his decisive move
on September 1, 1939, when German forces crossed the border and attacked
Poland's army. The following speech was made before the German parliament on that day. In it, Hitler outlines his reasons for going to war, placing
particular emphasis on the disputed "Corridor" region and the city of
Danzig (now Gdańsk, Poland) that had been part of Germany until the
1919 Treaty of Versailles placed it under Polish control. He also refers to the
nonaggression pact that Germany had just negotiated with the Soviet Union.
Throughout his speech, Hitler brazenly mischaracterizes both world events
and his own motives.*

*France and Great Britain were allied with Poland, so Germany's invasion
left them little choice but to declare war on Nazi Germany. Hitler's invasion
of Poland, then, was the event that set World War II into motion. The
destruction and chaos of this conflict formed the backdrop for the Holocaust.*

Members of the German Reichstag:

For months we have been tormented by a problem once imposed upon us
by the Dictate of Versailles and which, in its deterioration and corruption, has
now become utterly intolerable. Danzig is a German City. The Corridor was and
is German. All these territories owe their cultural development exclusively to the
German people, without whom absolute barbarism would reign in these Eastern
territories. Danzig was separated from us. The Corridor was annexed by Poland.
The German minorities living there were mistreated in the most appalling manner. Already during the years 1919/20 more than one million people of German
blood were driven from their homes. As usual, I have tried to change this intolerable state of affairs through proposals for a peaceful revision. It is a lie if it is
claimed throughout the world that we insure all our revisions only by applying
pressure. There was ample opportunity for fifteen years before National Socialism assumed power to carry through revisions by means of a peaceful understanding. This was not done. In every single case did I then take the initiative,

not once but many times, to bring forward proposals for the revision of absolutely intolerable conditions.

As you know, all these proposals were rejected. I need not enumerate them in detail: proposals for a limitation of armaments, if necessary even for the abolition of armaments, proposals for restrictions on methods of warfare, proposals for eliminating methods of modern warfare which, in my opinion, are scarcely compatible with international law. You know my proposals for the necessity of the restoration of German sovereign rights over the territories of the German Reich, the countless attempts for a peaceful solution of the Austrian problem which I have made, and later, on the problem of the Sudetenland, Bohemia, and Moravia. It was all in vain. One thing, however, is impossible: to demand that a peaceful revision should be made of an intolerable state of affairs, and then obstinately refuse such a peaceful revision. It is equally impossible to assert that in such a situation to act on one's own initiative in making a revision is to violate a law. For us Germans the Dictate of Versailles is not a law. It does not work to force somebody at the point of a pistol and by threatening to starve millions of people into signing a document and afterwards proclaim that this document with its forced signature was a solemn law.

In the case of Danzig and the Corridor I have again tried to solve the problems by proposing peaceful discussions. It was obvious that they had to be solved! That the deadline for this solution may perhaps be of little interest to the Western Powers is conceivable. But for us this deadline is not a matter of indifference! First and foremost, it was not and could not be a matter of indifference to the suffering victims. In Conferences with Polish diplomats I have discussed the ideas which you have heard me express here in my last speech before the Reichstag. No one can say that this was an improper procedure or even unreasonable pressure.

I then had the German proposals clearly stated and I feel bound to repeat once more that nothing could be fairer or more modest than those proposals submitted by me. And now I want to tell the world that only I could afford to make such proposals. Because I know very well that at that time I placed myself in a position contrary to the conception of millions of Germans by acting the way I did.

These proposals were rejected. But not only that! They were answered by mobilization, by increased terrorism, by intensified pressure on the people of German blood living in these territories, and by a gradual economic, political and, during the past few weeks, even military strangulation and blockade of the Free City of Danzig. Furthermore, Poland virtually began the war against the Free City of Danzig. Furthermore, she was not prepared to settle the problems of the Corridor in a fair manner satisfying the interests of both parties. And lastly, she did not even dream of fulfilling her obligations with regard to the minorities. I have to state here that Germany has fulfilled her obligations in this respect!

Minorities living in Germany are not subject to persecution. Let any Frenchman get up and declare that French citizens living in the Saar territory are being oppressed, ill-treated, or deprived of their rights. No one can make such an assertion.

For four months I have watched these developments without taking action but not without issuing repeated warnings. Recently I have made these warnings more and more emphatic. Over three weeks ago, the Polish ambassador was, at my request informed that if Poland persisted in sending further notes in the nature of an ultimatum to Danzig and in further oppressing the people of German blood, or if she should attempt to ruin Danzig economically through customs measure, Germany could no longer look on without taking action. I have left no room for doubt that in this respect the Germany of today is not to be confused with the Germany that existed before.

> *"Germany has no interests in the West, our fortifications in the West shall be the frontiers of the Reich for all times. We have no other aims in the future, and this attitude of the Reich will remain unchanged."*

Attempts have been made to justify the action against the German minorities by declaring that they had provoked them. I am wondering in what the "provocation" [of] … the women and children who are being mistreated and deported [consist of,] … or the "provocations" of those who were tortured in the most beastly and most sadistic manner and finally killed! One thing, however, I do know: there is not one single great power with any honor who would tolerate such conditions for any length of time.

In spite of it all I have made one last attempt. Although I am deeply convinced that the Polish Government—perhaps also because of its being dependent on an unrestraint, wild military rabble—is not seriously interested in a real understanding. I have nevertheless accepted a proposal by the British Government for mediation. The latter proposed that it would not carry on any negotiations but assured me that it would establish a direct contact between Poland and Germany in order to get the discussion going once more.

I must here state the following: I accepted that proposal. For these discussions I had drawn up the fundamentals which are known to you. And then I and my Government were sitting for two whole days waiting for the Polish Government to make up its mind whether to finally dispatch a plenipotentiary or not! Until last night it had not sent any plenipotentiary but informed us through its ambassador that at present it was considering the question whether and to what extent it might be able to accept the British proposals; it would inform England of its decision.

Members of the Reichstag! If such treatment is meted out to the German Reich and its Chief, and the German Reich and its Chief were to submit to such treatment, then the German Nation would deserve no better than to disappear from the political scene. My love of Peace and my endless patience must not be mistaken for weakness, much less for cowardice. Therefore, I have last night informed the British Government that things being as they are, I have found it impossible to detect any inclination on the part of the Polish Government to enter into a really serious discussion with us.

Thus, these proposals for mediation are wrecked, for in the meantime the answer to these offers had been, firstly, the order for Polish general mobilization, and secondly new grave atrocities. Repetitions of the latter incidents occurred last night. Only recently twenty-one frontier incidents had occurred, there were fourteen last night. Three of them were very grave.

For that reason, I have now decided to talk to Poland in the same language Poland has been using toward us for months.

If there are statesmen in the West who declare that their interests are involved, I can only regret such a declaration; however, not for one single minute could that persuade me to deviate from the execution of my duties. I have solemnly declared and repeat once more that we have no claims at all on these Western powers, and shall never demand anything from them. I repeatedly offered Britain our friendship, and if necessary closest cooperation. Love, however, is not to be offered by one partner only; it'll have to find response from the other. Germany has no interests in the West, our fortifications in the West shall be the frontiers of the Reich for all times. We have no other aims in the future, and this attitude of the Reich will remain unchanged.

Some of the other European powers understand our attitude. First of all I'd like to thank Italy for having supported us all this time. But you'll also understand that we do not want to make an appeal for any foreign help in this struggle. This task of ours we shall solve ourselves.

The neutral powers have assured us of their neutrality just like we have previously guaranteed their neutrality. This assurance we consider a sacred obligation, and as long as nobody breaks their neutrality, we, too, shall observe it painstakingly. What could we desire or want from them?

I am happy to be able to inform you here of an event of special importance. You are aware of it that Russia and Germany are governed by two different doctrines. There was only one single question to be cleared up: Germany has no intention of exporting her doctrine, and the minute Russia does not intend to export her own doctrine to Germany, I no longer see any reason why we should ever be opponents again. Both of us agreed on this one point: any struggle between our two people would only result in benefits for others. We have therefore resolved to enter into an agreement which will exclude any application of force between us in the future, which compels us to consult each other in certain European questions, which makes economic cooperation possible and above all makes sure that these two great powers don't exhaust their energies in fighting each other.

Any attempt on the part of the Western Powers to alter these facts will prove futile, and in that connection I should like to state one thing: this political decision signifies an enormous change for the future and is absolutely final.

I believe that the whole German people will welcome this political attitude. In the World War, Russia and Germany fought each other and up to the end they both suffered. That shall not happen a second time! The nonaggression and consultation pact was yesterday finally ratified in Moscow and in Berlin.

In Moscow, the pact was acclaimed just as you have acclaimed it here. I approve of every word in the speech made by Mr. Molotov, the Russian Commissar for Foreign Affairs.

Our aims I am determined to solve:

Firstly, the question of Danzig;

Secondly, the question of the Corridor;

Thirdly, to see to it that a change shall take place in Germany's relations to Poland, which will insure a peaceful coexistence of the two powers.

I am determined to fight until either the present Polish Government is willing to effect this change or another Poland Government is prepared to do so.

I am determined to eliminate from the German frontiers the element of insecurity, the atmosphere which permanently resembles civil war. I shall see to it that peace on the Eastern frontier shall be the same as it is on our other frontiers.

I shall carry out all necessary actions in such a manner that they shall not contradict the proposals which I have made known to you here, members of the Reichstag, as my proposals to the rest of the world.

That is, I will not wage war against women and children! I have instructed my air force to limit their attacks to military objectives. However, if the enemy should conclude from this that he might get away with waging war in a different manner he will receive an answer that he'll be knocked out of his wits!

Last night for the first time regular soldiers of the Polish Army fired shots on our territory. Since 5.45 a.m. we have been returning their fire. From now on, every bomb will be answered by another bomb. Whoever fights with poison gas will be fought with poison gas. Whoever disregards the rules of human warfare can but expect us to do the same.

I will carry on this fight, no matter against whom, until such time as the safety of the Reich and its rights are secured!

For more than 6 years now I have been engaged in building up the German armed forces. During this period more than 90 billion Reichsmark were spent building up the Wehrmacht. Today, ours are the best equipped armed forces in the world and they are far superior to those of 1914. My confidence in them can never be shaken.

If I call upon the Wehrmacht and if I ask sacrifices of the German people and, if necessary, unlimited sacrifices, then I am in the right to do so, for I myself am just as ready today as I was in the past to make every personal sacrifice. I don't ask anything of any German which I myself was not prepared to do at any moment for more than four years. There shall not be any deprivations for Germans in which I myself shall not immediately share. From this moment on my whole life shall belong more than ever to my people. I now want to be nothing but the first soldier of the German Reich.

Thus I have put on once again the coat which has always been the most sacred and dearest to me. I shall not put it aside until after victory—or I shall not live to see the end.

Should anything happen to me in this war, my first successor shall be Party member Goering. Should anything happen to Party member Goering, his successor shall be Party member Hess. To these men as your leaders you would then owe the same absolute loyalty and obedience that you owe to me. In the event that something fatal should happen to Party Member Hess, I am about to make legal provisions for the convocation of a senate appointed by me, who shall then elect the worthiest, that is to say the most valiant among themselves.

As a National Socialist and a German soldier I enter upon this fight with a stout heart! My whole life has been but one continuous struggle for my people, for its resurrection, for Germany, and this whole struggle has been inspired by one single conviction: faith in this people!

One word I have never known: capitulation. And if there was anybody who'd think that hard times are ahead of us I'd like him not to forget the fact that at one time a Prussian king with a ridiculously small staff confronted one of the greatest coalitions ever known and came forth victoriously after three campaigns because he possessed that strong and firm faith which is required of us in these times.

As for the rest of the world, I can only assure them that a November 1918 shall never occur again in German history.

I ask of every German what I myself am prepared to do at any moment: to be ready to pay with his life for his people and for his country.

Whoever believes to have a chance to evade this patriotic duty directly or indirectly, shall perish. We will have nothing to do with traitors. We all are acting only in accordance with our old principle: our own life matters nothing, all that matters is that our people, that Germany shall live.

I expect of you, as deputies of the Reich, that you will do your duty in whatever position you are called upon to fulfill. You must carry the banner of resistance, cost what may. Let no one report to me at any time that in his province, in his district or in his group or in his cell the morale is low. Bearers, responsible bearers of the morale are you! I am responsible for the province your district! None has the right to shun this responsibility. The sacrifice that is demanded of us is not greater than the sacrifice which has been made by many generations in the past. All those men who before us have traveled the most bitter and hardest road did nothing different from what we are called upon to do; the sacrifice they made was no less costly, no less painful, and therefore no easier than the sacrifice that may be demanded of us.

I also expect every German woman to take her place with unflinching discipline in this great fighting community.

German youth, needless to say, will do with heart and soul what is expected and demanded of it by the nation and by the National Socialist State.

If we form this community, forged together, ready for everything, determined never to capitulate, then our strong will shall master every emergency.

I conclude with the words with which I once started my fight for power in the Reich. At that time I said: "If our will is so strong that it cannot be broken through any distress, then our will and our German state will be able to master and subjugate distress."

Germany—Sieg Heil!

Source: Hitler, Adolf. Speech to the Reichstag, September 1, 1939. Reprinted as Document 2322-PS in *Nazi Conspiracy and Aggression*. Vol. 4. Washington, DC: United States Government Printing Office, 1946.

7.2
Creating Jewish Ghettos – 1939
Reinhard Heydrich's Resettlement Instructions to the Chiefs of the Einsatzgruppen

The German army conquered Poland in a matter of weeks, and the Nazis immediately put plans in place to resettle Jews living in the occupied territory. In the following September 21, 1939, memo, S.S. head Reinhard Heydrich details the methods to be used in dealing with Poland's Jewish population. The document represents the first written instructions regarding the creation of Jewish ghettos and calls for the establishment of Jewish councils (Judenrat) to administer the ghettos. In the opinion of some historians, the document's reference to a "final aim" may also indicate that Nazi leaders had already arrived at their decision to undertake the Holocaust.

Heydrich's instructions were sent to the chiefs of the Einsatzgruppen—
*mobile security squads that went into operation once the German army had
taken over enemy territory. These squads were responsible for the deaths of
many of the 5,000 Jewish civilians who were murdered in the conquest of
Poland, as well as the murder of an even larger number of non-Jewish Poles
who were perceived as dangerous. These killings were but a small hint of the
large-scale slaughter that would be perpetrated by the* Einsatzgruppen *later
in the war.*

SECRET

To: *Chiefs of all Einsatzgruppen of the Security Police*

Subject: Jewish question in the occupied territory

I refer to the conference held in Berlin today and once more point out that the
planned overall measures (i.e., the final aim) are to be kept *strictly secret.*

Distinction must be made between:

   (1) The final aim (which will require extended periods of time),
       and

   (2) The stages leading to the fulfillment of this final aim (which
       will be carried out in short terms).

The planned measures demand the most thorough preparation in their technical as well as economic aspects.

It is obvious that the tasks that lie ahead cannot be laid down in full detail
from here. The instructions and guidelines below will at the same time serve the
purpose of urging the chiefs of the Einsatzgruppen to give the matter their practical thought.

I

For the time being, the first prerequisite for the final aim is the concentration
of the Jews from the countryside into the larger cities. This is to be carried out with
all speed.

In doing so, distinction must be made:

   (1) between the areas of Danzig and West Prussia, Posen, Eastern
       Upper Silesia, and

   (2) the rest of the occupied territories.

As far as possible, the area mentioned (in *item* 1) is to be cleared of Jews; at
least the aim should be to establish only a few cities of concentration.

In the areas mentioned in *item* 2, as few concentration points as possible are
to be set up, so as to facilitate subsequent measures.

In this conjunction, it is to be borne in mind that only cities which are rail junctions, or at least are located along railroad lines are to be designated as concentration points.

On principal, Jewish communities of *fewer* than 500 persons are to be dissolved and to be transferred to the nearest city of concentration.

This decree does not apply to the area of Einsatzgruppe 1, which is situated east of Cracow and is bounded roughly by Polanico, Jaroslaw, the new line of demarcation, and the former Slovak-Polish border. Within this area, only an improvised census of Jews is to be carried out. Furthermore, Councils of Jewish Elders, as discussed below, are to be set up.

II

Councils of Jewish Elders [Jüdishe Ältestenräte]

(1) In each Jewish community, a Council of Jewish Elders is to be set up, to be composed, as far as possible, of the remaining influential personalities and rabbis. The council is to comprise up to 24 male Jews (depending on the size of the Jewish community).

The council is to be made *fully responsible*, in the literal sense of the word, for the exact punctual execution of all directives issued or yet to be issued.

(2) In case of sabotage of such instructions, the councils are to be warned of the severest measures.

(3) The Jewish councils are to take an improvised census of the Jews in their local areas—broken down if possible by sex (age groups): a) up to 16 years of age, b) from 16 to 20 years of age, and c) over, as well as by principal occupation groups—and are to report the results in the shortest possible time.

(4) The Councils of Elders are to be informed of the dates and deadlines for departure, departure facilities, and finally departure routes. They are then to be made personally responsible for the departure of the Jews from the countryside.

The reason to be given for the concentration of the Jews into the cities is that Jews have most influentially participated in guerrilla attacks and plundering actions.

(5) The Councils of Elders in the cities of concentration are to be made responsible for appropriately housing the Jews moving in from the countryside.

For general reasons of security, the concentration of Jews in the cities will probably necessitate orders altogether barring Jews from certain sections of cities, or, for example, forbidding them to leave the ghetto or go out after a designated evening hour, etc. However, economic necessities are always to be considered in this connection.

(6) The Councils of Elders are also to be made responsible for appropriate provisioning of the Jews during the transport to the cities.

No objections are to be voiced in the event that migrating Jews take their movable possessions with them, to the extent that this is technically possible.

(7) Jews who do not comply with the order to move into the cities are to be allowed a short additional period of grace where circumstances warrant. They are to be warned of strictest punishment if they should fail to comply with this latter deadline.

III

On principal, all necessary measures are always to be taken in closest accord and cooperation with the German civil administration agencies and locally competent military authorities.

In carrying them out, care must be taken that the economic security of the occupied territories not be impaired.

(1) Above all, the needs of the army must be considered.

For example, for the time being it will hardly be possible to avoid leaving behind some Jew traders here and there, who in the absence of other possibilities simply must stay for the sake of supplying the troops. In such cases, however, prompt Aryanization of these enterprises is to be sought and the emigration of the Jews is to be completed later, in accord with the locally competent German administrative authorities.

(2) For the preservation of German economic interests in the occupied territories, it is obvious that Jewish-owned essential or war industries and enterprises, as well as those important for the Four Year Plan, must be kept up for the time being.

In these cases also, prompt Aryanization is to be sought, and the emigration of the Jews is to be completed later.

(3) Finally, the food situation in the occupied territories must be taken into consideration. For instance, as far as possible, real estate owned by Jewish settlers is to be provisionally entrusted to the care of neighboring German or even Polish farmers, to be worked by them together with their own, so as to assure harvesting of the crops still in the fields or renewed cultivation.

With regard to this important question, contact is to be made with the agricultural expert of the Chief of the Civil Administration.

(4) In all cases in which the interests of the Security Police on one hand and those of the German Civil Administration on the other hand cannot be reconciled, I am to be informed in the fastest way before the particular measures in question are to be carried out, and my decision is to be awaited.

IV

The chiefs of the Einsatzgruppen will report to me continuously on the following matters:

(1) Numerical survey of the Jews present in their territories (broken down as indicated above, if possible). The numbers of Jews who are being evacuated from the countryside and of those who are already in the cities are to be reported separately.

(2) Names of the cities which have been designated as concentration points.

(3) Deadlines set for the Jews to migrate to the cities.

(4) Survey of all Jewish-owned essential or war industries and enterprises, as well as those important for the Four Year Plan, within their areas.

If possible, the following should be specified:

a. Kind of enterprise (also statement on possible conversion into enterprises that are truly essential or war related, or important for the Four Year Plan);

b. Which of these enterprises need to be Aryanized most promptly (in order to forestall any kind of loss)?

What kind of Aryanization is suggested? German or Poles? (This decision depends on the importance of the enterprise.)

c. How large is the number of Jews working in these enterprises (including leading positions)?

Can the enterprise simply be kept up after the removal of the Jews, or will such continued operation require assignment of German or Polish workers? On what scale?

Insofar as Polish workers have to be introduced, care should be taken that they are mainly brought in from the former German provinces, so as to begin the weeding out of the Polish element there. These questions can be carried out only through involvement and participation of the German labor offices which have been set up.

V

For the attainment of the goals set, I expect total deployment of all forces of the Security Police and the Security Service.

The chiefs of neighboring Einsatzgruppen are to establish contact with each other immediately so that the territories concerned will be covered completely.

VI

The High Command of the Army, the Plenipotentiary for the Four Year Plan (Attention: Secretary of State *Neumann*), the Reich Ministries of the Interior

155

(Attention: Secretary of State *Stuckart*), for Food and for Economy (Attention: Secretary of State *Landfried*), as well as the Chiefs of Civil Administration of the Occupied Territory have all received copies of this decree.

Source: Heydrich, Reinhard. Instructions to Chiefs of Einsatzgruppen, September 21, 1939. Reprinted in *A Holocaust Reader*. Edited by Lucy S. Dawidowicz. New York: Behrman House, 1976.

7.3
Directive for the Deportation of Jews and Poles – 1939
Excerpt from an SS Memorandum

Soon after securing their Polish territory, the Nazis began deporting Jews and selected Poles from the occupied areas that were made part of the German nation. The organization responsible for this action was the Higher SS and Police Leaders (HSSPF), which was overseen by Reinhard Heydrich's Reich Chief Security Office. The following excerpt from an HSSPF directive dated November 12, 1939, provides instructions on how the deportation was to be carried out. The section concerning the items that the deportees could take with them underscores the fact that those who were forcibly removed had most of their belongings and assets taken from them in the process.

1. In his capacity as Reich Commissioner for the Strengthening of the German Nationality the *Reichsführer* SS and Chief of German Police has ordered that the following people should be deported from the former Polish territories which now belong to the Reich:

(*a*) all Jews and

(*b*) all those Poles who either belong to the intelligentsia or because of their Polish nationalist attitudes might constitute a threat to the strengthening of German nationhood. Criminal elements are to be treated in the same way.

The deportation is intended (*a*) to purge and secure the new German territories. (*b*) to create accommodation and employment opportunities for the immigrant ethnic Germans. These goals must definitely be achieved by the evacuation action without regard for other considerations.

2. It was decided at a meeting with the Governor General in Cracow that the deportations from the Warthegau will initially include 200,000 Poles and 100,000 Jews during the period 15 November 1939-28 February 1940.

Reprinted by permission of University of Exeter Press.

3. The reception area for those being deported from here will be the territory south of Warsaw and Lublin.

4. In this first action all Jews from the country districts are to be deported and, in addition, at least 2,000 Poles from the smallest districts and a correspondingly larger number from the larger ones . . .

The area will only have been effectively purged and secured when the intellectual leadership, the whole of the intelligentsia, as well as all political and criminal elements have been removed. All those who are politically aware are also to be deported. In the case of the intelligentsia, deportation is not restricted to those involved in actual political or anti-German activities.

In addition, full consideration must be given to the need to create accommodation and jobs for the immigrant Reich and ethnic Germans. All aspects must be taken into account in determining which persons and circles are politically dangerous: among other things, membership of national political organisations, of political parties of every persuasion, of Catholic clerical and lay circles, etc.

The deportations will as far as possible proceed in such a way that comprehensive expulsions are carried out district by district. Transport will be solely by the Reich railways. The available trains can carry 900-1,000 persons ... Each train must be provided with an escort unit composed of six police officials and thirty self-defense people....

9. The Poles and Jews to be deported may take with them:

(a) Provisions for the period of their stay in the deportation camp and their rail journey.

(b) A suitcase with essential clothing and equipment.

(c) Cash solely in Polish currency up to a limit of 200 Zl. per head. It is forbidden to take bonds, foreign exchange, precious metals, jewelry, art objects. In the case of Jews, the amount of everything which they are permitted to take with them must be considerably reduced. The amount of cash must not exceed 50 Zl. per head.

The *Oberbürgermeister* and *Landräte* are responsible for the evacuation measures in their areas. All agencies of the Party and State are required to provide all necessary assistance and cooperation in the execution of this historic task which has been set by the Führer.

Source: *Nazism 1919-1945: Vol. 3, Foreign Policy, War, and Racial Extermination. A Documentary Reader.* Edited by J. Noakes and G. Pridham. Exeter, UK: University of Exeter Press. New edition with index, 2001.

7.4

A German General Objects to Nazi Policies – 1940

Letter Protesting the Treatment of Jews and Poles by Johannes Blaskowitz

The deportations and killings of Jewish and Polish civilians were opposed by some members of the German military. This memorandum from February 1940 was written by Johannes Blaskowitz, a German general serving in Poland who expresses concerns about the negative effects of these policies. He complains about the Third Reich's murderous policies on both strategic and moral grounds. There were other instances where officers objected to the actions of the S.S. (The S.S. personnel operated independently of the regular German military—the Wehrmacht.) Such objections had little effect, and those who made them usually put their careers at risk. Blaskowitz was later relieved of his command.

It is misguided to slaughter tens of thousands of Jews and Poles as is happening at present; because in view of the huge population neither the concept of a Polish State nor the Jews will be eliminated by doing so. On the contrary, the way in which this slaughter is being carried out is causing great damage; it is complicating the problems and making them much more dangerous than they would have been with a considered and systematic approach. The consequences are:

(a) Enemy propaganda is provided with material which could nowhere have been more effectively devised. It is true that what the foreign radio stations have broadcast so far is only a tiny fraction of what has happened in reality. But we must reckon that the clamour of the outside world will continually increase and cause great political damage, particularly since the atrocities have actually occurred and cannot be disproved.

> "If high officials of the SS and police demand acts of violence and brutality and praise them publicly, then in a very short time we will be faced with the rule of the thug."

(b) The acts of violence against the Jews which occur in full view of the public inspire among the religious Poles not only deep disgust but also great pity for the Jewish population, to which up to now the Poles were more or less hostile. In a very short time we ... shall reach the point at which our arch-enemies in the eastern sphere—the Pole and the Jew, who in addition will receive the particular support of the Catholic Church—will, in their hatred against their tormentors, combine against Germany right along the line.

(c) The role of the armed forces, who are compelled impotently to watch this crime and whose reputation, particularly with the Polish population, suffers irreparable harm, need not be referred to again.

(d) But the worst damage which will accrue to the German nation from the present situation is the brutalization and moral debasement which, in a very short time, will spread like a plague among valuable German manpower.

If high officials of the SS and police demand acts of violence and brutality and praise them publicly, then in a very short time we will be faced with the rule of the thug. Like-minded people and those with warped characters will very soon come together so that, as is now the case in Poland, they can give full expression to their animal and pathological instincts. It is hardly possible to keep them any longer in check, since they can well believe themselves officially authorized and justified in committing any acts of cruelty.

The only way of resisting this epidemic is to subordinate those who are guilty and their followers to the military leadership and courts as quickly as possible.

Source: *Nazism 1919-1945: Vol. 3, Foreign Policy, War, and Racial Extermination. A Documentary Reader.* Edited by J. Noakes and G. Pridham. Exeter, UK: University of Exeter Press. New edition with index, 2001.

7.5
The Madagascar Plan – 1940
Excerpt from a Memorandum by Nazi Official Franz Rademacher

The Nazis hatched a number of plans to banish Jews from the European territory under German control. One of the more elaborate was a scheme to deport them to the island of Madagascar, off the southeast coast of Africa. The possibility of using Madagascar for this purpose came about after Germany's quick victory over France in June 1940 (the peace treaty referred to in the document concerns the official document that was drawn up between France and the Third Reich following Germany's conquest). The island had previously been a French colony, and the Nazis assumed it would now come under their control. But even though some preliminary steps were taken to carry out the Madagascar Plan—including the forced removal of Jews to southern France in anticipation of shipping them to the island—the project was never implemented. In this July 3, 1940, document, an official in the Department of German Internal Affairs named Franz Rademacher outlines his thoughts on how Germany might accomplish the deportation.

THE JEWISH QUESTION IN THE PEACE TREATY

The imminent victory gives Germany the possibility, and in my opinion also the duty, of solving the Jewish question in Europe. The desirable solution is : All Jews out of Europe. The task of the Foreign Ministry in this is:

a. to anchor this demand in the peace treaty and to put through the same demand by means of separate negotiations with the European countries not affected by the peace treaty;

b. to assure in the peace treaty the necessary territory for settling the Jews and to determine the principles for the cooperation of the enemy countries in this problem;

c. to determine the position of the new Jewish overseas settlement area under international law;

d. as preparatory work:

1. clarification of the wishes and plans of the interested party, Government, and scientific offices inside Germany and to harmonize these plans with the wishes of the Foreign Minister; for this the following is also necessary:

2. preparation of a survey of the objective data available at various places (number of Jews in different countries); making use of their assets through an international bank,

3. taking up negotiations with our ally Italy on these questions.

With regard to beginning the preparatory work, Referat D III has already approached the Foreign Minister with suggestions via the department for German Internal Affairs, and has been instructed by him to institute this preparatory work at once. There have already been discussions with the office of the Reichsführer SS in the Ministry of the Interior and with a number of party offices. These offices approve the following plan of Referat D III:

Referat D III suggests as a solution to the Jewish question: In the peace treaty France must make the island of Madagascar available for the solution of the Jewish question and must resettle approximately 25,000 French people living there and compensate them. The island will be transferred to Germany as a mandate. The strategically important Diégo Suarez Bay as well as the harbor of Antsirane, will be German naval bases (if the navy should so desire perhaps these naval bases could also be expanded to include the harbors—open roadsteads—of Tamatave, Andevorante, Mananjary, etc.). In addition to these naval bases, suitable portions of the country will be detached from the Jewish territory for construction of air bases. The portion of the island not needed for military purposes will be placed under the administration of a German police governor, who will be under the control of the Reichsführer SS. In this territory the Jews otherwise have self-administration: their own mayors, police, postal and railroad administrations, etc. The Jews will be jointly liable for the value of the island. Their former European assets will be transferred for liquidation to a European bank to be set up for the purpose. In so far as these assets are insufficient to pay for the land which they will get and for the necessary purchase of commodities in Europe needed for developing the island, bank credits will be made available to the Jews by the same bank.

Since Madagascar will be only a mandate, the Jews who live there will not acquire German citizenship. On the other hand, all Jews deported to Madagascar will from the time of deportation be denied the citizenship of the various European countries by these countries. Instead they will be citizens of the mandate of Madagascar.

This arrangement will prevent the possible establishment of a Vatican State of their own in Palestine by the Jews, thus preventing them from using for their own purposes the symbolic value which Jerusalem has for the Christian and Moslem portions of the world. Moreover, the Jews will remain in German hands as a pledge for the future good conduct of the members of their race in America.

We can utilize for propaganda purposes the generosity which Germany shows the Jews by granting them self-government in the fields of culture, economics, administration, and justice, and can stress that our German sense of responsibility to the world does not permit us to give a race that has not had national independence for thousands of years an independent state immediately; for this they must still prove themselves to history.

Source: Rademacher, Franz. "The Jewish Question in the Peace Treaty," July 3, 1940. Reprinted as Document No. 101, "Document by an Official of the Department for German Internal Affairs," in *Documents on German Foreign Policy 1918-1945*. Washington, DC: United States Government Printing Office, 1957.

7.6
Nazi Deportation of German Jews – 1940
Nazi Report on the Deportation of Jews from Baden and the Palatinate

While the initial deportations took place in Poland in 1939, the Nazis applied the practice the following year in parts of southwestern Germany, along the border with France. Jews affected by these deportation actions were sent to concentration camps in southern France. As the following report mentions, the original plan was to send these people to Madagascar. When that plan failed to materialize, many of them ended up perishing in the camps.

Reprinted by permission of University of Exeter Press.

The deportation of Jews from Baden and the Palatinate was carried out in such a way that, according to the Gauleiters' [the local Nazi ruler's] order, "all persons of Jewish race" must be deported "in so far as they are fit to travel", without regard to age or sex. Only the partners of existing mixed marriages were excluded. Even men who had participated in the World War of 1914-1918 on the German side as front soldiers and, in some cases, as officers of the old *Wehrmacht* had to be sent off. The old people's homes in Mannheim, Karlsruhe, Ludwigshafen etc. were evacuated. Men and women who were incapable of walking were ordered to be transported to the trains on stretchers. The oldest person deported was a ninety-seven-year-old man from Karlsruhe. The time limit given to those being deported to get ready varied from a quarter of an hour to two hours depending on the locality. A number of men and women used this time to escape deportation by committing suicide. In Mannheim alone there had been eight suicides by Tuesday morning, in Karlsruhe three. *Wehrmacht* vehicles were made available to transport people from remote places to assembly points. Those deported were obliged to leave behind their belongings, capital and real estate. It is being held in trust until the Gauleiters have reached a final decision about it. Since in many cases the emigration did not take place according to the rules, i.e. without having fulfilled the legal provisions, e.g. payment of the Reich emigration [lit. "flight"] tax, the property had been impounded. Sums of cash of between 10 and 100 RM could be taken and were changed into French francs. The dwellings were sealed by the police.

According to available reports, the transports consisting of twelve sealed trains have arrived in concentration camps in the south of France at the foot of the Pyranees after a journey of several days. Since there is a shortage of food and suitable accommodation for the deportees, who consist mainly of old men and women, it is believed that the French government is intending to send them on to Madagascar as soon as the sea routes have reopened.

Source: *Nazism 1919-1945: Vol. 3, Foreign Policy, War, and Racial Extermination. A Documentary Reader.* Edited by J. Noakes and G. Pridham. Exeter, UK: University of Exeter Press. New edition with index, 2001.

7.7

Stuttgart Jews Receive An Evacuation Notice – 1941
Excerpt from a Notice of Evacuation Issued by the Jewish Cultural Association of Württemberg

As the war progressed and the Nazis' plans for the Holocaust became better established, Jews were transported to locations in Eastern Europe for the express purpose of killing them. One of the first signs of this new process came in October 1941, when Jews were prohibited from emigrating from all

German-controlled areas of Europe. Soon thereafter, the resettlement of the Jewish population in Western Europe began.

The following notice was issued in Stuttgart, Germany, on November 17, 1941, notifying Jewish families that they were being sent to "the East." The people who received this notice were transported to Riga, Latvia, where they were sent to concentration camps. Most died from the poor conditions in the camps or were shot. This particular document was issued by a Jewish organization, a common occurrence in many of the areas affected by such deportations. The Nazis misled or coerced such groups into aiding the resettlements. Most of the Jewish organizations that took part were unaware of the true character of the deportations and were probably trying to make the best of a horrible situation by helping the Jewish community prepare for the journey.

Re: Evacuation.

On the orders of the Secret State Police regional headquarters in Stuttgart we are obliged to inform you that you and the children mentioned above have been assigned to an evacuation transport to the East. At the same time, you, together with the above-mentioned children who have been assigned to the transport, are hereby obliged to hold yourself in readiness from Wednesday 26 November 1941 onwards in your present abode, and not to leave it even temporarily without the express permission of the authorities.

Employment, even in important plants, does not provide exemption from the evacuation. Any attempt to resist the evacuation or to avoid it is pointless and may have serious repercussions for the person concerned.

The enclosed declaration of assets must be filled in carefully for each member of the family involved, including each child, and delivered to the local police authority within three days.

Enclosed is a list of the most essential items to be brought with you. Each participant in the transport is entitled to take with them up to 50kg of luggage whether in the form of suitcases, rucksacks or shoulder bags. You are recommended to carry a large part of the luggage in a rucksack. It must be assumed that the members of the transport will have to carry their own luggage for part of the time. Suitcases, rucksacks, and travel rugs should be marked with the transport number noted above without fail; in addition, you are strongly advised to add your full name. If possible use indelible ink, other wise used fixed tags.

In addition, you are advised to put on warm underwear, warm clothing, the strongest possible boots and shoes, galoshes, coats and caps rather than hats.

Apart from hand luggage, it will probably be possible to take with you in addition mattresses, some bedding, some kitchen equipment—but without kitchen fur-

Reprinted by permission of University of Exeter Press.

niture—cooking materials, tins of food, first aid materials, sewing equipment, needles, all tools and gardening equipment. Some stoves with chimneys and sewing machines, preferably portable ones, will probably be able to be taken. Spades, shovels and such like as well as building tools are particularly important.

We request that you get such objects ready in your flat and if possible pack them up, with sharp tools covered with protective packing, and mark these things clearly too, particularly mattresses, with the transport number, if necessary with a cardboard label. These objects should be mentioned on the form but with a note 'are being taken with me'.

With the delivery of this letter you have been officially banned from disposing of your property. Thus you are no longer permitted to sell, give away, lend, pawn or in any way dispose of your property.

Every member of the transport will receive RM 50 in Reich credit notes and two food parcels worth RM 7.65, of which one contains food for consuming on the journey, while the second parcel …will be carried as luggage.

You should pay the required sum of RM 57.65 per person immediately to the Jewish Cultural Association of Württemberg, Stuttgart, Hospitalstrasse 36 or to the special W account of the Württemberg branch of the Reich Association of German Jews at the Gymnasialstrasse branch of the Deutsche Bank.

If you are unable to pay the amount, inform the Jewish Cultural Association immediately.

Prior to your departure, you must return your ration cards for the period after 1 December to the local office for a receipt.

Finally, we ask you not to delay; the efforts of our members, particularly in the employment field, entitle us to hope that this new and most difficult task can be mastered as well.

Jewish Cultural Association of Württemberg
Ernst Israel Moos Theodor Israel Rothschild Alfred Israel Fackenheim

Source: *Nazism 1919-1945: Vol. 3, Foreign Policy, War, and Racial Extermination. A Documentary Reader.* Edited by J. Noakes and G. Pridham. Exeter, UK: University of Exeter Press. New edition with index, 2001.

7.8
The Nazis Widen Their Net – 1942
Foreign Office Notice of Evacuation of Jews from Foreign Territories

As the Holocaust proceeded, the Nazis continuously sought to expand the Jewish deportations from all areas under their control or where they had friendly relations with the government in power. This September 24, 1942, document from the foreign office addresses the various evacuation initiatives the German government was pursuing in 1942.

NOTICE

The RAM (Reich Foreign Minister) has instructed me today by telephone to hasten as much as possible the evacuation of Jews from different countries in Europe since it is certain that Jews incite against us everywhere and must be made responsible for acts of sabotage and attacks. After a short lecture on the evacuations now in process in Slovakia, Croatia, Rumania and the occupied territories, the RAM has ordered that we are to approach the Bulgarian, Hungarian and Danish Governments with the goal of getting the evacuation started in these countries.

In respect to the regulation of the Jewish question in Italy, the RAM has reserved further steps to himself. This question is to be discussed personally either at a conference between the Fuehrer and the Duce or between the RAM and Count Ciano.

Source: "Foreign Office Notice of Evacuation of Jews from Foreign Territories," September 24, 1942. Reprinted as Document 3688-PS in *Nazi Conspiracy and Aggression.* Vol. 6. Washington, DC: United States Government Printing Office, 1946.

7.9
Seizure of Jewish Art Possessions – 1943
Letter and Report from Alfred Rosenberg to Adolf Hitler

As Jews fled or were removed from German-occupied territories, their possessions were seized by the Nazis. Among the items captured were valuable artworks owned by Jewish collectors. The looting of these items was overseen by Alfred Rosenberg, a key advisor to Adolf Hitler on racial and cultural issues. (Rosenberg was convicted of several war crimes at the Nuremberg Trials and executed in 1946.) In the following correspondence with Hitler, Rosenberg details some of the art treasures that had been seized between 1940 and 1943. Many of these artworks passed into other hands after World War II ended, and debate continues about their rightful ownership. In some cases, the descendents of the Jewish owners have been successful in regaining the possessions once held by their families.

16 April 1943
673/R/Ma

Mr Fuehrer:

In my desire to give you, my Fuehrer, some joy for your birthday I take the liberty to present to you a folder containing photos of some of the most valuable paintings which my special purpose staff [Einsatzstab], in compliance with your order, secured from ownerless Jewish art collections in the occupied western territories. These photos represent an addition to the collection of 53 of the most valuable objects of art delivered some time ago to your collection. This folder also shows only a small percentage of the exceptional value and extent of these objects of art, seized by my service command [Dienststelle] in France, and put into a safe place on the Reich.

I beg of you, my Fuehrer, to give me a chance during my next audience to report to you orally on the whole extent and scope of this art seizure action. I beg you to accept a short written intermediate report of the progress and extent of the art seizure action which will be used as a basis for this later oral report, and also accept 3 copies of the temporary picture catalogues which, too, only show part of the collection you own. I shall deliver further catalogues which are now being compiled, when they are finished. I shall take the liberty during the requested audience to give you, my Fuehrer, another 20 folders of pictures, with the hope that this short occupation with the beautiful things of art which are nearest to your heart will send a ray of beauty and joy into your revered life.

Heil, my Fuehrer

Intermediate Report of the Seizure of Ownerless Jewish Art Possessions, by the Special Purpose Staff [Einsatzstab] of Reichsleiter Rosenberg in the Occupied Western Territories.

The seizure action began in compliance with the Fuehrer order of 17 Sept 1940. At first those art collections were seized which the Jews, fleeing from occupied territories, left behind in Paris. The seizure action was extended to all remaining cities and villages of the occupied French territory where it was thought that Jewish art collections might be hidden. By using all possible ways and means we discovered and seized all Jewish art collections which were hidden either in Jewish homes in Paris, in castles in the provinces or in warehouses and other storage places. The seizure action was in part very difficult and tedious and, up to now, not all completed. The escaped Jews knew how to camouflage the hiding places of these objects of art, and to find them was made more difficult by the Frenchmen originally charged with the administration of the hiding places. The special purpose staff [Einsatzstab] in connection with the security police [Sicherheitsdienst-SD], the squad for the protection of the foreign currency market [Devisenschutzkommando] and by using their own ingenuity succeeded in securing the main part of art collections, left behind by the escaped Jews, and bringing it safely to the Reich. The most important part of the action was the securing of 79 collections of well-known Jewish art collectors in France. The list of collections is attached hereto. Top place on the list is taken by the famous collections of the Jewish family of Rothschild. The difficulty of the seizure action is shown by the fact that the Rothschild collections were distributed over various places in Paris, in Bordeaux and in the Loire castles of the Rothschilds, and could only be found after a long and tedious search. Although the action covered the past 2 years, we discovered and secured, through the use of trusted agents, quite a large part of the Rothschild collection in 1942.

Besides the seizure of these complete Jewish art collections, we also searched all vacant Jewish apartments in Paris and other places for single art objects which might have been left behind. The main job in this action was to ascertain all addresses of Jews, escaped from the occupied territories, since we had to overcome quite a few difficulties on the part of the French police force which naturally tried their best to retard our progress. During this search through hundreds of single Jewish apartments a large amount of art objects were secured....

During the time from 17 Sept 1940 to 7 April 1943, 10 transports of 92 cars or a total of 2775 crates were sent to Germany. The contents of the crates were: paintings, antique furniture, Gobelins, objects of art, etc. Besides all this another special transport of 53 art objects was shipped to the Fuehrerbau in Muenchen, and 594 pieces (paintings, plastics, furniture, textiles) delivered to Reichs Marshal [Goering].

Castle Neuschwanstein was designated as the first shelter. After this castle was filled, the Bavarian administration for state-owned castles and parks saw fit to relinquish several rooms in the castle Herrenchiemsee for further shipments.

Since these 2 shelters were not enough and since the Bavarian administration could not supply any more we rented 2 more in the neighborhood; it was made possible through the intervention of the State Treasurer [Reichsschatzmeister]. We rented several rooms in the former Salesianer monastery at Buxheim near Memmingen in Schwaben and the privately owned castle Kogl near Voecklabruck at Upper Austria [Oberdonau]....

9455 articles in the aforementioned shelters have been completely inventoried, as of 1 April 1943. The inventory is as follows:

5255 Paintings
297 Sculptures
1372 Pieces antique furniture
307 Textiles
2224 Small objects of art, including East-Asiatic art....

Since the number of technicians was small, the time short, and the necessity of a quick expert from Paris was paramount, only the most valuable objects were inventoried in Paris. Therefore the inventory has to be continued in the shelters. According to the latest count there are approximately 10,000 more objects to be inventoried.

At present there are 400 crates in Paris, ready for shipment which will be sent to the Reich as soon as necessary preliminary work in Paris is completed. Should the present 4 shelters not prove sufficient for consequent shipments, 2 more places, namely the castle Bruck near Linz and the camp Seisenegg near Amstetten on the lower Danube have been prepared....

The action of seizure [Fassungaktion] in Paris and occupied Western territories will be continued, although on a reduced scale, since there are still new art objects of great value to be found. The administration of the East not only will seize furniture, but also the art objects which might yet be found there. Here too valuable art objects were found in the last months. These art objects, found during the collection of furniture, were also sent to the shelters and will receive the same treatment as the others. Besides these objects, whose art value is established, hundreds of modern French paintings were seized which from the German standpoint are without value as far as the national-socialist art conception is concerned. These works of modern French painters will be listed separately, for a later decision as to their disposition.

On orders from the Reichs Marshal some of the works of modern and degenerate French art were exchanged in Paris for paintings of known value. The exchange was of great advantage to us, since we received 87 works by Italian, Dutch and German masters who are known to be of great value. We shall continue to trade whenever a chance presents itself. At the completion of the action a proposal as to the disposition of the modern and degenerate French paintings will be presented.

Source: Rosenberg, Alfred. Letter to Adolf Hitler, April 16, 1943. Reprinted as Document 015-PS in *Nazi Conspiracy and Aggression*. Vol. 3. Washington, DC: United States Government Printing Office, 1946.

8

ARRIVING AT THE
"FINAL SOLUTION"

Nazi Reich Marshal Hermann Göring, seen here at a 1943 Nazi rally, instructed SS head
Reinhard Heydrich to prepare a "Final Solution" to the Jewish problem.

INTRODUCTION

Though the Nazis' genocidal campaign against Jews did not commence until after the advent of World War II, there were several earlier steps that served as precedents. From the beginning of their reign, the Nazis had used the power of the state as a weapon against those they saw as genetically inferior. The Law for the Prevention of Genetically Diseased Offspring, issued in July 1933, provided for the sterilization of citizens who were mentally retarded or suffering from psychological problems, hereditary diseases, or alcoholism. Inspired by their eugenic beliefs, the Nazis wanted to prevent such people from reproducing because they felt that they harmed the overall genetic quality of the German people. Systematic murder began in the late 1930s, when the government began collecting information on babies that were born mentally retarded or physically deformed. About 5,000 of these children were later collected in special hospitals where they were killed by lethal injection.

In 1939 Adolf Hitler himself approved a new euthanasia program, known as T-4, which was aimed at adults. Though the official order used the term "mercy death," these state-sponsored executions were anything but merciful. T-4 resulted in the murder of an estimated 70,000 people who suffered from mental or physical disabilities. Many of them were put to death in early versions of the gas chambers that would later kill millions of Jews. In addition, many of the doctors who worked in the T-4 Program later played key roles in carrying out the Holocaust. Though it was meant to be secret, the T-4 Program drew a lot of criticism, especially from church officials. These complaints probably played a part in the Nazi Party's decision to suspend the program in 1941.

The exact point when Nazi leaders decided to exterminate the Jewish population under their control is a matter of debate. Some scholars believe that the plan was formulated before the war. The primary piece of evidence supporting this view is the January 1939 speech made by Hitler in which he predicted that "the annihilation of the Jewish race in Europe" would take place if a war were to break out. In addition, an official document issued shortly after the Nazis took over Poland speaks of an unspecified "final goal" and calls for the establishment of Jewish "concentration points" along rail lines—perhaps an indication that mass killings had already been decided upon. This document was written by Reinhard Heydrich, the head of the intelligence unit of the S.S. and one of the men most responsible for carrying out the Nazis' genocidal policies against the Jews.

Other historians believe that the decision to undertake mass killings took place at a later date, and they often point to the spring or summer of 1941. The first widespread massacres began with the German invasion of Soviet-controlled territory in June of that year. Soon after, on July 31, Nazi official Hermann Göring issued a memo to Heydrich that makes direct reference to a "complete solution," to the "Jewish question." (A similar term—"final solution"—became a well-used euphemism among the Nazis and has been widely used to refer to the Holocaust in the decades since.)

The Holocaust Begins

By the fall of 1941 extermination camps with gas chambers were being readied, and in October of that year Nazi officials halted Jewish emigration from German-controlled areas of Europe. Emigration had slowed considerably after the war started, but some Jews received official permission to depart to foreign lands between September 1939 and October 1941. This change of policy clearly indicated that the Nazis had settled on another fate for the Jewish people under their control.

Another key date is January 20, 1942, when Heydrich held a meeting to discuss the Final Solution. Known as the Wannsee Conference—a reference to the suburb of Berlin where the meeting took place—the gathering addressed details such as the total Jewish population in various occupied areas and the need to evacuate those people to "the East," meaning Poland. No direct reference to mass executions is included in the minutes of the meeting, but the participants were told that Jews would be assigned to work gangs where "a large part will undoubtedly disappear through natural diminution." The remainder would be "appropriately dealt with."

Historians have also debated the identities of the early Nazi architects of the Holocaust. One central issue is whether Adolf Hitler personally initiated the extermination of Europe's Jews or whether the idea came from other Nazi leaders operating without Hitler's direct input. Because no evidence of a direct order from Hitler has been found, some historians have argued that lesser leaders took the initiative, especially those in charge of specific regions in the Nazi empire. This school of thought holds that these regional authorities sometimes undertook the killings in hopes of currying favor with their superiors or as a ruthless means to address food and housing shortages and other administrative problems. An opposing theory advanced by other scholars holds that central figures of the Nazi Party—Hitler and S.S. commander Heinrich Himmler, in particular—carefully orchestrated the launch of the Final Solution. A sort of middle ground, summed up by historian Yehuda Bauer in *A History of the Holocaust,* contends that while regional authorities willingly carried out genocidal policies, they were specifically ordered to carry out these measures by Nazi leaders in Berlin.

DOCUMENTS

8.1
The First Nazi Sterilization Laws – 1933
The Law for the Prevention of Genetically Diseased Offspring

One the earliest indications that the Nazis intended to take strong measures to control the make-up of Germany's population came with the enactment of the Law for the Prevention of Genetically Diseased Offspring on July 14, 1933. This measure, personally signed by German Chancellor Adolf Hitler, allowed for the sterilization of citizens who suffered from a variety of ailments that the government classified as hereditary. By taking this action, the Nazis believed that they would prevent these conditions from being passed on to future generations.

The Reich Government has passed the following law, which is hereby announced:

PAR. 1

1 Anyone who is suffering from a hereditary disease can be sterilized by a surgical operation if, according to the experiences of medical science, it is to be expected with great probability that his offspring will suffer from serious hereditary physical or mental defects.

2 Those who suffer from any of the following diseases are considered to be suffering from a hereditary disease within the meaning of this law:

(1) Mental deficiency from birth
(2) Schizophrenia
(3) Circular (manic-depressive) illness
(4) Hereditary epilepsy
(5) Hereditary St. Vitus' Dance (Huntington's Disease)
(6) Hereditary blindness
(7) Hereditary deafness
(8) Serious hereditary physical deformation.

3 Furthermore, persons suffering severely from alcoholism can be sterilized.

PAR. 2

1 The person to be sterilized has the right to make an application. If this person is incapacitated or under tutelage because of mental deficiency or is not yet 18,

the legal representative has the right to make an application but needs the consent of the court dealing with matters of guardianship to do so. In other cases of limited capacity the application needs the consent of the legal representative. If someone who has attained his or her majority has received someone to look after his or her person, the consent of the latter is necessary.

2 A certificate from a physician approved for the German Reich is to be attached to the application, to the effect that the person to be sterilized has been informed of the nature and results of sterilization.

3 The application can be withdrawn.

PAR. 3

Sterilization can also be applied for by the following:

1 The civil service physician

2 For the inmates of a sanatorium, hospital, nursing home, or prison, by the head thereof.

PAR. 4

The application is to be made to the office of the Genetic Health Court…

PAR. 12

1 Once the Court has made its final decision for sterilization it must be carried out even against the will of the person to be sterilized. The civil service physician has to request the necessary measures from the police authorities. Where other measures are insufficient, direct force may be used.

2 If facts that necessitate a renewed investigation of the case come out, the Genetic Health Court must reopen the proceedings and suspend the sterilization. If the application was refused, it is only permissible to reopen the case if new facts have arisen that justify sterilization…

PAR. 18

This law comes into force on 1 January 1934.

Source: "Law for the Prevention of Genetically Diseased Offspring," July 14, 1933. Reprinted in *The Nazi Germany Sourcebook*. Edited by Roderick Stackelberg and Sally A. Winkle. London: Routledge, 2002.

8.2
Hitler Approves "Mercy Deaths" – 1939
Adolf Hitler Endorses the Nazi T-4 Program

With this brief document Adolf Hitler gave his endorsement to a program that would become known as T-4. It would result in the murder of approximately 70,000 people who were deemed unfit to live by the Third Reich because of mental or physical impairments. T-4 allowed the Nazis to refine their ability to kill large numbers of people with poison gas. It also may have taught Hitler to take greater care in personally signing off on potentially controversial programs, even if he wholeheartedly supported them. When T-4 drew the criticism of church officials, the Führer may have taken the uproar as a lesson. Historians speculate that the T-4 controversy may be one reason why no written order from Hitler about carrying out the Holocaust has ever been found.

Berlin 1 Sept 1939
Reichsleiter Bouhler and Dr. Brandt, M.D.

are charged with the responsibility of enlarging the authority of certain physicians to be designated by name in such a manner that persons who, according to human judgment, are incurable can, upon a most careful diagnosis of their condition of sickness, be accorded a mercy death.

Signed: A. HITLER
[Handwritten note]
given to me by Bouhler on 27 August 1940
signed: Dr. Guertner

Source: Hitler, Adolf. Endorsement of the Nazi T-4 Program, September 1, 1939. Reprinted as Document 630-PS in *Nazi Conspiracy and Aggression*. Vol. 3. Washington, DC: United States Government Printing Office, 1946.

8.3
Church Officials Protest Nazi Euthanasia Policies – 1941
Text of a Letter from Antonius Hilfrich, the Bishop of Limburg

As the murderous reality of T-4 became widely known, it drew the criticism of a number of prominent church officials. The Bishop of Limburg, Dr. Antonius Hilfrich, sent the following letter of protest to the Reich Minister of Justice on August 13, 1941. Perhaps as a result of these complaints, the T-4 program was officially suspended in 1941, although it is believed that similar killings continued in secret for the duration of the Third Reich.

Regarding the report submitted on July 16 (Sub IV, pp 6-7) by the Chairman of the Fulda Bishops' Conference, Cardinal Dr. Bertram, I consider it my duty to present the following as a concrete illustration of destruction of so-called "useless life."

About 8 kilometers from Limburg, in the little town of Hadamar, on a hill overlooking the town, there is an institution which had formerly served various purposes and of late had been used as a nursing home; this institution was renovated and furnished as a place in which, by consensus of opinion, the above mentioned euthanasia has been systematically practiced for months—approximately since February 1941. The fact has become known beyond the administrative district of Wiesbaden, because death certificates from a Registry Hadamar-Moenchberg are sent to the home communities. (Moenchberg is the name of this institution because it was a Franciscan monastery prior to its secularization in 1803.)

Several times a week buses arrive in Hadamar with a considerable number of such victims. School children of the vicinity know this vehicle and say: "There comes the murder-box again." After the arrival of the vehicle, the citizens of Hadamar watch the smoke rise out of the chimney and are tortured with the ever-present thought of the miserable victims, especially when repulsive odors annoy them, depending on the direction of the wind.

The effect of the principles at work here are: children call each other names and say, "You're crazy; you'll be sent to the baking oven in Hadamar." Those who do not want to marry, or find no opportunity, say, "Marry, never! Bring children into the world so they can be put into the bottling machine!" You hear old folks say, "Don't send me to a state hospital! After the feeble-minded have been finished off, the next useless eaters whose turn will come are the old people."

All God-fearing men consider this destruction of helpless beings as crass injustice. And if anybody says that Germany cannot win the war, if there is yet a just God, these expressions are not the result of a lack of love of fatherland but of a deep concern for our people. The population cannot grasp that systematic actions are carried out which in accordance with Par. 211 of the German criminal code are punishable with death! High authority as a moral concept has suffered a severe shock as a result of these happenings. The official notice that N. N. had died of a contagious disease and that for that reason his body has to be burned, no longer finds credence, and such official notices which are no longer believed have further undermined the ethical value of the concept of authority.

Officials of the Secret State Police, it is said, are trying to suppress discussion of the Hadamar occurrences by means of severe threats. In the interest of public peace, this may be well intended. But the knowledge and the conviction and the indignation of the population cannot be changed by it; the conviction will be increased with the bitter realization that discussion is prohibited with threats but that the actions themselves are not prosecuted under penal law.

Facta loquuntur.

I beg you most humbly, Herr Reich Minister, in the sense of the report of the Episcopate of July 16 of this year, to prevent further transgressions of the Fifth Commandment of God.

[Signed] Dr. Hilfrich

I am submitting copies of this letter to the Reich Minister of the Interior and the Reich Minister for Church Affairs.

Source: Hilfrich, Antonius. Letter to Reich Minister of Justice, August 13, 1941. Reprinted as Document 615-PS in *Nazi Conspiracy and Aggression*. Vol. 3. Washington, DC: United States Government Printing Office, 1946.

8.4
Hitler Addresses the "Jewish Question" – 1939
Excerpt from a January 1939 Speech by Adolf Hitler

Adolf Hitler left no written proof of his direct approval of the Holocaust, but on January 30, 1939, he did make a strikingly prophetic comment that seemed to forecast the mass killing of the Jews. These remarks came in a speech at the Reichstag, at a time when fears of an impending war were running high. In his speech, Hitler vowed that if a second world war commenced it would lead to "the annihilation of the Jewish race in Europe."

Hitler's speech also provides a crash course in the ideology that the Nazis had been promoting throughout the 1930s; it essentially blames "international Jewry" for all of Germany's difficulties. This speech has led some historians to conclude that Hitler had decided upon the Jewish genocide before World War II commenced. Others view this threat as another example of the Führer's posturing; they believe that the Nazi leadership did not dedicate itself to planning and carrying out the Holocaust until later.

The German nation has no feeling of hatred towards England, America, or France; all it wants is peace and quiet. But these other nations are being continually stirred up to hatred of Germany and the German people by Jewish and non-Jewish agitators. And so, should the war-mongers achieve what they are aiming at, our own people would be landed in a situation for which they would be psychologically quite unprepared and which they would thus fail to grasp. I therefore consider it necessary that from now on our propaganda and our press should always make a point of answering these attacks, and above all bring them to the notice of the German people. The German nation must know who the men are who want to bring about a war by hook or by crook. It is my conviction that these people are mistaken in their calculations, for when once National Socialist propaganda is devoted to the answering of the attacks, we shall succeed just as we succeeded inside Germany herself in overcoming, through the convincing power of our propaganda, the Jewish world-enemy. The nations will in a short time realize that National Socialist

Reprinted by permission of the Royal Institute of International Affairs (Chatham House), London.

Germany wants no enmity with other nations; that all the assertions as to our intended attacks on other nations are lies—lies born of morbid hysteria, or of a mania for self-preservation on the part of certain politicians; but that in certain States these lies are being used by unscrupulous profiteers to salvage their own finances. That, above all, international Jewry may hope in this way to satisfy its thirst for revenge and gain, but that on the other hand this is the grossest defamation which can be brought to bear on a great and peace-loving nation...

But there is one thing that everyone should realize: these attempts cannot influence Germany in the slightest as to the way in which she settles her Jewish problem. On the contrary, in connection with the Jewish question I have this to say: it is a shameful spectacle to see how the whole democratic world is oozing sympathy for the poor tormented Jewish people, but remains hard-hearted and obdurate when it comes to helping them—which is surely, in view of its attitude, an obvious duty. The arguments that are brought up as an excuse for not helping them actually speak for us Germans and Italians.

For this is what they say:

1. "We," that is the democracies, "are not in a position to take in the Jews." Yet in these empires there are not 10 people to the square kilometre. While Germany, with her 135 inhabitants to the square kilometre, is supposed to have room for them!

2. They assure us: We cannot take them unless Germany is prepared to allow them a certain amount of capital to bring with them as immigrants.

For hundreds of years Germany was good enough to receive these elements, although they possessed nothing except infectious political and physical diseases. What they possess today, they have by a very large extent gained at the cost of the less astute German nation by the most reprehensible manipulations.

To-day we are merely paying this people what it deserves. When the German nation was, thanks to the inflation instigated and carried through by Jews, deprived of the entire savings which it had accumulated in years of honest work, when the rest of the world took away the German nation's foreign investments, when we were divested of the whole of our colonial possessions, these philanthropic considerations evidently carried little noticeable weight with democratic statesmen.

To-day I can only assure these gentlemen that, thanks to the brutal education with which the democracies favoured us for fifteen years, we are completely hardened to all attacks of sentiment. After more than eight hundred thousand children of the nation had died of hunger and undernourishment at the close of the War, we witnessed almost one million head of milking cows being driven away from us in accordance with the cruel paragraphs of a dictate which the humane democratic apostles of the world forced upon us as a peace treaty. We witnessed over one million German prisoners of war being retained in confinement for no reason at all for a whole year after the War was ended. We witnessed over one and a half million Germans being torn away from all that they possessed in the territories lying on our frontiers, and being whipped out with practically only what they wore on their backs. We had to endure having millions of our fellow countrymen torn from us without their consent, and without their being afforded the slightest possibility of existence. I could supplement these examples with dozens of the most cruel kind. For this reason we ask to be spared all sentimental talk. The German nation does not wish its interests to be determined and controlled by any foreign nation. France to the French, England to the English, America to the Americans, and Germany to the Germans. We are resolved to prevent the settlement in our country of a strange people which was capable of snatching for itself all the leading positions in the land, and to oust it. For it is our will to educate our own nation for these leading positions. We have hundreds of thousands of very intelligent children of peasants and of the working classes. We shall have them educated—in fact we have already begun—and we wish that one day they, and not the representatives of an alien race, may hold the leading positions in the State together with our educated classes. Above all, German culture, as its name alone shows, is German and not Jewish, and therefore its management and care will be entrusted to members of our own nation. If the rest of the world cries out with a hypocritical mien against this barbaric expulsion from Germany of such an irreplaceable and culturally eminently valuable element, we can only be astonished at the conclusions they draw from this situation. For how thankful they must be that we are releasing these precious apostles of culture, and placing them at the disposal of the rest of the world. In accordance with their own declarations they cannot find a single reason to excuse themselves for refusing to receive this most valuable race in their own countries. Nor can I see a reason why the members of this race should be imposed upon the German nation, while in the States, which are so enthusiastic about these "splendid people," their settlement should suddenly be refused with every imaginable excuse. I think that the sooner this problem is solved the better; for Europe cannot settle down until the Jewish question is cleared up. It may very well be possible that sooner or later an agreement on this problem may be reached in Europe, even between those nations which otherwise do not so easily come together.

The world has sufficient space for settlements, but we must once and for all get rid of the opinion that the Jewish race was only created by God for the purpose of being in a certain percentage a parasite living on the body and the productive work of other nations. The Jewish race will have to adapt itself to sound constructive activity as other nations do, or sooner or later it will succumb to a crisis of an inconceivable magnitude.

One thing I should like to say on this day which may be memorable for others as well as for us Germans: In the course of my life I have very often been a prophet, and have usually been ridiculed for it. During the time of my struggle for power it was in the first instance the Jewish race which only received my prophecies with laughter when I said that I would one day take over the leadership of the

State, and with it that of the whole nation, and that I would then among many other things settle the Jewish problem. Their laughter was uproarious, but I think that for some time now they have been laughing on the other side of their face. To-day I will once more be a prophet: If the international Jewish financiers in and outside Europe should succeed in plunging the nations once more into a world war, then the result will not be the bolshevization of the earth, and thus the victory of Jewry, but the annihilation of the Jewish race in Europe!...

The nations are no longer willing to die on the battle-field so that this unstable international race may profiteer from a war or satisfy its Old Testament vengeance. The Jewish watchword "Workers of the world unite" will be conquered by a higher realization, namely "Workers of all classes and of all nations, recognize your common enemy!"

Source: Hitler, Adolf. *The Speeches of Adolf Hitler, April 1922-August 1939.* An English translation of representative passages arranged under subjects and edited by Norman H. Baynes. London: Oxford University Press for the Royal Institute of International Affairs, 1942.

8.5
Authorizing the "Complete Solution" – 1941
Text of a Letter from Hermann Göring to Reinhard Heydrich

This document from Göring, a senior member of Adolf Hitler's inner circle, to Reinhard Heydrich, head of the Reich Chief Security Office (RSHA), is generally recognized as the official authorization that led to the Holocaust. Nonetheless, it too has caused a fair amount of debate among historians of the Nazi era. The use of the euphemism "complete solution" is less than clear, though the similar "final solution" became widely used by other Nazi leaders to refer to the Third Reich's genocidal murder of the Jews. The date of the memo adds to the controversy. At this point—late July 1941—the Einsatzgruppen *were already carrying out the mass killings in eastern Europe that have been viewed as the first stage of the Holocaust. Thus, the order seems rather late in coming. Some scholars have explained the discrepancy by noting that the Nazis often issued written orders well after a verbal order had set events in motion. Others contend that the decision to proceed with the "complete solution" was reached after the* Einsatzgruppen *had begun their deadly work.*

Berlin, 31 July 1941

To: The Chief of the Security Police and the Security Service;

SS-Gruppenfuehrer Heydrich

Complementing the task that was assigned to you on 24 January 1939, which dealt with the carrying out of emigration and evacuation, a solution of the Jewish problem, as advantageous as possible, I hereby charge you with making all necessary preparations in regard to organizational and financial matters for bringing about a complete solution of the Jewish question in the German sphere of influence in Europe.

Wherever other governmental agencies are involved, these are to cooperate with you.

I charge you furthermore to send me, before long, an overall plan concerning the organizational, factual and material measures necessary for the accomplishment of the desired solution of the Jewish question.

Signed: GOERING

Source: Göring, Hermann. Letter to Reinhard Heydrich, July 31, 1941. Reprinted as Document 710-PS in *Nazi Conspiracy and Aggression*. Vol. 3. Washington, DC: United States Government Printing Office, 1946.

8.6
Targeting Jews for "Liquidation" in Poland – 1941
Excerpt from a Speech by Hans Frank

The head of the General Government of Poland (a Polish region occupied by the Nazis but not annexed to Germany), Hans Frank was involved in many of the repressive and violent actions that were carried out against Polish civilians during the war. He was convicted of committing war crimes at the Nuremberg trials and was executed in 1946. Frank compiled a diary during the war years and portions of it were used as evidence at the trials. The following excerpt from the diary records a speech he made on December 16, 1941, at the Government Building in Krakow. In it, he openly declares that the millions of Jews under his administration must be "done away with" and hints that this directive has come from unnamed authorities in Berlin. The "great discussion" that he mentions that will take place in Berlin is likely a reference to the Wannsee Conference held the following month, during which plans for carrying out the Holocaust were refined.

As far as the Jews are concerned, I want to tell you quite frankly, that they must be done away with in one way or another. The Fuehrer said once: should united Jewry again succeed in provoking a world-war, the blood of not only the nations, which have been forced into the war by them, will be shed, but the Jew will have found his end in Europe. I know, that many of the measures carried out against the Jews in the Reich, at present, are being criticized. It is being tried intentionally, as is obvious from the reports on the morale, to talk about cruelty, harshness, etc. Before I continue, I want to beg you to agree with me on the following formula: We will principally have pity on the German people only, and nobody else in the whole world. The others, too had no pity on us. As an old National-Socialist, I must say: This war would only be a partial success, if the whole lot of Jewry would survive it, while we would have shed our best blood in order to save Europe. My attitude towards the Jews will, therefore, be based only on the expectation that they must disappear. They must be done away with. I have entered negotiations to have them deported to the East. A great discussion concerning that question will take place in Berlin in January, to which I am going to delegate the State-Secretary Dr. Buehler. That discussion is to take place in the Reich-Security Main-Office with SS-Lt. General Heydrich. A great Jewish migration will begin, in any case.

But what should be done with the Jews? Do you think they will be settled down in the "Ostland", in villages [Siedlungdoerfer]? This is what we were told in Berlin: Why all this bother? We can do nothing with them either in the "Ostland" nor in the "Reichkommissariat". So, liquidate them yourself.

Gentlemen, I must ask you to rid yourself of all feeling of pity. We must annihilate the Jews, wherever we find them and wherever it is possible, in order to maintain there the structure of the Reich as a whole. This will, naturally, be achieved by other methods than those pointed out by Bureau Chief Dr. Hummel. Nor can the judges of the Special Courts be made responsible for it, because of the limitations of the frame work of the legal procedure. Such outdated views cannot be applied to such gigantic and unique events. We must find at any rate, a way which leads to the goal, and my thoughts are working in that direction.

> *"Gentlemen, I must ask you to rid yourself of all feeling of pity. We must annihilate the Jews, wherever we find them and wherever it is possible."*

The Jews represent for us also extra-ordinarily malignant gluttons. We have now approximately 2,500,000 of them in the general government, perhaps with the Jewish mixtures and everything that goes with it, 3,500,000 Jews. We cannot shoot or poison those 3,500,000 Jews, but we shall nevertheless be able to take measures, which will lead, somehow, to their annihilation, and this in connection with the gigantic measures to be determined in discussions from the Reich. The general government must become free of Jews, the same as the Reich. Where and how this is to be achieved is a matter for the offices which we must appoint and create here. Their activities will be brought to your attention in due course.

Source: Frank, Hans. Speech in Krakow, Poland, December 16, 1941. Reprinted as Document 2233-PS in *Nazi Conspiracy and Aggression.* Vol. 4. Washington, DC: United States Government Printing Office, 1946.

8.7

Heinrich Himmler Discusses "Extermination of the Jewish Race" – 1943

Excerpt from a Speech at the Meeting of S.S. Major-Generals

Heinrich Himmler was the head of the S.S., the military corps that ran the death camps, so he was perhaps the most prominent Nazi leader to be intimately involved in the logistics of the Holocaust. On October 4, 1943 (at which point the genocide was well underway), he addressed a meeting of S.S. officers at Posen, Germany, and discussed the "extermination of the Jewish race." Himmler also notes the extreme secrecy that must be maintained about the Holocaust, comparing it to the silence that surrounded the murders that took place on the "Night of the Long Knives" in 1934, when a number of Nazi Party members were purged.

I also want to talk to you, quite frankly, on a very grave matter. Among ourselves it should be mentioned quite frankly, and yet we will never speak of it publicly. Just as we did not hesitate on June 30th, 1934 to do the duty we were bidden, and stand comrades who had lapsed up against the wall and shoot them, so we have never spoken about it and will never ... speak of it. It was that tact which is a matter of course and which I am glad to say, is inherent in us, that made us never discuss it among ourselves, never to speak of it. It appalled everyone, and yet everyone was certain that he would do it the next time if such orders are issued and if it is necessary.

I mean the clearing out of the Jews, the extermination of the Jewish race. It's one of those things it is easy to talk about—"The Jewish race is being exterminated", says one party member, "that's quite clear, it's in our program—elimination of the Jews, and we're doing it, exterminating them." And then they come, 80 million worthy Germans, and each one has his decent Jew. Of course the others are vermin, but this one is an A-1 Jew. Not one of all those who talk this way has witnessed it, not one of them has been through it. Most of *you* must know what it means when 100 corpses are lying side by side, or 500 or 1000. To have stuck it out and at the same time—apart from exceptions caused by human weakness—to have remained decent fellows, that is what has made us hard. This is a page of glory in our history which has never been written and is never to be ... written, for we know how difficult we should have made it for ourselves, if—with the bombing raids, the burdens and the deprivations of war—we still had Jews today in every town as secret saboteurs, agitators and trouble-mongers. We would now probably have reached the 1916/17 stage when the Jews were still in the German national body.

We have taken from them what wealth they had. I have issued a strict order, which SS-Obergruppenfuehrer Pohl has carried out, that this wealth should, as a matter of course, be handed over to the Reich without reserve. We have taken none of it for ourselves. Individual men who have lapsed will be punished in accordance with an order I issued at the beginning, which gave this warning; Whoever takes so much as a mark of it, is a dead man. A number of SS men—there are not very many of them—have fallen short, and they will die, without mercy. We had the moral right, we had the duty to our people, to destroy this people which wanted to destroy us. But we have not the right to enrich ourselves with so much as a fur, a watch, a mark, or a cigarette or anything else. Because we have exterminated a bacterium we do not want, in the end, to be infected by the bacterium and die of it. I will not see so much as a small area of sepsis appear here or gain a … hold. Wherever it may form, we will cauterize it. Altogether however, we can say, that we have fulfilled this most difficult duty for the love of our people. And our spirit, our soul, our character has not suffered injury from it.

Source: Himmler, Heinrich. Speech to S.S. Officers, October 4, 1943. Reprinted as Document 1919-PS in *Nazi Conspiracy and Aggression*. Vol. 4. Washington, DC: United States Government Printing Office, 1946.

9

ATROCITIES IN THE
WAR ZONES

German soldiers look on as an SS officer prepares to shoot a
Ukrainian Jew kneeling on the edge of a mass grave filled with corpses.

INTRODUCTION

Though the gas chamber is the form of execution most commonly associated with the Holocaust, death came in many forms. The initial wave of killing was primarily carried out with firearms. Most of it took place after June 1941, when German Chancellor Adolf Hitler decided to abandon his 1939 truce with Soviet leader Joseph Stalin and conquer the Communist state that he loathed.

As the German forces advanced deep into Soviet territory, they were accompanied by special *Einsatzgruppen* or mobile security units of the S.S. These units were authorized to execute anyone deemed a threat in the newly captured territories, but one of their primary tasks was to exterminate as many Jews as possible. Operating in chaotic war zones, the *Einsatzgruppen* used methods that were quick and brutally effective. Victims were lined up in front of large trenches and mowed down with machine gun or rifle fire. The death toll from these operations could be astonishing—10,000 people or more per day in a single location. By the end of 1942, German forces had killed about 1.4 million Jews in the Soviet Union and in Eastern European states formerly under Soviet control.

Often, the *Einsatzgruppen* received assistance from local non-Jewish residents, including armed units of anti-Soviet partisans who allied themselves with the Germans. Many of these groups were extremely anti-Semitic and were eager to assist in wiping out the Jews. In some cases, regular German soldiers took part in the killings, though operations were generally directed by the S.S. On the other hand, the path of carnage left by the *Einsatzgruppen* was not always welcomed by the regular commanders in the German Army. Some lodged official complaints about what they had observed. These objections were not necessarily motivated by compassion for the Jews, however. In some cases they were based solely on concerns that Germany's murderous policies would spark greater unrest among Poles, or damage the Third Reich's reputation on the world stage.

9.1
Murder in the Ukraine – 1942
Statement on the Killings at Dubno, Ukraine, by Hermann Friedrich Graebe

Most historians date the beginning of the systematic extermination of the Jews to June 1941, when the Einsatzgruppen *of the S.S. began carrying out mass shootings of Jews. These murderous actions became commonplace as the German army advanced against the Soviets, and these massacres occurred in locations all across eastern Europe, including present-day eastern Poland, Lithuania, Belorussia, the Ukraine, and Russia.*

One of the most horrifying descriptions of these killings came from Hermann Friedrich Graebe, a German who worked in the Ukraine as a civilian contractor building railroad communications structures for the occupying German army. During the course of the war, Graebe used his position to protect large numbers of helpless Jews in the Ukraine from death at the hands of the Germans and their Ukrainian henchmen. He deliberately sought out and accepted more assignments and contracts than his company could possibly handle for the sole purpose of hiring more Jews who could be protected as "essential" for the German war effort. Graebe's actions eventually aroused the suspicions of his superiors, however, and in September 1944 he defected to the American lines. Over the next several years he worked closely with the War Crimes Branch of the U.S. Army, and he became the only German to testify for the prosecution at the Nuremberg Trials. The following statement was taken from his testimony at Nuremberg.

I, Hermann Friedrich Graebe, declare under oath:

From September 1941 until January 1944 I was manager and engineer-in-charge of a branch office in Sdolbunow, Ukraine, of the Solingen building firm of Josef Jung. In this capacity it was my job to visit the building sites of the firm. Under contract to an Army Construction Office, the firm had orders to erect grain storage buildings on the former airport of Dubno, Ukraine.

On 5 October 1942, when I visited the building office at Dubno, my foreman Hubert Moennikes of 21 Aussenmuehlenweg, Hamburg-Haarburg, told me that in the vicinity of the site, Jews from Dubno had been shot in three large pits, each about

30 meters long and 3 meters deep. About 1500 persons had been killed daily. All of the 5000 Jews who had still been living in Dubno before the pogrom were to be liquidated. As the shootings had taken place in his presence he was still much upset.

Thereupon I drove to the site, accompanied by Moennikes and saw near it great mounds of earth, about 30 meters long and 2 meters high. Several trucks stood in front of the mounds. Armed Ukrainian militia drove the people off the trucks under the supervision of an SS-man. The militia men acted as guards on the trucks and drove them to and from the pit. All these people had the regulation yellow patches on the front and back of their clothes, and thus could be recognized as Jews.

> "Without screaming or weeping these people undressed, stood around in family groups, kissed each other, said farewells and waited for a sign from another SS-man, who stood near the pit, also with a whip in his hand."

Moennikes and I went directly to the pits. Nobody bothered us. Now I heard rifle shots in quick succession, from behind one of the earth mounds. The people who had got off the trucks—men, women, and children of all ages—had to undress upon the order of an SS-man, who carried a riding or dog whip. They had to put down their clothes in fixed places, sorted according to shoes, top clothing and underclothing. I saw a heap of shoes of about 800 to 1000 pairs, great piles of under-linen and clothing. Without screaming or weeping these people undressed, stood around in family groups, kissed each other, said farewells and waited for a sign from another SS-man, who stood near the pit, also with a whip in his hand.

During the 15 minutes that I stood near the pit I heard no complaint or plea for mercy. I watched a family of about 8 persons, a man and woman, both about 50 with their children of about 1, 8 and 10, and two grown-up daughters of about 20 to 24. An old woman with snow-white hair was holding the one-year old child in her arms and singing to it, and tickling it. The child was cooing with delight. The couple were looking on with tears in their eyes. The father was holding the hand of a boy about 10 years old and speaking to him softly; the boy was fighting his tears. The father pointed toward the sky, stroked his head, and seemed to explain something to him. At that moment the SS-man at the pit shouted something to his comrade. The latter counted off about 20 persons and instructed them to go behind the earth mound. Among them was the family, which I have mentioned. I well remember a girl, slim and with black hair, who, as she passed close to me, pointed to herself and said, "23". I walked around the mound, and found myself confronted by a tremendous grave. People were closely wedged together and lying on top of each other so that only their heads were visible. Nearly all had blood running over their shoulders from their heads.

Some of the people shot were still moving. Some were lifting their arms and turning their heads to show that they were still alive. The pit was already 2/3 full. I estimated that it already contained about 1000 people. I looked for the man who did the shooting. He was an SS-man, who sat at the edge of the narrow end of the pit, his feet dangling into the pit. He had a tommy gun on his knees and was smoking a cigarette. The people, completely naked, went down some steps which were cut in the clay wall of the pit and clambered over the heads of the people lying there, to the place to which the SS-man directed them. They lay down in front of the dead or injured people; some caressed those who were still alive and spoke to them in a low voice. Then I heard a series of shots. I looked into the pit and saw that the bodies were twitching or the heads lying already motionless on top of the bodies that lay before them. Blood was running from their necks. I was surprised that I was not ordered away, but I saw that there were two or three postmen in uniform nearby. The next batch was approaching already. They went down into the pit, lined themselves up against the previous victims and were shot. When I walked back, round the mound I noticed another truckload of people which had just arrived. This time it included sick and infirm people. An old, very thin woman with terribly thin legs was undressed by others who were already naked, while two people held her up. The woman appeared to be paralyzed. The naked people carried the woman around the mound. I left with Moennikes and drove in my car back to Dubno.

On the morning of the next day, when I again visited the site, I saw about 30 naked people lying near the pit—about 30 to 50 meters away from it. Some of them were still alive; they looked straight in front of them with a fixed stare and seemed to notice neither the chilliness of the morning nor the workers of my firm who stood around. A girl of about 20 spoke to me and asked me to give her clothes, and help her escape. At that moment we heard a fast car approach and I noticed that it was an SS-detail. I moved away from the site. 10 minutes later we hear shots from the vicinity of the pit. The Jews still alive had been ordered to throw the corpses into the pit—then they had themselves to lie down in this to be shot in the neck.

I make the above statement at Wiesbaden, Germany, on 10th November 1945. I swear before God that this is the absolute truth.

Hermann Friedrich Graebe

Source: Graebe, Hermann F. Nuremberg Testimony, November 10, 1945. Reprinted as Document 2992-PS in *Nazi Conspiracy and Aggression*. Vol. 5. Washington, DC: United States Government Printing Office, 1946.

9.2

Operations of Einsatzgruppen "Action-Groups" – 1941
Excerpts from a Report by an Action-Group Commander

> *The* Einsatzgruppen *of the S.S. were divided into several different "Action-Groups." ("Action" was a commonly-used term among the Nazis; it usually was employed in connection with the murder or oppression of Jews.) The following document is a report issued by Franz Walter Stahlecker, the commander of Action-Group A, which operated in the Baltic region that included Lithuania [spelled Lithouania in the report], Latvia, and Estonia. It documents the murders of Jews and Communists in precise detail. Stahlecker's report also discusses the Nazis' efforts to incite local citizens to take part in the killings.*

At the start of the Eastern Campaign it became obvious with regard to the *Security Police* that its special work had to be done not only in the rear areas, as was provided for in the original agreements, with the High Command of the Army, but also in the combat areas, and this for two reasons. On the one hand, the development of the rear area of the armies was delayed because of the quick advance and on the other hand, the undermining communist activities and the fight against partisans was most effective within the area of actual fighting—especially when the Luga sector was reached.

To carry out the duties connected with security police, it was desirable to move into the larger towns together with the armed forces. We had our first experiences in this direction when a small advance detachment under my leadership entered Kowne together with the advance units of the Armed Forces on 25 June 1941. When the other larger towns, especially Libau, Mitau, Riga, Dorpat, Reval, and the larger suburbs of Leningrad were captured, a detachment of the Security Police was always with the first army units. Above all, communist functionaries and communist material had to be seized, and the armed forces themselves had to be secured against surprises inside the towns; the troops themselves were usually not able to take care of that because of their small numbers. For this purpose the Security Police immediately after capture formed volunteer detachments from reliable natives in all three Baltic provinces; they carried out their duties successfully under our command. For example, it may be mentioned that the armed forces suffered not inconsiderable losses through guerillas in Riga, on the left of the Duena river; on the right bank of the Duena river, however, after these volunteer detachments had been organized in Riga not a single soldier was injured, although these Latvian detachments suffered some killed and wounded in fighting with Russian stragglers.

Similarly, native anti-Semitic forces were induced to start pograms [pogroms] against Jews during the first hours after capture, though this inducement proved to be very difficult. Following our orders, the Security Police was determined to solve the Jewish question with all possible means and most decisively. But it was desirable that the Security Police should not put in an immediate appearance, at least in the beginning, since the extraordinarily harsh measures were apt to stir even German circles. It had to be shown to the world that the native population itself took the first action by way of natural reaction against the suppression by Jews during several decades and against the terror exercised by the Communists during the preceding period....

Cleansing and Securing the Area of Operations.

1. *Instigation of self-cleansing actions.* Considering that the population of the Baltic countries had suffered very heavily under the government of Bolshevism and Jewry while they were incorporated in the USSR, it was to be expected that after the liberation from that foreign government, they (i.e. the population themselves) would render harmless most of the enemies left behind after the retreat of the Red Army. It was the duty of the Security Police to set in motion these self-cleansing movements and to direct them into the correct channels in order to accomplish the purpose of the cleansing operations as quickly as possible. It was no less important in view of the future to establish the unshakable and provable fact that the liberated population themselves took the most severe measures against the Bolshevist and Jewish enemy quite on their own, so that the direction by German authorities could not be found out.

In Lithouania this was achieved for the first time by partisan activities in Kowno [also spelled Kovno]. To our surprise it was not easy at first to set in motion an extensive pogrom against Jews. Klimatis, the leader of the partisan unit, mentioned above, who was used for this purpose primarily, succeeded in starting a pogrom on the basis of advice given to him by a small advanced detachment acting in Kowno, and in such a way that no German order or German instigation was noticed from the outside. During the first pogrom in the night from 25. [the 25th] to 26.6 [the 26th of June] the Lithouanian partisans did away with more than 1.500 Jews, set fire to several Synagogues or destroyed them by other means and burned down a Jewish dwelling district consisting of about 60 houses. During the following nights about 2,300 Jews were made harmless in a similar way. In other parts of Lithouania similar actions followed the example of Kowno, though smaller and extending to the Communists who had been left behind.

These self-cleansing actions went smoothly because the Army authorities who had been informed showed understanding for this procedure. From the beginning it was obvious that only the first days after the occupation would offer the opportunity for carrying out pogroms. After the disarmament of the partisans the self-cleansing actions ceased necessarily.

It proved much more difficult to set in motion similar cleansing actions in *Latvia*. Essentially the reason was that the whole of the national stratum of leaders had been assassinated or destroyed by the Soviets, especially in Riga. It was possible though through similar influences on the Latvian auxiliary to set in motion a pogrom against Jews also in Riga. During this pogrom all synagogues were destroyed and about 400 Jews were killed. As the population of Riga quieted down quickly, further pogroms were not convenient.

So far as possible, both in Kowno and in Riga evidence by film and photo was established that the first spontaneous executions of Jews and Communists were carried out by Lithouanians and Latvians.

In *Estonia* by reason of the relatively small number of Jews no opportunity presented itself to instigate pogroms. The Estonian self-protection units made harmless only some individual Communists whom they hated especially, but generally they limited themselves to carrying out arrests.

2. *Combating Communism.* Everywhere in the area of operation counteractions against communism and Jewry took first place in the work of the Security Police.

The Soviet officials and the functionaries of the Communist Party had fled with the Soviet Army. In view of the experiences made during the Bolshevist oppression which lasted more than one year, the population of the Baltic countries realized that all remainders of Communism left behind after the retreat of the Red Army had to be removed. Such basic opinion facilitated essentially the work of the Security Police with regard to cleansing in this sphere, especially since active nationalist people cooperated in this cleansing, viz. in Lithouania the partisans, in Latvia and Estonia the self-protection units...

****

3. *Action against Jewry.* From the beginning it was to be expected that the Jewish problem in the East could not be solved by pogroms alone. In accordance with the basic orders received, however, the cleansing activities of the Security Police had to aim at a complete annihilation of the Jews. Special detachments reinforced by selected units—in Lithouania partisan detachments, in Latvia units of the Latvian auxiliary police—therefore performed extensive executions both in the town and in rural areas. The actions of the execution detachments were performed smoothly. When attaching Lithouanians and Latvian detachments to the execution squads, men were chosen whose relatives had been murdered or removed by the Russians.

Especially severe and extensive measures became necessary in *Lithouania.* In some places—especially in Kowno—the Jews had armed themselves and participated actively in franctireur war [guerrilla fighting] and committed arson. Besides these activities the Jews in Lithouania had collaborated most actively hand in glove with the Soviets.

The sum total of the Jews liquidated in Lithouania amounts to 71.105.

During the programs in Kowno 3.800 Jews were eliminated, in smaller towns about 1.200 Jews.

In *Latvia* as well the Jews participated in acts of sabotage and arson after the invasion of the German Armed Forces. In Duensburg so many fires were lighted by the Jews that a large part of the town was lost. The electric power station burnt down to a mere shell. The streets which were mainly inhabited by Jews remained unscathed.

In Latvia up to now 30.000 Jews were executed in all. 500 were made harmless by pogroms in Riga.

Most of the 4.500 Jews living in Esthonia at the beginning of the Eastern Campaign fled with the retreating Red Army. About 200 stayed behind. In Reval alone there lived about 1.000 Jews.

The arrest of all male Jews of over 16 years of age has been nearly finished. With the exception of the doctors and the Elders of the Jews who were appointed by the Special Commandos, they were executed by the Self-Protection Units under the control of the Special Detachment 1a. Jewesses in Pernau and Reval of the age groups from 16 to 60 who are fit for work were arrested and put to peat-cutting or other labor.

At present a camp is being constructed in Harku, in which all Estonian Jews are to be assembled, so that Estonia will be free of Jews within a short while.

After the carrying out of the first larger executions in Lithouania and Latvia it became soon apparent that an annihilation of the Jews without leaving any traces could not be carried out, at least not at the present moment. Since a large part of the trades in Lithouania and Latvia are in Jewish hands and others carried on nearly exclusively by Jews (especially those of glaziers, plumbers, stovebuilders, cobblers) many Jewish partisans are indispensable at present for repairing installations of vital importance for the reconstruction of towns destroyed and for work of military importance. Although the employers aim at replacing Jewish labor with Lithouanian or Latvian labor, it is not yet possible to displace all employed Jews especially not in the larger towns. In co-operation with the labor exchange offices, however, all Jews who are no longer fit for work are being arrested and shall be executed in small batches.

In this connection it may be mentioned that some authorities of the Civil Administration offered resistance, at times even a strong one, against the carrying out of larger executions. This resistance was answered by calling attention to the fact that it was a matter of carrying out basic orders.

Apart from organizing and carrying out measures of execution, the creation of *Ghettos* was begun in the larger towns at once during the first days of operations. This was especially urgent in Kowno because there were 30.000 Jews in a total population of 152.400. Therefore, at the end of the first pogrom a Jewish Committee was summoned who were informed that the German authorities so far had not seen any reason to interfere in the quarrels between Lithouanians and

Jews. The sole basis for creating a normal situation would be to construct a Jewish Ghetto. Against remonstrations made by the Jewish Committee, it was declared that there was no other possibility to prevent further pogroms. On this the Jews at once declared themselves ready to do everything in their power to transfer their co-racials to the town district of Viriampol which was intended as a Jewish Ghetto and with the greatest possible speed. This own district lies in the triangle between the Mamel river and a tributary; it is connected with Kowno by one bridge only and can, therefore, easily be locked off.

In Riga the so-called "Moskau suburb" was designated as a Ghetto. This is the worst dwelling district of Riga, already now mostly inhabited by Jews. The transfer of the Jews into the Ghetto-district proved rather difficult because the Latvians dwelling in that district had to be evacuated and residential space in Riga is very crowded. 24,000 of the 28,000 Jews living in Riga have been transferred into the Ghetto so far. In creating the ghetto, the Security Police restricted themselves to mere policing duties, while the establishment and administration of the Ghetto as well as the regulation of the food supply for the inmates of the Ghetto were left to Civil Administration; the Labor Offices were left in charge of Jewish labor.

In the other towns with a larger Jewish population Ghettos shall be established likewise.

Marking of the Jews by a yellow star, to be worn on the breast and the back which was ordered in the first instance by provisional orders of the Security Police, was carried out within a short time on the basis of regulations issued by the Commander of the Rear area and later by the Civil Administration…

Source: Stahlecker, Franz Walter. Action Group A Report. Reprinted as Document L-180 in *Nazi Conspiracy and Aggression*. Vol. 7. Washington, DC: United States Government Printing Office, 1946.

9.3
Jewish Labor and the German War Effort – 1941
Letter from an Armament Inspector in the Ukraine

> *The actions of the* Einsatzgruppen *were sometimes opposed by other members of the German military. This memo from an unnamed armaments inspector in the Ukraine to German military officials in Berlin argues that the Jews are an important part of the regional economy and that killing them may harm the German war effort. The inspector also refutes the argument that Jewish civilians constituted a threat to the German military. The author of the memo contends that they pose no great danger.*

For the personal information of the Chief of the Industrial Armament Department I am forwarding a total account of the present situation in the Reichskommissariat Ukraine in which the difficulties and tensions encountered so far and the problems which give rise to serious anxiety are stated with unmistakable clarity.

Intentionally I have desisted from submitting such a report through official channels or to make it known to other departments interested in it because I do not expect any results that way but, to the contrary, am apprehensive, that the difficulties and tensions and also the divergent opinions might only be increased due to the peculiarity of the situation...

Regulation of the Jewish question in the Ukraine was a difficult problem because ... the Jews constituted a large part of the urban population. We therefore have to deal—just as in the General Government [gg.]—with a mass problem of policy concerning the population. Many cities had a percentage of Jews exceeding 50%. Only the rich Jews had fled from the German troops. The majority of Jews remained under German administration. The latter found the problem more complicated through the fact that *these Jews represented almost the entire trade* and even *a part of the manpower in small and medium industries* besides the business which had in part become superfluous as a direct or indirect result of the war. *The elimination therefore necessarily had far-reaching economic consequences and even direct consequences for the armament industry* (production for supplying the troops).

The attitude of the Jewish population was anxious—obliging from the beginning. They tried to avoid everything that might displease the German administration. That they hated the German administration and army inwardly goes without saying and cannot be surprising. However, there is no proof that Jewry as a whole or even to a greater part was implicated in acts of sabotage. Surely, there were some terrorists or saboteurs among them just as among the Ukrainians. But it cannot be said that the Jews as such represented a danger to the German armed forces. The output produced by Jews who, of course, were prompted by nothing but the feeling of fear, was satisfactory to the troops and the German administration.

The Jewish population remained temporarily unmolested shortly after the fighting. Only weeks, sometimes months later, specially detached formations of the police [Ordnungspolizei] executed a planned shooting of Jews. This action as a rule proceeded from east to west. It was done entirely in public with the use of the Ukrainian militia and unfortunately in many instances also with members of the armed forces taking part voluntarily. The way these actions which included men and old men, women and children of all ages were carried out was horrible. The great masses executed make this action more gigantic than any similar measure taken so far in the Soviet Union. So far about 150,000 to 200,000 Jews may have been executed in the part of the Ukraine belonging to the Reichskommissariat [RK]; no consideration was given to the interests of economy.

Summarizing it can be said that the kind of solution of the Jewish problem applied in the Ukraine which obviously was based on the ideological theories as a matter of principle had the following results:

a. Elimination of a part of partly superfluous eaters in the cities.

b. Elimination of a part of the population which hated us undoubtedly.

c. Elimination of badly needed tradesmen who were in many instances indispensable even in the interests of the armed forces.

d. Consequences as to foreign policy—propaganda which are obvious.

e. Bad effects on the troops which in any case get indirect contact with the executions.

f. Brutalizing effect on the formations which carry out the executions—regular police—(Ordnungspolizei).

Scooping off the agricultural surplus in the Ukraine for the purpose of feeding the Reich is therefore only feasible if traffic in the interior of the Ukraine is diminished to a minimum. The attempt will be made to achieve this

1. by annihilation of superfluous eaters (Jews, population of the Ukrainian big cities, which like Kiev do not receive any supplies at all);

2. by extreme reduction of the rations allocated to the Ukrainians in the remaining cities;

3. by decrease of the food of the farming population.

It must be realized that in the Ukraine eventually only the Ukrainians can produce economic values by labor. If we shoot the Jews, let the prisoners of war perish, condemn considerable parts of the urban population to death by starvation and also lose a part of the farming population by hunger during the next year, the question remains unanswered: Who in all the world is then supposed to produce economic values here? In view of the manpower bottleneck in the German Reich there is no doubt that the necessary number of Germans will not be available either now or in the near future. However, if the Ukrainian is supposed to work he has to be maintained physically not due to sentiments but due to very sober economic considerations. Part of these is also the creation of an orderly correlation between currency, prices of goods and wages.

(Summary)

Population.

The attitude of the Ukrainian population is still obliging in spite of the deterioration of its economic situation during the last few months. A change of attitude is to be expected with continued deterioration which is certainly to be anticipated.

The Germans [Volksdeutsche] in the Ukraine do not constitute an element on which the administration and the economy of the country can lean.

A considerable proportion of the Jews who partly represented more than half of the population in the cities of the RK has been executed. Thereby the majority of tradesmen has been eliminated thus hurting also interests of the armed forces (supplies for troops, billets).

Billeting, food, clothing and health of the prisoners of war is bad, mortality very high. The loss of tens of thousands even hundreds of thousands during this winter is to be expected. Among them is manpower which could have been utilized successfully for the Ukrainian economy, also skilled specialists and tradesmen.

Source: Letter from a Ukrainian Armament Inspector. Reprinted as Document 3257-PS in *Nazi Conspiracy and Aggression*. Vol. 5. Washington, DC: United States Government Printing Office, 1946.

9.4
Non-German Participation in the Murder of Jews – 1941
An Account of the Liquidation of the Borissov Ghetto

Non-Germans played a large role in the massacre discussed below, which took place in Borissov (also spelled Borrisov and Borisov) in Belorussia or Belarus in October 1941. The shootings were organized by David Ehof, who headed the local security police. He made use of law enforcement officers— many of them brought in from neighboring Latvia—to carry out much of the actual massacre of the Jewish ghetto residents. The following is an excerpt from Ehof's personal account to Soviet authorities of the murderous action in the Borissov Ghetto (the bracketed dates, which appear in the original, are the actual dates when the described events took place).

For two days and two nights they were placed under the influence of alcohol and ideologically prepared to inflict atrocities on innocent people. For this purpose I organized a party with a banquet in a restaurant in the town for the participants during which the policemen had the opportunity of imbibing alcoholic drinks to excess. The following were guests of honour: Obersturmführer Kraffe [Rudolph Grave], the mayor of the Borrisov district, Stankewitsch, as well as officials of the Gestapo and the Secret Field Police (GFP).

I was the first to speak at the banquet. In my speech I congratulated those present on the victories won by Germany, praised the fascist German army and urged them to wage a merciless fight against anti-German activities. In order to stimulate a hatred of Jews among those present, I tried to justify the Nazi policy of exterminating the Jews in my speech and urged the policemen not to express any feelings of compassion and humanity towards either the adult Jews or the children. Similar speeches, which served to prepare the police ideologically for mass terror, were held by the GFP official of the town of Borrisov [Steiler], the mayor of Borrisov, Stankewitsch, the local garrison commander of Borrisov as well as other senior officials…

On Kraffe's instructions, I sealed off the ghetto during the night of 9-9 November [19-20 October] with additional guards. By this time, three graves had been dug near the airfield about 2 km. from Borrisov by prisoners of war under the direction of the Secret Field Police. They were about 400 metres long, 3 metres wide and up to 2 metres deep and were intended for burying the corpses.

Early in the morning of the 9 November [19 October], we assembled the police, who were not yet sober, in front of the security administration building and explained to them that we were now to begin shooting all the Jews in the ghetto. I also announced that I had been put in charge of shooting the Jews. I then once again called for a merciless reckoning with the Jews.

I then ordered my deputy Kowalski [sic!] and the police platoon leader, Pipin, to organize the transport of the Jews to the place of execution and ensure that they were guarded. After the number of guards round the ghetto had been increased we sent the police in groups into the ghetto and sent in the lorries to carry away the Jewish population which had been condemned to be shot. The police broke into the Jewish houses, chased the people to the square in the centre of the ghetto, drove them into vehicles by force and transported them to the place of execution. There was no mercy shown either to old people, children, pregnant women, or the sick. Anyone who offered resistance was shot on the spot on my orders—in the square, in the houses, on the trip to the place of execution—or they were beaten half to death.

> "At the place of execution there were snacks and schnaps. The police drank schnaps and had a snack in the intervals between shooting the groups of Jews and then got back to their bloody work in a state of intoxication."

The condemned people were not only brought in lorries but also on foot in groups of 70 or 80 persons and were mercilessly beaten in the process.

The people who were brought to the place of execution were placed about fifty metres from the graves and guarded until it was their turn to be shot. Twenty or twenty-five people at a time were led to the place of execution, to the graves. At the graves they were undressed; they even had their good quality underclothes torn from their bodies. Having been completely undressed they were driven to the graves and forced to lie face down. The police and Germans shot them with rifles and automatic weapons. In this way more and more groups were driven to the graves and shot. They too were made to lie face down on the corpses of those who had been previously shot.

At the place of execution there were snacks and schnaps. The police drank schnaps and had a snack in the intervals between shooting the groups of Jews and then got back to their bloody work in a state of intoxication.

I arrived at the place of execution about 11 o'clock in the morning and saw an indescribably horrific sight—the place of execution was filled with groans and cries and the continual shrieks of horror of the women and children.

The dehumanized and drunken policemen beat those who offered resistance, who did not step to the edge of the grave, with rifle butts and kicked them. The children were thrown into the grave and shot there.

During the first few minutes this horrific picture even shook me although by then I had shot hundreds of people. I was roused from this mood of uncertainty and depression, which had gripped me against my will under the impression of what I had seen, by the official of the Minsk SD, Kraffe [*sic!*] who accused me of sympathising with the Jews.

The police who had been egged on by me, Kraffe, and the other SD officials exterminated no fewer than 7,000 people on the first day of the mass shooting. On the third day, i.e. on 10 November 1941 [21 October] we continued with the "cleansing" of the ghetto of Jews. On my orders, the police searched all the houses and other buildings, arrested all the Jews hiding there and brought them to the place of execution. On this day another one thousand people approximately were discovered and shot in the same way.

Source: *Nazism 1919-1945: Vol. 3, Foreign Policy, War, and Racial Extermination. A Documentary Reader.* Edited by J. Noakes and G. Pridham. Exeter, UK: University of Exeter Press. New edition with index, 2001.

9.5
Rationalizing the Massacre of Jews – 1942
Memo on the "Combating of Partisans and Action against Jews in the District General of White Ruthenia"

During World War II, Wilhelm Kube served as the Third Reich's Commissioner General for White Ruthenia—the region now known as Belorussia. In that capacity, Kube wrote the following July 31, 1942, memo on ongoing efforts to eliminate the region's Jewish population. He asserts in his report that the Jews in the district are a threat because they would aid the partisans—local residents who were fighting against the German army. This justification was commonly used for the murders, but it was discounted by other German authorities. Kube also alludes to a dispute among the Nazis that preoccupied them for much of World War II—whether the Jews should be completely wiped out or whether some should be allowed to live so that their labor could be enlisted to support the occupying German forces.

… In all the clashes with partisans in White Ruthenia it has been proven that Jewry, in the former Polish section as well as in the former Soviet sections of the District General, together with the Polish movement of resistance in the East and the Red Guards from Moscow, is the main bearer of the partisan movement in the East. In consequence, the treatment of Jewry in White Ruthenia, in view of the endangering of the entire economics, is a matter of political prominence, which should in consequence not be solved only according to an economic, but also according to a political viewpoint. In exhaustive discussions with the SS Brigadier General Zenner and the exceedingly capable Leader of the SD, SS lieutenant Colonel Dr. jur. Strauch, we have liquidated in the last ten weeks about 55,000 Jews in White Ruthenia. In the territory Minsk-Land [county] Jewry has been completely eliminated, without endangering the manpower commitment. In the predominantly Polish territory Lida 16,000 Jews, in Zlonin 8,000 Jews, and so forth, have been liquidated. Owing to an encroachment in the army rear zone, already reported thither, the preparations made by us for liquidation of the Jews in the area Glebokie, have been disturbed. The army rear zone, without contacting me, has liquidated 10,000 Jews, whose systematical elimination had been provided for by us in any event. In Minsk-City approximately 10,000 Jews were liquidated on the 28 and 29 of July, 6500 of them Russian Jews, predominantly aged persons, women and children—the remainder consisted of Jews unfit for commitment of labor who, in their overwhelming majority were deported to Minsk in November of last year from Vienna, Bruenn, Bremen and Berlin, by order of the Fuehrer.

The area of Luzk too, has been relieved of several thousand Jews. The same applies to Novogrodek and Wilejka. Radical measures are imminent for Baranowitschi and Hanzewitschi. In Baranowitschi alone, approximately 10,000 Jews are still living in the city itself; of these, 9,000 Jews will be liquidated next month.

In Minsk City 2,600 Jews from Germany are left over. In addition to that all the 6,000 Russian Jews and Jewesses, who remained as employees with such units, which employed them during the action, are still alive. Even in the future, Minsk will still retain its character as the strongest center of the Jewish element, necessitated for the present by the concentration of the armament industries and the tasks of the railroad. In all the other areas, the number of Jews to be drafted for labor commitment, will be limited by the SD and by me to 800 at the most, but if possible to 500, so that after completion of future actions as announced, we will retain a remainder of 8,600 Jews in Minsk and of about 7,000 in the other 10 areas, including the Jewless areas of Minskland [county]. The danger, that the partisans can rely essentially upon Jewry in the future, will then exist no longer. Naturally, after the termination of demands of the armed forces, the SD and I would like it best, to eliminate Jewry once and for all in the District General of White Ruthenia. For the time being, the necessary demands of the armed forces, which are the main employers of Jewry, are considered. Besides the fact of this unequivocal attitude toward the Jewry, the SD in White Ruthenia has in addition the grave task to transfer continually new contingents of Jews from the Reich to their destiny. This is an excessive strain on the physical strength of the men in the SD and keeps them away from their duties, which are awaiting them in the area of White Ruthenia proper.

Therefore, I would be grateful if the Reich Commissioner could possibly stop additional deportations of Jews to Minsk at least until the peril of the Partisan movement has been subdued conclusively. I need the SD in its total force (100% commitment) against the partisans and against the Polish Resistance movement, both of which are occupying the entire strength of the not overwhelmingly strong SD units.

After completion of the action against the Jews in Minsk, SS Lieutenant Colonel Dr. Strauch reported to me tonight with just indignation, that suddenly, without directives of the Reichleader SS, and without notification to the Commissioner General, a transport of 1000 Jews from Warshow has arrived for this airforce administrative-command. I beg the Reich Commissioner (already prepared by telegram) to prevent transports of such a kind, in his capacity as supreme Plenipotentiary for the Eastern Territory. The Polish Jew is, exactly like the Russian Jew, an enemy of Germanism. He represents a politically dangerous element, the political danger of which exceeds by far his value as a skilled worker. Under no circumstances may administrative offices of the armed forces or of the air forces import Jews to an area of civil administration without the approval of the Reich Commissioner or from the Government General or any other place, as they will endanger the entire political work and the safeguarding of the District General. I fully agree with the commander of the SD in White Ruthenia, that we shall liquidate every shipment of Jews, which is not ordered or announced by our superior offices, to prevent further disturbances in White Ruthenia.

Source: Kube, Wilhelm, "Combating of Partisans and Action against Jews in the District General of White Ruthenia," July 31, 1942. Reprinted as Document 3428-PS in *Nazi Conspiracy and Aggression*. Vol. 6. Washington, DC: United States Government Printing Office, 1946.

9.6
Questioning German Pacification Tactics – 1943
Excerpts from a German Officer's Memo on the Pacification of Occupied Eastern Territory

This document, written by an unknown Nazi official, is representative of several official objections to the murderous pacification campaigns that Germany undertook in occupied Eastern territories during World War II. But as with other Nazi documents that were critical of this effort, the objections contained in this document are focused more on the brutal methods used to pursue pacification, not on the immorality of the killings themselves. In this memorandum, for instance, the anonymous author seems primarily concerned about the potential public relations fallout of the Nazis' brutal pacification campaign in the region. Note that the official employs the term "special treatment" in regard to the treatment of Jews. This was a common Nazi euphemism for murder.

… The fact that Jews receive special treatment requires no further discussion. However it appears hardly believable that this is done in the way described in the report of the General Commissar of 1 June 1943! What is Katyn against that? [A reference to the massacre of Poles by Soviet forces in 1940.] Imagine only that these occurrences would become known to the other side and exploited by them. Most likely such propaganda would have no effect only because people who hear and read about it, simply would not be ready to believe it.

The fight against bands also is taking on forms which are highly questionable if pacification and exploitation of the several territories are the aims of our policy. Thus, the dead who were suspected of belonging to bands and whose number was indicated in the report of 5 June 1943 about the "Cottbus" project to have amounted to 5,000, in my opinion, with few exceptions would have been suitable for forced labor in the Reich.

It should not be ignored in this connection that in view of the difficulties of making oneself understood as generally in such clean-up operations, it is very hard to distinguish friend from foe. Nevertheless, it should be possible to avoid atrocities and to bury those who have been liquidated. To lock men, women and children into barns and to set fire to these, does not appear to be a suitable method of combatting bands, even if it is desired to exterminate the population. This method is not worthy of the German cause and hurts our reputation severely.

I am asking that you take the necessary action.

Source: Memorandum on the Pacification of Nazi-Occupied Territory, 1943. Reprinted as Document R-135 in *Nazi Conspiracy and Aggression.* Vol. 8. Washington, DC: United States Government Printing Office, 1946.

9.7
Dealing Death in the Ukraine – 1942
Excerpts of Letters from an Einsatzkommando

The S.S. soldiers who served in the mobile killing squads were known as Einsatzkommandos. The following letters were written by an Einsatzkommando known only as Jacob based in southwestern Ukraine. It is written to a German acquaintance, a high-ranking officer in the S.S. This letter, like many others written by German soldiers of the Third Reich, features a strange blend of humanity and inhumanity. This correspondence, for instance, features both heartfelt statements of love for absent family members and chilling statements of irrational hatred toward Jews.

[May 5, 1942]

I have been here at Kamenetz-Podolsk for a month. The territory I administer with twenty-three men and 500 Ukrainian police, is as big as a German *Regierungsbezirk* [governmental district]. Most of the work is done for me by the police, the good-for-nothings. No surprise. Yesterday half-Bolsheviks and today wearing the honourable police uniform. There are some hard-working chaps among them but the percentage is low. As commanding officer, I am simultaneously prosecuting council, judge, executioner etc.

Naturally, we are cleaning up considerably, especially among the Jews. But the population has to be kept firmly in check too. One has to keep one's eyes open. We act fast. Well, we shall be able to get home all the sooner. My family is very unhappy. I have been away for two years.

I have a cosy flat in a former children's home (asylum). One bedroom and a living room with all amenities. Nothing is missing. Apart of course from my wife and children. You will understand me. My Dieter and my little Liese write often in their own way. Sometimes I could weep. It is not good to love one's children as I do. I hope that the war will soon be over and with it the period of service in the East.

After receiving a reply from his acquaintance telling him that he must accept the hardships of war service, Jacob wrote the following:

[June 21, 1942]

I am replying to your letter of 10th immediately … I am grateful for your reprimand. You are right. We men of the new Germany must be strict with ourselves even if it means a long separation from our family. For we must finish matters once and for all and finally settle accounts with the war criminals, in order to create a better and eternal Germany for our heirs. We are not sleeping here. There are three or four operations a week. Sometimes Gypsies, another time Jews, partisans and all sorts of trash … We are not carrying on a lawless regime here, but when an action requires immediate atonement we contact the SD and justice takes its course. If the official judicial system were operating, it would be impossible to exterminate a whole family when only the father is guilty.

I do not know if you Herr *Obergruppenführer* ever saw such frightful kinds of Jews in Poland. I am grateful for having been allowed to see this bastard race close

---

up. If fate permits, I shall have something to tell my children. Syphilitics, cripples, idiots were typical of them. One thing was clear: they were materialists to the end. They were saying things like: 'We are skilled workers, you are not going to shoot us'. They were not men but monkeys in human form.

Ah well, there is only a small percentage of the 24,000 Jews of Kamenetz-Podolsk left. The yids in the surrounding area are also clients of ours. We are ruthlessly making a clean sweep with a clear conscience and then '... the waves close over, the world has peace.'

Source: *Nazism 1919-1945: Vol. 3, Foreign Policy, War, and Racial Extermination. A Documentary Reader.* Edited by J. Noakes and G. Pridham. Exeter, UK: University of Exeter Press. New edition with index, 2001.

10

LIFE AND DEATH
IN THE GHETTO

Two destitute children sit on the cobblestone pavement in a square in the Warsaw ghetto.

INTRODUCTION

Beginning with their resettlement of the Jewish population of Poland, the Nazis created ghettos in their newly conquered territories—special segregated areas in towns and cities where the Jewish population was massed together. In most cases these areas were "closed"—walled off from the rest of the town, with armed guards posted to prevent the Jewish residents from traveling to outside areas except for authorized reasons such as work.

The ghettos served multiple purposes for the Nazis. First, they were a means of controlling the Jewish population that the Germans saw as dangerous and undesirable. Also, they were treated as a source of labor. The Nazis organized ghetto residents into supervised work details that were sent to outside areas, and factories and workshops charged with manufacturing goods for the German war effort were located within the ghettos. The Jewish workers were essentially slaves: wages were very low or nonexistent.

In time, the ghettos became an integral part of the Final Solution. They served as convenient staging areas where Jews from a given region could be gathered together before their shipment to the death camps. In some places, such as Lithuania and other territories taken from the Soviets, a simpler form of mass killing took place: once brought together in a ghetto, some or all of the residents would be taken to nearby areas, shot, and buried in mass graves. Finally, the ghettos were instruments of death in and of themselves. The residents were seldom supplied with sufficient food, and the overcrowded conditions bred epidemics. In terms of malnutrition and disease, the Jewish districts served as a ghastly preview of the conditions in the extermination camps. In addition, Nazi troops frequently employed deadly force against the residents. All told, about a million Jews perished in the ghettos.

Despite the grim circumstances under which they existed, though, the ghetto dwellers showed a remarkable ability to persevere. Schools were set up, welfare commissions were established to aid the most desperate, and cultural groups staged plays and concerts to help lift community spirits. Resistance groups were formed and sometimes forged links with anti-Nazi rebels outside the ghetto.

These efforts were aided by the fact that ghetto residents had a limited degree of self-rule. A *Judenrat* or Jewish council oversaw affairs within the walled enclosures, though the Nazis were the ultimate authority over the ghetto. The *Judenrat* could be a positive force for the ghetto residents. But some councils were plagued by corruption, susceptible to bribes from residents who wanted to secure better living conditions or food rations or work assignments.

Whatever their merits or failures, it bears remembering that the members of the *Judenrat* operated in a morally murky environment. To cooperate with the Germans was to participate in the oppression and murder of their own people, yet *Judenrat* members knew that outright resistance to the Nazis could trigger wholesale slaughter of the people under their wing. Many *Judenrat* leaders decided to cooperate because they reasoned that a calm and productive Jewish work force might be kept alive long enough to be liberated. But doing so forced them to undertake terrible tasks. The most agonizing of these duties was selecting which Jews among the ghetto population were to be "resettled." Officially, this meant relocation to another area for work, but in most cases the evacuees were being sent elsewhere and killed—a fact that became increasingly well known in the ghettos as time went by.

Few ghettos survived until the end of the war. Despite desperate attempts to placate their overseers, most were eventually "liquidated," to use the official Nazi term. Ghetto after ghetto was emptied by the Nazis in the war's later years, the residents shipped to Polish prison camps that had been specifically designed to destroy vast numbers of people.

10.1
The Struggle to Find Food in the Łódź Ghetto – 1941
Excerpt from The Diary of Dawid Sierakowiak

One of the largest ghettos constructed by the Nazis was in the city of Łódź. which had the second-largest Jewish population in Poland after Warsaw. Located in the western region of Poland occupied by Germany in 1939, Łódź became the focal point of Nazi efforts to remove Jews from that entire region and send them to the Government General of Poland.

When the Nazis began forcing the Jews of Łódź and surrounding areas into the ghetto in 1940, Dawid Sierakowiak was fifteen years old. He kept a diary of his daily experiences in a series of notebooks, several of which were discovered after the war in the apartment his family had lived in. The Łódź ghetto was more tightly sealed off from the outside world than were the Jewish districts in cities such as Warsaw, which made it more difficult to smuggle in food and other essentials. As a result, hunger was severe and widespread in Łódź, and much of Sierakowiak's diary—including these 1941 diary excerpts—is taken up with the subject of food or, more precisely, the lack of it. Despite the grim conditions, the children of the ghetto were able to attend a school that was organized by the Judenrat. *Though he was thankful for the chance to study, Sierakowiak was critical of Mordechai Rumkowski, a controversial leader of the Łódź* Judenrat *who advocated cooperation with the Nazis.*

Sierakowiak died in August 1943, probably from a combination of tuberculosis and malnutrition. Within another year, the population of the Łódź ghetto had been almost completely wiped out, with the ghetto's last residents forced into the Auschwitz-Birkenau death camp.

Tuesday, April 22. Łódź. Rumkowski has come up with a splendid idea to prevent workers in the bread cooperatives from eating on the job. Starting tomorrow a 2-kilo loaf of bread will be given to each person as a ration for five days. This way, weighing, slicing, and eating bread will be avoided in the cooperatives. Furthermore, the private sale of wood (which usually comes from the theft of fence parts, latrines, and all other wooden structures in the ghetto that have not yet been torn down by the ghetto administration) will be prohibited. Wood now costs 80 pf a kilo. (It's been months since the last allocation of coal was issued, and the last time Rumkowski gave wood was in the beginning of February.) So we will again have to satisfy ourselves with a single soup a day from the community kitchen because even though our supplementary allocations include potatoes, barley, and vegetables, we will have nothing to cook them with. If they don't beat us with a stick, they'll beat us with a club. The inevitability of death by starvation grows more evident. Also tomorrow the administration is instituting an action to clean up the ghetto to protect us from epidemics. It is about time.

I have registered at the school secretariat at Dworska Street. On Sunday, the third and fourth levels will be reopened for the students living on our side of the bridge. The *gymnasium* [school] is located at 6 Smugowa Street. There will be additional nutrition in school, but details won't be known until Friday. So I'll go to school again (of course, only if I don't have some other job to do). There will finally be an end to the anarchy in my daily activities and, I hope, an end to too much philosophizing and depression.

Wednesday, April 23. Łódź. It's constantly cold and rainy. I don't think there was one single sunny day during this unfortunate year. I still don't have any work to do because the rutabagas haven't arrived yet. It certainly makes people furious because they've been waiting for two weeks. Although I did not have any work to do, I ran to the workshop almost every hour to learn whether the rutabagas arrived, whether they needed me. It took me almost the whole day, and of course they will not pay me for it.

Thursday, April 24. Łódź. Rutabagas have finally arrived, and I worked all day. I received my coupon and was able to take my portion before the "finishing off" of the load.

Friday, April 25. Łódź. We've finally finished distributing the rutabagas, but it means that my job has ended. I have just found out that we will not be paid for the number of days we worked, but for the total amount of rutabagas we distributed. Thus I can't count on more than 10 to 12 RM for two full weeks of running around.

Saturday, April 26. Łódź. School starts at nine o'clock tomorrow. We'll have five months to cover the fourth grader at best, and it's a whole lot of material. I only hope that no new obstacles get in our way.

Sunday, April 27. Łódź. The first day of school. The trip to Marysin is quite long, but the worst thing about it is the awful mud from the incessant rain. I must cross all kinds of fields, and my shoes are in terrible shape. They are beginning to "go," but any repair is out of the question. I suppose I'll soon have to rush to school barefoot.

The school is located in a tiny building that can hardly hold our benches. There are no other supplies (not even a blackboard). Nor is there a cloakroom, and we sit in the classroom wearing our coats. We had six classes today. During the last class, Rumkowski himself arrived for a visit accompanied by Praszkier [Rumkowski's special assignments chief], Karo (the "minister" of education), and a number of other ghetto "dignitaries." Rumkowski toured the kitchen, tasted the soup (which was simply delicious, probably for his sake), and addressed the students. He spoke about the difficulties connected with opening the school, and said he will try to get more for us; he demanded that we work diligently, keep clean, and behave well.

After Rumkowski's speech (incidentally, he has grown fat and looks incredibly younger) I went up to Praszkier, director of the kitchen department, to find out about my application, which he was supposed to submit to the president [Rumkowski] for me. He informed me that I won't get the job because my role is to study (!), and that Mom will be the one who will receive a job from him. I wonder if he will keep his word this time. I have not been paying for the soup for several months because I was officially allowed to register for subsidy. But we are not eligible anymore, since Father's earnings exceed the amount allowed. So now again, study, study, study.

Monday, April 28. Łódź. The Germans win one victory after another. The fighting in Yugoslavia and Greece is coming to an end, and the last English troops are leaving in a hurry; in Africa, where Germans are arriving through France (using French ships to reach French Tunis), the English are beginning to take heavy losses. Although they talk again about tensions in German-Soviet relations, these are naturally only consoling rumors. The Devil has taken too much of a hold over us, and nothing good can happen very soon in the world. We will certainly suffer much more here.

Tuesday, April 29. Łódź. Classes at school have been very good from the outset. Every day we have six solid lessons, even though the conditions in which the classes are held are still very uncomfortable.

This is the second month of incessant rain and extreme cold. Even the oldest people in the ghetto can't remember such a bad spring, but if the days were hot, on the other hand, who knows how many epidemics there might be in the ghetto. In this respect spring is passing relatively calmly, even though fears are enormous…

Saturday, May 24. Łódź. I've been catching up with classes all day today. I'm damnably hungry because there isn't even a trace left of the small loaf of bread that was supposed to feed me through Tuesday. I console myself that I'm not the only one in such a dire situation. When I receive my ration of bread, I can hardly control myself and sometimes suffer so much from exhaustion that I have to eat whatever food I have, and then my small loaf of bread disappears before the next ration is issued, and my torture grows. But what can I do? There's no help. Our grave will apparently be here.

Sunday, May 25. Łódź. It's really like May now. Even though the emaciated, famished people (like me) can't yet afford to fully "summerize" their garb, winter coats have finally been put away. It's already dry everywhere, and the smell of spring in Marysin makes your heart break with the memory of prewar times. In normal times we would now be three weeks away from the *gymnasium* pregraduation exams, and the longed-for vacation. There would certainly be an excursion and after that a camping trip or a visit to the country. Damn it! You feel like crying when you remember those things. Blast it!

Monday, May 26. Łódź. At school everything proceeds normally. We're working on Cicero's often praised speech against Cataline, and will start metrics next week; in mathematics we're doing exponential equations, and before long we'll start on the measurement of volumes. We are falling behind in other subjects, though not in German. Dinners in school are relatively substantial, and my extra portion of soup comes in awfully handy. Even five such portions would not be too much. A school paper is being organized. I've submitted a caricature for it, and perhaps one of my articles in Yiddish will be accepted as well. (All the others I wrote turned out to be unacceptable to the censors. The ghetto has its own precisely formulated bourgeois ideology.)

Even though Mom has a job, things are not too well at home. She leaves at seven and comes back at nine in the evening. Father works from eight to eight. So all our housekeeping falls on Nadzia's shoulders; she takes care of all the food lines, cleaning, etc., and she performs all these efforts, having only one soup and 30 dkg of bread a day. (Just like Mom, she gives away 10 dkg of her bread to Father. He doesn't know, however, how to appreciate it, and his attitude toward them is bad and reveals unmitigated egotism, just as it does toward me.)

We don't cook at home anymore because we have nothing to cook. We can't get any potatoes because they are not available in the ghetto. Any increase in the daily portion of bread is beyond hope.

Tuesday, May 27. Łódź. Everybody is anxiously awaiting Roosevelt's speech, which was scheduled for today. People are saying that it was on May 27 that the United States declared war on Germany in 1917. Unfortunately, I don't have a textbook to check this fact, but even if it is true, it doesn't seem to be a reason for the United States to join the war today. I hope I'm proven wrong, though. Otherwise, everyone is ready to tyrannize me endlessly for my relentless pessimism. Too bad they always have to admit I've been right. That's what killing me …

Wednesday, May 28. Łódź. According to Roosevelt, we must wait, wait, and wait. Listening to this disgusting blabber drives you crazy. The statistics show an unbelievable increase in the number of children and young people sick from tuberculosis here, and the hearse is as busy as ever. Meanwhile, over there they wait. Damn them!

216

Thursday, May 29. Łódź. Rumkowski once again presented us with a real treat as he was issuing a tiny portion of food for the holidays [Shavuot, the Jewish holiday honoring God's giving of the Torah to Moses]. Namely, he announced that the next allocation of bread will be given for only four days instead of five days, which means 50 dkg a day. If the larger portions of bread remain for longer it will be really something. But now people will just encourage their stomachs, and later it will be even worse. All the excitement is about a single common, dry piece of bread. It's horrible. All this weighing of portions, the squabbling "about weight," grabbing for crumbs—will it ever end?

Friday, May 30. Łódź. Getocajtung [the official newspaper of the ghetto's Jewish Administration] has published an article by Rumkowski in which he writes that since there is nothing to be cooked, instead of supplementary soup, workers will receive 20 dkg of bread, 5 dkg of sausage, and a cup of ersatz coffee with saccharine for 25 pf a day.

In school I managed to finagle a third soup. After everybody had their soup and after several quite brutal refusals, I persuaded the kitchen manager with my begging to give me an extra portion. But even with the weight of the soup I lapped up in my stomach, I was as hungry as before. I don't think I'll ever be able to satiate my hunger.

Source: Sierakowiak, Dawid. *The Diary of Dawid Sierakowiak: Five Notebooks from the Łódź Ghetto.* Edited by Alan Adelson. Translated from the Polish by Kamil Turowski. New York: Oxford University Press, 1996.

10.2
The "Great Action" in Lithuania – 1941
Excerpt from Surviving the Holocaust: The Kovno Ghetto Diary *by Avraham Tory*

Sooner or later all ghettos became way stations to the Holocaust. Some of the first Jewish districts to serve this function were located in the areas of eastern Europe conquered by the German army in 1941. The following eyewitness account by Avraham Tory, deputy secretary of the Jewish council in Kovno, concerns the so-called "Great Action" undertaken by the Nazis in Kovno, Lithuania, on October 28 and 29, 1941. This was a massacre of more than 11,000 Jews from Kovno (called Kaunas in Lithuanian, Kovno is the Hebrew name for the city). Tory's account captures both the terror felt by Jewish residents caught in the Nazis' genocidal machine and the desperate bravery of men like Dr. Elchanan Elkes, the head of Kovno's Jewish council, who worked feverishly to deliver ghetto residents from death.

Many Jewish residents of the Kovno ghetto kept secret archives, diaries, photographs, and drawings to document the Nazi crimes being perpetuated against their community. Tory was one of these secret recordkeepers of Kovno's dark history. He carefully documented events in Kovno from June 1941 to January 1944, when he escaped from the ghetto and went into hiding. Both he and his diary survived the Holocaust. His daily record of events in Kovno was later used in trials against several Nazi war criminals.

The main Nazi discussed in this excerpt is Helmut Rauca, an S.S. master sergeant who was in charge of the ghetto. He disappeared after the war, but in 1982 he was discovered living comfortably in Toronto. He was extradited to West Germany and charged with aiding and abetting in the murder of more than 11,500 Jews in Kovno between 1941 and 1943. Rauca died during legal proceedings, before he could be brought to trial for his crimes.

Immediately after their visit to the chief rabbi, members of the Council convened for a special meeting and decided to publish the decree. So it was that on October 27, 1941, announcements in Yiddish and in German were posted by the Council throughout the Ghetto. Their text was as follows:

> The Council has been ordered by the authorities to publish the following official decree to the Ghetto inmates:
>
> All inmates of the Ghetto, without exception, including children and the sick, are to leave their homes on Tuesday, October 28, 1941, at 6 A.M., and to assemble in the square between the big blocks and the Demokratu Street, and to line up in accordance with police instructions.
>
> The Ghetto inmates are required to report by families, each family being headed by the worker who is the head of the family.
>
> It is forbidden to lock apartments, wardrobes, cupboards, desks, etc....
>
> After 6 A.M. nobody may remain in his apartment.
>
> Anyone found in the apartments after 6 A.M. will be shot on sight.

The wording was chosen by the Council so that everyone would understand that it concerned a Gestapo order; that the Council had no part in it.

The Ghetto was agog. Until the publication of this order everyone had carried his fears in his own heart. Now those fears and forebodings broke out. The rumors about the digging of pits in the Ninth Fort, which had haunted people like a nightmare, now

Reprinted by permission of the publisher from *Surviving the Holocaust: The Kovno Ghetto Diary* by Avraham Tory, edited by Martin Gilbert, translated by Jersy Michaelowicz, with textual and historical notes by Dina Porat, 43-58, Cambridge, Mass: Harvard University Press, Copyright © 1990 by the President and Fellows of Harvard College.

acquired tangible meaning. The Ghetto remembered well the way the previous "actions" had been prepared, in which some 2,800 people had met their deaths…

Tuesday morning, October 28, was rainy. A heavy mist covered the sky and the whole Ghetto was shrouded in darkness. A fine sleet filled the air and covered the ground in a thin layer. From all directions, dragging themselves heavily and falteringly, groups of men, women, and children, elderly and sick who leaned on the arms of their relatives or neighbors, babies carried in their mothers' arms, proceeded in long lines. They were all wrapped in winter coats, shawls, or blankets, so as to protect themselves from the cold and the damp. Many carried in their hands lanterns or candles, which cast a faint light, illuminating their way in the darkness.

Many families stepped along slowly, holding hands. They all made their way in the same direction—to Demokratu Square. It was a procession of mourners grieving over themselves. Some thirty thousand people proceeded that morning into the unknown, toward a fate that could already have been sealed for them by the bloodthirsty rulers.

A deathlike silence pervaded this procession tens of thousands strong. Every person dragged himself along, absorbed in his own thoughts, pondering his own fate and the fate of his family whose lives hung by a thread. Thirty thousand lonely people, forgotten by God and by man, delivered to the whim of tyrants whose hands had already spilled the blood of many Jews.

All of them, especially heads of families, had equipped themselves with some sort of document, even a certificate of being employed by one of the Ghetto institutions, or a high school graduation diploma, or a German university diploma—some paper that might perhaps, perhaps, who knows, bring them an "indulgence" for the sin of being a Jew. Some dug out commendations issued by the Lithuanian Army; perhaps these might be of help…

The square was surrounded by machine-gun emplacements. [Helmut] Rauca [the Gestapo agent in charge of Jewish affairs in Kovno] positioned himself on top of a little mound from which he could watch the great crowd that waited in the square in tense and anxious anticipation. His glance ranged briefly over the column of the Council members and the Jewish Ghetto police, and by a movement of his hand he motioned them to the left, which, as it became clear later, was the "good" side. Then he signaled with the baton he held in his hand and ordered the remaining columns: "Forward!" The selection had begun.

The columns of employees of the Ghetto institutions and their families passed before Rauca, followed by other columns, one after another. The Gestapo man fixed his gaze on each pair of eyes and with a flick of the finger of his right hand passed sentence on individuals, families, or even whole groups. Elderly and sick persons, families with children, single women, and persons whose physique did not impress him in terms of labor power, were directed to the right. There, they immediately fell into the hands of the German policemen and the Lithuanian partisans, who showered them with shouts and blows and pushed them toward an opening especially made in the fence, where two Germans counted them and then reassembled them in a different place.

At first, nobody knew which was the "good" side. Many therefore rejoiced at finding themselves on the right. They began thanking Rauca, saying "Thank you kindly," or even "Thank you for your mercy." There were many men and women who, having been directed to the left, asked permission to move over to the right and join their relatives from whom they had been separated. Smiling sarcastically, Rauca gave his consent.

Those who tried to pass over from the right to the left, in order to join their families, or because they guessed—correctly, as it turned out—that that was the "good" side, immediately felt the pain of blows dealt by the hands and rifle butts of the policemen and the partisans, who brutally drove them back again to the right. By then everyone realized which side was the "good" and which the "bad" one.

When some old or sick person could not hold out any longer and collapsed to the ground, the Lithuanians set upon him instantly, kicking him with their boots, beating him, and threatening to trample him underfoot if he did not get up at once. Drawing the last ounce of strength, he would rise to his feet—if he could—and try to catch up with his group. Those unable to get up were helped by their companions in trouble, who lifted them up, supported them, and helped them along to reach the assembly spot in the small Ghetto, to which they were marched under heavy guard.

In most cases these were old people, women, and children, frightened and in a state of shock, turned by screams and blows into a panic-stricken herd which felt it was being driven by a satanic, omnipotent force. It was a force which banished all thought and seemed to allow no hope of escape.

In especially shocking cases where members of a family were separated, when pleas and cries were heartrending, Dr. Elkes tried to come to the rescue, and at times he even succeeded in transferring whole families to the left. Among others, he intervened on behalf of a veteran public figure, the director of the hospital, a skillful artisan, and a number of activists of Zionist and non-Zionist underground circles. Unfortunately he did not succeed in transferring everyone to the left.

The commander of the Jewish police, Kopelman, who stayed with Dr. Elkes near Rauca, also succeeded in saving Jews and whole families. The number of such survivors, throughout this bitter and hurried day, reached into the hundreds.

Rauca directed the job of selection composedly, with cynicism, and with the utmost speed, by mere movements of the finger of his right hand. When the meaning of the movement of his finger was not grasped instantly, he would roar: "To the right!" or "To the left!" And when people failed to obey at once he shouted at them: "To the right, you lousy curs!" Throughout the selection he did not exhibit any sign of fatigue or sensitivity at the wailing, pleas, and cries, or at the sight of the heartrending spectacles which took place before his eyes when children were separated from their parents, or parents from their children, or husbands and wives from each other—all those tragedies did not penetrate his heart at all.

From time to time, Rauca feasted on a sandwich—wrapped in wax paper lest his blood-stained hands get greasy—or enjoyed a cigarette, all the while performing his fiendish work without interruption.

When a column composed mostly of elderly people, or of women or children, appeared before him, he would command contemptuously: "All this trash to the right!" or "All this pile of garbage goes to the right!" To Dr. Elkes, when he tried to intervene in an attempt to save their lives, he would say: "Wait, you'll be grateful to me for having rid you of this burden."

Whenever Rauca condescended to respond favorably to Dr. Elkes's intercession, he would say carelessly: "Well, as far as I am concerned ..." and then order the German policeman: "This fat one, or this short one, or this one with the glasses on, bring him back to me."

Now and then Rauca would be handed a note with a number written on it, copied from the notebook kept by the German who diligently applied himself to the task of recording the number of Jews removed to the small Ghetto.

Rauca was quick to dispense "mercy" to those who, having found themselves on the left side, asked to be reunited with their families motioned to the right. In such cases he would say: "You want to be together—all right, everybody to the right!'

Everyone passing in front of Rauca would wave a document he held in his hand. This brought a scornful smile to Rauca's lips. He acted in accordance with his own criteria...

Dr. Elkes stood there, his pale face bearing an expression of bottomless grief. Since 6 A.M. this sixty-five-year-old man had been standing on his feet, refusing to sit on the stool that had been brought to him. Now and then, when he was overcome by a fit of weakness, those near him asked him to sit down to regain his strength, or offered him a piece of bread. He refused, murmuring: "Thank you, thank you, gentlemen; terrible things are happening here; I must remain standing on guard in case I can be of assistance." Whenever he succeeded in transferring someone from the bad to the good side, and the person saved would try to shake his hand, he would refuse, saying : "Leave me alone, leave me alone." Sometimes, when in his efforts to transfer somebody to the left side he would inadvertently step too close to the guard unit charged with keeping order at the dividing line, he would be showered with curses and threats from the Lithuanian partisans: "Get away, you old, stupid Zhid, or else you'll go together with them." ...

The Jewish Ghetto policemen were instructed to keep order in that part of the square where those who had passed the selection were assembled. On that day the Jewish policemen displayed initiative, daring, and resourcefulness—they cheered up the dispirited, they lent a hand to those who collapsed on the ground or fainted, and gave them water. They even worked wonders: while lining up the survivors in a new column, they seized every opportunity of transferring individuals—and even whole families still waiting for their turn—over to the good side. They did this with cunning and deftness; they would signal by a wink, or a movement of the hand, to slip away, to jump quickly, or to crouch and crawl toward them without drawing the attention of the guards. Whenever such a person drew near them, the Jewish policemen would set upon him screaming and push him brutally to the good side, pretending that they were forcing him back to his correct place. But whenever they did not succeed in deceiving the guards, a hail of curses and blows would pour on the unfortunate policeman caught in the act.

The selection was completed only after nightfall, but not before Rauca made sure that the quota had been fulfilled and that some 10,000 people had been transferred to the small Ghetto. Only then were those who had passed through the selection, and had remained standing in the square, allowed to return to their homes.

About 17,000 out of some 27,000 people slowly left the vast square where they had been standing for more than twelve hours. Hungry, thirsty, crushed, and dejected, they returned home, most of them bereaved or orphaned, having been separated from a father, a mother, children, a brother or a sister, a grandfather or a grandmother, an uncle or an aunt. A deep mourning descended on the Ghetto. In every house there were now empty rooms, unoccupied beds, and the belongings of those who had not returned from the selection. One-third of the Ghetto population had been cut down. The sick people who had remained in their homes in the morning had all disappeared. They had been transferred to the Ninth Fort during the day.

The square was strewn with several dozen bodies of elderly and sick people who had died of exhaustion. Here and there stools, chairs, and empty baby carriages were lying about.

On his way back Dr. Elkes muttered: "It wasn't worthwhile living for more than sixty years in order to witness a day like this! Who can bear all this when you are being appealed to with heartrending cries and there is nothing much you can do? I can't bear it any longer!"

When we reached Dr. Elkes's house we found many people besieging his door. All of them wanted to know what had happened to the people who had been taken to the small Ghetto. Men and women implored him to save their parents, wives, children, brothers, sisters, or other relatives. Everyone had a moving story of his own to tell.

Deadly tired and crushed by the day's horrors as he was, Dr. Elkes listened to every one. In vain he tried to explain that he had no idea of the German plans regarding the people transferred to the small Ghetto and that he was powerless to get them out of there. Nonetheless he promised to do all he could and to intervene with the authorities to comply with their requests. He wrote down the names of those he had been asked to rescue, including details such as occupation or skill which might produce some result with the Germans.

Among the Jews transferred to the small Ghetto there were pessimists who felt that all was lost, whereas others refused to give up all hope. But everyone tried to keep his head above water in case a miracle might occur. As more and more people were transferred there, there was more conflict and even competition among them. Each family tried to take possession of a better apartment, to gather more wood for fuel, to get indispensable household utensils, and so on. Some people set about tidying up and improving apartments that had long ago been abandoned by their previous occupants, filling up holes in the wall and fixing windows to protect against wind and rain. The more industrious got together during the night to discuss how to organize their lives in the new quarters. Some even proposed to elect immediately a Council on the patter of the Council in the large Ghetto. All night long they debated and haggled among themselves, but were unable to agree about the composition of the proposed Council, the distribution of apartments, and so on.

> *"Thousands of inmates from the large Ghetto flocked to the fence and, with tearful eyes and frozen hearts, watched the horrible procession trudging slowly up the hill."*

It was an autumnal, foggy, and gloomy dawn when German policemen and drunken Lithuanian partisans broke into the small Ghetto, like so many ferocious beasts, and began driving the Jews out of their homes. The assault was so unexpected and brutal that the wretched inmates did not have a single moment to grasp what was going on. The partisans barked out their orders to leave the houses and to line up in rows and columns. Each column was immediately surrounded by partisans, shouting "Forward march, you scum, forward march," and driving the people by rifle butts out of the small Ghetto toward the road leading to the Ninth Fort. It was in the same direction that the Jews had been led away in the "action" commanded by Kozlovski on September 26, 1941 [when 1,200 Jews had been shot], and in the "action" of the liquidation of the small Ghetto on October 4, 1941. The same uphill road led Jews in one direction alone—to a place from which no one returned.

It was a death procession. The cries of despair issuing from thousands of mouths were hovering above them. Bitter weeping could be heard from far off.

223

Column after column, family after family, those sentenced to death passed by the fence of the large Ghetto. Some men, even a number of women, tried to break through the chain of guards and flee to the large Ghetto, but were shot dead on the spot. One woman threw her child over the fence, but missed her aim and the child remained hanging on the barbed wire. Its screams were quickly silenced by bullets.

Thousands of inmates from the large Ghetto flocked to the fence and, with tearful eyes and frozen hearts, watched the horrible procession trudging slowly up the hill. Many recognized a brother, a sister, parents or children, relatives or friends, and called to them by name. They were thrust back brutally by the reinforced guard of the Lithuanian partisans, who pointed to the signs posted on the fence. In German, Lithuanian, and Yiddish the signs warned: "Death zone! Whoever approaches within two meters of the fence will be shot on the spot without warning."

Dr. Elkes and the head of the Jewish Ghetto police, Kopelman, accompanied by their assistants, arrived at the fence. No sooner was Dr. Elkes seen than the cries and pleas went up from those being marched up the hill, as well as from those crowding into one big outburst that rose up to heaven: "Save us!'

Dr. Elkes asked that Rauca be found with the utmost urgency. He was traced before long by Kopelman's men at the German Ghetto command. Elkes addressed him immediately, asking to "allow him to remove from the small Ghetto those people who had fallen victim to error during the selection." Rauca consented, but limited the number of men and women to be removed to 100. Dr. Elkes kept in his pocket a list of people whose relatives had pleaded with him during the night and morning to save them, but their number far exceeded the figure of 100.

Accompanied by two sentries from the German Ghetto Guard, Dr. Elkes passed into the area of the small Ghetto, where he was immediately assailed by a throng of people already lined up in a column ready for departure. They begged him to save their lives. One seized his hand, another took hold of the tail of his coat, while another clasped his neck and refused to let go. Those who surrounded him knew full well that by leaving the column they endangered their lives, but they kept crying: "It is better for us to be killed here. We won't let go of you, Doctor—save us!" Within seconds the entire column faltered. For a moment it seemed that those condemned to death had rebelled. The Lithuanian guards intervened immediately, and with blows and kicks pushed people back into their places and hurried the whole column toward the road to catch up with the other columns that had moved ahead.

Dr. Elkes himself was ordered by the guards to clear out at once—if not, they threatened, they would take him too to the Ninth Fort. Dr. Elkes insisted on his right to remove 100 people, as permitted by Rauca. Thereupon the Lithuanian partisans pounced upon him, hitting him with their fists. One of them brought down the butt of his rifle upon his head. Dr. Elkes collapsed on the ground, unconscious and bleeding profusely.

Jewish policemen and other Ghetto inmates (myself included) rushed from behind the fence to help. We lifted him up and carried him on our shoulders to the large Ghetto across the road, and put him inside the first house near the fence. He lay there for several days. Physicians stitched his open head wounds and nursed him, until he was able to stand on his feet again and return to his home. His efforts to save a number of Jews from the small Ghetto had almost cost him his own life.

The procession, numbering some 10,000 people, and proceeding from the small Ghetto to the Ninth Fort, lasted from dawn until noon. Elderly people, and those who were sick, collapsed by the roadside and died. Warning shots were fired incessantly, all along the way, and around the large Ghetto. Thousands of curious Lithuanians flocked to both sides of the road to watch the spectacle, until the last of the victims was swallowed up by the Ninth Fort.

In the fort, the wretched people were immediately set upon by the Lithuanian killers, who stripped them of every valuable article—gold rings, earrings, bracelets. They forced them to strip naked, pushed them into pits which had been prepared in advance, and fired into each pit with machine guns which had been positioned there in advance. The murderers did not have time to shoot everybody in one batch before the next batch of Jews arrived. They were accorded the same treatment as those who had preceded them. They were pushed into the pit on top of the dead, the dying, and those still alive from the previous group. So it continued, batch after batch, until the 10,000 men, women, and children had been butchered.

Source: Tory, Avraham. "October 28, 1941." In *Surviving the Holocaust: The Kovno Ghetto Diary.* Edited by Martin Gilbert. Translated by Jerzy Michalowicz. Cambridge, MA: Harvard University Press, 1990.

10.3
Lithuanian Participation in the "Great Action" in the Kovno Ghetto - 1941
Excerpt from an Interview with Holocaust Survivor Marcia Ceitlin Spies

A member of a wealthy Jewish family in Kovno, Lithuania, Marcia Ceitlin Spies was eleven years old when the German Army invaded her homeland in the summer of 1941. Because her parents had previously been sent to a prison in the Soviet Union, Spies resided with her aunt and uncle and, with them, was confined to one of Kovno's ghetto neighborhoods. In the following interview, she recalls the horrors of the Nazis' "Great Action" of October 1941, in which more than 11,000 Jewish residents of the Kovno ghetto were

Marcia Ceitlin Spies, Videotaped interview conducted by Joyce Tapper, 31 July 1995. Survivors of the Shoah Visual History Foundation, Beverly Hills, CA, USA.

murdered. Spies notes that non-Jewish Lithuanians played a large role in the atrocities carried out against the Jews of Kovno.

They immediately drove all of us out into the street in the ghetto. And the Germans, I remember them to this day, went around and said "right, left, right, left." Right meant survival and left meant death... My cousin ... had a boyfriend, and they were both pictures of health. And [Aunt Paula] thought perhaps they would be spared. You know, to see two young, beautiful people—of course they needed them for work. But unfortunately, it did not happen... [Aunt Paula] sent my cousin ... off with her boyfriend to stand in the lineup, and they were separated, and the [boyfriend's] whole family was killed, together with my twenty-year-old cousin. And my Aunt Paula never forgave herself for that. So that was the big blow in our family because she was really the first one, and I must say, the only one who was killed during the ghetto years...

We were all outside, and I remember standing with ... the whole family, right with the children. But my uncle somehow found out right away which [side] was death and which one was life, and so we were alerted right away so we made sure that we were separated, you know, into life... This went on for I think a whole day, and after that day we were told that we could go back to our houses and that the other people were just going to be evacuated to another city for work...

Then later on that night, we started hearing gunshots. The next day, or a couple days later, some people ... told us what had happened... They just lined up these people, 10,000 people, around a hole. And there were machine guns that just shot them all. And the Germans were standing, actually, with the [non-Jewish] Lithuanians who were standing right there. And just threw them in, whoever was there just fell in. And whoever was not dead, they would just push them into that grave and then put dirt on top of it. And they were still hearing the cries of the people. So a few escaped. They just dug their way out of the graves and came back to Kovno... [But] many, many Jews ... were killed right there...

The Lithuanians were even more cold-blooded murderers than the Germans. Some of the atrocities that went on, the Germans couldn't even bear looking at it, whereas the Lithuanians were immediately—with vengeance—after the Jews, especially. And I remember them saying that "Hitler opened our eyes up—that our eyes were closed." Because most of the Jewish population in Kovno were quite well off, and we lived quite a very good life...

Thereafter there were small separations and killings... Every time we were driven out of our homes into the streets. And the Germans would come through, and ... especially they picked the ones who were old and sick. They would separate them immediately and kill them off. Take them out, again, under the camouflage that they were just sending them for better care, to hospitals and so on.

Source: Spies, Marcia Ceitlin. Videotaped interview conducted by Joyce Tapper, 31 July 1995. Survivors of the Shoah Visual History Foundation Testimony 4963.

10.4
A Warsaw Ghetto Resettlement Notice – 1942
Text of an Announcement From S.S. Officer Hermann Höfle

During World War II, Poland's capital city of Warsaw became home to the largest Jewish ghetto created by the Nazis; it eventually held more than 400,000 people. On July 22, 1942, the Nazis began removing groups of Jews from the district. The Nazis claimed that they were being "resettled," but they were actually being sent on the short rail journey to the Treblinka death camp, where they were murdered. More than 300,000 Jews from Warsaw were loaded on trains to Treblinka over the next two and a half months. Hermann Höfle, the S.S. officer in charge of the "resettlement," issued the following official announcement to the Warsaw Judenrat *on the day the deportations began.*

The Jewish Council is hereby informed of the following:

1. All Jewish persons irrespective of age or sex who live in Warsaw will be resettled to the east.

2. The following are excluded from the resettlement:

(*a*) all Jewish persons who are employed by the German authorities or by German agencies and can provide proof of it.

(*b*) all Jewish persons who belong to the Jewish Council and are employees of the Jewish Council. (The qualifying date is the date of publication of the order.)

(*c*) all Jewish persons who are employed by German firms and can provide proof of it.

(*d*) all Jews capable of work who have not hitherto been employed. They are to be placed in barracks in the ghetto.

(*e*) all Jewish personnel who are members of the personnel of the Jewish hospitals. Similarly, the members of Jewish disinfection troops.

(*f*) all Jewish persons who belong to the Jewish police force.

(*g*) all Jewish persons who are close relatives of the persons referred to in (*a*)-(*f*). Such relatives are restricted to wives and children.

(*h*) all Jewish persons who on the first day of the resettlement are in one of the Jewish hospitals and are not capable of being released. The fitness for release will be decided by a doctor to be designated by the Jewish Council.

3. Every Jewish person being resettled may take 15 kg. of his property as personal luggage. All valuables may be taken: gold, jewellery, cash, etc.

Food for three days should be taken.

Reprinted by permission of University of Exeter Press.

4. The resettlement begins on 22 July 1942 at 11 o'clock ...

II. The Jewish Council is responsible for providing the daily quota of Jews for transportation. To carry out this task the Jewish Council will use the Jewish police force (100 men). The Jewish Council will ensure that every day from 22 July onwards, by 16.00 at the latest, 6,000 Jews are assembled at the collecting point. The collecting point for the whole period of the evacuation will be the Jewish hospital in Stawki street. On 22 July, the 6,000 Jews will be assembled directly on the loading platform near the transfer office. To start with, the Jewish Council may take the quotas of Jews from the whole population. Later, the Jewish Council will receive special instructions according to which particular streets and blocks of flats are to be cleared...

VIII. Punishments:

(a) Any Jewish person who leaves the ghetto at the start of the resettlement without belonging to the categories of persons spelled out in 2(a) and (c), and in so far as they were not hitherto entitled to do so, will be shot.

(b) any Jewish person who undertakes an act which is calculated to evade or disturb the resettlement measures will be shot.

(c) Any Jewish person who assists in an act which is calculated to evade or disturb the resettlement measures will be shot.

(d) All Jews who, on completion of the resettlement, are encountered in Warsaw and do not belong to the categories referred to in 2 (a)-(h) will be shot.

The Jewish Council is hereby informed that, in the event that the orders and instructions are not carried out 100%, an appropriate number of hostages who have been taken in the meantime will be shot ...

Source: *Nazism 1919-1945: Vol. 3, Foreign Policy, War, and Racial Extermination. A Documentary Reader.* Edited by J. Noakes and G. Pridham. Exeter, UK: University of Exeter Press. New edition with index, 2001.

10.5
Life in Warsaw under the Shadow of the Swastika – 1942
Excerpt from Scroll of Agony *by Chaim A. Kaplan*

> *The founder and principal of a Hebrew school before the war, Chaim A. Kaplan kept a detailed account of life in the Warsaw ghetto under Nazi rule. The pandemonium that ensued as German troops began deporting Jews from the ghetto in 1942 is recorded in the following passages from his diary. Kaplan notes that the roundup of Warsaw residents was largely carried out by members of the Jewish police and that, at least in the beginning, it was the poorer members of the population who were deported, as wealthier residents were often able to bribe the authorities. As his own deportation*

became imminent, Kaplan gave his diary notebooks to a friend who was able to smuggle them out of the ghetto. After being hidden away for years (some were stored in a kerosene can and buried in the ground), the notebooks were delivered to historians in the 1950s and 1960s—one of many remarkable feats of preservation that helped historians piece together the story of the wartime ghettos. Though his diary survived, Kaplan did not. He and his wife are believed to have died at Treblinka in December 1942 or January 1943.

July 23, 1942 ...

The expulsion has already begun. It is being carried out by the Jewish people under German supervision. On the first day the Jewish police furnished the requisite number of 6,000 people; the second day of the expulsion, the police could round up only 4,700 men, women and children. The Nazis filled in the deficit. We remember the words of the elegist: "On this night my sons will weep." In these two days the emptiness of the ghetto has been filled with cries and wails. If they found no way to the God of Israel it is a sign He doesn't exist.

July 26, 1942

The terrible events have engulfed me; the horrible deeds committed in the ghetto have so frightened and stunned me that I have not the power, either physical or spiritual, to review these events and perpetuate them with the pen of a scribe. I have no words to express what has happened to us since the day the expulsion was ordered. Those people who have gotten some notion of historical expulsions from books know nothing. We, the inhabitants of the Warsaw ghetto, are now experiencing the reality. Our only good fortune is that our days are numbered—that we shall not have long to live under conditions like these, and that after our terrible sufferings and wanderings we shall come to eternal rest, which was denied us in life. Among ourselves we fully admit that this death which lurks behind our walls will be our salvation; but there is one thorn. We shall not be privileged to witness the downfall of the Nazis, which in the end will surely come to pass.

Some of my friends and acquaintances who know the secret of my diary urge me, in their despair, to stop writing. "Why? For what purpose? Will you live to see it published? Will these words of yours reach the ears of future generations? How? If you are deported you won't be able to take it with you because the Nazis will watch your every move, and even if you succeed in hiding it when you leave Warsaw, you will undoubtedly die on the way, for your strength is ebbing. And if you don't die from lack of strength, you will die by the Nazi sword. For not a single deportee will be able to hold out to the end of the war."

And yet in spite of it all I refuse to listen to them. I feel that continuing this diary to the very end of my physical and spiritual strength is a historical mission which must not be abandoned. My mind is still clear, my need to record unstilled, though it is now five days since any real food has passed my lips. Therefore I will not silence my diary! ...

July 27, 1942

Anyone who could see the expulsion from Warsaw with his own eyes would have his heart broken. The ghetto has turned into an inferno. Men have become beasts. Everyone is but a step away from deportation; people are being hunted down in the streets like animals in the forest. It is the Jewish police who are cruelest toward the condemned. Sometimes a blockade is made of a particular house, sometimes of a whole block of houses. In every building earmarked for destruction they begin to make the rounds of the apartments and to demand documents. Whoever has neither documents that entitle him to remain in the ghetto not money for bribes is told to make a bundle weighing 15 kilos—and on to the transport which stands near the gate. Whenever a house is blockaded a panic arises that is beyond the imagination. Residents who have neither documents or money hide in nooks and crannies, in the cellars and in the attics. When there is a means of passage between one courtyard and another the fugitives begin jumping over the roofs and fences at the risk of their lives; in time of panic, when the danger is imminent, people are not fussy about methods. But all these methods only delay the inevitable, and in the end the police take men, women, and children. The destitute and impoverished are the first to be deported. In an instant the truck becomes crowded. They are all alike: poverty makes them equal. Their cries and wails tear the heart out.

> *"I feel that continuing this diary to the very end of my physical and spiritual strength is a historical mission which must not be abandoned. My mind is still clear, my need to record unstilled."*

The children, in particular, rend the heavens with their cries. The old people and the middle-aged deportees accept the judgement in silent submission and stand with their small parcels under their arms. But there is no limit to the sorrow and tears of the young women; sometimes one of them makes an attempt to slip out of the grasp of her captors, and then a terrible battle begins. At such times the horrible scene reaches its peak. The two sides fight, wrestle. On one side a woman with wild hair and a torn blouse rages with the last of her strength at the Jewish thieves, trying to escape from their hands. Anger flows from her mouth and she is like a lioness ready for the kill. And on the other side are the two policemen, her "brothers in misfortune," who pull her back to her death. It is obvious that the police win. But during the fight the wailing of the captives increases sevenfold, and the whole street cries with them.

But isolated incidents don't hold up the operation. The police do what is incumbent upon them. After the completion of the arrest in one house, they move on to another. The *Judenrat* prepares a daily list of houses in which blockades will be made that day. And here a new source of income is opened up for the graft-chasing police. The wealthy and the middle class have yet to be brought to the transports. For those who have no documents, banknotes turn into documents. There is almost a fixed price for ransom, but for some it is cheaper, all according to the class of the ransomed one and the number of people in his household.

Two actual cases are known to me. One of the members of our family ransomed himself off with a substitute for money. In place of the ready cash which he didn't have at the time of the hunt, he gave a silk umbrella as a "gift" not to be returned. An acquaintance of mine, a Hebrew teacher, a downtrodden pauper with a crippled son, was forced to give 300 zloty—his last nest egg, since he has no expectation of new earnings from teaching Hebrew. In this instance the price was high, for expulsion of a cripple means expulsion to the gates of death. Sick people and cripples are killed by the Nazis while still en route.

But from the time they began to hunt down passerby on the street, the sorrow of the expulsion became even greater. For this barbarism the beloved *Judenrat* will find no atonement. One who is seized in his apartment supplies himself with some clothing and food for the journey. His loved ones take their leave of him, fall on his neck. Not so one who is seized on the street. He is taken to the transport as he is, without extra clothing, without food and sustenance, and usually without a penny. No entreaties avail him. He is led out to the transfer point like a lamb to the slaughter.

Life in the ghetto has been turned upside down. Panic is in its streets, fear on every face, wails and cries everywhere you turn. Trade has ceased; bargaining has been silenced; and most important, smuggling has stopped. When there is no smuggling, costs go up, so that the price of bread has reached 60 zloty. Prices have increased tenfold, all businesses have ceased to exist. Everyone's staff of bread has been broken. From whence cometh our help? We are lost! We are lost! ...

August 2, 1942

Jewish Warsaw is in its death throes. A whole community is going to its death! The appalling events follow one another so abundantly that it is beyond the power of a writer of impressions to collect, arrange, and classify them; particularly when he himself is caught in their vise—fearful of his own fate for the next hour, scheduled for deportation, tormented by hunger, his whole being filled with the fear and dread which accompanies the expulsion. And let this be known: From the beginning of the world, since the time when man first had dominion over another man to do him harm, there has never been so cruel and barbaric an expulsion as this one. From hour to hour, even from minute to minute, Jewish Warsaw is being demolished and destroyed, reduced and decreased. Since the day the exile was decreed, ruin and destruction, exile and wandering, bereavement and widowhood have befallen us in all their fury.

For five days now the Nazis have been "helping" the Jewish police. Since then the expulsion has begun to leave a trail of innocent blood behind it. A man who is ordered to leave his apartment must go as he is, for if he tarries a single moment he is put to death at once.

After Nowolipie, henceforward to be known as Schultz Street, came the turn of Leszno Street from the corner of Zelazna to Solna. The population of Leszno was not struck by the evacuation order, but rather by the degree of expulsion. A blockade was made on Leszno Street, and within two hours about 2,000 people were brought to the transfer point. All of them went forth empty-handed, naked and half-dressed. Woe to that family which must be routed out by the Nazis or their minions, the "alert" Ukrainians and Lithuanians. The victims emerge beaten and sore, naked as the day they were born.

Today the population of the "little ghetto" drank the cup of hemlock. At four the murderers set upon their task, and at seven a crowd of 5,000 people was led out through Smocza to the transfer point. All their possessions were left in the hands of the enemy.

Jewish Warsaw is turning into a city of slave laborers who have nothing of their own. The German companies that own the factories concentrate their employees in one section. To achieve this, they confiscate all the houses near a factory and settle the workers and their families in them. Without them there would be no Jewish community. Every activity in the ghetto, and all its establishments, are being brought to an end. Jews who are not employed in one of the factories will be expelled from Warsaw. For the time being they are busy with schemes and plans for hiding until the wrath passes, but the wrath of the Nazis never passes. On the contrary, it increases. Concessions granted on paper never materialize in practice. All of the various *Ausweisen* [documents of identification] are voided and nullified. In the end, everyone will be expelled.

Today I heard from Dr. Lajfuner, who in turn heard it from rumor, that the houses from 12 to 21 Nowolipki Street will be confiscated and turned over to the workers of a brush factory. This news will affect us both, for he is a resident at Number 14 and I at Number 20. If the rumor proves true I shall have no place to lay my head. And his fate is like mine. We shall both sleep out of doors—until we are caught and deported. Meanwhile we are without food—not even enough for a single meal.

We have no information about the fate of those who have been expelled. When one falls into the hands of the Nazis he falls into the abyss. The very fact that the deportees make no contact with their families by letters bodes evil. Nothing that is related—and many things are related—is based on exact information. One person says that a certain family has received news of one of its members who was deported, that he arrived in the place intended for him alive and well—but he doesn't name the place nor give his address, and he doesn't ask them to write to him. Certain other unconfirmed reports are widespread, but no one knows their source nor lends much credence to them. Nevertheless, there is some local information about one segment of the deportees—the sick, the aged, the crippled and the other invalids, the weak ones who need the care and help of other people. They have returned to the city, not to the living but rather to the dead—to the cemetery. There they have found rest for their oppressed souls, and there they attain eternal peace. I have not yet verified this information myself. I record it as I heard it from the rumor.

August 4, 1942...
In the evening hours

I have not yet been caught; I have not yet been evicted from my apartment; my building has not yet been confiscated. But only a step separates me from all these misfortunes. All day my wife and I take turns standing watch, looking through the kitchen window which overlooks the courtyard, to see if the blockade has begun. People run from place to place like madmen.

On the very day that I packed my possessions to turn them over to the relative who is my protector, my friend M. from Nowolipki Street brought me some of his belongings because he had heard that his block was in danger of blockade. My friend M. is "kosher" [a Hebrew word, meaning okay or protected in this context] by virtue of the fact that he has an administrative position at the *Judenrat*. His documents are valid and carry full privileges. But the size of the ghetto is being steadily decreased, and there is therefore a danger that the function of an administrator will cease to exist. What did he do? He looked for some kind of factory, and found one, but only upon payment of ransom. Because he had no cash, he gave its equivalent, a precious stone worth several thousand zloty. This was the last of his savings for the bad times to come. When he handed over the stone he was destitute.

My lot is even worse because I have neither money nor a factory job, and therefore am a candidate for expulsion if I am caught. My only salvation is in hiding. This is an outlaw's life, and a man cannot last very long living illegally. My heart trembles at every isolated word. I am unable to leave my house, for at every step the devil lies in wait for me.

There is the silence of death in the streets of the ghetto all through the day. The fear of death is in the eyes of the few people who pass by on the sidewalk opposite our window. Everyone presses himself against the wall and draws into himself so that they will not detect his existence or his presence.

Today my block was scheduled for a blockade with Nazi participation. Seventy Jewish policemen had already entered the courtyard. I thought, "The end has come." But a miracle happened, and the blockade was postponed. The destroyers passed on to the Nalewki-Zamenhof block.

When the danger was already past I hurried to escape. Panic can drive a man out of his mind and magnify the danger even when it no longer exists. But already there is a fear that my block will be blockaded tomorrow. I am therefore trying to lay plans to escape with the dawn. But where will I flee? No block is secure.

Thousands of people in the Nalewki-Zamenhof block were driven from their homes and taken to the transfer point. More than thirty people were slaughtered. In the afternoon, the furies subsided a bit. The numbers of passersby increased, for the danger of blockade was over. By four in the afternoon, the quota was filled: 13,000 people had been seized and sent off, among them 5,000 who came to the transfer of their own free will. They had had their fill of the ghetto life, which is a life of hunger and fear of death. They escaped from the trap. Would that I could allow myself to do as they did!

If my life ends—what will become of my diary?

Source: Kaplan, Chaim A. *Scroll of Agony: The Warsaw Diary of Chaim A. Kaplan.* Translated by Abraham I. Katsh. New York: Macmillan, 1965.

10.6
Deportation of Children from the Łódź Ghetto – 1942
Excerpt from an Address by Judenrat Leader Mordechai Rumkowski

Mordechai Rumkowski, who was the head of the Łódź Judenrat during World War II, was heavily criticized within the Jewish community for his dictatorial behavior and his cooperative attitude toward their Nazi persecutors. Rumkowski, though, believed that the best way to keep some of the city's Jewish population alive was to prove that the ghetto residents were productive, well-behaved workers. Rumkowski's accommodation with the Nazis forced him to organize the periodic selections of Jews to be "resettled"—that is, sent away, usually to be killed. In the following address made on September 4, 1942, he explains to the ghetto residents why children and elderly residents must be handed over to the Nazis.

Jewish residents of Łódź did survive longer than those in most other ghettos established by Nazi Germany during World War II. But in the end, the Nazi appetite for genocide was too great, and its population was liquidated in 1944. Rumkowski ended up dying at Auschwitz-Birkenau, as did most of the other residents removed from Łódź.

The ghetto has been struck a hard blow. They demand what is most dear to it—children and old people. I was not privileged to have a child of my own and therefore devoted my best years to children. I lived and breathed together with children. I never imagined that my own hands would be forced to make this sacrifice on the altar. In my old age I am forced to stretch out my hands and to beg: "Brothers and sisters, give them to me!—Fathers and mothers, give me your children…" (Bitter weeping shakes the assembled public)… Yesterday, in the course of the day, I was given the order to send away more than 20,000 Jews from the ghetto, and if I did not "we will do it ourselves." The question arose: "Should we have accepted this and carried it out ourselves, or left it to others?" But as we were guided not by the thought: "how many will be lost?" but "how many can be saved?" we arrived at the conclusion—those closest to me at work, that is, and myself—that however difficult it was going to be, we must take upon ourselves the carrying out of this decree. I must carry out this difficult and bloody operation, I must cut off limbs in order to save the body! I must take away children, and if I do not, others too will be taken, God forbid … (terrible wailing).

I cannot give you comfort today. Nor did I come to calm you today, but to reveal all your pain and all your sorrow. I have come like a robber, to take from you what is dearest to your heart. I tried everything I knew to get the bitter sentence cancelled. When it could not be cancelled, I tried to lessen the sentence. Only yesterday I ordered the registration of nine-year-old children. I wanted to save at least one year—children from nine to ten. But they would not yield. I succeeded in one thing—to save the children over ten. Let that be our consolation in our great sorrow.

There are many people in this ghetto who suffer from tuberculosis, whose days or perhaps weeks are numbered. I do not know, perhaps this is a satanic plan, and perhaps not, but I cannot stop myself from proposing it: "Give me these sick people, and perhaps it will be possible to save the healthy in their place." I know how precious each one of the sick is in his home, and particularly among Jews. But at a time of such decrees one must weigh up and measure who should be saved, who can be saved and who may be saved.

Common sense requires us to know that those must be saved who can be saved and who have a chance of being saved and not those whom there is no chance to save in any case…

Source: Trunk, I. *Lodzsher Geto (Lodz Ghetto)*. New York, n.p., 1962. Reprinted in *Documents on the Holocaust: Selected Sources on the Destruction of the Jews of Germany and Austria, Poland, and the Soviet Union*. Edited by Yithak Arad, Yisrael Gutman, and Abraham Margaliot. Translations by Lea Ben Dor. Jerusalem: Yad Vashem, 1981.

10.7
Rumors of the Holocaust in the Warsaw Ghetto – 1944
Excerpt from a Report by Yitzhak Cukierman

The Nazis went to great lengths to keep the truth about the death camps from becoming known in the ghettos. Despite their efforts, however, dark rumors began to circulate within these terrorized Jewish communities. The degree to which these stories were believed varied from person to person, as the following report indicates. It was written by Yitzhak Cukierman (also spelled Yitzhak Zuckerman and Icchak Cukierman), who was a leader in the Warsaw ghetto uprising in 1943. He survived the ghetto fighting and was living secretly in Nazi-occupied Warsaw when he compiled this report in March 1944 (after most of the ghettos had been liquidated). The report was smuggled to London by members of the anti-Nazi Polish Underground. Cukierman survived the war, and in the years that followed he helped large numbers of Jews relocate to Palestine, where the nation of Israel was established.

The liquidation of the Jews in the Government-General began at Passover 1942. The first victims were the Jews of the city of Lublin, and shortly after that the Jews of the whole District of Lublin. They were evacuated to Belzec, and there they were killed in new gas-chambers that had been built specially for this purpose. The Jewish Underground newspapers gave detailed descriptions of this mass slaughter. But [the Jews of] Warsaw did not believe it! Common human sense could not understand that it was possible to exterminate tens and hundreds of thousands of Jews. They decided that the Jews were being transported for agricultural work in the parts of Russia occupied by the Germans. Theories were heard that the Germans had begun on the productivization of the Jewish lower-level bourgeoisie! The Jewish press was denounced and charged with causing panic, although the *descriptions* of the "rooting out" of the population corresponded accurately to the reality. Not only abroad were the crimes of the Germans received with disbelief, but even here, close by Ponary, Chelmno, Belzec and Treblinka, did this information get no hearing! This unjustified optimism developed together with the lack of information, which was the result of total isolation from the outside world and the experience of the past. Had not the Germans for two and a half years carried out many deportations of Jews from Cracow, from Lublin, from the Warsaw District and from the "Reich?" Certainly there had been not a few victims and blood had been shed during these deportations, but total extermination?

There were some people who believed it, however. The events at Ponary and Chelmno were a fact, but it was said "that was just a capricious act of the local authorities." For, after all, the German authorities in the Government-General did not have the same attitude to the ghettoes in the cities and the small towns, not until death brought an equal fate to all. More than once, in various places, the reaction to the information we had about the liquidation of the Jews was: "That cannot happen to us here."

Yitzhak Cukierman's Report "Jewish Population Disbelieves Report of the Extermination." Original Polish Title: "Raport:Powstanie ZOB" PUMST archival reference number: MSW, t. 46. Reprinted with permission of the Polish Underground Movement (1939-1945) Study Trust.

It was of course the Germans themselves who created these optimistic attitudes. Through two and a half years they prepared the work of exterminating the three and a half million Jews of Poland with German thoroughness. They rendered the Jewish masses helpless with the aid of individual killings, oppression and starvation, with the aid of ghettos and deportations. In years of unceasing experiments the Germans perfected their extermination methods. In Vilna they had needed several days to murder a thousand Jews, in Chelmno half an hour was enough to kill a hundred, and at Treblinka ten thousand were murdered every day!

Source: Yitzhak Cukierman's Report "Jewish Population Disbelieves Report of the Extermination." Original Polish Title: "Raport:Powstanie ZOB" PUMST archival reference number: MSW, t. 46. English translation from Yad Vashem Archives, O-25/96. Reprinted in *Documents on the Holocaust: Selected Sources on the Destruction of the Jews of Germany and Austria, Poland, and the Soviet Union.* Edited by Yithak Arad, Yisrael Gutman, and Abraham Margaliot. Translations by Lea Ben Dor. Jerusalem: Yad Vashem, 1981.

10.8
Liquidation of the Rowno Ghetto – 1942
Excerpt from Testimony by Hermann Freidrich Graebe

Hermann Friedrich Graebe was a German who worked in the Ukraine as a civilian contractor building railroad communications structures for the occupying German army. During the course of the war, Graebe used his position to protect large numbers of helpless Jews in the Ukraine from death at the hands of the Germans and their Ukrainian henchmen. He deliberately sought out and accepted more assignments and contracts than his company could possibly handle for the sole purpose of hiring more Jews who could be protected as "essential" for the German war effort. Graebe's actions eventually aroused the suspicions of his superiors, however, and in September 1944 he defected to the American lines. Over the next several years he worked closely with the War Crimes Branch of the U.S. Army, and he became the only German to provide testimony for the prosecution at the Nuremberg Trials.

In the following excerpt from his testimony, Graebe recounts how the Jewish ghetto in Rowno (also spelled Rovno and Równe), Ukraine, was "liquidated." As Graebe testifies, he was able to save some of the Jewish residents who worked for him, and he later rescued an additional twenty-five persons by providing them with false identification papers and transporting them to a safer area. For these efforts—and his assistance in bringing Nazi war criminals to justice—he was given the honor of Righteous among the Nations by Yad Vashem, the Holocaust remembrance organization based in Israel.

237

I, Hermann Friedrich Graebe, declare under oath:

From September 1941 until January 1944 I was manager and engineer-in-charge of a branch office in Sdolbunow, Ukraine, of the Solingen building firm of Josef Jung. In this capacity it was my job to visit the building sites of the firm. The firm had, among others, a site in Rowno, Ukraine.

> *"In the street women cried out for their children and children for their parents. That did not prevent the SS from driving the people along the road ... until they reached a waiting freight train."*

During the night of 13th July 1942 all inhabitants of the Rowno Ghetto, where there were still about 5000 Jews, were liquidated.

I would describe the circumstances of my being a witness of the dissolution of the Ghetto, and the carrying out of the pogrom [Aktion] during the night and the morning, as follows:

I employed for the firm, in Rowno, in addition to Poles, Germans, and Ukrainians about 100 Jews from Sdolbunow, Ostrog, and Mysotch. The men were quartered in a building,—5 Bahnhofstrasse, inside the Ghetto, and the women in a house at the corner of Deutsche Strasse,—98.

On Saturday, 11 July 1942, my foreman, Fritz Einsporn, told me of a rumor that on Monday all Jews in Rowno were to be liquidated. Although the vast majority of the Jews employed by my firm in Rowno were not natives of this town, I still feared that they might be included in this pogrom which had been reported. I therefore ordered Einsporn at noon of the same day to march all the Jews employed by us—men as well as women—in the direction of Sdolbunow, about 12 km from Rowno. This was done.

The Senior Jew [Judenrat] had learned of the departure of the Jewish workers of my firm. He went to see the Commanding Officer of the Rowno SIPO and SD, SS Major [SS Sturmbannfuehrer] Dr. Puetz, as early as the Saturday afternoon to find out whether the rumor of a forthcoming Jewish pogrom—which had gained further credence by reason of the departure of Jews of my firm—was true. Dr. Puetz dismissed the rumor as a clumsy lie, and for the rest had the Polish personnel of my firm in Rowno arrested. Einsporn avoided arrest by escaping from Sdolbunow. When I learned of this incident I gave orders that all Jews who had left Rowno were to report back to work in Rowno on Monday, 13 July 1942. On Monday morning I myself went to see the Commanding Officer, Dr. Puetz, in order to learn, for one thing, the truth about the rumored Jewish pogrom and secondly to obtain information on the arrest of the Polish office personnel. SS Major [SS—Sturmbannfuehrer] Puetz stated to me that no pogrom [Aktion] whatever was planned. Moreover such a pogrom would be stupid because the firms and the Reichsbaden would lose valuable workers.

An hour later I received a summons to appear before the Area Commissioner of Rowno. His deputy, Stableiter and Cadet Officer [Ordensjunker] Beck, subjected me to the same questioning as I had undergone at the SD. My explanation that I had sent the Jews home for urgent delousing appeared plausible to him. He then told me—making me promise to keep it a secret—that a pogrom would in fact take place on the evening of Monday 13 July 1942. After lengthy negotiation I managed to persuade him to give me permission to take my Jewish workers to Sdolbunow—but only after the pogrom had been carried out. During the night it would be up to me to protect the house in the Ghetto against the entry of Ukrainian militia and SS. As confirmation of the discussion he gave me a document, which stated that the Jewish employees of Messrs. Jung were not affected by the pogrom [Original attached.]

On the evening of this day I drove to Rowno and posted myself with Fritz Einsporn in front of the house in the Bahnhofstrasse in which the Jewish workers of my firm slept. Shortly after 22:00 the Ghetto was encircled by a large SS detachment and about three times as many members of the Ukrainian militia. Then the electric arclights which had been erected in and around the Ghetto were switched on. SS and militia squads of 4 to 6 men entered or at least tried to enter the houses. Where the doors and windows were closed and the inhabitant did not open at the knocking, the SS men and militia broke the windows, forced the doors with beams and crowbars and entered the houses. The people living there were driven on to the street just as they were, regardless of whether they were dressed or in bed. Since the Jews in most cases refused to leave their houses and resisted, the SS and militia applied force. They finally succeeded, with strokes of the whip, kicks and blows with rifle butts in clearing the houses. The people were driven out of their houses in such haste that small children in bed had been left behind in several instances. In the street women cried out for their children and children for their parents. That did not prevent the SS from driving the people along the road, at running pace, and hitting them, until they reached a waiting freight train. Car after car was filled, and the screaming of women and children, and the cracking of whips and rifle shots resounded unceasingly. Since several families or groups had barricaded themselves in especially strong buildings, and the doors could not be forced with crowbars or beams, these houses were now blown open with hand grenades. Since the Ghetto was near the railroad tracks in Rowno, the younger people tried to get across the tracks and over a small river to get away from the Ghetto area. As this stretch of country was beyond the range of the electric lights, it was illuminated by signal rockets. All through the night these beaten, hounded and wounded people moved along the lighted streets. Women carried their dead children in their arms and legs down the road toward the train. Again and again the cries "Open the door!" "Open the door!" echoed through the Ghetto.

About 6 o'clock in the morning I went away for a moment, leaving behind Einsporn and several other German workers who had returned in the meantime. I thought the greatest danger was past and that I could risk it. Shortly after I left, Ukrainian militia men forced their way into 5 Bahnhofstrasse, and brought 7 Jews out and took them to a collecting point inside the Ghetto. On my return I was able to prevent further Jews from being taken out. I went to the collecting point to save these 7 men. I saw dozens of corpses of all ages and both sexes in the streets I had to walk along. The doors of the houses stood open, windows were smashed. Pieces of clothing, shoes, stockings, jackets, caps, hats, coats, etc., were lying in the street. At the corner of a house lay a baby, less than a year old with his skull crushed. Blood and brains were spattered over the house wall and covered the area immediately around the child. The child was dressed only in a little shirt. The commander, SS Major Puetz, was walking up and down a row of about 80-100 male Jews who were crouching on the ground. He had a heavy dog whip in his hand. I walked up to him, showed him the written permit of Stabsleiter Beck and demanded the seven men whom I recognized among those who were crouching on the ground. Dr. Puetz was very furious about Beck's concession and nothing could persuade him to release the seven men. He made a motion with his hand encircling the square and said that anyone who was once here would not get away. Although he was very angry with Beck, he ordered me to take the people from 5 Bahnjofstrasse out of Rowno by 8 o'clock at the latest. When I left Dr. Puetz, I noticed a Ukrainian farm cart, with two horses. Dead people with stiff limbs were lying on the cart. Legs and arms projected over the side boards. The cart was making for the freight train. I took the remaining 74 Jews who had been locked in the house to Sdolbunow.

Several days after the 13th of July 1942 the Area Commissioner of Sdolbunow, Georg Marschall, called a meeting of all firm managers, railroad superintendents, and leaders of the Organization Todt and informed them that the firms, etc., should prepare themselves for the "resettlement" of the Jews which was to take place almost immediately. He referred to the pogrom in Rowno where all the Jews had been liquidated, i.e., had been shot near Kostolpol.

I made the above statement in Wiesbaden, Germany, on 10 November 1945. I swear by God that this is the absolute truth.

Hermann Friedrich Graebe

Source: Graebe, Hermann F. Nuremberg Testimony, November 10, 1945. Reprinted as Document 2992-PS in *Nazi Conspiracy and Aggression*. Vol. 5. Washington, DC: United States Government Printing Office, 1946.

11

MURDER IN THE DEATH CAMPS

This photograph of the bodies of former prisoners outside the crematorium at the Dachau concentration camp in Germany was taken by an American soldier after the camp's 1945 liberation.

INTRODUCTION

The Nazis had made use of concentration camps since taking power in 1933, but a new type of prison was established when they began carrying out the Holocaust. The primary function of these death camps was to kill perceived enemies of the Third Reich. German leaders devised the conceptual framework for these camps after determining that the methods of open slaughter employed by the *Einsatzgruppen* had too many flaws. They were concerned by several factors: the *Einsatzgruppen* murders attracted unwanted attention, they inflicted a heavy psychological toll on the people who did the actual shooting, and they usually resulted in mass graves, which left evidence of the atrocities. The technologically advanced extermination camps, on the other hand, employed poison gas as a means of killing and used crematoriums to dispose of the bodies of the victims. The death camps thus enabled the Nazis to cloak the Holocaust under a veil of secrecy and to make the whole genocidal process more impersonal.

The majority of the camps were located in thinly populated regions of Poland. The Nazis believed that the prisons would attract less attention in rural areas of Poland than they would in more heavily populated areas such as Germany itself (although a few death camps, such as Majdanek, were situated in more highly populated areas). The Nazis also concentrated the death camps in Poland for "production" reasons; Poland and surrounding regions contained the highest population densities of Jews identified by the Third Reich for extermination.

The initial victims of the death camps were Poles, most of whom were pulled from the ghettos. Beginning in the summer of 1942, trains from the other parts of Europe under Nazi control—Germany, Holland, France, Belgium, Italy, Czechoslovakia, Hungary, and more—began delivering victims to the death camps. These shipments continued until the fall of 1944.

The first extermination camp, Chelmno, began operation in early December 1941 and eventually accounted for as many as 360,000 deaths (estimates of the final death toll vary for this camp, as for most of the others). At Chelmno the Nazis utilized gas vans—buses that had been reconfigured so that their exhaust fumes could be directed into the rear area of the vehicle to asphyxiate the victims. The Nazis found this method inefficient, and the camps that began operating in the spring and summer of 1942—which included Belzec, Sobibór, Treblinka, and Majdanek—employed specially constructed gas chambers. All together, the administrators and guards at Belzec, Sobibór, and Treblinka murdered around 1.6 million Jews. These camps generally operated for a year or less.

Auschwitz-Birkenau

The deadliest and most notorious of the extermination camps was Auschwitz-Birkenau in western Poland. Sometimes referred to simply as Auschwitz, it was actually a complex of camps located close together, with Auschwitz and Birkenau being the two largest. After some initial experiments, gassings began in these camps in April 1942 and continued until November 1944. According to various estimates, between 900,000 and 1.3 million Jews were murdered there, as were tens of thousands of other victims: Roma (also known as Gypsies), Poles, Russian prisoners of war, and others. It was not unusual for 8,000 people a day to be killed at Auschwitz-Birkenau, sometimes more. It was there that the Nazis developed the use of prussic acid, a pesticide manufactured under the name of Zyklon B, as the fatal gas for its Final Solution operations.

At its peak of operation, Auschwitz-Birkenau had five gas chamber/crematory complexes in operation. Even then, the camp commanders sometimes had difficulty keeping up with their ghastly work. When huge numbers of Hungarian Jews were brought to the camp in the summer of 1944, the gas chambers were killing people faster than the crematories could dispose of them. This led camp commanders to order the burning of large numbers of bodies in huge outdoor pits. The stench from these pits further added to the sickening smell that hung over the camp. The odor of incinerated flesh and the sight of the crematory chimneys spewing smoke and flame night and day served as nightmarish reminders to camp prisoners of their likely eventual fate.

Some prisoners did manage to avoid the gas chamber. As with the ghettos, the camps were utilized as a source of slave labor. Immediately upon arrival, the new prisoners underwent their first "selection": those deemed weak, along with nearly all young children and their mothers, were sent immediately to the gas chambers; men and women who looked like they might be productive were sent to camp barracks and were assigned to work crews. These crews sometimes toiled at the main camp and sometimes were sent to other locations.

Prisoners in the death camps also learned that that the Nazis did not require poison gas to kill. Fed a starvation diet of bread and soup, the inmates were forced to perform hard labor and were housed in overcrowded barracks with little heat and poor sanitation. Only the hardiest and luckiest could survive these conditions. The rest were claimed by disease (typhus and typhoid were two of the biggest killers), starvation, or capricious violence doled out by sadistic camp guards. Conditions and treatment were so severe that even those prisons such as Mauthausen in Austria that lacked a large-scale gas chamber still functioned as death camps. The prisoners were simply brutalized until they died.

As horrific as these conditions were, the Nazis found a way to make the camps even more sinister. Many prisoners were selected for inhumane medical experiments. Some of these unfortunate prisoners were exposed to dangerous viruses and diseases. Others were sterilized through heavy exposure to x-rays and chemicals. And still others were subjected to various tortures by Nazi doctors conducting experiments on the limits of human endurance. The most infamous doctor to engage in these terrifying experiments at Auschwitz-Birkenau was Josef Mengele, who came to be known as the "Angel of Death." Mengele devoted much of his time to murderous studies on twins, with whom he had a peculiar fascination. But he conducted sadistic experiments on many other prisoners as well. In addition, Mengele frequently greeted transport trains when they arrived at the camp. As the prisoners disembarked, Mengele calmly selected some prisoners for immediate gassing and others for hard labor or medical experiments.

11.1
Nazi Use of Murderous "Gas Vans" – 1942
Excerpt from a Report on the Effectiveness of Gas Van Operations

The first Nazi attempts at mass execution by means other than gunfire utilized so-called gas vans, which were bus-type vehicles that had been reengineered so that the exhaust fumes could be directed to a passenger compartment in order to kill the occupants by asphyxiation. The first death camp to go into operation, Chelmno, utilized these vans beginning in December 1941, though the vehicles were also employed on a limited basis by the Einsatzgruppen in eastern Europe. The following document was written in May 1942 by an S.S. commander who used the gas vans in the Ukraine. His memo does not spend any time pondering the morality of using the vans as a tool of execution; instead, it focuses entirely on ways in which the vans do not meet performance expectations.

TOP SECRET

… The overhauling of vans by groups D and C is finished. While the vans of the first series can also be put into action if the weather is not too bad, the vans of the second series *(Saurer) stop completely in rainy weather.* If it has rained for instance for only one half hour, the van cannot be used because it simply skids away. It can only be used in absolutely dry weather. It is only a question now whether the van can only be used standing at the place of execution. First the van has to be brought to that place, which is possible only in good weather. The place of execution is usually 10-15 km away from the highways and is difficult to access because of its location; in damp or wet weather it is not accessible at all. If the persons to be executed are driven or led to that place, then they realize immediately what is going on and get restless, which is to be avoided as far as possible. There is only one way left; to load them at the collecting point and to drive them to the spot.

I ordered the vans of group D to be camouflaged as house-trailers by putting one set of window shutters on each side of the small van and two on each side of the larger vans, such as one often sees on farm-houses in the country. The vans became so well-known, that not only the authorities, but also the civilian population called the van "death van", as soon as one of these vehicles appeared. It is my opinion, the van cannot be kept secret for any length of time, not even camouflaged.

The Saurer-van which I transported from Simferopol to Taganrog suffered damage to the brakes on the way. The Security Command [SK] in Mariupol found the cuff of the combined oil-air brake broken at several points. By persuading and bribing the H.K.P…we managed to have a form machined, on which the cuffs were cast. When I came to Stalino and Gorlowka a few days later, the drivers of the vans complained about the same faults. After having talked to the commandants of those commands I went once more to Mariupol to have some more cuffs made for those cars too. As agreed two cuffs will be made for each car, six cuffs will stay in Mariupol as replacements for group D and six cuffs will be sent to SS-Untersturmfuehrer Ernst in Kiev for the cars of group C. The cuffs for the groups B and A could be made available from Berlin, because transport from Mariupol to the north would be too complicated and would take too long. Smaller damages on the cars will be repaired by experts of the commands, that is of the groups in their own shops.

Because of the rough terrain and the indescribable road and highway conditions the caulkings and rivets loosen in the course of time. I was asked if in such cases the vans should be brought to Berlin for repair. Transportation to Berlin would be much too expensive and would demand too much fuel. In order to save those expenses I ordered them to have smaller leaks soldered and if that should no longer be possible, to notify Berlin immediately by radio… Besides that I ordered that during application of gas all the men were to be kept as far away from the vans as possible, so they should not suffer damage to their health by the gas which eventually would escape. I should like to take this opportunity to bring the following to your attention: several commands have had the unloading after the application of gas done by their own men. I brought to the attention of the commanders of those S.K. concerned the immense psychological injuries and damages to their health which that work can have for those men, even if not immediately, at least later on. The men complained to me about head-aches which appeared after each unloading. Nevertheless they don't want to change the orders, because they are afraid prisoners called for that work, could use an opportune moment to flee. To protect the men from these damages, I request orders be issued accordingly.

The application of gas usually is not undertaken correctly. In order to come to an end as fast as possible, the driver presses the accelerator to the fullest extent. By doing that the persons to be executed suffer death from suffocation and not death by dozing off as was planned. My directions now have proved that by correct adjustment of the levers death comes faster and the prisoners fall asleep peacefully. Distorted faces and excretions, such as could be seen before, are no longer noticed.

Today I shall continue my journey to group B, where I can be reached with further news.

Signed: Dr. Becker
SS Untersturmfuehrer

Source: Report on Gas Van Operations, May 1942. Reprinted as Document 501-PS in *Nazi Conspiracy and Aggression*. Vol. 3. Washington, DC: United States Government Printing Office, 1946.

11.2
Deathwatch at Belżec – 1942
Kurt Gerstein Recalls Genocidal Procedures at the Nazi Death Camps

The following graphic description of the mass murder procedures used in the Nazi death camps is one of the few first-hand accounts to survive the war. Considerable controversy has swirled around this chronicle, however. Gerstein was once a member of the Nazi Party, but he was also an outspoken critic of Adolf Hitler's government because its actions clashed with his strong Christian beliefs. His protests caused him to be imprisoned in a concentration camp in the late 1930s, though he was subsequently released. Several years later Gerstein was able to join the Waffen S.S. He later claimed that he did so because he was angered over reports of the Nazi euthanasia program and wanted to investigate the issue himself. Because his job in the S.S. involved using pesticides to disinfect clothing and buildings, he became ensnared in efforts to develop prussic acid as the primary means of gassing prisoners. It was in this capacity that Gerstein visited several of the Nazi death camps scattered across occupied Poland in August 1942.

At the end of the war Gerstein reported his death camp experiences to French authorities, who confined him in a Paris jail under suspicion of committing war crimes. He was found dead in his cell in July 1945. French officials reported that he hanged himself, but suspicions that he was murdered have persisted.

Gerstein gave several different versions of his experiences at the death camps in official depositions, and these accounts were recorded in both French and German. Discrepancies between the different reports have become a source of controversy, and Gerstein's psychological state at the time of his depositions has also been questioned. In addition, his estimations of the dimensions of the Belżec gas chambers seem small for the number of victims they held. That said, the details of how the killings were carried out match those of other witnesses, and most historians accept Gerstein's account as a generally accurate record of how the Nazi gas chambers operated.

In January 1942, I was appointed head of the Department of Sanitation Techniques and at the same time to the parallel position for the same sector of the SS and Police Medical Office. In this capacity I took over the entire technical service of disinfection, including disinfection with highly toxic gases. On June 8, 1942, SS Sturmbannführer Günther of the *Reichssicherheitshauptamt* [RSHA—Reich Security Main Office], dressed in civilian clothes, walked into my office. He was unknown to me. He ordered me to obtain for him, for a top secret mission, 100 kilos of prussic acid and to take it to a place known only to the truck driver. A few weeks later, we set out for the potash plant near Kolin (Prague).

I understood little the nature of my mission. But I accepted. To this day, I believe that it was luck, strangely resembling Providence, that gave me the opportunity to see what I was trying to find out. Out of hundreds of other possible assignments, I was put in charge of that post which was closest to the area that interested me...

On the way to Kolin, we were accompanied by SS Obersturmbannführer and M.D., Professor Pfannenstiel, Professor of Hygiene at the University of Marburg/Lahn.

From my deliberately bizarre technical questions, the people at the Kolin prussic acid plant could understand that the acid was going to be used to kill human beings. I did this in order to spread rumors among the population.

We then set off with the truck for Lublin (Poland). SS Gruppenführer [Odilo] Globocnik was waiting for us. He told us: "This is one of our most secret matters, indeed the most secret. Anyone who talks about it will be shot. Only yesterday two babblers were shot." He then explained to us: "At present"—this was August 17, 1942—"there are three installations":

(1) Bełżec, on the Lublin-Lwów road. Maximum per day: 15,000 persons (seen)!

(2) Sobibór, I don't know exactly where: not seen: 20,000 persons per day.

(3) Treblinka, 120 km. northeast of Warsaw: 25,000 persons per day; seen.

(4) Majdanek, near Lublin; seen in preparation.

Except for the last one, I made a thorough inspection of all these camps, accompanied by Police Chief [Christian] Wirth [an S.S. officer], the head of all these death factories. Wirth had earlier been put in charge by Hitler and Himmler of the murder of the insane at Hadamar, Grafeneck, and various other places.

Globocnik said: "You will have to disinfect large quantities of clothing ten or twenty times, the whole textile accumulation. It is only being done to conceal that the source of clothing is Jews, Poles, Czechs, etc. Your other duty will be to improve the service in our gas chambers, which function on diesel engine exhaust. We need gas which is more toxic and works faster, such as prussic acid. The Führer and Himmler—they were just here on August 15, the day before yesterday—instructed me to accompany personally all those who have to see these installations." ...

We left for Bełżec two days later. A small special station with two platforms was set up on a yellow sand hill, immediately to the north of the Lublin-Lwów railway. To the south, near the road, were some service buildings and a notice: "Sonderkommando of the Waffen-SS in Bełżec." Globocnik presented me to the SS

Hauptstrumführer Obermeyer of Pirmasens, who showed great reserve when taking me over the installations. We saw no dead that day, but a pestilential odor blanketed the whole region and millions of flies were everywhere. Alongside the station was a large barrack marked "Cloak Room," with a ticket window inside marked "Valuables." Further on, a room with about a hundred chairs, "Barber." Then a passageway about 150 meters long, in the open, barbed wire on both sides, and notices: "To the Baths and Inhalators." In front of us was a building of the bathhouse type, with large pots of geraniums and other flowers. Then stairs and then left and right 3 enclosures 5 meters square, 1.90 meters high, with wooden doors like garages. At the rear wall, not properly visible in the darkness, large wooden platform doors. On the roof, a copper Star of David. On the building, the inscription: "Heckenholt Foundation." That afternoon I saw nothing else.

> *"At the corner stood a heavy SS man, who told the poor people in a pastoral voice: 'No harm will come to you! You just have to breathe very deeply, that strengthens the lungs, inhaling is a means of preventing contagious diseases. It's a good disinfection!'"*

Next morning, a few minutes before seven, I was told: "In ten minutes the first train will arrive." Indeed, a few minutes later a train arrived from Lemberg, with 45 cars holding 6,700 people, of whom 1,450 were already dead on arrival. Behind the small barbed-wire window, children, young ones, frightened to death, women, men. The train pulled in: 200 Ukrainians detailed for the task tore open the doors and with their leather whips drove the Jews out of the cars. A loudspeaker issued instructions: to remove all clothing, even artificial limbs and eyeglasses; to tie their shoes together with small pieces of string handed out by a little Jewish boy; to turn in all valuables, all money at the ticket window "Valuables," without voucher, without receipt. Women and girls were to have their hair cut off in the "Barber's" barrack. (An SS sergeant on duty told me: "That's to make something special for submarine crews.")

Then the march began. To the left and right, barbed wire; behind, two dozen Ukrainians, guns in hand.

They approached. Wirth and I, we were standing on the ramp in front of the death chambers. Completely nude, men and women, young girls, children, babies, cripples, filed by. At the corner stood a heavy SS man, who told the poor people in a pastoral voice: "No harm will come to you! You just have to breathe very deeply, that strengthens the lungs, inhaling is a means of preventing contagious diseases. It's a good disinfection!" They asked what was going to happen to them. He told them: "The men will have to work, building roads and houses. But the women won't be

251

obliged to do so; they'll do housework, cooking." For some of these poor creatures, this was a last small hope, enough to carry them, unresisting, as far as the death chambers, most without a word, pushed forward by those behind them. One Jewish woman of about forty, her eyes flaming torches, cursed the murderers: after several whiplashes by Captain Wirth in person, she disappeared into the gas chamber. Many people pray, while others ask: "Who will give us water for washing the dead?" [a reference to *taharah,* the traditional Jewish rite of washing the dead body before burial].

Inside the chambers, SS men crowded the people. "Fill them up well," Wirth had ordered, "700-800 of them to every 25 square meters." The doors are shut. Meanwhile, the rest of the people from the train, naked, wait. I am told "naked even in winter!" "But they may catch their death!" "But that's what they're here for!" was the reply. At that moment I understood the reason for the inscription "Heckenholt." Heckenholt was the driver of the diesel truck whose exhaust gases were to be used to kill these unfortunates. SS Unterscharführer Heckenholt was making great efforts to get the engine running. But it doesn't go. Captain Wirth comes up. I can see he is afraid because I am present at a disaster. Yes, I see it all and I wait. My stop watch showed it all, 50 minutes, 70 minutes, and the diesel did not start! The people wait inside the gas chambers. In vain. They can be heard weeping, "like in the synagogue," says Professor Pfannenstiel, his eyes glued to a window in the wooden door. Furious, Captain Wirth lashes the Ukrainian assisting Heckenholt, 12, 13 times in the face. After two hours and 49 minutes—the stop watch recorded it all—the diesel started. Up to that moment, the people shut up in those four crowded chambers were still alive, four times 750 persons in four times 45 cubic meters! Another 25 minutes elapsed. Many were already dead, that could be seen through the small window because an electric lamp inside lit up the chamber for a few minutes. After 28 minutes, only a few were still alive. Finally, after 32 minutes, all were dead.

On the far side members of the work commando opened the wooden doors. They—themselves Jews—were promised their lives and a small percentage of the valuables and money collected for this terrible service. Like pillars of basalt, the dead were still erect, not having any space to fall, or to lean. Even in death, families could be seen still holding hands. It is hard to separate them as the chambers are emptied for the next load; corpses are tossed out… Two dozen workers were busy checking the mouths of the dead, which they opened with iron hooks. "Gold to the left, without gold to the right!" … Dentists hammered out gold teeth, bridges and crowns. In the midst of them stood Captain Wirth. He was in his element, and showing me a large can of teeth, he said: "See for yourself the weight of that gold! It's only from yesterday and the day before. You can't imagine what we find here every day—dollars, diamonds, gold! You'll see yourself!" …

Then the bodies were flung into large trenches, 100 x 20 x 12 meters, located near the gas chambers… Subsequently, I was told, the bodies were piled on train rails and burned in diesel oil so that they would disappear.

The next day we drove in Captain Wirth's car to Treblinka about 120 km. northeast of Warsaw. The equipment in that place of death was almost the same as at Bełżec, but even larger. Eight gas chambers and veritable mountains of clothing and underwear, about 35-40 meters high. Then, in our honor, a banquet was held for all those employed at the establishment. Obersturmbannführer Professor Doctor Pfannenstiel, Professor of Hygiene at the University of Marburg/Lahn, made a speech: "Your work is a great work and a very useful and very necessary duty." To me, he spoke of the establishment as "a kindness and a humanitarian thing." To all present, he said: "When one sees the bodies of the Jews, one understands the greatness of your work."

Source: Gerstein, Kurt. Account of Nazi Death Camps. Published in *A Holocaust Reader*, edited by Lucy S. Dawidowicz. New York: Behrman House, 1976.

11.3
The Commander at Auschwitz Recalls His Genocidal Work – 1940-1943
Excerpt from Rudolf Höss's Testimony before the International Military Tribunal

As the commandant of Auschwitz-Birkenau in the early 1940s, Rudolf Höss oversaw the creation and operation of the largest and most lethal of the Nazi death camps. After the war, Höss testified at the war crimes hearings at Nuremberg (his name is spelled Hoess throughout the Nuremberg transcript). During his testimony, he detailed the procedures and methods used to "process" Jews and other groups targeted by the Nazis at Auschwitz. He also noted various "improvements" that he instituted to make the process of mass killing more "efficient." Höss made no effort to deny the mass executions that took place at Auschwitz and other Nazi camps; in fact, his estimates of the number of people killed at Auschwitz-Birkenau are higher than the totals put forth by most historians. The only defense he offered for his behavior was that he was following the orders of others, including his superior S.S. officer, Heinrich Himmler. Höss was a witness at Nuremberg rather than a defendant, but he was later put on trial in Poland. He was found guilty of various war crimes and executed on April 7, 1947.

Höss's interrogators during the portions of Nuremberg testimony excerpted here were Dr. Kurt Kauffmann, defense counsel for Ernst Kaltenbrunner, one of the Nazi defendants; and U.S. Colonel John Harlen Amen, who was part of the prosecution team.

DR. KAUFFMANN: When were you commander at Auschwitz?

253

HOESS: I was commander at Auschwitz from May 1940 until December 1943.

DR. KAUFFMANN: What was the highest number of human beings, prisoners, ever held at one time at Auschwitz?

HOESS: The highest number of internees held at one time at Auschwitz, was about 140,000 men and women.

DR. KAUFFMANN: Is it true that in 1941 you were ordered to Berlin to see [SS commander Heinrich] Himmler? Please state briefly what was discussed.

HOESS: Yes. In the summer of 1941 I was summoned to Berlin to Reichsführer SS Himmler to receive personal orders. He told me something to the effect—I do not remember the exact words—that the Führer had given the order for a final solution of the Jewish question. We, the SS, must carry out that order. If it is not carried out now then the Jews will later on destroy the German people. He had chosen Auschwitz on account of its easy access by rail and also because the extensive site offered space for measures insuring isolation…

DR. KAUFFMANN: When did you meet [Adolf] Eichmann?

HOESS: I met Eichmann about 4 weeks after having received that order from the Reichsführer. He came to Auschwitz to discuss the details with me on the carrying out of the given order. As the Reichsführer had told me during our discussion, he had instructed Eichmann to discuss the carrying out of the order with me and I was to receive all further instructions from him.

DR. KAUFFMANN: Will you briefly tell whether it is correct that the camp of Auschwitz was completely isolated, describing the measures taken to insure as far as possible the secrecy of carrying out of the task given to you?

HOESS: The Auschwitz camp as such was about 3 kilometers away from the town. About 20,000 acres of the surrounding country had been cleared of all former inhabitants, and the entire area could be entered only by SS men or civilian employees who had special passes. The actual compound called "Birkenau," where later on the extermination camp was constructed, was situated 2 kilometers from the Auschwitz camp. The camp installations themselves, that is to say, the provisional installations used at first were deep in the woods and could from nowhere be detected by the eye. In addition to that, this area had been declared a prohibited area and even members of the SS who did not have a special pass could not enter it. Thus, as far as one could judge, it was impossible for anyone except authorized persons to enter that area.

DR. KAUFFMANN: And then the railway transports arrived. During what period did these transports arrive and about how many people, roughly, were in such a transport?

HOESS: During the whole period up until 1944 certain operations were carried out at irregular intervals in the different countries, so that one cannot speak of a continuous flow of incoming transports. It was always a matter of 4 to 6 weeks. During those 4 to 6 weeks two to three trains, containing about 2,000 persons each, arrived daily. These trains were first of all shunted to a siding in the Birkenau region and the locomotives then went back. The guards who had accompanied the transport had to leave the area at once and the persons who had been brought in were taken over by guards belonging to the camp.

They were there examined by two SS medical officers as to their fitness for work. The internees capable of work at once marched to Auschwitz or to the camp at Birkenau and those incapable of work were at first taken to provisional installations, then later to the newly created crematoria...

DR. KAUFFMANN: And after the arrival of the transports were the victims stripped of everything they had? Did they have to undress completely; did they have to surrender their valuables? Is that true?

HOESS: Yes.

DR. KAUFFMANN: And then they immediately went to their death?

HOESS: Yes.

DR. KAUFFMANN: I ask you, according to your knowledge, did these people know what was in store for them?

HOESS: The majority of them did not, for steps were taken to keep them in doubt about it and suspicion would not arise that they were to go to their death. For instance, all doors and all walls bore inscriptions to the effect that they were going to undergo a delousing operation or take a shower. This was made known in several languages to the internees by other internees who had come in with earlier transports and who were being used as auxiliary crews during the whole operation.

DR. KAUFFMANN: And then, you told me the other day, that death by gassing set in with a period of 3 to 15 minutes. Is that correct?

HOESS: Yes.

DR. KAUFFMANN: You also told me that even before death finally set in, the victims fell into a state of unconsciousness?

HOESS: Yes. From what I was able to find out myself or what was told me by medical officers, the time necessary for reaching unconsciousness or death varied according to the temperature and the number of people present in the chambers. Loss of consciousness took place within a few seconds or a few minutes.

DR. KAUFFMANN: Did you yourself ever feel pity with the victims, thinking of your own family and children?

HOESS: Yes.

DR. KAUFFMANN: How was it possible for you to carry out these actions in spite of this?

HOESS: In view of all these doubts which I had, the only one and decisive argument was the strict order and the reason given for it by the Reichsführer Himmler.

DR. KAUFFMANN: I ask you whether Himmler inspected the camp and convinced himself, too, of the process of annihilation?

HOESS: Yes. Himmler visited the camp in 1942 and he watched in detail one processing from beginning to end.

DR. KAUFFMANN: Does the same apply to Eichmann?

HOESS: Eichmann came repeatedly to Auschwitz and was intimately acquainted with the proceedings...

[A recess was taken.]...

COL. AMEN: Witness, you made an affidavit, did you not, at the request of the Prosecution?

HOESS: Yes.

COL. AMEN: I ask the witness be shown document 3868-PS, which will become Exhibit USA-819.

[The document was submitted to the witness.]

COL. AMEN: You signed that affidavit voluntarily, Witness?

HOESS: Yes.

COL. AMEN: And the affidavit is true in all respects?

HOESS: Yes.

COL. AMEN: This, if the Tribunal please, we have in four languages.

[Turning to the witness.] Some of the matters covered in this affidavit you have already told us about in part, so I will omit some parts of the affidavit. If you will follow along with me as I read, please. Do you have a copy of the affidavit before you?

HOESS: Yes.

COL. AMEN: I will omit the first paragraph and start with Paragraph 2:

> "I have been constantly associated with the administration of concentration camps since 1934, serving at Dachau until 1938; then as Adjutant in Sachsenhausen from 1938 to 1 May 1940, when I was appointed Commandant of Auschwitz. I commanded at Auschwitz until 1 December 1943, and estimate that at least 2,500,000 victims were executed and exterminated there by gassing and burning, and at least another half million succumbed to starvation and disease making a total dead of about 3,000,000. This figure represents about 70 or 80 percent of all persons sent to Auschwitz as prisoners, the remainder having been selected and used for slave labor in

the concentration camp industries; included among the executed and burned were approximately 20,000 Russian prisoners of war (previously screened out of prisoner-of-war cages by the Gestapo) who were delivered at Wehrmacht transports operated by regular Wehrmacht officers and men. The remainder of the total number of victims included about 100,000 German Jews, and great numbers of citizens, mostly Jewish, from Holland, France, Belgium, Poland, Hungary, Czechoslovakia, Greece, or other countries. We executed about 400,000 Hungarian Jews alone at Auschwitz in the summer of 1944."

That is all true, Witness?

HOESS: Yes, it is.

COL. AMEN: ...

"6. The 'final solution' of the Jewish question meant the complete extermination of all Jews in Europe. I was ordered to establish extermination facilities at Auschwitz in June 1941. At that time there were already in the General Government three other extermination camps: Belzek, Treblinka, and Wolzek. These camps were under the Einsatzkommando of the Security Police and SD. I visited Treblinka to find out how they carried out their exterminations. The camp commandant at Treblinka told me that he had liquidated 80,000 in the course of one-half year. He was principally concerned with liquidating all the Jews from the Warsaw Ghetto. He used monoxide gas, and I did not think that his methods were very efficient. So when I set up the extermination building at Auschwitz, I used Cyklon B [more often known as Zyklon B], which was a crystallized prussic acid which we dropped into the death chamber from a small opening. It took from 3 to 15 minutes to kill the people in the death chamber, depending upon climatic conditions. We knew when the people were dead because their screaming stopped. We usually waited about one-half hour before we opened the doors and removed bodies. After the bodies were removed our special Kommandos took off the rings and extracted gold from the teeth of the corpses."

Is that all true and correct, Witness?

HOESS: Yes.

COL. AMEN: Incidentally, what was done with the gold which was taken from the teeth of the corpses, do you know?

HOESS: Yes.

COL. AMEN: Will you tell the Tribunal?

HOESS: The gold was melted down and brought to the Chief Medical Office of the SS in Berlin.

COL. AMEN:

"7. Another improvement we made over Treblinka was that we built gas chambers to accommodate 2,000 people at one time whereas at Treblinka their 10 gas chambers only accommodated 200 people each. The way we selected our victims was as follows: We had two SS doctors on duty at Auschwitz to examine the incoming transports of prisoners. The prisoners would be marched by one of the doctors who would make spot decisions as they walked by. Those who were fit for work were sent to the camp. Others were sent immediately to the extermination plants. Children of tender years were invariably exterminated since by reason of their youth they were unable to work. Still another improvement we made over Treblinka was that at Treblinka the victims almost always knew that they were to be exterminated and at Auschwitz we endeavored to fool the victims into thinking that they were going through a delousing process. Of course, frequently they realized our true intentions and we sometimes had riots and difficulties due to that fact. Very frequently women would hide their children under the clothes, but of course when we found them we would send the children in to be exterminated. We were required to carry out these exterminations in secrecy but of course the foul and nauseating stench from the continuous burning of bodies permeated the entire area and all of the people living in the surrounding communities knew that exterminations were going on at Auschwitz."

Is that all true and correct, Witness?

HOESS: Yes.

Source: "One Hundred and Eighth Day, Monday, 15 April 1946." *Trial of the Major War Criminals before the International Military Tribunal, Nuremberg, 14 November 1945-1 October 1946.* Vol. 11, *Proceedings 8 April 1946-17 April 1946.* Nuremberg, Germany: International Military Tribunal, 1947.

11.4

A Holocaust Survivor Recalls His Journey to the Death Camps – 1944
Excerpt from Night *by Elie Wiesel*

The trains that the Third Reich used to take the deportees away from their homes and deliver them to the death camps were instruments of torture in themselves. In most cases, dozens of people were forced into individual rail cars that were intended for freight or livestock. They would remain inside for days on end as the trains labored across the countryside. Deportees were usually provided with very little food or water, and they had to improvise their toilet facilities as well as they could. Hunger, thirst, and exposure to the heat or cold often claimed lives even before the train reached its grim destination. The sheer terror of the experience took a terrible mental toll on many passengers as well. In the following excerpt from his famous autobiographical work Night, *Holocaust survivor Elie Wiesel recounts his family's deportation from their hometown in Hungary. In Wiesel's case, the year was 1944, and the train on which he rode was bound for a nightmarish destination.*

Saturday, the day of rest, was chosen for our expulsion.

The night before, we had the traditional Friday evening meal. We said the customary grace for the bread and wine and swallowed our food without a word. We were, we felt, gathered for the last time round the family table. I spent the night turning over thoughts and memories in my mind, unable to find sleep.

At dawn, we were in the street, ready to leave. This time there were no Hungarian police. An agreement had been made with the Jewish Council that they should organize it all themselves.

Our convoy went toward the main synagogue. The town seemed deserted. Yet our friends of yesterday were probably waiting behind their shutters for the moment when they could pillage our homes.

The synagogue was like a huge station: luggage and tears. The altar was broken, the hangings torn down, the walls bare. There were so many of us that we could scarcely breathe. We spent a horrible twenty-four hours there. There were men downstairs; women on the first floor. It was Saturday; it was as though we had come to attend the service. Since no one could go out, people were relieving themselves in a corner.

The following morning, we marched to the station, where a convoy of cattle wagons was waiting. The Hungarian police made us get in—eighty people in each car. We were left a few loaves of bread and some buckets of water. The bars at the window were checked, to see that they were not loose. Then the cars were sealed. In each car one person was placed in charge. If anyone escaped, he would be shot.

Two Gestapo officers strolled about on the platform, smiling: all things considered, everything had gone off very well.

A prolonged whistle split the air. The wheels began to grind. We were on our way.

Lying down was out of the question, and we were only able to sit by deciding to take turns. There was very little air. The lucky ones who happened to be near a window could see the blossoming countryside roll by.

After two days of traveling we began to be tortured by thirst. Then the heat became unbearable.

Free from all social constraint, young people gave way openly to instinct, taking advantage of the darkness to flirt in our midst, without caring about anyone else, as though they were alone in the world. The rest pretended not to notice anything.

We still had a few provisions left. But we never ate enough to satisfy our hunger. To save was our rule; to save up for tomorrow. Tomorrow might be worse.

The train stopped at Kaschau, a little town on the Czechoslovak frontier. We realized then that we were not going to stay in Hungary. Our eyes were opened, but too late.

The door of the car slid open. A German officer accompanied by a Hungarian lieutenant-interpreter, came up and introduced himself.

"From this moment, you come under the authority of the German army. Those of you who still have gold, silver, or watches in your possession must give them up now. Anyone who is later found to have kept anything will be shot on the spot. Secondly, anyone who feels ill may go to the hospital car. That's all."

The Hungarian lieutenant went among us with a basket and collected the last possessions from those who no longer wished to taste the bitterness of terror.

"There are eighty of you in this wagon," added the German officer, "If anyone is missing, you'll all be shot, like dogs…"

They disappeared. The doors were closed. We were caught in a trap, right up to our necks. The doors were nailed up; the way back was finally cut off. The world was a cattle wagon hermetically sealed.

We had a woman with us named Madame Schächter. She was about fifty; her ten-year-old son was with her, crouched in a corner. Her husband and two eldest sons had been deported with the first transport by mistake. The separation had completely broken her.

I knew her well. A quiet woman with tense, burning eyes, she had often been to our house. Her husband, who was a pious man, spent his days and nights in study, and it was she who worked to support the family.

Madame Schächter had gone out of her mind. On the first day of the journey she had already begun to moan and to keep asking why she had been separated from her family. As time went on, her cries grew hysterical.

On the third night, while we slept, some of us sitting one against the others and some standing, a piercing cry split the silence:

"Fire! I can see a fire! I can see a fire!"

There was a moment's panic. Who was it who had cried out? It was Madame Schächter. Standing in the middle of the wagon, in the pale light from the windows, she looked like a withered tree in a cornfield. She pointed her arm toward the window, screaming:

"Look! Look at it! Fire! A terrible fire! Mercy! *Oh, that fire!*"

Some of the men pressed up against the bars. There was nothing there; only the darkness.

The shock of this terrible awakening stayed with us for a long time. We still trembled from it. With every groan of the wheels on the rail, we felt that an abyss was about to open beneath our bodies. Powerless to still our own anguish, we tried to console ourselves:

"She's mad, poor soul…"

Someone had put a damp cloth on her brow, to calm her, but still her screams went on:

"Fire! Fire!"

> *"She continued to scream, breathless, her voice broken by sobs. 'Jews, listen to me! I can see a fire! There are huge flames! It is a furnace!'"*

Her little boy was crying hanging onto her skirt, trying to take hold of her hands. "It's all right, Mummy! There's nothing there… Sit down…" This shook me even more than his mother's screams had done.

Some women tried to calm her. "You'll find your husband and your sons again … in a few days…"

She continued to scream, breathless, her voice broken by sobs. "Jews, listen to me! I can see a fire! There are huge flames! It is a furnace!"

It was as though she were possessed by an evil spirit which spoke from the depths of her being.

We tried to explain it away, more to calm ourselves and to recover our own breath than to comfort her. "She must be very thirsty, poor thing! That's why she keeps talking about a fire devouring her."

But it was in vain. Our terror was about to burst the sides of the train. Our nerves were at breaking point. Our flesh was creeping. It was as though madness were taking possession of us all. We could stand it no longer. Some of the young men forced her to sit down, tied her up, and put a gag in her mouth.

Silence again. The little boy set down by his mother, crying. I had begun to breathe normally again. We could hear the wheels churning out that monotonous rhythm of a train traveling through the night. We could begin to doze, to rest, to dream…

An hour or two went by like this. Then another scream took our breath away. The woman had broken loose from her bonds and was crying out more loudly than ever:

"Look at the fire! Flames, Flames everywhere…"

Once more the young men tied her up and gagged her. They even struck her. People encouraged them:

"Make her be quiet! She's mad! Shut her up! She's not the only one. She can keep her mouth shut…"

They struck her several times on the head blows that might have killed her. Her little boy clung to her; he did not cry out; he did not say a word. He was not even weeping now.

An endless night. Toward dawn, Madame Schächter calmed down. Crouched in her corner, her bewildered gaze scouring the emptiness, she could no longer see us.

She stayed like that all through the day, dumb, absent, isolated among us. As soon as night fell, she began to scream: "There's a fire over there!" She would point at a spot in space, always the same one. They were tired of hitting her. The heat, the thirst, the pestilential stench, the suffocating lock of air—these were as nothing compared with these screams which tore us to shreds. A few days more and we should all have started to scream too.

But we had reached a station. Those who were next to the windows told us its name:

"Auschwitz."

No one had ever heard that name.

The train did not start up again. The afternoon passed slowly. Then the wagon doors slid open, Two men were allowed to get down to fetch water.

When they came back, they told us that, in exchange for a gold watch, they had discovered that this was the last stop. We would be getting out here. There was a labor camp. Conditions were good. Families would not be split up. Only the young people would go to work in the factories. The old men and invalids would be kept occupied in the fields.

The barometer of confidence soared. Here was a sudden release from the terrors of the previous nights. We gave thanks to God.

Madame Schächter stayed in her corner, wilted, dumb, indifferent to the general confidence. Her little boy stroked her hand.

As dusk fell, darkness gathered inside the wagon. We started to eat our last provisions. At ten in the evening, everyone was looking for a convenient position in which to sleep for a while, and soon we were all asleep. Suddenly:

"The fire! The furnace! Look, over there! …"

Waking with a start, we rushed to the window. Yet again we had believed her, even if only for a moment. But there was nothing outside save the darkness of night. With shame in our souls, we went back to our places, gnawed by fear, in spite of ourselves. As she continued to scream, they began to hit her again, and it was with the greatest difficulty that they silenced her.

The man in charge of our wagon called a German officer who was walking about on the platform, and asked him if Madam Schächter could be taken to the hospital car.

"You must be patient," the German replied. "She'll be taken there soon."

Towards eleven o'clock the train began to move. We pressed against the windows. The convoy was moving slowly. A quarter of an hour later, it slowed down again. Through the windows we could see barbed wire; we realized that this must be the camp.

We had forgotten the existence of Madame Schächter. Suddenly, we heard terrible screams:

"Jews, look! Look through the window! Flames! Look!"

And as the train stopped, we saw this time that flames were gushing out of a tall chimney into the black sky.

Madam Schächter was silent herself. Once more she had become dumb, indifferent, absent, and had gone back to her corner.

We looked at the flames in the darkness. There was an abominable odor floating in the air. Suddenly, our doors opened. Some odd-looking characters dressed in striped shirts and black trousers leapt into the wagon. They held electric torches and truncheons. They began to strike out to right and left, shouting:

"Everybody get out! Everyone out of the wagon! Quickly!"

We jumped out. I threw a last glance toward Madame Schächter. Her little boy was holding her hand.

In front of us flames. In the air that smell of burning flesh. It must have been about midnight. We had arrived—at Birkenau, reception center for Auschwitz.

Source: Wiesel, Elie. *Night*. Translated from the French by Stella Rodway. New York: Hill and Wang, 1960.

11.5
Arrival and Survival at Auschwitz-Birkenau – 1944
Excerpt from an Interview with Holocaust Survivor David Mandel

As the following account indicates, the gas chambers were just one aspect of the terror experienced by prisoners at the death camps. Born in 1929, David

Mandel was a native of Munkacs (also known as Mukacevo), a town that was part of Czechoslovakia following World War I and later became part of Hungary. In May 1944, he and other Jewish residents of the town were forced into train cars and transported to the extermination camp of Auschwitz-Birkenau in Poland. Mandel was fourteen at the time. With him were his parents, five brothers, and a sister, as well as members of his extended family.

We arrived. I remember, they started yelling … "*schnell*. Get out. Leave all your belongings behind. It's going to follow you. Stand in line. All able-bodied men to the left. All women and children to the right." And there were these people with striped garb. We didn't know who they were or where we were. They kept saying … "go to work." My father understood. I was fourteen and a half years old. He told me to stand tall and lie about my age—tell them I'm eighteen.

I had my brother who was [two years] younger [with me], and he had this little bag of food. And by that time my mother, my [two youngest] brothers, and my sister, and my aunt, and my cousins went to the right. And my father told my [younger] brother to take over the foodstuff to my mother, cause we didn't know how long before we'd see one another again. And [after he took the food to my mother] they wouldn't let my little brother back [to the left side].

And then all these people who went on the right, they marched them off to this building. I remember there was some stench in the air. There was a big chimney. We didn't know anything. And we know now these people were marched to these buildings. They were asked to undress, to put their clothes neatly [aside]… And they were ushered into this room where it looked like showers. And now we know instead of showers they turned on this Zyklon B gas faucets, and they gassed these poor souls. That's the kind of death my family met…

With my [older] brother and my dad, we were ushered the other way on the double. We ran to these barracks, following orders, hoping, you know, to see the family. We had to undress. They sheared our hair from all over our body… And we had to take a shower. All we could hold onto was our shoes and our belt. They took all of our clothing away. We were naked. I remember I held onto pictures of my family I dared take along. While in the shower I put them inside my shoe.

Then we had to line up, and they tattooed us. My brother has got A9237, I have A9238, my father was tattooed A9239. They did it with pen and ink. It hurt. Our arms got swollen. Anyone who cried or screamed was beaten. We had to endure. We were branded. No longer David Mandel. I was reduced to a number.

They didn't feed us [at first]. I remember after a day or so they gave us a bowl of soup, and it *stunk*. There were some fellow prisoners. We were like separated

David Mandel, Videotaped interview conducted by Elissa Schosheim, 1 February 1996. Survivors of the Shoah Visual History Foundation, Beverly Hills, CA, USA.

through barbed wire. They extended their skinny arms. They wanted that soup, and they ate it. We couldn't understand how anybody can eat anything like that, that has that foul smell... Later on, we were so hungry, that soup was the most delicious thing we ever had.

We were there for a few days, then they marched us off from Birkenau to Auschwitz, which was about maybe three kilometers. I remember going through this gate. It said *"Arbeit Macht Frei"*—"Work Makes You Free." Another lure to keep us calm...

About the second or third day my father was pulled out as a strong man [to do work in another camp]. He was put on a truck and carted off. And my brother and I were left there. My brother was seventeen. I was fifteen years old. We were just a couple of skinny kids. My brother found a piece of moldy bread, and he ate it, and he got violently ill. They took him to a *krankenbau*, which is a hospital like. Meantime I was alone while he was in the *krankenbau*. A truck came. They put the remaining group onto a truck, and they carted me off to a nearby satellite camp of Auschwitz, near Krakow...

So I was fifteen years old—not quite fifteen years old—all by myself. I was on a detail. I worked in a power plant. I was unloading brick. I remember we had to hand four bricks at a time, like a chain gang, and the brick was like sandpaper. The tips of my fingers became nothing but flesh...

Our regime consisted of, we had to get up about four o'clock in the morning, and we had to stand in line, and they counted us. They called that *appell*. And they gave us some kind of a hot substance, a tea-like, a grassy type of water, and that's all we had for breakfast. And after that, we had to line up again as we were heading for work. And as we left the gate they counted us. While we arrived to the work-place they counted us. As they broke us down into the details they counted us.

At noon we had to assemble again in the middle of the workplace. They counted us. We had to line up, and they dished out a bowl of soup. I remember, if we were lucky, we got the bottom of the barrel that was thicker. If we were unlucky, we got the watery part of it that was on the top. And anybody who moved out of line and in and out got a terrible, cruel beating. We didn't dare move up.

At night, while we came back, ... after work, they counted us. When we left the place of work, they counted us. As we entered the camp again, they counted us. We had to line up in front of every barrack. They counted us. And after that they gave us our bread, which was a piece of black bread. Sometimes it had a slice of margarine with it, sometimes a slice of liverwurst. And that was our meager rations. It was a starving rations. I don't know how many calories, but it just wasn't enough to survive on.

I was one of the youngest ones in the camp. Eventually I moved from this power plant. I worked in a coal mine. I was switching tracks. I was a kid [so] there was a civil

Polish engineer who would give me a piece of bread once in a while. I would help out in the kitchen [to get extra food]. Now that I look back, maybe fellow inmates saw to it that I get a [good] job, that I survive. We didn't think that anybody would survive these unsurvivable conditions, but I was given a chance, and I was a little bit better off than most. And they wanted me, perhaps, [to] be a eyewitness to what took place.

I witness father and son fighting over a piece of bread—son stealing from the father. I witness what went on. I was sort of glad that I wasn't with my father and my brother. It reminds me of a drowning man, somebody trying to save him and they both drown.

Source: Mandel, David. Videotaped interview conducted by Elissa Schosheim, 1 February 1996. Survivors of the Shoah Visual History Foundation Testimony 11722.

11.6

A French Political Prisoner at Auschwitz – 1943-1945
Excerpt from the Nuremberg Testimony of Marie Claude Vaillant-Couturier

A native of Paris, Marie Claude Vaillant-Couturier became a member of the underground French Resistance after Germany invaded France in 1940. She was arrested in 1942 by agents of the Nazi-controlled Vichy government of France and was sent to Auschwitz-Birkenau in January 1943 with a group of other non-Jews. Though the treatment of these political prisoners was slightly better than that afforded the Jewish inmates, they still experienced most of the dangers and horrors of camp life. Vaillant-Couturier also witnessed a variety of atrocities that were directed at other prisoners. The following is an excerpt from her testimony before the International Military Tribunal at Nuremberg in 1946. She is being questioned in this excerpt by French prosecutor Charles Dubost.

MME. VAILLANT-COUTURIER: We arrived at Auschwitz at dawn. The seals on our cars were broken, and we were driven out by blows with the butt end of a rifle, and taken to the Birkenau camp, a section of the Auschwitz Camp. It is situated in the middle of a great plain, which was frozen in the month of January. During this part of the journey we had to drag our luggage. As we passed through the door we knew only too well how slender our chances were that we would come out again, for we had already met columns of living skeletons going to work; and as we entered we sang "The Marseillaise" [the French national anthem] to keep up our courage.

We were led to a large shed, then to a disinfecting station. There our heads were shaved and our registration numbers were tattooed on the left forearm. Then we were taken into a large room for a steam bath and a cold shower. In spite of the fact that we were naked, all this took place in the presence of SS men and women. We were then given clothing which was soiled and torn, a cotton dress and jacket of the same material.

All this had taken several hours, we saw from the windows of the block where we were, the camp of the men; and toward evening an orchestra came in. It was snowing and we wondered why they were playing music. We then saw that the camp foremen were returning to the camp. Each foreman was followed by men who were carrying the dead. As they could hardly drag themselves along, every time they stumbled they were put on their feet again by being kicked or by blows with the butt end of a rifle.

After that we were taken to the block where we were to live. There were no beds but only bunks, measuring 2 by 2 meters, and there nine of us had to sleep the first night without any mattress or blanket. We remained in blocks of this kind for several months. We could not sleep all night, because every time one of the nine moved—this happened unceasingly because we were all ill—she disturbed the whole row.

At 3:30 in the morning the shouting of the guards woke us up, and with cudgel blows we were driven from our bunks to go to roll call. Nothing in the world could release us from going to the roll call; even those who were dying had to be dragged there. We had to stand there in rows of five until dawn, that is, 7 or 8 o'clock in the morning in the winter; and when there was a fog, sometimes until noon. Then the commandos [the members of the labor crews] would start on their way to work.

M. DUBOST: Excuse me, can you describe the roll call?

MME. VAILLANT-COUTURIER: For roll call we were lined up in rows of five; and we waited until daybreak, until the Aufseherinnen, the German women guards in uniform, came to count us. They had cudgels and they beat us more or less at random.

We had a comrade, Germaine Renaud, a school teacher from Azay-le-Rideau in France, who had her skull broken before my eyes from a blow with a cudgel during the roll call.

The work at Auschwitz consisted of clearing demolished houses, road building, and especially the draining of marsh land. This was by far the hardest work, for all day long we had our feet in the water and there was the danger of being sucked down. It frequently happened that we had to pull out a comrade that had sunk in up to the waist.

During the work the SS men and women who stood guard over us would beat us with cudgels and set their dogs on us. Many of our friends had their legs torn by the dogs. I even saw a woman torn to pieces and die under my very eyes when Tauber, a member of the SS, encouraged his dog to attack her and grinned at the sight.

267

The causes of death were extremely numerous. First of all, there was the complete lack of washing facilities. When we arrived at Auschwitz, for 12,000 internees there was only one tap of water, unfit for drinking, and it was not always flowing. As this tap was in the German wash house we could reach it only by passing through the guards, who were German common-law women prisoners, and they beat us horribly as we went by. It was therefore almost impossible to wash ourselves or our clothes. For more than 3 months we remained without ever changing our clothes. When there was snow, we melted some to wash in. Later in the spring, when we went to work we would drink from a puddle by the road-side and then wash our underclothes in it. We took turns washing our hands in the dirty water. Our companions were dying of thirst, because we got only half a cup of some herbal tea twice a day.

M. DUBOST: Please describe in detail one of the roll calls at the beginning of February.

MME. VAILLANT-COUTURIER: On 5 February there was what is called general roll call.

M. DUBOST: In what year was that?

MME. VAILLANT-COUTURIER: In 1943. At 3:30 the whole camp…

M. DUBOST: In the morning at 3:30?

MME. VAILLANT-COUTURIER: In the morning at 3:30 the whole camp was awakened and sent out on the plain, whereas normally the roll call was at 3:30 but inside the camp. We remained out in front of the camp until 5 in the afternoon, in the snow, without any food. Then when the signal was given we had to go through the door one by one, and we were struck in the back with a cudgel, each one of us, in order to make us run. Those who could not run, either because they were too old or too ill, were caught by a hook and taken to Block 25, "waiting block" for the gas chamber. On that day 10 of the French women of our convoy were thus caught and taken to Block 25.

When all the internees were back in the camp, a party to which I belonged was organized to go and pick up the bodies of the dead which were scattered over the plain as on a battlefield. We carried to the yard of Block 25 the dead and the dying without distinction, and they remained there stacked up in a pile.

This Block 25, which was the anteroom of the gas chamber, if one may express it so, is well known to me because at that time we had been transferred to Block 26 and our windows opened on the yard of number 25. One saw stacks of corpses piled up in the courtyard, and from time to time a hand or head would stir among the bodies, trying to free itself. It was a dying woman attempting to get free and live. The rate of mortality in that block was even more terrible than elsewhere because, having been condemned to death, they received food or drink only if

268

there was something left in the cans in the kitchen; which means that very often they went for several days without a drop of water.

One of our companions, Annette Épaux, a fine young woman of 30, passing the block one day, was over come with pity for those women who moaned from morning till night in all languages, "Drink. Drink. Water!" She came back to our block to get a little herbal tea, but as she was passing it through the bars of the window she was seen by the Aufseherin, who took her by the neck and threw her into Block 25. All my life I will remember Annette Épaux. Two days later I saw her on the truck which was taking the internees to the gas chamber. She had her arms around another French woman, old Line Porcher, and when the truck started moving she cried "Think of my little boy, if you ever get back to France." Then they started singing "The Marseillaise."

In Block 25, in the courtyard, there were rats as big as cats running about and gnawing the corpses and even attacking the dying who had not enough strength left to chase them away.

Another cause of mortality and epidemics was the fact that we were given food in large red mess tins, which were merely rinsed in cold water after each meal. As all the women were ill and had not the strength during the night to go to the trench which was used as a lavatory, the access to which was beyond description, they used these containers for a purpose for which they were not meant. The next day the mess tins were collected and taken to a refuse heap. During the day another team would come and collect them, wash them in cold water, and put them in use again.

Another cause of death was the problem of shoes. In the snow and mud of Poland leather shoes were completely destroyed at the end of a week or two. Therefore our feet were frozen and covered with sores. We had to sleep with our muddy shoes on lest they be stolen, and when the time came to get up for roll call cries of anguish could be heard: "My shoes have been stolen." Then one had to wait until the whole block had been emptied to look under the bunks for odd shoes. Sometimes one found two shoes for the same foot, or one shoe and one sabot. One could go to roll call like that but it was an additional torture for work, because sores formed on our feet which quickly became infected for lack of care. Many of our companions went to the Revier [the infirmary] for sores on their feet and legs and never came back.

M. DUBOST: What did they do to the internees who came to roll call without shoes?

MME. VAILLANT-COUTURIER: The Jewish internees who came without shoes were immediately taken to Block 25.

M. DUBOST: They were gassed then?

MME. VAILLANT-COUTURIER: They were gassed for any reason whatsoever. Their conditions were moreover absolutely appalling. Although we were crowd-

269

ed 800 in a block and could scarcely move, they were 1,500 to a block of similar dimensions, so that many of them could not sleep or even lie down during the whole night.

M. DUBOST: Can you talk about the Revier?

MME. VAILLANT-COUTURIER: To reach the Revier one had to go first to the roll call. Whatever the state was …

M. DUBOST: Would you please explain what the Revier was in the camp?

MME. VAILLANT-COUTURIER: The Revier was the blocks where the sick were put. This place could not be given the name of hospital, because it did not correspond in any way to our idea of a hospital.

To go there one first had to obtain authorization from the block chief who seldom gave it. When it was finally granted we were led in columns to the infirmary where, no matter what weather, whether it snowed or rained, even if one had a temperature of 40° (centigrade) one had to wait for several hours standing in a queue to be admitted. It frequently happened that patients died outside before the door of the infirmary, before they could get in. Moreover, lining up in front of the infirmary was dangerous because if the queue was too long the SS came along, picked up all the women who were waiting, and took them straight to Block Number 25.

M. DUBOST: That is to say, to the gas chamber?

MME. VAILLANT-COUTURIER: That is to say, to the gas chamber. That is why very often the women preferred not to go to the Revier and they died at their work or at roll call. Every day, after evening roll call in winter time, dead were picked up who had fallen into the ditches.

The only advantage of the Revier was that as one was in bed, one did not have to go to roll call; but one lay in appalling conditions, four in a bed of less than one meter in width, each suffering from a different disease, so that anyone who came for leg sores would catch typhus or dysentery from neighbors. The straw mattresses were dirty and they were changed only when absolutely rotten. The bedding was so full of lice that one could see them swarming like ants. One of my companions, Marguerite Corringer, told me that when she had typhus, she could not sleep all night because of the lice. She spent the night shaking her blanket over a piece of paper and emptying the lice into a receptacle by the bed, and this went on for hours.

There were practically no medicines. Consequently the patients were left in their beds without any attention, without hygiene, and unwashed. The dead lay in bed with the sick for several hours; and finally, when they were noticed, they were simply tipped out of the bed and taken outside the block. There the women porters would come and carry the dead away on small stretchers, with heads and legs dangling over the sides. From morning till night the carriers of the dead went from the Revier to the mortuary.

During the big epidemics, in the winters of 1943 and 1944, the stretchers were replaced by carts, as there were too many dead bodies. During those periods of epidemics there were from 200 to 350 dead daily...

M. DUBOST: What do you know about the convoy of Jews which arrived from Romainville about the same time as yourself?

MME. VAILLANT-COUTURIER: When we left Romainville the Jewesses who were there at the same time as ourselves were left behind. They were sent to Drancy and subsequently arrived at Auschwitz, where we found them again 3 weeks later, 3 weeks after our arrival. Of the original 1,200 only 125 actually came to the camp; the others were immediately sent to the gas chambers. Of these 125 not one was left alive at the end of 1 month.

The transports operated as follows:

When we first arrived, whenever a convoy of Jews came, a selection was made; first the old men and women, then the mothers and the children were put into trucks together with the sick or those whose constitution appeared to be delicate. They took in only the young women and girls as well as the young men who were sent to the men's camp.

Generally speaking, of a convoy of about 1,000 to 1,500, seldom more than 250—and this figure really was the maximum—actually reached the camp. The rest were immediately sent to the gas chamber.

At the selection they also picked out the women in good health between the ages of 20 and 30, who were sent to the experimental block; and young girls and slightly older women, or those who had not been selected for that purpose, were sent to the camp where, like ourselves, they were tattooed and shaved.

There was also, in the spring of 1944, a special block for twins. It was during the time when large convoys of Hungarian Jews—about 700,000 arrived. Dr. Mengele, who was carrying out the experiments, kept back from each convoy twin children and twins in general, regardless of their age, so long as both were present. So we had both babies and adults on the floor of that block. Apart from blood tests and measuring I do not know what was done to them.

M. DUBOST: Were you an eye witness of the selections on the arrival of the convoys?

MME. VAILLANT-COUTURIER: Yes, because when we worked in the sewing block in 1944, the block where we lived directly faced the stopping place of the trains. The system had been improved. Instead of making the selection at the place where they arrived, a side line now took the train practically right up to the gas chamber; and the stopping place, about 100 meters from the gas chamber, was right opposite of our block though, of course, separated from us by two rows of barbed wire. Consequently, we saw the unsealing of the cars and the soldiers letting men, women, and children out of them. We then witnessed heart-rending scenes; old couples forced to part from each other, mothers made to abandon their young daughters, since the latter were sent to the camp, whereas mothers and children were sent to the gas chambers. All these people were unaware of the fate awaiting them. They were merely upset at being separated, but they did not know that they were going to their death. To render their welcome more pleasant at this time—June-July 1944—an orchestra composed of internees, all young and pretty girls dressed in little white blouses and navy blue skirts, played during the selection, at the arrival of the trains, gay tunes such as "The Merry Widow," the "Barcarolle" from "The Tales of Hoffman," and so forth. They were then informed that this was a labor camp and since they were not brought into the camp they saw only the small platform surrounded by flowering plants. Naturally, they could not realize what was in store for them…

Source: "Forty-Fourth Day, Monday, 28 January 1946." *Trial of the Major War Criminals before the International Military Tribunal, Nuremberg, 14 November 1945-1 October 1946. Vol. 6, Proceedings 22 January 1946-4 February 1946.* Nuremberg, Germany: International Military Tribunal, 1947.

11.7
Sorting Valuables at Auschwitz-Birkenau – 1944-1945
Holocaust Survivor George Gottlieb Recalls His Work as Part of the "Canada Group"

A Hungarian Jew who grew up in the town of Bicske, near Budapest, George Gottlieb was sent to Auschwitz in 1944 at age fifteen along with the other members of his family—his parents, an older brother, and a grandfather. Upon arrival at the concentration camp, Gottlieb and his brother were chosen for a work group while his father and grandfather went immediately to the gas chamber. He was unsure of his mother's fate. In the following recollection, Gottlieb described the job he and his brother later performed as part of the Canada Group—the inmates who collected and sorted the belongings of newly arrived prisoners at the Auschwitz train station. (The nickname apparently came from the fact that the members of the group handled a lot of valuable merchandise and Canada was viewed as a wealthy country.) This prized job allowed the brothers to obtain more food and brought them into contact with an S.S. guard who performed a rare act of humanity in the midst of the camp's horror and misery. But their duties at the train station also exposed them to Dr. Josef Mengele, the infamous Nazi doctor who selected prisoners for medical experiments and sometimes designated new arrivals for gassing or work details.

George Gottlieb, Videotaped interview conducted by Joan Karen Benbasat, 24 September 1996. Survivors of the Shoah Visual History Foundation, Beverly Hills, CA, USA.

My brother and I, thankfully, we were selected to go work what they called the *Kanadisch* Group—the Canadian Group. Our work was to go to the railroad station, and we were those famous guys who were yelling and screaming to the [passengers on the] incoming trains to get off and form the line of five. And our job was to remove everything from the train, everything that the people brought in, and sort them—different piles that we had to sort, children's clothes, men's clothes, ladies' clothes, books, … and basically get rid of anything which was perishable. They didn't want it should rot there—get rid of it. But also at the same time … we had real valuables. It's unbelievable, it's amazing, that if you think about it, that people … going into a ghetto, they brought silverware with them. So that silverware came to Auschwitz/Birkenau. They had jewelry. They had necklaces and etcetera, which was hidden in pockets. They had money. I mean they had all kind of different things, what basically we were not allowed to touch. That was something where they had a box for smaller jewelry, another one for bigger one, and we had to pile the clothes and suitcases, shoes, everything separate…

We were all continuously under SS guard… When we left camp to the railroad station, we were strip-searched, that nothing should come out of the camp. [When we] come *back* to camp, once again strip-searched, that nothing can come from the railroad station back. That way we couldn't manipulate, we couldn't organize anything [that is, keep some of the valuables for their own use]. Always the same SS guard who took us. It was a twelve-hour shift… We had to be at the station at seven, we stayed through seven at night. I was always with my brother, by the way, together, always on a day shift while we did this work.

But we found out the whole operation. We saw … I had the unpleasant thing of seeing Dr. Mengele everyday. Suddenly we knew, we saw the big chimneys, and we know the chimney is basically the crematorium, and we saw where the gas chamber is. And also what we have seen, where the smell comes from. The smell came—that even with the tremendous German precision, that they were precise in everything, but they did not calculate it properly. That it took somewhere around forty minutes to burn the bodies, and the gas chamber took ten to eleven minutes to kill the people. So that crematoriums could not supply fast enough to get rid of the bodies. So they were digging huge ditches, and those ditches [filled with bodies] were doused with gasoline and just put on fire. Outside. And that was an unbelievable smell, and it was an unbelievable knowledge that that was happening. I mean, once you are that close, so close to that happening…

Physically it was the best job available. There was no better job. For the simple reason, … you see food coming in from ghettos. First of all, you know the food comes from another Jewish family [and] you stuff your mouth, … even if the punishment is harsh. Punishment could have been, at that time, a shot, but you stuffed your mouth and you ate, so basically that was the best job available…

The same SS guard was a pleasant-looking fellow. He was a German SS. By the way, … you had a lot of Ukrainian and Lithuanian SS in Auschwitz also. And this guy was pleasant. I mean he basically never did anything. He yelled, screamed, but he was never rough to us. I was brash, young, and not thinking. [One day] I grabbed like a handful of good jewelry, … I thought it was good jewelry, and just put it in his hand. So he looked at me first, and his reaction was, "it goes to the box." I just picked my shoulders up like "here you are," and I turned away, and my brother saw that he turned away and put it in his pocket. So when we saw that he put the jewelry in the pocket, it was quite a good feeling. Our feeling was that okay, he's a comrade in crime. I'm stealing, he's taking. I have no use for it. To me, it could have been diamond or rubies or God knows what, because what's the difference? Let him have it. What's the difference who has it? I prefer that he should have it than the German Reich should have it—that the government should have it. Maybe he can do something…

> "Somebody heard Mom's voice. Mom was a beautiful lady. And suddenly you see somebody running to you, bald, with a long sack gown … We gave her the goodies. We kissed. And the twenty minutes were gone. And that's the last time I saw Mom."

Through the wires, you were yelling and screaming continuously. [We] yell and scream what try to find out if Mommy's there [alive in the women's camp]. We knew that right next to us was another men's camp, but the camp right next to it was a ladies' camp. You know, like in rows there were many, many camps. And one day we got the unbelievable relief news by saying, through the rumors, that, yes, Mommy's alive. Naturally the same rumor brought it back most probably to her that *we* are alive. Naturally she had no idea who is the "we." We knew by having our job, the so-called *Kanadisch* Group, the Canadian Group, that Dad and Grandpa immediately went to gas chamber and crematorium—at least we hope it was the gas chamber and crematorium, but anyway, we knew exactly where they went. They were on the wrong side of the track. So our aim, our duty, our desire to live was to find out if Mommy's alive, how is she, and what she's doing. And then we found this one up, and as a matter of fact a couple of days later, once again through this rumor mill, even the barrack number was given to us, where she is. She was in Barrack Fourteen.

And, shamelessly, I went over to the SS guard, the same SS guard who was quite nice, and ask him the question, is there any way we can let Mom know that we are alive and with her and what? And he just turned around, kicked me in the … pants, and told me to get back into line. I got a healthy kick from him. And I didn't expect too much more. Really didn't expect any miracle from him.

And a couple of days later, maybe a week later, on the morning when we were leaving [for work], he selected [a group] out of the 110 people, which included my brother and I. And there was a pushcart there—you know with the two big wheels?—with some blankets or some clothing on top of it… He took … ten of us. We pushed that cart, and we had no idea, where we are going, what are we doing.

And suddenly with the pushcart, suddenly he stopped in front of the ladies' camp. He handed some documents over to the guard, and the gate opened up, and we went in… In front of Barrack Fourteen he stopped and handed me and my brother a brown paper bag. The paper bag had food bread in it—German bread, what they were eating, not our garbage. Must have been a pound or a kilo, I don't know how much, butter. Sausage. And a pocket knife. He looked at his watch. He said, "you have twenty minutes. Find your mother." …

We were looking, and somebody heard Mom's voice. Mom was a beautiful lady. And suddenly you see somebody running to you, bald, with a long sack gown …

We gave her the goodies. We kissed. And the twenty minutes were gone. And that's the last time I saw Mom. It's a tough sight. And a tougher memory. A beautiful, beautiful woman, looking like that.

Until today, I hear her saying, "be proud of your heritage." And the last words: "be proud of your name." I hope we can be…

That's the last time I saw Mom. That's the last time that *we* saw Mom. But we knew that she was alive. And we knew that she going to be strong… And basically that's what kept us fighting…

The basic idea is that if you ask, what made you fight?, what made you survive?, it's the very, very, very few conversation between the two brothers—my brother and I. We said to each other that we must survive because we are the men and we have to take care of Mom. We knew that Dad is gone. Grandpa is gone. And we knew that she's alive. That gave us the strength to fight.

Source: Gottlieb, George. Videotaped interview conducted by Joan Karen Benbasat, 24 September 1996. Survivors of the Shoah Visual History Foundation Testimony 20035.

11.8
The Collection of Jewish Assets at the Reichsbank – 1942-1945
Excerpt from a Statement by Emil Puhl, Director of the Reichsbank

A small percentage of the valuables and personal items seized from incoming prisoners at the Nazi death camps found their way to the camp's black market. Most of the more valuable commodities such as jewelry and cash, though, went to the S.S. leadership. As the following statement by the director of the Reichsbank (one of Germany's central banks) shows, some portion of the plunder made it all the way to senior Nazi officials in Berlin. While theft of Jewish assets was not the primary motivation for the Holocaust, Nazi officials took maximum advantage of this source of riches. After the war, Jewish survivors and descendants of the dead had some success in recovering art treasures, money, and other valuables that had been looted during the Holocaust.

...

2. In the summer of 1942, the Reichsbank President and Reich Economics Minister, Walter Funk, had a conversation with me and with Herr Friedrich Wilhelm, a member of the board of the Reichsbank. Funk told me that he had made arrangements with the Reichsführer Himmler to receive gold and jewellery from the SS for safe-keeping. Funk gave instructions to me to make the necessary arrangements with [Oswald] Pohl, who was head of the economic department of the SS and to whom the economic side of the concentration camps was subordinated.

3. I asked Funk where the gold, jewellery and cash and other items which were to be delivered by the SS came from. Funk replied that it was confiscated property from the occupied eastern territories and that I should not ask any further questions. I protested against the Reichsbank taking over these assets. Funk replied that we should make the necessary arrangements for taking over the assets and keep the matter absolutely secret.

4. Thereupon I made the necessary arrangements for receiving the assets with the officials responsible for the safes and, at its next board meeting, I reported to the board of the Reichsbank about the measures which had been taken. On the same day, Pohl of the Economic Department of the SS rang me up and asked me whether I was informed of the matter. I refused to discuss the matter on the telephone, whereupon he came to see me and said that the SS had some jewellery which it wished to hand over to the Reichsbank for safe-keeping. I made the necessary arrangements with him for the transfer and, from then onwards, deliveries were made from time to time from August 1942 through the following years.

5. Among the items deposited by the SS were jewellery, watches, spectacle frames, gold fillings, and other objects in large quantities which had been removed by the SS from the Jews, concentration camp victims, and other persons. We became aware of this when the SS attempted to transform this material into cash and, with Funk's knowledge and approval, made use of Reichsbank personnel for this purpose. Apart from gold, jewellery, and other such items, the SS delivered paper money, foreign exchange, and bonds to the Reichsbank which were dealt with in the legal way usual for such items. As far as the jewellery and gold were concerned, Funk told me that Himmler and the Reich Finance Minister, von Krosigk, had reached an agreement whereby gold and similar items were deposited

under the State's account and amounts which were later realised by the sale of these items were credited to the State.

6. In pursuance of my duties, I visited the safes of the Reichsbank from time to time and saw what was stored there. Funk too visited the safes from time to time in pursuance of his duties.

7. Following Funk's instructions, the Gold Discount Bank established a current account, which finally contained 10-12 million Reich Marks, and which was put at the disposal of the economic administration of the SS for financing the production of material in factories under SS control by workers from concentration camps.

Source: *Nazism 1919-1945: Vol. 3, Foreign Policy, War, and Racial Extermination. A Documentary Reader.* Edited by J. Noakes and G. Pridham. Exeter, UK: University of Exeter Press. New edition with index, 2001.

11.9
A Buchenwald Inmate Remembers Nazi Medical Experiments – 1944-1945
Excerpt from Alfred Balachowsky's Testimony at Nuremberg

The Nazis performed monstrous medical experiments on prisoners at a number of concentration camps. The following testimony, provided at the Nuremberg War Crimes Trials after the war, concerns the "research" carried out at Buchenwald, a camp inside Germany. Buchenwald held a variety of prisoners, including political detainees, prisoners of war, and—especially at the end of the war—Jews who had been evacuated from the Polish camps. Alfred Balachowsky was an inmate at Buchenwald who worked in the medical unit. He is being questioned in this excerpt by French prosecutor Charles Dubost.

M. DUBOST: ... Will you now testify to the criminal practices of the SS Medical Corps in the camps, criminal practices in the form of scientific experiments?

BALACHOWSKY: I was recalled to Buchenwald the 1st of May 1944, and assigned to Block 50, which was actually a factory for the manufacture of vaccines against exanthematous typhus. I was recalled from Dora [another concentration camp] to Buchenwald, because in the meantime, the management of the camp had learned that I was a specialist in this sort of research, and consequently they wished to use my services in Block 50 for the manufacture of vaccines....

Block 50 ... was under Sturmbannführer Schuler, who was a doctor.... This same Sturmbannführer Schuler was also in charge of another block in the Buchenwald Camp. This other block was Block 46, the infamous block for experiments, where the internees were utilized as guinea pigs.

Blocks 46 and 50 were both run by one office.... All archives, index cards pertaining to the experiments—as well as Block 50, were sent to the ... office of Block 50.

The secretary of Block 50 was an Austrian political prisoner, my friend, Eugene Kogon. He and a few other comrades had, consequently, opportunities of looking through all the archives of which they had charge. Therefore they were able to know, day by day, exactly what went on either in Block 50, our block, or in Block 46. I myself was able to get hold of most of the archives of Block 46, and even the book in which the experiments were recorded has been saved. It is in our possession, and has been forwarded to the Psychological Service of the American Forces....

M. DUBOST: Were the men who were subjected to these experiments volunteers or not?

BALACHOWSKY: The human beings subjected to the experiments were recruited not only in the Buchenwald Camp, but also outside the camp. They were not volunteers; in most cases they did not know that they would be used for experiments until they entered Block 46. The recruitment took place among criminals, perhaps in order to reduce their large numbers in that way. But the recruitment was also carried out among political prisoners and I have to point out that recruits for Block 46 came also from Russian prisoners of war....

The experiments carried out in Block 46 did without doubt serve a medical purpose, but for the greater part they were of no service to science. Therefore, they can hardly be called experiments. The men were used for observing the effects of drugs, poisons, bacterial cultures, *èt cetera*. I take, as an example, the use of the vaccine against exanthematous typhus. To manufacture this vaccine it is necessary to have bacterial cultures of typhus. For experiments such as are carried out at the Pasteur Institute and the other similar institutes of the world, cultures are not necessary as typhus patients can always be found for samples of infected blood. Here it was quite different. From the records and the chart you have in your hand, we could ascertain in Block 46 12 different cultures of typhus germs, designated by the letter BU, (meaning Buchenwald) and numbered Buchenwald 1 to Buchenwald 12. A constant supply of these cultures was kept in Block 46 by means of the contamination of healthy individuals through sick ones; this was achieved by artificial inoculation of typhus germs by means of intravenous injection of 0.5 to 1 cubic centimeter of infected blood drawn from a patient at the height of the crisis. Now, it is well-known that artificial inoculation of typhus by intravenous injection is invariably fatal. Therefore all these men who were used for bacterial culture during the whole time such cultures were required (from October 1942 to the liberation of the camp) died, and we counted 600 victims sacrificed for the sole purpose of supplying typhus germs.

M. DUBOST: They were literally murdered to keep typhus germs alive?

BALACHOWSKY: They were literally murdered to keep typhus germs alive. Apart from these, other experiments were made as to the efficacy of vaccines....

278

In 1944 experiments were also made on the effects of vaccines. One hundred and fifty men lost their lives in these experiments. The vaccines used by the German Army were not only those manufactured in our Block 46, but also ones which came from Italy, Denmark, Poland, and the Germans wanted to ascertain the value of these different vaccines. Consequently, in August 1944 they began experiments on 150 men who were locked up in Block 46.

Here, I should like to tell you how Block 46 was run. It was entirely isolated and surrounded by barbed wire. The internees had no roll call and no permission to go out. All the windows were kept closed, the panes were of frosted glass. No unauthorized person could enter the block. A German political prisoner was in charge of the Block. This German political prisoner was Kapo Dietzsch, an asocial individual who had been in prisons and in camps for 20 years and who worked for the SS. It was he who gave the injections and inoculations and who executed people upon order. Strangely enough, there were weapons in the block, automatic pistols, and hand grenades, to quell any possible revolt, either outside or inside the block.

I can also tell you that an order slip for Block 46, sent to the office … at Block 50 in January 1945, mentioned three strait jackets to be used for those who refused to be inoculated.

Now I come back to the typhus and vaccine experiments. You will see how they were carried out.

The 150 prisoners were divided into 2 groups: those who were to be used as tests and those who were to be the subjects. The latter only received (ordinary) injections of the different types of vaccines to be tested. Those used for testing were not given any injections. Then, after the vaccination of the subject, inoculations were given (always by means of intravenous injections) to everybody selected for this experiment, those for testing as well as the subjects. Those used for tests died about two weeks after the inoculation—as such is approximately the period required before the disease develops its fatal issue. As for the others, who received different kinds of vaccines, their deaths were in proportion to the efficacy of the vaccines administered to them… After the conclusion of the experiments, no survivors were allowed to live, according to the custom prevailing in Block 46. All the survivors of the experiments were "liquidated" and murdered in Block 46, by the customary methods which some of my comrades have already described to you, that is by means of intracardiac injections of phenol.…

I now come to experiments with phosphorus, particularly made on prisoners of Russian origin. Phosphorus burns were inflicted in Block 46 on Russian prisoners for the following reason. Certain bombs dropped in Germany by the Allied aviators caused burns on the civilians and soldiers which were difficult to heal. Consequently, the Germans tried to find a whole series of drugs which would hasten the healing of the wounds caused by these burns. Thus, experiments were carried out in Block 46 on Russian prisoners who were artificially burned with phosphorous products and then treated with different drugs supplied by the German chemical industry....

M. DUBOST: What were the results of these experiments?

BALACHOWSKY: All these experiments resulted in death.

M. DUBOST: Always in death? So each experiment is equivalent to a murder for which the SS are collectively responsible?

BALACHOWSKY: For which those who established this institution are responsible.

M. DUBOST: That is the SS as a whole, and the German medical corps in particular?

BALACHOWSKY: Definitely so, as the orders came from the Versuchsabteilung 5 (Research Station 5). The SS were responsible as the orders were issued by that section at Leipzig and, therefore, came from the Supreme Command of the Waffen SS.

Source: "Forty-Fifth Day, Tuesday, 29 January 1946." *Trial of the Major War Criminals before the International Military Tribunal, Nuremberg, 14 November 1945-1 October 1946.* Vol. 6, *Proceedings 22 January 1946-4 February 1946.* Nuremberg, Germany: International Military Tribunal, 1947.

11.10
The Nazi Order for the Evacuation or Liquidation of Prisoners – 1944
Excerpt from a Nazi Memorandum on the "Clearance of Prisons"

As the Germans retreated westward before Soviet military forces in 1944, the fighting drew ever closer to the death camps and other prisons maintained by the Nazis in Poland. The Nazis were determined to keep the Red Army from liberating any of these prisoners—presumably because they were witnesses to their murderous activities. Nazi officials thus ordered inmates to be evacuated, if possible, or else killed. The majority of the prisoners in the death camps were indeed evacuated as the Russians approached. The following document is dated July 1944 and comes from the commander of Nazi security forces in one of the Polish regions.

4143 TOP SECRET

To: The Branch Office for the attention of SS-Hauptsturmfuehrer Thiel—or acting deputy—in Tomaschow.

Subject: Clearance of Prisons.

... I again stress the fact that the number of inmates of the Sipo [*Sicherheit-spolizei*—Nazi security police] and SD [*Sicherheitsdienst*—S.S. security police] prisons must be kept as low as possible. In the present situation, particularly those suspects, handed over by the Civil Police [*Ordnungspolizei*] need *only be subjected to a short, formal interrogation,* provided there are no serious grounds for suspicion. They are then to be sent by the quickest route to a concentration camp, should no court-martial proceedings be necessary or should there be no question of discharge. *Please keep the number of discharges very low.* Should the situation at the front necessitate it, early preparations are to be made for the total clearance of prisons. Should the situation develop suddenly in such a way that it is impossible to evacuate the prisoners, the prison inmates are to be liquidated and their bodies disposed of as far as possible (burning, blowing up the building, etc.). If necessary, *Jews* still employed in the armament industry or on other work are to be dealt with in the same way.

The liberation of prisoners or Jews by the enemy ... must be avoided under all circumstances nor may they fall into their hands alive.

Source: "Clearance of Prisons," July 1944. Reprinted as Document L-53 in *Nazi Conspiracy and Aggression.* Vol. 7. Washington, DC: United States Government Printing Office, 1946.

12

RESISTANCE

Of all the Jewish resistance movements that erupted in ghetto areas during World War II, the most famous took place in Warsaw, Poland. Nazi SS troops finally set much of the ghetto afire to suppress the uprising, which raged for almost a month in the spring of 1943.

INTRODUCTION

Despite the overwhelming death toll of the Holocaust, many victims resisted their persecution and murder by a variety of means, including armed struggle. Poland was the site of some of the most valiant defense efforts. Even while imprisoned in the ghettos, Jewish groups did what they could to assist Polish partisans who carried out acts of sabotage against the Nazis. Those Jews who were able to escape from the ghettos sometimes joined existing partisan bands or formed their own guerrilla units.

The most strident resistance came within the ghettos themselves. All of these uprisings were eventually crushed but not before making the Nazis suffer deaths of their own. The largest revolt took place in Warsaw. After watching the deportation of more than 300,000 Jews from the city (most were killed at the Treblinka death camp), an organized band of ghetto fighters led by Mordecai Anilewicz rose up against the Nazis in April 1943. Fierce fighting roared through the Warsaw Ghetto for almost a month. The Jews had very few weapons, but they made skilled use of underground bunkers they had built beneath the buildings of the ghetto. In the end, the Germans burned most of the ghetto to remove the Jewish fighters. Another courageous form of resistance was carried out by underground operatives who assisted the ghetto fighters and aided escaped Jews in Poland. Many of these figures were Jewish women who went into hiding among the non-Jews in order to ferry information, money, and arms to insurgent groups.

Even the prisoners in the extermination camps were sometimes able to organize uprisings. This was a considerable accomplishment given the close supervision of the camps, the weakened physical condition of the prisoners, and the difficulty of obtaining weapons. Rebellions took place in six different camps. One of the most elaborate took place at Sobibór, where prisoners conspired to kill a dozen Nazi guards and then launched a large-scale prison break. Most of the 400 escapees were killed but 60 prisoners were never found by their Nazi pursuers. At Auschwitz, members of the *Sonderkommando*—the prisoners forced to assist in the gas chambers—staged an uprising and escape in October 1944. Most of the rebels were killed during or after the attack, and all of the escapees were recaptured. Most of the other prison rebellions were put down in a similar manner.

The failure of Jewish resistance efforts can be attributed to the conditions the victims found themselves in rather than a lack of resolve. The overwhelming force of an army and a police state was directed against a poorly armed civilian population, making opposition very difficult. Furthermore, for a long time the Jews caught up in the Holocaust did not fully understand the extent of the Nazi threat. Even when they began to grasp the awful truth—that friends and family members allegedly being "resettled" from the ghettos were actually being murdered, for instance—open resistance was not an easy choice. To take just one example, ghetto residents knew that they stood little chance of overcoming the well-armed Germans in an uprising. Also, would-be rebels knew that if they were defeated they would be sacrificing not only their own lives but those of everyone else around them. Given these factors, many reached the grim conclusion that their best hope for survival was to avoid rebellion and pray for liberation.

DOCUMENTS

12.1
A Defiant Voice in Munich – 1942
Text of the Second Leaflet Issued by The White Rose

Many historians have noted that the majority of German citizens expressed few objections to the actions of Hitler's government, including its persecution of the Jews and other groups. Indeed, many Germans, their views poisoned by years of exposure to anti-Semitism, approved of Nazi efforts to eradicate Jews from German life. There were exceptions, however. One of the most courageous resistance efforts was carried out by The White Rose, a small group of young German college students based in Munich. In 1942 they began issuing anonymous leaflets that were openly critical of the Nazi government—an astounding and dangerous activity considering the presence of Hitler's ever-watchful secret police. In addition, the leaflets contained withering condemnations of the German people for their failure to oppose the Third Reich. In the Second Leaflet, reprinted below, they even discussed the murder of Jews in Poland.

The group issued six leaflets in all, each of them urging Germans to reclaim their country from Adolf Hitler and the Nazi Party. In February 1943 members of the White Rose even painted anti-Nazi graffiti on buildings in Munich, a daring slap in the face to the Nazi empire. The White Rose evaded the Gestapo for months, but on February 18, 1943, two of the group's six members, brother and sister Hans and Sophie Scholl, were captured while attempting to distribute leaflets at the University of Munich. A third member, Christoph Probst, was arrested soon after. All three were convicted of treason and beheaded. The other three members of the White Rose—students Alexander Schmorell and Willi Graf and professor Kurt Huber—were arrested and executed a short time later. Today, the members of The White Rose are memorialized all across Germany, and a square at the University of Munich is named after Hans and Sophie Scholl.

It is impossible to engage in intellectual discourse with National Socialism because it is not an intellectually defensible program. It is false to speak of a

From Students against Tyranny: The Resistance of the White Rose, Munich, 1942-1943, by Inge Scholl. Copyright 1970 Wesleyan University Press. Reproduced with permission of Wesleyan University Press; permission conveyed via Copyright Clearance Center, Inc.

National Socialist philosophy, for if there were such an entity, one would have to try by means of analysis and discussion either to prove its validity or to combat it. In actuality, however, we face a totally different situation. At its very inception this movement depended on the deception and betrayal of one's fellow man; even at that time it was inwardly corrupt and could support itself only by constant lies. After all, Hitler states in an early edition of "his" book … : "It is unbelievable, to what extent one must betray a people in order to rule it." If at the start this cancerous growth in the nation was not particularly noticeable, it was only because there were still enough forces at work that operated for the good, so that it was kept under control. As it grew larger, however, and finally in an ultimate spurt of growth attained ruling power, the tumor broke open, as it were, and infected the whole body. The greater part of its former opponents went into hiding. The German intellectuals fled to their cellars, there, like plants struggling in the dark, away from light and sun, gradually to choke to death. Now the end is at hand. Now it is our task to find one another again, to spread information from person to person, to keep a steady purpose, and to allow ourselves no rest until the last man is persuaded of the urgent need to struggle against this system. When thus a wave of unrest goes through the land, when "it is in the air," when many join the cause, then in a great final effort this system can be shaken off. After all, an end with terror is preferable to terror without end.

> "Why do the German people behave so apathetically in the face of all these abominable crimes, crimes so unworthy of the human race? … The German people slumber on in their dull, stupid sleep and encourage these fascist criminals."

We are not in a position to draw up a final judgment about the meaning of our history. But if this catastrophe can be used to further the public welfare, it will be only by virtue of the fact that we are cleansed by suffering; that we yearn for the light in the midst of deepest night, summon our strength, and finally help in shaking off the yoke which weighs our world.

We do not want to discuss here the question of the Jews, nor do we want in this leaflet to compose a defense or apology. No, only by way of example do we want to cite the fact that since the conquest of Poland *three hundred thousand* Jews have been murdered in this country in the most bestial way. Here we see the most frightful crime against human dignity, a crime that is unparalleled in the whole of history. For Jews, too, are human beings—no matter what position we take with respect to the Jewish question—and this crime was perpetrated against human beings. … Why tell you all these things, since you are fully aware of them—or if not of these, then of other equally grave crimes committed by this frightful sub-humanity? Because here we touch on a problem which involves us deeply and forces us all to take thought.

Why do the German people behave so apathetically in the face of all these abominable crimes, crimes so unworthy of the human race? Hardly anyone thinks about that. It is accepted as fact and put out of mind. The German people slumber on in their dull, stupid sleep and encourage these fascist criminals; they give them the opportunity to carry on their depredations; and of course they do so. Is this a sign that the Germans are brutalized in their simplest human feelings, that no chord within them cries out at the sight of such deeds, that they have sunk into a fatal consciencelessness from which they will never, never awake? It seems so, and will certainly be so, if the German does not at last start up out of his stupor, if he does not protest wherever and whenever he can against this clique of criminals, if he shows no sympathy for these hundreds of thousands of victims. He must evidence not only sympathy, no, much more: a sense of *complicity* in guilt. For through his apathetic behavior he gives these evil men the opportunity to act as they do; he tolerates this "government" which has taken upon itself such an infinitely great burden of guilt; indeed, he himself is to blame for the fact that it came about at all! Each man wants to be exonerated of a guilt of this kind, each one continues on his way with the most placid, the calmest conscience. But he cannot be exonerated; he is *guilty, guilty, guilty*! It is not too late, however, to do away with this most reprehensible of all miscarriages of government, so as to avoid being burdened with even greater guilt. Now, when in recent years our eyes have been opened, when we know exactly who our adversary is, it is high time to root out this brown horde. Up until the outbreak of the war the larger part of the German people was blinded; the Nazis did not show themselves in their true aspect. But now, now that we have recognized them for what they are, it must be the sole and first duty, the holiest duty of every German to destroy these beasts…

Please make as many copies as possible of this leaflet and distribute them.

Source: School, Inge. *Students against Tyranny: The Resistance of the White Rose. Munich, 1942-1943.* Translated by Arthur R. Schultz. Middletown, CT: Wesleyan University Press, 1970.

12.2
Resistance in the Warsaw Ghetto – 1943
Text of a Pamphlet Distributed by the Jewish Military Organization in the Warsaw Ghetto

During World War II, armed resistance against Nazi persecutors erupted in a number of Jewish ghettos. Of these outbreaks, the Jewish residents of Warsaw staged the most prolonged ghetto revolt against the Nazis. This notice was issued in January 1943 by Zydowski Zwiazek Wojskowy (ZZW)— the Jewish Military Organization in Warsaw. It shows that residents of the ghetto were well aware of the existence of the Treblinka death camp, the place where hundreds of thousands of former Warsaw residents had been killed the previous year. A small revolt took place at about the same time that this notice appeared but was quickly crushed. A larger uprising began three months later and raged across Warsaw for nearly a month before German troops were able to put it down.

We are rising up for war!

We are of those who have set themselves the aim of awakening the people. Our wish is to take this watchword to our people:

> *Awake and fight!*

> *Do not despair of the road to escape!*

Know that escape is not to be found by walking to your death passively, like sheep to the slaughter. It is to be found in something much greater: in war!

Whoever defends himself has a chance of being saved! Whoever gives up self-defense from the outset—he has lost already!

Nothing awaits him except only a hideous death in the suffocation-machine of Treblinka.

> *Let the people awaken to war!*

Find the courage in your soul for desperate action!

Put an end to our terrible acceptance of such phrases as:

We are all under sentence of death!

It is a lie!!!

We were destined to live! We too have a right to life!

One only needs to know how to fight for it!

It is no great art to live when life is given to you *willingly!*

But there is an art to life just when they are trying to rob you of this life.

> *Let the people awaken and fight for its life!*

Let every mother be a lioness defending her young!

Let no father stand by and see the blood of his children in silence!

Let not the first act of our destruction be repeated!

An end to despair and lack of faith!

An end to the spirit of slavery amongst us!

Let the tyrant pay with the blood of his body for every soul in Israel!

Let every house become a fortress for us!

> *Let the people awaken to war!*

In war lies your salvation!

Whoever defends himself has a hope of escape!

We are rising in the name of the war for the lives of the helpless masses whom we seek to save, whom we must arouse to action! It is not for ourselves alone that we wish to fight. We will be entitled to save ourselves only when we have completed our duty! *As long as the life of a Jew is still in danger, even one, single, life, we have to be ready to fight!!!!*

Our watchword is:

Not even one more Jew is to find his end in Treblinka!

Out with the traitors to the people!

War for life or death on the conqueror to our last breath!

> *Be prepared to act!*
> *Be ready!*

Source: Jewish Historical Institute, Warsaw, Poland; Ringelblum Archive, file number Ring 11/333. Reprinted in *Documents on the Holocaust, Selected Sources on the Destruction of the Jews of Germany and Austria, Poland, and the Soviet Union.* Edited by Y. Arad, Y. Gutman, and A. Margaliot. Jerusalem: Yad Vashem, 1981.

12.3
Communique from the Warsaw Ghetto Uprising – 1943
Excerpt from a Letter Written by Mordecai Anilewicz

The armed revolt that began in Warsaw in April 1943 became a prolonged battle that stretched well into May. One of the foremost leaders of the uprising was twenty-four-year-old Mordecai Anilewicz. The following is a letter he wrote to one of his compatriots who was outside the ghetto while the fighting was going on. In the end Anilewicz and most of the other Jewish fighters were killed.

Dear Itzhak:

… Let's leave out this time personal matters. I must tell you how I and my comrades feel; something happened beyond our wildest dreams: the Germans twice ran away from the ghetto. One of our units held out 40 minutes, another more than six hours. The mine we laid in the area of the brushmakers' shop exploded. When we heard that members of the P.P.R. attacked the Germans and the radio station "Swit" broadcast wonderful news about our self-defense—I had the feeling of perfection. There is, of course, plenty of work to do yet, but what was done until now was done perfectly…

Many fires in the ghetto. Yesterday the hospital was burning. Whole blocks of houses are on fire… By day we sit in hiding places.

I cannot describe to you the conditions under which Jews live. Only exceptional individuals will survive. The rest will die, sooner or later. Their fate is sealed. In all the bunkers where our comrades are hiding it is already impossible to light a candle for lack of air.

As of this evening we are switching to partisan methods of action. Three units are going out tonight, with two tasks: armed patrol and acquisition of weapons.

You should know that the pistol is of no use. We hardly made use of it. What we need is grenades, rifles, machine guns and explosives.

I don't know what else to write to you. I can imagine that you have many questions, but let this be enough for you this time.

Keep well. Perhaps we'll still see each other. What's most important: the dream of my life has become a reality. I lived to see Jewish defense in the ghetto in all its greatness and splendor.

Mordecai
23, April 1943

Source: Meed, Vladka. *On Both Sides of the Wall: Memoirs from the Warsaw Ghetto.* Beit Lohamei Haghetaot, Israel: Ghetto Fighters' House and Hakibbutz Hameuchad Publishing House, 1972.

12.4
Battling German Troops in the Streets of Warsaw – 1943
Excerpt from a Shoah *Interview with Simha Rottem*

> *Simha Rottem (also known as "Kajik") was one of the few Warsaw ghetto fighters who survived the uprising. In this recollection, which was featured in the acclaimed documentary film* Shoah, *he describes the grim conditions endured by the fighters.*

At Passover time we felt something was going to happen in the ghetto. We could feel the pressure. On Passover eve the Germans attacked. Not just the Germans, but the Ukrainians too, along with the Lithuanians, the Polish police, and the Latvians, and this massive force entered the ghetto. We felt this was the end. On the morning the Germans went into the ghetto, the attack was concentrated on the central ghetto. We were a little away from it; we heard blasts, shots, the echo of the gunfire, and we knew the fighting was fierce in the central ghetto.

During the first three days of fighting, the Jews had the upper hand. The Germans retreated at once to the ghetto entrance, carrying dozens of wounded with them. From then on, their onslaught came entirely from the outside, through air attack and artillery. We couldn't resist the bombing, especially their method of setting fire to the ghetto. The whole ghetto was ablaze. All life vanished from the streets and houses. We hid in the cellars and bunkers. From there we made our sorties. We went out at night. The Germans were in the ghetto mostly by day, leaving at night. They were afraid to enter the ghetto at night.

> *"Besides fighting the Germans, we fought hunger, and thirst. We had no contact with the outside world; we were completely isolated, cut off from the world."*

The bunkers were prepared by the residents, not by the fighters. When we could no longer stay in the streets, we fell back on the bunkers. All the bunkers were alike inside. The most striking thing was the crowding, for there were a lot of us, and the heat. It was so hot you couldn't breathe. Not even a candle could burn in those bunkers. To breathe in that intense heat, you sometimes had to lie with your face to the ground. The fact that we fighters hadn't prepared bunkers proves we didn't expect to survive our fight against the Germans.

I don't think the human tongue can describe the horror we went through in the ghetto. In the streets, if you can call them that, for nothing was left of the streets, we had to step over heaps of corpses. There was no room to get around them. Besides fighting the Germans, we fought hunger, and thirst. We had no contact with the outside world; we were completely isolated, cut off from the world. We were in such a state that we could no longer understand the very meaning of why we went on fighting. We thought of attempting a breakout to the Aryan part of Warsaw, outside the ghetto.

Just before May 1 Sigmund and I were sent to try to contact Antek in Aryan Warsaw. We found a tunnel under Bonifratérska Street that led out into Aryan Warsaw. Early in the morning we suddenly emerged into a street in broad daylight. Imagine us on that sunny May 1, stunned to find ourselves in the street, among normal people. We'd come from another planet. People immediately jumped on us, because we certainly looked exhausted, skinny, in rags. Around the ghetto there were always suspicious Poles who grabbed Jews. By a miracle, we escaped them. In Aryan Warsaw, life went on as naturally and normally as before. The cafés operated normally, the restaurants, buses, streetcars, and movies were open. The ghetto was an isolated island amid normal life.

Our job was to contact Itzhak Zuckermann to try to mount a rescue operation, to try to save the few fighters who might still be alive in the ghetto. We managed to contact Zuckermann. We found two sewer workers. On the night of May

8-9 we decided to return to the ghetto with another buddy, Rijek, and the two sewer men. After the curfew we entered the sewers. We were entirely at the mercy of the two workmen, since only they knew the ghetto's underground layout. Halfway there they decided to turn back, they tried to drop us, and we had to threaten them with our guns. We went on through the sewers until one of the workmen told us we were under the ghetto. Rijek guarded them so they couldn't escape. I raised the manhole cover to go up into the ghetto.

At bunker Mila 18 [the headquarters of the Jewish Combat Organization], I missed them by a day. I had returned the night of May 8-9. The Germans found the bunker on the morning of the eighth. Most of its survivors committed suicide, or succumbed to gas in the bunkers. I went to bunker Francziskanska 22. There was no answer when I yelled the password, so I had to go on through the ghetto. I suddenly heard a woman calling from the ruins. It was darkest night, no lights, you saw nothing. All the houses were in ruins, and I heard only one voice. I thought some evil spell had been cast on me, a woman's voice talking from the rubble. I circled the ruins. I didn't look at my watch, but I must have spent a half hour exploring, trying to find the woman whose voice guided me, but unfortunately I didn't find her.

Were there fires?

Strictly speaking, no, for the flames had died down, but there was still smoke, and that awful smell of charred flesh of people who had surely been burned alive. I continued on my way, going to other bunkers in search of fighting units, but it was the same everywhere. I'd give the password: "Jan."

That's a Polish first name, Jan?

Right. And I got no answer. I went from bunker to bunker, and after walking for hours in the ghetto, I went back toward the sewers…

I was alone all the time. Except for that woman's voice, and a man I met as I came out of the sewers, I was alone throughout my tour of the ghetto. I didn't meet a living soul. At one point I recall feeling a kind of peace, of serenity. I said to myself: "I'm the last Jew. I'll wait for morning, and for the Germans."

Source: Lanzmann, Claude. *Shoah: An Oral History of the Holocaust.* New York: Pantheon Books, 1985.

12.5
"The Warsaw Ghetto is No More" – 1943
Official Report on the Destruction of the Warsaw Ghetto by Jürgen Stroop

Jürgen Stroop was the German S.S. commander who was placed in charge of putting down the Jewish resistance in the Warsaw Ghetto. He composed the following report at the conclusion of the fighting. His report details the tenacious attacks carried out by the Jewish fighters, both women and men.

THE WARSAW GHETTO IS NO MORE ...

I myself arrived in Warsaw on 17 April 1943 and took over the command of the action on 19 April 1943, 0800 hours, the action itself having started the same day at 0600 hours.

Before the large-scale action began, the limits of the former Ghetto had been blocked by an external barricade in order to prevent the Jews from breaking out. This barricade was maintained from the start to the end of the action and was especially reinforced at night.

When we invaded the Ghetto for the first time, the Jews and the Polish bandits succeeded in repelling the participating units, including tanks and armored cars, by a well-prepared concentration of fire. When I ordered a second attack, about 0800 hours, I distributed the units, separated from each other by indicated lines, and charged them with combing out the whole of the Ghetto, each unit for a certain part. Although firing commenced again, we now succeeded in combing out the blocks according to plan. The enemy was forced to retire from the roofs and elevated bases to the basements, dug-outs, and sewers. In order to prevent their escaping into the sewers, the sewerage system was dammed up below the Ghetto and filled with water, but the Jews frustrated this plan to a great extent by blowing up the turning off valves. Late the first day we encountered rather heavy resistance, but it was quickly broken by a special raiding party. In the course of further operations we succeeded in expelling the Jews from their prepared resistance bases, sniper holes, and the like, and in occupying during the 20 and 21 April the greater part of the so-called remainder of the Ghetto to such a degree that the resistance continued within these blocks could no longer be called considerable.

The main Jewish battle group, mixed with Polish bandits, had already retired during the first and second day to the so-called Muranowski Square. There, it was reinforced by a considerable number of Polish bandits. Its plan was to hold the Ghetto by every means in order to prevent us from invading it. The Jewish and Polish standards were hoisted at the top of a concrete building as a challenge to us. These two standards, however, were captured on the second day of the action by a special raiding party. SS Untersturmfuehrer Dehmke fell in this skirmish with the bandits; he was holding in his hand a hand-grenade which was hit by the enemy and exploded, injuring him fatally. After only a few days I realized that the original plan had no prospect of success, unless the armament factories and other enterprises of military importance distributed throughout the Ghetto were dissolved. It was therefore necessary to approach these firms and to give them appropriate time for being evacuated and immediately transferred. Thus one of these firms after the other was dealt with, and we very soon deprived the Jews and bandits of their chance to take refuge time and again in these enterprises, which were under the supervision of the Armed Forces. In order to decide how much time was necessary to evacuate these enterprises thorough inspections were necessary. The conditions discovered there are indescribable. I cannot imagine a greater chaos than in the Ghetto of Warsaw. The Jews had control of everything, from the chemical substances used in manufacturing explosives to clothing and equipment for the Armed Forces. The managers knew so little of their own shops that the Jews were in a position to produce inside these shops arms of every kind, especially hand grenades, Molotov cocktails, and the like.

Moreover, the Jews had succeeded in fortifying some of these factories as centers of resistance. Such a center of resistance in an Army accommodation office had to be attacked as early as the second day of the action by an Engineer's Unit equipped with flame throwers and by artillery. The Jews were so firmly established in this shop that it proved to be impossible to induce them to leave it voluntarily; I therefore resolved to destroy this shop the next day by fire...

The number of Jews forcibly taken out of the buildings and arrested was relatively small during the first few days. It transpired that the Jews had taken to hiding in the sewers and in specially erected dug-outs. Whereas we had assumed during the first days that there were only scattered dug-outs, we learned in the course of the large-scale action that the whole Ghetto was systematically equipped with cellars, dug-outs, and passages. In every case these passages and dug-outs were connected with the sewer system. Thus, the Jews were able to maintain undisturbed subterranean traffic. They also used this sewer network for escaping subterraneously into the Aryan part of the city of Warsaw. Continuously, we received reports of attempts of Jews to escape through the sewer holes. While pretending to build air-raid shelters they had been erecting dug-outs within the former Ghetto ever since the autumn of 1942. These were intended to conceal every Jew during the new evacuation action, which they had expected for quite a time, and to enable them to resist the invaders in a concerted action. Through posters, handbills, and whisper propaganda, the communistic resistance movement actually brought it about that the Jews entered the dug-outs as soon as the new large-scale operation started. How far their precautions went can be seen from the fact that many of the dug-outs had been skillfully equipped with furnishings sufficient for entire families, washing and bathing facilities, toilets, arms and munition supplies, and food supplies sufficient for several months. There were differently equipped dug-outs for rich and for poor Jews. To discover the individual dug-outs was difficult for the units, as they had been efficiently camouflaged. In many cases, it was possible only through betrayal on the part of the Jews.

When only a few days had passed, it became apparent that the Jews no longer had any intention to resettle voluntarily, but were determined to resist evacuation with all their force and by using all the weapons at their disposal. So-called battle groups had been formed, led by Polish-Bolshevists; they were armed and paid any price asked for available arms.

During the large-scale action we succeeded in catching some Jews who had already been evacuated and resettled in Lublin or Troolinka, but had broken out from there and returned to the Ghetto, equipped with arms and ammunition. Time and again Polish bandits found refuge in the Ghetto and remained there undisturbed, since we had no forces at our disposal to comb out this maze. Whereas it had been possible during the first days to catch considerable numbers of Jews, who are cowards by nature, it became more and more difficult during the second half of the action to capture the bandits and Jews. Over and over again new battle groups consisting of 20 to 30 or more Jewish fellows, 18 to 25 years of age, accompanied by a corresponding number of women kindled new resistance. These battle groups were under orders to put up armed resistance to the last and if necessary to escape arrest by committing suicide. One such battle group succeeded in mounting a truck by ascending from a sewer in the so-called Prosta, and in escaping with it (about 30 to 35 bandits). One bandit who had arrived with this truck exploded 2 hand grenades, which was the agreed signal for the bandits waiting in the sewer to climb out of it. The bandits and Jews—there were Polish bandits among these gangs armed with carbines, small arms, and in one case a light machine gun, mounted the truck and drove away in an unknown direction. The last member of this gang, who was on guard in the sewer and was detailed to close the lid of the sewer hole, was captured. It was he who gave the above information. The search for the truck was unfortunately without result.

During this armed resistance the women belonging to the battle groups were equipped the same as the men; some were members of the Chaluzim movement. Not infrequently, these women fired pistols with both hands. It happened time and again that these women had pistols or hand grenades (Polish "pineapple" hand grenades) concealed in their bloomers up to the last moment to use against the men of the Waffen SS, Police, or Wehrmacht.

The resistance put up by the Jews and bandits could be broken only by relentlessly using all our force and energy by day and night. *On 23 April 1943 the Reichs Fuehrer SS issued through the higher SS and Police Fuehrer East at Cracow his order to complete the combing out of the Warsaw Ghetto with the greatest severity and relentless tenacity.* I therefore decided to destroy the entire Jewish residential area by setting every block on fire, including the blocks of residential buildings near the armament works. One concern after the other was systematically evacuated and subsequently destroyed by fire. The Jews then emerged from their hiding places and dug-outs in almost every case. Not infrequently, the Jews stayed in the burning buildings until, because of the heat and the fear of being burned alive[,] they preferred to jump down from the upper stories after having thrown mattresses and other upholstered articles into the street from the burning buildings. With their bones broken, they still tried to crawl across the street into blocks of buildings which had not yet been set on fire or were only partly in flames. Often Jews changed their hiding places during the night, by moving into the ruins of burnt-out buildings, taking refuge there until they were found by our patrols. Their stay in the sewers also ceased to be pleasant after the first week. Frequently from the street, we could hear loud voices coming through the sewer shafts. Then the men of the Waffen SS, the Police or the Wehrmacht Engineers courageously climbed down the shafts to bring out the Jews and not infrequently they then stumbled over Jews already dead, or were shot at. It was always necessary to use smoke candles to drive out the Jews. Thus one day we opened 183 sewer entrance holes and at a fixed time lowered smoke candles into them, with the result that the bandits fled from what they believed to be gas to the center of the former Ghetto, where they could then be pulled out of the sewer holes there. A great number of Jews, who could not be counted, were exterminated by blowing up sewers and dug-outs.

The longer the resistance lasted, the tougher the men of the Waffen SS, Police, and Wehrmacht became; they fulfilled their duty indefatigably in faithful comradeship and stood together as models and examples of soldiers. Their duty hours often lasted from early morning until late at night. At night, search patrols with rags wound round their feet remained at the heels of the Jews and gave them no respite. Not infrequently they caught and killed Jews who used the night hours for supplementing their stores from abandoned dug-outs and for contacting neighboring groups or exchanging news with them…

Only through the continuous and untiring work of all involved did we succeed in catching a total of 56,065 Jews whose extermination can be proved. To this should be added the number of Jews who lost their lives in explosions or fires but whose numbers could not be ascertained…

The large-scale action was terminated on 16 May 1943 with the blowing up of the Warsaw synagogue at 2015 hours.

Now, there are no more factories in the former Ghetto. All the goods, raw materials, and machines there have been moved and stored somewhere else. All buildings etc., have been destroyed. The only exception is the so-called Dzielna Prison of the Security Police, which was exempted from destruction.

III.

Although the large-scale operation has been completed, we have to reckon with the possibility that a few Jews are still living in the ruins of the former Ghetto; therefore, this area must be firmly shut off from the Aryan residential area and be guarded. Police Battalion III/23 has been charged with this duty. This Police Battalion has instructions to watch the former Ghetto, particularly to prevent anybody from entering the former Ghetto, and to shoot immediately anybody found inside the Ghetto without authority. The Commander of the Police Battalion will continue to receive further direct orders from the SS and Police Fuehrer. In this way, it should be possible to keep the small remainder of Jews there, if any, under constant pressure and to exterminate them eventually. The remaining Jews and bandits must be deprived of any chance of survival by destroying all remaining buildings and refuges and cutting off the water supply.

It is proposed to change the Dzielna Prison into a concentration camp and to use the inmates to remove, collect and hand over for reuse the millions of bricks, the scrap-iron, and other materials.

IV.

Of the total of 56,065 Jews caught, about 7,000 were exterminated within the former Ghetto in the course of the large-scale action, and 6,929 by transporting them to T.II, which means 14,000 Jews were exterminated altogether. Beyond the number of 56,065 Jews an estimated number of 5,000 to 6,000 were killed by explosions or in fires.

The number of destroyed dug-outs amounts to 631...

Apart from 8 buildings (Police Barracks, hospital, and accommodations for housing working-parties) the former Ghetto is completely destroyed. Only the dividing walls are left standing where no explosions were carried out. But the ruins still contain a vast amount of stones and scrap material which could be used.

Warsaw, 16 May, 1943.

The SS and Police Fuehrer in the District of Warsaw.
SS Brigadefuehrer and Majorgeneral of Police.

Source: Stroop, Jürgen. "The Warsaw Ghetto is No More," May 16, 1943. Reprinted as Document 1061-PS in *Nazi Conspiracy and Aggression.* Vol. 3. Washington, DC: United States Government Printing Office, 1946.

12.6
An S.S. Commander Describes Jewish Resistance Efforts in One Polish District – 1943
Excerpt from "Solution of the Jewish Problem in the District of Galicia" by Fritz Katzmann

Fritz Katzmann was the S.S. and Police Leader in the District of Galicia in Poland. In this report, dated June 30, 1943, Katzmann details some of the Jewish resistance efforts that the German forces faced in Poland. Throughout his report, he refers to the Jewish men and women who took up arms against their murderous tormentors as "gangsters."

The smaller the number of Jews remaining in the district, the harder their resistance. Arms of all kinds, among them those of Italian make, were used for defense. The Jews purchased these Italian arms from Italian soldiers stationed in the District for high sums in Zloty currency. The ensuing photos give a small selection from the arms confiscated. Especially dangerous were the sawed-off carbines of all kinds. [Photographs omitted.]

Underground bunkers were found with entrances concealed in a masterly manner opening some times into flats, some times into the open. In most cases the entrances had only so much width that just one person could crawl through it. The access was concealed in such a manner that it could not be found by persons not acquainted with the locality. Here nothing succeeded but the assistance of some Jews to whom anything whatever was promised in exchange. What these dug-outs looked like will be shown by the ensuing photographs together with their comments: [Photographs omitted.]

In the course of the evacuation action we furthermore discovered that the Jews attempted more than ever to escape to foreign countries. These attempts were made by Jews in possession of considerable amounts of money, jewels, and of forged papers. They tried every means to effect their purpose and often approached members of the German and allied Forces with the request to transport them to or beyond the frontier by way of military cars. They offered in exchange disproportionally high amounts, in many cases up to 5,000 Zl. And more a person. Although in a few cases members of foreign forces, especially Hungarians, came to an agreement with them and fulfilled their part, in by far the most cases the Security Police was informed in time by V-men so that the necessary counter-measures were applied, the Jews caught, and the valuables confiscated. By way of illustration some cases are described:

In September 1942 the office of the SS & Police Leader was informed by an Italian soldier (of German blood resident in Switzerland) that some Jews were concealed within the Italian barracks in Lwow, who were to be smuggled across the frontier by members of the Italian Forces within the next days. Shortly before they intended to start, two leaders in mufti entered the barracks and succeeded in arresting a group of seven persons and confiscating 3,200 gold dollars and a large amount of diamonds and jewels. They made the interesting discovery that already 970 gold dollars had been paid for bribing 4 members of the Italian Forces. This money was confiscated also. The Italian soldiers thereupon were sent home.

On 13 May 1943 two German Drivers of the Luftwaffe Headquarters in Cracow reported that a Jew had approached them with the request to transport about 20 to 30 Jews from the Jewish camp Lwow to Brody; some of them were in possession of arms; they would provide forged transport orders; directed to these military drivers. In exchange they offered 20,000 Zl. The drivers were ordered to accept the offers, to load the Jews on the Luftwaffe car the 15 May at 5 p.m., to start in the direction of Brody, but to turn the car as soon as it passed the office of NSKK Lwow which was situated at this street, and to drive into the court yard of this office. In fact the car, manned with 20 Jews and one Pole, arrived in this court yard at 5:30 p.m. The Jews, some of whom were armed with charged pistols and sawed-off carbines with the safety devices released, were overwhelmed by a waiting detachment and disarmed...

After a diligent search, considerable valuables were found and confiscated. A diligent interrogation of the arrested Jews led to the discovery that a certain Jew by the name of Horowitz who was staying in the woods near Brody together with a larger group of Jews, used to organize such transports. As a result of this interrogation it was possible moreover to arrest those Jews who forged identity papers for fugitives. The Pole who was arrested at the same time, confessed to be a member of the Polish Resistance Movement "PPR". Furthermore he named the Jew Horowitz as the Chief Executive of the "PPR" in Lwow. The place of communication in the woods near Brody having been discovered by these interrogations, the whole of this wood area was surrounded and combed out by detachments of the Gendarmerie and of the Ukrainian Police, and two companies of the German Army on the same day. These forces met smaller forces of armed bandits who had established themselves in several furnished dug-outs and trenches dating from the Russian occupation. The bandits in all cases used their arms, but they all were overwhelmed and rendered harmless.

33 Jewish bandits were shot. Some sawed-off carbines and some quick-firing rifles and pistols of Russian make were confiscated. Polish game-keeper taking part in the combing-out action was shot dead by the bandits. During the arrests in Lwow, one SS-man was wounded by a shot into the left shank. The 2 German drivers were paid as recompense for their exemplary conduct 2,000 Zl. Each. The forged marching-orders and transport orders found in possession of the Jews are reproduced below. [Transport order omitted.]

In the same way we succeeded on May 21, 1943 in destroying a Jewish gang who again were armed with 0.8 cal. Pistols of Italian origin. (In the meantime all Italian soldiers left the district of Galicia.)

Only some days later, the 31 May, we succeeded again, during a new comb-out, in destroying 6 dug-outs of major size containing 139 Jewish bandits.

On June 2, 1943, again some Jews who attempted to escape to Hungary by means of a military car owned by the Hungarian Army, were arrested and, since they resisted, shot. Here again considerable values were confiscated. The Hungarian soldiers participating in the action were adequately rewarded.

The evacuation having been completed, nevertheless, still minor actions are necessary in order to track Jews in hiding and concealment. This is proved by the fact that every day some persons are caught in possession of forged identity cards and passes. Some forged identity cards, passes, marching orders, and leave passes are enclosed herewith. [Cards and photographs omitted.]

Since we received more and more alarming reports on the Jews becoming armed in an ever increasing manner, we started during the last fortnight in June 1943 an action throughout the whole of the district of Galicia with the intent to use strongest measures to destroy the Jewish gangsterdom. Special measures were found necessary during the action to dissolve the Ghetto in Lwow where the dug-outs mentioned above had been established. Here we had to act brutally from the beginning, in order to avoid losses on our side; we had to blow up or to burn down several houses. On this occasion the surprising fact arose that we were able to catch about 20,000 Jews instead of 12,000 Jews who had registered. We had to pull at least 3,000 Jewish corpses out of every kind of hiding places; they had committed suicide by taking poison.

Our own losses suffered in these actions:

Spotted Fever:	dead-1 man	fallen ill:	120 men
Shot by Jews:	dead-7 men	wounded:	12 men
Stabbed by Jews:	dead-1 man		

Lost by accident in evacuation action: dead: 2 men, wounded: 5 men.

Despite the extraordinary burden heaped upon every single SS-Police Officer during these actions, mood and spirit of the men were extraordinarily good and praiseworthy from the first to the last day.

Only thanks to the sense of duty of every single leader and man have we succeeded to get rid of this PLAGUE in so short a time.

Source: Katzmann, Fritz. "Solution of the Jewish Problem in the District of Galicia," June 30, 1943. Reprinted as Document L-18 in *Nazi Conspiracy and Aggression*. Vol. 7. Washington, DC: United States Government Printing Office, 1946.

13

HIDING AND ESCAPE

Numerous Jewish families sought to escape the Nazi nightmare by going into hiding. Clara and Frieda Isaacman (right and left, respectively) successfully hid out with their parents and brother in Nazi-occupied Antwerp, Belgium, for more than two years.

INTRODUCTION

The most successful efforts in evading the Nazi murder machine came not from mass uprisings but from the efforts of individuals to shield themselves or others. Jews went into hiding to avoid all manner of Nazi persecution, including the early concentration camp arrests of the 1930s, the confinement to ghettos, and the deportations to the extermination camps. Of course, hiding meant that the Jews had to somehow make themselves invisible or indistinguishable to the gentile world, which usually required the help of non-Jews. It is here that the history of the Holocaust, which is dominated by accounts of astonishing cruelty and avarice, unveils inspiring tales of selflessness and courage on the part of people whose strong sense of compassion led them to put their own lives at risk.

Memoirs such as Clara Isaacman's *Clara's Story,* meanwhile, showed the courage of ordinary Jewish people threatened by Nazi terror. Indeed, the most famous piece of Holocaust literature, Anne Frank's *The Diary of a Girl,* tells the true story of two Jewish families—the Franks and the Van Daans—who hid in an Amsterdam office building for two years after the Nazis invaded the Netherlands. Throughout these months of fear and confinement, Frank and the other seven Jews in hiding relied on non-Jewish friends to keep them safe and fed. Their presence was eventually discovered by an informer, however, and on August 4, 1944, the Gestapo raided the hideout and arrested everyone. A month later they were deported to Auschwitz-Birkenau. Several of the hideaways died there, while others perished in other camps or death marches. Anne and her sister ended up in at the concentration camp in Belsen, Germany, where they both died of disease and starvation in late February or early March 1945. The only person to survive was Anne's father, Otto, who oversaw publication of Anne's diary following the war. While Frank's story and many others ended tragically, many Jewish families saved themselves by going into hiding or by arranging other forms of escape.

In one memorable instance, hiding and rescuing Jews became a nationwide undertaking. Denmark, which had come under German control in 1940, had a population of about 8,000 Jews. In 1943 the Nazis planned to begin deporting them to the death camps. The operation was scheduled to begin on October 1, but news of the impending arrests spread through the country in advance. In a widespread action that involved hundreds of non-Jewish Danes, more than 7,000 Jews went into hiding and were smuggled to safety in Sweden aboard small Danish fishing boats. In the end, fewer than 100 of the Jews residing in Denmark at the beginning of the occupation were killed by the Nazis. Denmark's refusal to submit to the Nazi evil constitutes one of the most successful acts of defiance in the Holocaust story.

Another admirable saga of rescue took place in Hungary in 1944, where Raoul Wallenberg, a Swedish citizen, managed to save thousands of people who would have otherwise faced deportation to the death camps. Basing himself at the Swedish embassy in Budapest and drawing on the financial backing of the United States and international Jewish agencies, Wallenberg devised a variety of schemes to shield potential Holocaust victims. He issued an estimated 20,000 passports, giving diplomatic protection to those who received them. He also deposited 12,000 people at safe houses that were declared extensions of the embassy, thereby granting the residents diplomatic immunity. After the war, Wallenberg was detained by Soviet authorities who accused him of being a U.S. spy, and he disappeared from public view. The Soviets later reported that he died in their custody in 1947, but several testimonies have claimed that Wallenberg was still alive in the Soviet prison system as late as the 1960s.

13.1
A Jewish Girl Recalls Going into Hiding – 1942
Excerpt from Clara's Story *by Clara Isaacman*

Born in Romania, Clara Isaacman moved to Antwerp, Belgium, with her parents when she was young. When the German army captured Belgium in 1940, the family tried to escape but failed. Soon the Nazis began implementing their typical anti-Jewish actions in Antwerp. Isaacman's older brother was forced into a labor camp and was eventually killed at Auschwitz-Birkenau. The rest of the family—her parents, sister Frieda, and brother Elie—decided to go into hiding in 1942 in order to avoid a similar fate. They spent the next two and a half years in hiding. It proved a wise decision, as all of them except for Isaacman's father survived the Nazi occupation. After the war was over and Adolf Hitler had been defeated, Isaacman said that "for many years I found it too difficult to talk about the cruelty and viciousness that I had witnessed." Over time, however, she decided that she could no longer remain silent, in part because "[so] many people had risked their lives to save mine. They were not all Jews, but they understood and practiced the ideals that are common to all faiths. They valued human life, regardless of religion or nationality. Some of these brave, selfless people perished in the attempt to save their country and to keep people like me and my family alive."

Isaacman's life as a fugitive began when Mr. Yeager, a member of the anti-Nazi resistance, found her family a place to stay. Soon their lives became a strange mixture of extreme fear and utter boredom, as the following excerpt from her memoir Clara's Story *shows.*

July-December 1942

"Arrangements have made for you to stay with a family named Adams," Mr. Yeager announced. "Clara, I think you know one of their sons. You will be taken to their home tonight, after dark. We must move you in two groups; you are less likely to arouse suspicion that way. Please make yourselves ready."

Reprinted from *Clara's Story,* © 1984 by Clara Isaacman, published by the Jewish Publication Society with the permission of the publisher.

With a nod to Daddy and a quick bow to Mama he was gone as quickly and as quietly as he had come. We packed our few belongings. After Daddy said the evening prayers, we ate the last of our food and settled down once more to wait.

At nine o'clock, just as the sky was turning dark, Mr. Yeager returned with Mr. Adams. Adams was a meek man, of average height, bald, and thin. He shook hands with Mama and Daddy. When they thanked him for helping us, he murmured that he was glad to do it. He was a trolley-car conductor and had obtained trolley tickets for everyone. Holding Elie's hand, Mama announced that she and Elie would go with Mr. Yeager. Daddy, Frieda, and I were to go with Mr. Adams.

The trip seemed endless, fraught with dangerous, unthinkable consequences. We were breaking so many regulations, traveling after curfew and sitting on the trolleys. But all this was necessary. We were pretending that we were not Jews, but Belgian citizens going about our normal business. Dear God, I prayed, please, please let us all arrive at Mr. Adams's house safely. Don't let any soldiers stop my family.

We arrived at a modest, two-story row house in a working-class neighborhood. As the two families were solemnly introduced to each other, the Adamses assured us that we were safe. They and their five children could be trusted not to tell anyone they were hiding Jews. Robert, the Adamses' oldest son, and I greeted each other gravely. We had been in some of the same classes in elementary school. Seeing a familiar face was somehow reassuring.

Mrs. Adams, a severe-looking woman, explained the living arrangements. Their family slept on the second floor. The first floor had four rooms. She led the way as we walked through the house. First was a living room, then a kitchen. Behind the kitchen was a small spare room. The only piece of furniture in the spare room was a narrow bed.

"This is your room," the woman announced. "The children will have to sleep on the floor."

We looked around our cramped quarters as she continued.

"You are to stay in your room except when you are preparing or eating your meals or using the bathroom. You will give me the money to buy your food. Mrs. Heller, you may use the kitchen when I am out or when we are through eating. Under no circumstances are you to answer a knock on the door or look out a window. You will please remember that. Because we are hiding Jews, we are risking as much as you."

We nodded our understanding to each of her conditions. I sensed that she was not happy about our being in her house. Apparently it had been Mr. Adams's idea to shelter Jews in danger. Mrs. Adams was cooperating only for the extra income we would provide.

At first it was strange to sleep on the floor in the same room as our parents and to spend whole days doing almost nothing, never going out. But we soon became accustomed to our surroundings, and our lives settled into a steady routine. Even though there were twelve people living in close quarters, sharing one bathroom and one kitchen, the two families lived completely independently of one another. Mrs. Adams had made it clear that this was the only way she could house another family. She and her husband were liberal-minded Catholics who felt that Jews were people like anyone else. But hiding them was strictly business.

On weekday mornings we stayed in our room until Mr. and Mrs. Adams were gone for the day. When school started in September, we heard the children getting ready to leave, Mrs. Adams preparing breakfast, Mr. Adams leaving for work. Once the house was quiet we were free to move about. Mrs. Adams spent most mornings at the local market. In the afternoon she liked to sit in the kitchen drinking whiskey, which made Mama nervous. We walked around the house without shoes and spoke in whispers, careful not to make any noise so that the neighbors on either side who shared walls with the Adamses would think the house was empty during the day. Each day was like the one before. There was no schedule. There was little to do. Our lives were punctuated by meals and by the coming and going of our hosts. We devised a system of knocks so that the Adamses could warn us if guests were coming. When we heard a warning knock, we would all run back to our room and wait in silence until the visitors left.

Of all the Adamses, Robert was the most sensitive to our situation. He often brought us games and books, and I thought he would have enjoyed spending more time with us had his mother not been so strict.

As days stretched into weeks, Mama and Daddy devised a program of instruction for us. They worried about all the schooling we were missing, so part of every day was spent studying. Mama was fluent in many languages. We spoke Yiddish among ourselves; but when she was growing up in Romania, she had spoken Romanian and German as well. She had studied French in school and had learned Flemish and English in the ten years she had been in Belgium. She and Daddy knew Hungarian, too, which they spoke when they did not want us to understand what they were saying. Mama started to teach us all the languages she knew, with special emphasis on English.

Daddy discussed philosophy and history with us. He and Mama always valued our opinions, so it seemed natural to us to examine our own situation with them in terms of history and ideas. Suddenly all the dry facts of Jewish history I had studied in school came alive as we talked. Daddy reminded us that the Jew's strength was also his burden. We had been persecuted through the ages because we had clung to our heritage. Our proud traditions and beliefs, which had become the basis for some of the world's other great religions, set us apart. We were fated always to appear different from other people, and this difference was often perceived by others as a threat. I had heard these words and ideas so many times—in classrooms, in synagogue, and in our home. But they never meant as much to me as when they were spoken in hiding, surrounded by terror and war. Daddy recounted the famous stories we all knew by heart: the Purim story about the struggle between Haman and the Jews of Shushan, when Esther's courage saved Jews from the gallows; the story of Masada, where Jews died rather than submit to Roman rule; the tales of the Spanish Inquisition, when the Marranos held fast to their Judaism in spite of the threat of torture and death by burning at the stake.

> *"I was terribly frightened each time [my father] went out and left us alone. I felt as though I hung suspended over a fearful chasm, dangling from a frayed rope."*

As my father spoke, a pattern began to emerge, a theme that helped me to see our own situation as the latest event in the long struggle for freedom. I also understood the difference between our troubles and those of our ancestors. In the last hundred years the world had become industrialized, mechanized. Haman's power in a small city in Mesopotamia thousands of years before was greatly multiplied by Hitler, who had all the resources of a modern republic at his command. Hitler had the means to exterminate the entire Jewish population of Europe.

"Our job, our sacred duty," Daddy said, "is to stay alive. You must not see our hiding as an act of cowardice. We must survive in order to preserve Judaism. We are soldiers in the struggle for survival, and our battle is just as important as what is happening on the front."

When we were not having discussions or reading, we played games. Everyone took turns keeping Elie occupied, playing chess and checkers for hours. Sometimes, especially when I was reading a good book, I almost forgot where I was. But then my attention would drift, and I had the feeling I was fading. Like words erased from a page, I seemed to exist only as a faint shadow.

Almost every afternoon when Mama went to the kitchen to prepare our evening meal, she found Mrs. Adams sitting at the kitchen table, a glass and a bottle of whiskey in front of her.

"A woman who drinks can't be trusted," Mama complained to Daddy. "How long will it be before she tells a neighbor about us."

"She's too frightened for her own safety to betray us," Daddy replied.

"She's using the money we pay her to buy liquor instead of food for her family," Frieda said.

"I don't think we can stay here much longer," insisted Mama. "And what about the Adams children? I'm so afraid they'll let something slip, that they'll whisper their secret to a friend at school."

"They're terribly curious about us," I said. "Last Sunday one of the little girls asked me why don't we go to church with them."

310

Daddy tried to reassure us, saying that these were good people who had put themselves in a dangerous situation. But Mama could not stop worrying. I noticed that she was smoking more and more. She had always enjoyed cigarettes, but she had smoked only occasionally at home. Now it seemed that she was always holding a cigarette. She could no longer buy regular cigarettes, so we took turns rolling some tobacco in a little piece of paper. At first it was like a game, but soon she seemed to need cigarettes more than anything else.

Our most basic need in hiding was money. Without the money that we used to pay the Adamses, we could not imagine what would happen to us. They certainly could not afford to maintain us on their own, no matter how good their intentions. Our supply of money was shrinking, and our parents worried about it.

The day we went into hiding, Daddy had brought with him all the money he had in the house as well as a few diamonds. Now our cash was all gone, and Daddy had to sneak out every few weeks to meet a Christian friend who bought his gems. I was terribly frightened each time he went out and left us alone. I felt as though I hung suspended over a fearful chasm, dangling from a frayed rope. It was as if any sudden motion might destroy my precarious balance and I would plunge into a great nothingness. I knew that my behavior could not ensure Daddy's safety, but I needed to feel that by being very still I was helping him return to us unharmed.

The days wore on in tedious succession. Outside, Antwerp was dressing in fall colors. Children were scuffling through crisp leaves on the sidewalks. The parks and the zoo were less crowded now; the old people who lined the park benches in summer had gone inside. Children no longer sailed toy boats in the ponds, but there were lovers strolling through the park, oblivious to the weather. And there were young mothers pushing prams, their little ones swaddled in wools to protect them from the chilly air.

At the Adamses fuel was in short supply. We had to put on extra sweaters. I began to spend long hours daydreaming about the world outside. I remembered the smell of burning leaves, the sight of giant elms, their golden leaves lit by the late afternoon sun, the sounds of children racing their bicycles in the park, laughing and shouting to one another. I longed for even a glimpse out the window.

"Just a little bit longer," Mama said when she saw me struggling with the confinement. "I'm sure it will be just a little bit longer."

Her calm certainty soothed my restlessness, and I went back to my book or played another game with Elie.

Our funds dwindled. We wondered whether the diamonds were still in their hiding place in the doorpost of our house on Leeuwerick Street [where they had been secreted before the family went into hiding]. Elie wanted to go for the diamonds, but Mama and Daddy wouldn't let him. Such an errand would be terribly dangerous, they argued, and there was a good chance the diamonds were no longer there. We had heard rumors of empty Jewish homes being looted, both by Belgian citizens and by Nazi soldiers.

In December, just before Hanukkah, my parents decided that someone would have to go for the diamonds.

"I want to go," Elie insisted.

"He's too young. Let me go, Daddy," I begged.

"Perhaps it should be an adult," Mama said, "If you or I go, none of the children will be in danger."

"That's not fair," Elie cried. "I asked first."

We knew that it would probably be easier for a child to slip into the house unseen than a grownup, but Mama and Daddy hesitated exposing any of us to such danger. There seemed to be no way to settle the argument.

"Let's pick straws," I suggested. "The one who pulls the short straw runs the errand."

Mama and Daddy relented. We used five of Mama's matches. Daddy broke one off in the middle, then he held them between his thumb and forefinger with all the heads lined up evenly, the bottoms concealed in his fist. One by one we each picked a match. First Mama: she picked a long one. Then me. I pulled slowly, but it was long. Frieda pulled a long one also. There were two matches left. If Elie picked a long one, Daddy would go. Elie quickly pulled one match out of Daddy's hand. We all gasped: he had gotten his wish.

Daddy arranged for Mr. Adams to accompany Elie as close to Leeuwerick Street as possible. They would have to take several trolleys, and it would be dark. Elie would travel the last part of the journey on foot, alone. Mr. Adams agreed to wait for him at a designated spot.

They decided to go at nightfall. Everything had to be accomplished by the 7 p.m. curfew. Anyone on the street after that hour could be questioned, even shot by patrolling soldiers.

The streets were busy with people going home from work. Mama bundled Elie up warmly in coats and scarves borrowed from the Adams children, holding him close for a few moments as though she wished her love could protect him. When Elie and Mr. Adams were both ready, Mama gave Elie one last embrace, Daddy shook their hands, we all whispered, "Good luck," and then they were out the door, swallowed by the night. I envied Elie his errand, not only because he was doing something important, but because he was outside, breathing fresh air.

We sat in our room and waited. We had spent months waiting, but this was a special kind of torment. Mama started smoking nervously, one cigarette after another. Her broad, handsome face, usually so calm, was contorted with worry. Daddy sat on the edge of the bed, his elbows on his knees, holding his head in his hands.

In our minds we were all with Elie. I could picture every part of his trip. I imagined him sitting on the trolley. There would be soldiers everywhere. Elie had been instructed to behave calmly. Thank goodness it's cold, I thought, with that hat on, no one can see how dark and curly his hair is. If a soldier questioned him, Elie would reply in Flemish. Once Elie and Mr. Adams were across town they would have to travel on foot. This was as dangerous as riding the trolley because our entire neighborhood had been emptied that night in July. Anyone entering an uninhabited street after dark would look suspicious to a soldier on patrol. Alone and without lights, Elie had to go to our house, remove the doorframe, retrieve the packet, and return to where Mr. Adams waited for him.

One hour passed and another. I could not even think about the possibility that Elie might get caught or that he might not get the diamonds. The hour for curfew was approaching, Just when I felt I would explode from the tension, we heard the front door open. We stayed in our room in case it was guests for the Adams family—or worse. Then we heard running footsteps, and Elie burst into the room. He tumbled into Frieda's arms and said, "I got them! I got them!" He laughed hysterically and yelled, "I got them! I got the *lokshen*! I got them!"

After so much hardship, Elie's success made us all deliriously happy. We suddenly took delight in the code word we used for diamonds—*lokshen* (noodles)—and laughed with him. "He's got them. He's got the *lokshen*," we laughed so hard that we were soon panting and once again mindful that we had to keep quiet.

That night, despite our confinement, our joy was complete. Elie's triumph belonged to all of us. He told us that he had found the house in shambles. People had stripped it bare of furniture and had searched everywhere but the secret doorframe for hidden treasure. Floor boards were torn up, wallpaper was ripped from the wall, even the stairs had been destroyed.

A week later, on the last night in December, Daddy went out to sell one of the stones that Elie had retrieved.

Source: Isaacman, Clara, and Joan Adess Grossman. *Clara's Story*. Philadelphia: The Jewish Publication Society of America, 1984.

13.2
Escaping the Death March – 1945
Excerpt from an Interview with Holocaust Survivor David Mandel

As the Russian Army approached the concentration camps in the Auschwitz-Birkenau area of Poland in January 1945, the Nazis decided to evacuate the prisoners held in these facilities. They forced the malnourished and poorly clad inmates to undertake a so-called death march through the winter cold back to Germany. Thousands of prisoners died along the way. David Mandel took part in one of these marches. As he notes below, the conditions were so brutal that some of the prisoners turned on one another for survival. But Mandel also realized that the chaotic circumstances of the march offered a chance to escape.

It was in January 1945. It was a cold night. It was snowing. They awakened us. We had to line up and put our clothes on. Our clothes consisted of a shirt made out of some kind of a cotton fabric with no collar, a pajama-cotton jacket with cotton pajama pants, a piece of cloth for socks, shoes that were canvas top with wooden soles. The soles must have been an inch thick. We had caps—cotton caps—we had a cotton coat, like a robe. We had to line up in the cold of the winter, and they were evacuating the camp. I guess the Russians started an invasion, and the Nazis didn't want to leave anybody behind. They were evacuating all camps. They were burning the barracks with all those sick who couldn't march. They didn't want any witnesses to tell the world of these atrocities that took place. At the time there were maybe three to five thousand of us.

We marched. It was difficult to go on the road with these wooden shoes. The snow clung to it—it was like walking on skates. Anybody who twisted an ankle and couldn't continue was shot. Anybody who tried to escape was shot. After about three nights we walked and slept in fives—the three in the middle slept, and two on the outside were walking, and you can sleep and walk. It's amazing how much a human being can endure… People were picking off clothes from the dead, from one another. Trying to change shoes. Anybody who lost a cap, you know, grab somebody else's cap. People were fending for themselves. We became worse than animals.

We finally arrived in a camp called Blechhammer… One time, I remember, we found out where the warehouse was, and we just went as a group and tried to break the door open. And we went in there, and we just brought all the foodstuff out. And people were just fighting and scratching, and I remember suddenly there was a machinegun erected, opposite, and they started machine-gunning us. This friend of mine and I, who I had befriended, another French boy—we were buddy-buddy—we were on the side. And somebody came through with some bread. We wrestled him to the ground, and we took the bread away from him… I remember barracks were burning. There were bodies strewn all over. Didn't bother me at all. (Now when I see blood, I faint.) I was frying potatoes, sitting on dead bodies. There were people begging for help. People were fending for themselves.

I am asked how I could survive. They say survivors have a guilty conscience. I didn't help. I looked out for myself. What went through my mind is that I had to

David Mandel, Videotaped Interview conducted by Elissa Schosheim, 1 February 1996. Survivors of the Shoah Visual History Foundation. Beverly Hills, CA, USA.

stay alive. I have three younger brothers. I have a sister. They need me. And that kept me going.

We were waiting. We knew already, word got out, you know, that the Russians are coming. But lo and behold one night we were awakened with gunshots. We had to stand in line. They went through with bayonets, into the sleeping quarters. They set the barracks on fire. They were shooting. We stood in line, I remember—left the camp. We were on the road again. Cold, snow. It's amazing how I never caught a cold.

We came to a village, I remember, about maybe two, three hours after we left the camp—middle of the night. We turned the corner. The guard hasn't turned the corner yet. I had a blanket with me, rolled-up blanket. I threw it. My friend and I, three others, ran off the road into this yard.

There was a fence. Snow—knee-deep. I jumped over the fence, these three after us—these three inmates. By that time the guard turned the corner. He hollered "halt!" "Stop!" But there was no stopping. We ran. They opened up fire. Those [other] three never made it. I remember this other kid who was about eighteen—I was fifteen—[we] crawled in the snow. We zigged and zagged. The bullets were flying. There was woods—a forest—nearby. We had to go across a little creek. It was frozen. My friend got hit. A bullet grazed his ankle. We were hiding out in these woods—a fifteen year old, an eighteen year old. We didn't know which way to go…

In the woods we found a cottage. Must have been a resort because it was something like a motel. It had rooms, and I remember it had a bomb shelter. And we were looking for footprints. We were sniffing for humans. We were like animals. We threw pebbles at the shutters to see whether anybody is around. And we finally convinced [ourselves] nobody was around. We went in there. We found pieces of frozen bread, a sack of sugar, some frozen potatoes. It was nourishment.

I remember we took mattresses from these rooms, and we piled them into one room, and we sort of created a hole in between the mattresses. That's where we slept. And at night we would open up the shutters, and we would get some snow and melt it for water.

And then one day, our shutter was open a little bit, and we noticed a couple of civilians approaching this cottage. And the thing opened. My friend jumped aside, and I was frozen. I couldn't move. These two civilians had that scared look on their face like they saw a living skeleton. And I was scared. And they told us the Russians had been in for a couple days. So we went to the road. I remember we had to go up an embankment. And the Russians were marching towards Germany.

And there was a Russian Jewish soldier who spoke to us in Yiddish. And he took us to this German family—husband and wife, an elderly couple. And he made them promise to feed us and take care of us. And he says, if not, he's going to come back. Well this German couple cooked for us, slowly.

315

And we ate. I swear I could see myself getting heavier.

Source: Mandel, David. Videotaped interview conducted by Elissa Schosheim, 1 February 1996. Survivors of the Shoah Visual History Foundation, Testimony 11722.

13.3
"Some People Were Very Nice" – 1944-1945
Holocaust Survivor Erna Roth Anolik Recalls Hiding Out during the War's Final Months

Born in Uzhorod, Czechoslovakia, in 1923, Erna Roth Anolik was twenty years old when she and her family were sent to Auschwitz-Birkenau in 1944. Upon arrival, her mother, younger brother, and older sister were almost immediately sent to the gas chamber. Her father also later died at Auschwitz. Anolik and another sister, Elizabeth, were the sole members of the family to survive the Holocaust.

Anolik and her sister spent six weeks in Auschwitz before being transferred to a work camp in Gelsenkirchen, Germany. After a brief stay there, they were selected for a factory workforce that was based in the city of Essen, Germany. In Essen both Anolik and her sister worked as slave laborers in very difficult and dangerous conditions. But Anolik's job in Essen also brought her into contact with Germans who treated her and other prisoners kindly. Eventually, some of these Germans helped Anolik, her sister, and several other Jewish women gain their freedom.

One day [in Gelsenkirchen] about four or five men came from Essen, Germany, from the Krupps Ammunition Factory, and they picked out women—about 500 of us—who they wanted to come and work for the ammunition factory in Essen. And my sister and I, and two of our friends who were with us all along [Rene and Agnes Kernigsberg], … we were taken to Essen… In fact, when my sister and I were picked out to go to work in Essen, the two of them [Rene and Agnes] had typhus in Gelsenkirchen, so they were very sickly and they were not picked to go to work. And I said to one of the men who picked me out that I am not going unless they can come with us. So he had them come also… We all stayed together and sort of looked after each other…

For instance, sleeping on the floor in winter was very cold. And since we just had that one dress and one blanket—no coat, but one blanket. So the blanket served as a cover for at night and also as a coat for during the day. And so one blan-

---

Erna Roth Anolik, Videotaped Interview conducted by Suzie Eisenstock, 10 November 1996. Survivors of the Shoah Visual History Foundation. Beverly Hills, CA, USA.

316

ket was not warm enough, so the four of us would sleep together and put the four blankets together. That way, all of us were warm enough. We kept each other warm...

And there [in Essen] we went to work every morning. We were woken up ... for the counting, and then we went to the train—a streetcar actually, I think it was a streetcar—and went to work in the factory. Some women worked at annealing ovens. I, myself, with a small group of women, worked outside again, cleaning up debris or bringing in raw material into the factory. I remember in the winter, for instance, we were bringing in metal sheets. Many times we'd bring them in, and we thought that our skin would come off with the sheets because it was so cold. And we did that every day. At night we'd go back to camp.

"One of the young S.S. soldiers always told us, 'You'll never get out alive. We'll always have the five minutes to kill you all.'"

And then I think it was around December 12th [1944]. For some reason, I don't know why, I remember that. But there was a bombing at the camp, and our barracks were bombed [by Allied aircraft who were targeting Essen]... And also in town, the train we used to take—the streetcar—was bombed, so it was out of commission. So from then on we had to march to work. We went by foot. So we had to get up even earlier because it was seven kilometers [about 4.3 miles] each way. So we marched to work, and one day my wooden shoes broke as we were marching to work. And there was nothing to do, so my sister and I stayed behind. We tore off a piece of my blanket and wrapped that around my foot, and we marched to work. Because, [we] couldn't escape—there was no place to go. I mean the way we looked everybody would have known right away that we are Jewish prisoners. And just couldn't escape, so we went back to work.

And one of the men working in the factory [an employee rather than a prisoner] saw that I didn't have shoes, and next day he brought shoes for me. Every once in a while you found some people who were very nice to us. They would bring in a piece of bread or whatever to help us. In fact, one time, one of the workers said that he knows of a German man who said, when time comes, if somebody needs help [in escaping], he's willing to help. But we didn't know how to go about it.

Until, in February [1945], when there was a bombing as we were in the camp at night. The S.S. people who guarded us went into shelters, but we were not allowed to go into shelters. And that's when one of the women, her name was Rose Katz—I never knew her before, but she approached my sister and me and asked if we would be willing to escape. And I said, "well where could we go?" She says she knows where one of the workers from the factory was, and he would help us.

So my sister and I and the two Kernigsberg girls and this Rose Katz and also a sixth girl, I think her name was Gisela Israel, we escaped while the S.S. guards were in the shelter... And we went into a Jewish cemetery—went into a building there, but then overnight there was a bombing, and the building was destroyed. So we went over to another side of the building and stayed there, and the next morning this Rose Katz and my sister went over to where the German [worker] lived. Rose Katz apparently knew where this German lived because she had done some work for him. And [they] told him that we are hiding, the six of us, and would he help in any way? So he would come over once a day and bring us either a bottle of water or a piece of bread or maybe a potato or whatever he had. And he said he also would see if he could get in touch with the man who said he knew somebody who would help us.

But then one day as we were hiding out in the cellar of the building in the cemetery, a German came in and asked who we were. We said we were German people, and we were from Duisberg, and our homes were bombed, and our parents were out looking for another place to live. That's why we are hiding here. And he left. But we were afraid he might be from the police, or even if he wasn't, he would probably know that what we told him was not true, and he would report us.

So we went over to the German and said we cannot stay there. So he took us to his place, but he was really a very poor man. He didn't have much. And he couldn't keep the six of us... He told us that he really cannot feed us. And again we told him about Mr. Schneider, who would know where this man who wanted to help us lived. So we went to look for Mr. Schneider, but his place was bombed out—his area [of the city]. But somehow we found him, and he took us to a Mr. Neerman—Fritz Neerman, who took us in—took four of us in. Rose Katz then went to somebody else, but the four of us, my sister and the two Kernigsberg girls and I, went to this Mr. Fritz Neerman who was the most wonderful person I have ever, ever encountered.

He took us in. He was a food wholesaler, and he had a big home. And separate from his home was an apartment, which he used to have rented out. There was no tenant there then. So he gave us this apartment or big room. And I remember we took our [prison] clothes off and burned them in a little stove that was in the room that he put us in. And he told us—he opened the closet; he had a wife and two daughters—and he said, "anything you want to take from the closet to wear, whatever you need." And we took out clothes and then burned our own, and we took a bath for the first time since we left home. And first time since we left home, we slept in beds, on white sheets. And he treated us very, very well. He had a maid who cooked for him, and he would see that she cooked for us also. And every day she would bring in the food for us.

And he would keep us informed how the war was going. He was just wonderful to us, really wonderful. I couldn't imagine that anybody can be this [good]. Because he endangered not only his life but his family's life. Because if he was caught with us hiding in his place, I'm sure that he would have been killed. And not only did he help *us*, but there were some Russian prisoners in town that he would have his maid cook in barrels and would bring it over to feed these Russian prisoners... It was done very secretly, and nobody knew that we were there. And he managed to hide us until liberation.

We were never afraid of being caught and dying. There was no risk for *us*. We knew what awaited us if we didn't escape or what awaited us if we stayed in camp. One of the young S.S. soldiers always told us, "you'll never get out alive. We'll always have the five minutes to kill you all." So there was no risk-taking, really. I mean, the alternative was definite death...

We stayed indoors all the time. All the time. Once in a while we would go into his apartment, like for instance on, I remember, Easter. We went into his apartment and had lunch... And the maid made waffles, which I had never in my life had waffles. We had waffles with strawberries. And he would always take out the map and let us know how the war was going. I guess he was hoping that it would be over soon. And sure enough, in April—I think it was around Easter time that was the very first time that we left the apartment. I guess we looked normal enough by then because we were wearing his daughter's clothing, and some of our hair grew back. And we went outside. And we saw a jeep with soldiers in it. We didn't know they were American soldiers. So we ran back in, and we told him that we saw a jeep with soldiers. And then went out and saw that it was American soldiers, so that's how we knew. That's where we were when we were liberated.

Source: Anolik, Erna Roth. Videotaped interview conducted by Suzie Eisenstock, 10 November 1996. Survivors of the Shoah Visual History Foundation, Testimony 22586.

14

LIBERATION

Survivors of the SS Death Camp in Mauthausen, Austria, tear down the Nazi eagle that hangs
above the entrance after their liberation in May 1945.

INTRODUCTION

In early 1943 the tide of war turned against Germany, especially on the eastern front. After pushing deep into Russia, the German army began to retreat westward with Soviet forces in pursuit. By the following year, the fighting reached Poland and began to close in on the remaining extermination camps. At last, the liberation that Jewish prisoners had hoped for was becoming a possibility, but many would not live to see it. The Nazis decided to evacuate the camps and march the remaining prisoners back toward Germany. In the case of Auschwitz-Birkenau, the evacuation took place in January 1945. Nearly 60,000 malnourished and poorly clad inmates were driven out into the winter cold to begin brutal death marches that continued for hundreds of miles. Thousands died along the way, overcome by exhaustion or exposure or shot by S.S. guards as soon as they began to lag behind. Luckier prisoners were able to avoid the death marches because they were housed in camp hospitals at the time of evacuation and unable to depart. Holocaust scholars believe that the S.S. planned to murder these patients after the other prisoners departed. But some patients were spared when the remaining German guards fled the Soviet onslaught.

Those prisoners that survived the death marches ended up in concentration camps in Germany. These prisons became extremely overcrowded as more and more prisoners arrived from the east. The Third Reich was now being squeezed between the Soviet army in the east and the American and British forces in the west. During these final weeks and months of the war, many prisoners finally succumbed to starvation, disease, and the cumulative impact of months of exhausting labor.

As order broke down in the final weeks before Germany's surrender, many of the camps suffered extreme shortages of food and water. Some of the worst condi-

323

tions prevailed at the Bergen-Belsen concentration camp, where 37,000 people died of starvation and disease in the weeks before the camp was liberated and an additional 14,000 perished even after the British arrived in mid-April. Other prisoners were simply murdered in the final days of the war, as their S.S. guards fulfilled their mission to kill Jews even as the Nazi state crumbled. In the most heartbreaking incidents, prisoners were gunned down just minutes before liberating armies reached them.

Finally, in early May 1945, the killing stopped. Adolf Hitler had committed suicide on April 30, spouting his anti-Semitic hatred to the very end. Germany officially surrendered on May 7. Many of the Holocaust camp survivors—200,000 in total—just barely escaped with their lives. They spent weeks or months in hospitals recovering from extreme malnutrition and debilitating illnesses. Once back on their feet, they faced the daunting task of attempting to stitch their lives back together again. Because so many prisoners had been separated from their families before or during their imprisonment, they had no idea if their parents, spouses, siblings, or other family members had survived the nightmare of the previous four years. This led them to search through the many displaced persons (D.P) camps that housed refugees throughout Europe and to return to the communities where they lived before the war, hoping to find some word about their family members. Sometimes miraculous reunions took place, even years later in far distant lands. But all too often the survivors came to realize that their loved ones were among the millions of victims cut down during the Holocaust.

14.1
Arrival of the Americans – 1945
Excerpt from an Interview with Auschwitz Survivor George Gottlieb

Even while millions of Jews were being exterminated in the concentration camps, others continued to be used as a source of slave labor to aid the Nazi war effort. Many prisoners were used in work projects at Auschwitz-Birkenau and other large camps, while others were shipped to smaller labor camps where they were assigned to specific tasks that included everything from toiling in coal mines to running machines in factories. Prisoners assigned to labor details in these camps were more likely to survive the Holocaust than others caught in the Nazi death machine. In some cases, such as the well-known example of German businessperson Oskar Schindler (of Schindler's List fame), sympathetic factory owners purposefully shielded Jews from harm, using the excuse that they needed them as workers. But many laborers still died in these camps, unable to endure prolonged exposure to brutal conditions and backbreaking labor. The most unfortunate of these Holocaust victims held on for months or even years, only to succumb mere days or weeks before their liberators arrived.

In 1944 Jewish prisoner George Gottlieb and his brother were shipped from Auschwitz-Birkenau to a labor camp in Germany. They thus avoided the Nazi death march out of Poland that took place several months later. Nonetheless, Gottlieb and his fellow prisoners were pushed to the brink of death as the war drew to a close. After completing yet another forced march to a camp near Brandenberg, Gottlieb collapsed in total exhaustion. A short time later, American troops unexpectedly liberated the camp. Tragically, however, some concentration camp victims died after liberation, when their acute malnourishment made it impossible for them to process even moderate amounts of regular food. Some camp survivors who had endured years of terror, backbreaking labor, and near starvation died after consuming distributed rations that their wrecked digestive systems could not handle.

In the following excerpt from a postwar interview with Gottlieb, he recalls the exhausting labor and desperate conditions that prevailed at the camp—

George Gottlieb, Videotaped Interview conducted by Joan Karen Benbasat, 24 September 1996. Survivors of the Shoah Visual History Foundation, Beverly Hills, CA, USA.

and recounts events that unfolded in the first hours after American troops arrived at the camp.

Sometime in the month of August [1944], suddenly we were pushed on a train. By the way, that's the first time that we went in a passenger train [as opposed to the cattle cars or freight cars that the Nazis often used to transport the Jews]. And we had no idea where we are going, and that train went on for two or three days. And finally we arrived in Germany. We know [the direction] we are heading, and we passed near Berlin, and geographically we knew enough where we are, and we are just northeast of Berlin, to a city called Braumschweig… Braumschweig is a comparatively large town where they had the Bussing Autoworks… Bussing, to the best of my knowledge, was or is a division of Mercedes Benz truck division. And there the train stopped, and probably a mile from the train station we had a big camp—big, big camp. A labor camp—this was strictly a labor camp. This was not an extermination camp. There was no final solution or extermination here. This was death by labor…

Immediately the next morning we started to go to work. The work was that we had to go from the railroad station to the factory. We carried from steel to wood to any material whatsoever that was necessary in fabrication of the trucks… Braumschweig was extremely hard labor, extremely hard. I mean the whole day outside, and fall came, winter came, and it was miserable. Miserable cold, miserable conditions. Food is exactly the same as in Auschwitz… We had German *kapos* only [the inmate overseers who supervised the squads of prisoners]… Here we had absolute criminals, absolute criminals. I mean the *kapo* that was in charge in our barrack, he looked like a weightlifter, I mean he looked like a specimen of health. And he had the biggest pleasure of kicking and punching and any kind of brutality, whatever he could do to anybody… "Jew pig," that was the [equivalent] greeting of "hello, I love you." That was the nicest what he could say.

But besides us, on the other side of the railroad tracks, there was a huge POW [prisoner of war] camp. The POW camp had French, English, and Russian soldiers. Not one American uniform that we have seen. They were working inside in the factory. We were never allowed into the factory. So the only contact [we had with them was] that we took from the railroad to the factory anything that would have to be brought there. By the way, no mechanized equipment. Everything is physical. And they are the ones who brought it in [the factory], and they worked, we assumed, on machines…

Once we started to work there … we [had] went through already three, four, five, six months without any kind of … hygiene—to wash your face, wash your clothes. No such thing—it's the same clothes, the same shoes, the same shirt, the same pants and jacket…. From day one in Auschwitz there is nothing else but the latrine. No such a thing as toilet paper. No such thing as soap or water or toothbrush or toothpaste or comb. Comb wasn't necessary really. The basic idea was that once a month they cut your hair on a brushcut basis. But in the middle of your head, with that head sheared, they cut … a [two-inch] stripe… They figured if you are such a genius that in your striped shirt you can escape—and most of the people with a tattoo on their arm—at least on your head, if you take off your hat or whatever it is, it is quite obvious that you're a concentration camp … prisoner.

Anyway, our work was not only hard, but an awful lot of people fell. We started out to be 28,000 at Braumschweig. And with a minimum of food and a tremendous amount of work, and the difficulty of the temperature and the rest of it, it was hard work—real hard work.

One day while we are marching for our famous lunch, I notice that the SS is feeding the German shepherds with potato peels. And that smell, the fumes came up, and it was just an unbelievable *temptation*—let's call it that way. You know, you're hungry. I broke line, and I jumped into the place where the shepherds were feeding, and I took away a dish of potato peels. My brother was hollering and screaming at me. You know the desperation came to the point of what can happen? They can kill me, but I have potato peels, so maybe I'm going to eat. I had probably stuffed my mouth with an awful lot of potato peels, but I tossed that dish towards my brother when the SS guard, for unknown reasons, instead of using his gun [firing a shot], he used the butt of his rifle and hit me in the back two or three times and asked me to spit it out. Actually I did not spit it out, I swallowed as much as I could. I found way later that at the time that he hit me, he broke one of my vertebrae.

But there is no such thing as being sick and no such a thing as not being able to do, because if you stayed sick, the next day you didn't live. But the people in our group, [then] they knew that I can't lift. Once [the load] was already up on the shoulder I could walk, but bending down and lifting, for a couple of weeks—it was hard. But the camaraderie was unbelievable. Not only camaraderie—everybody knew that if you have to help somebody, you help somebody.

By then already, many, many times—I mean it was a practically a daily affair—that from your group of six sometimes somebody didn't move if they're ordered to turn, and this person was dead. And bodies started to pile, and … you know it was an accepted fact that people die, that people cannot take it, and people are getting to the point where physically, mentally—but mostly physically—[they cannot go on]…

I have to say that march of going from the camp to the railroad station, we went through one part of town… Today, if somebody is telling you that "we didn't know about it," [the concentration camps], somehow ask the question that if you see 10,000 or 6,000 or 8,000, I don't know how many, at the same time march with stripes and basically feeble-looking or funny-looking people going through—don't you ask the question, who are they? Are they prisoners? What do you mean prisoners? Prisoners for *what*? I mean, that they didn't know about concentration camps? Don't tell me…

[By the spring of 1945] I was mentally, physically in such a condition that I didn't know if I'm dead or alive. Finally [one morning] I just lie down in the court-yard… We heard some shooting… Suddenly the S.S. guards started to assemble all those who were able to stand and walk. And I thought that we were going to be taken away on a new march. And I wasn't in a position even to get on my knees, never mind about getting up and marching.

Then the SS guard took all those who were standing in the middle of that courtyard and machine-gunned them down and killed them. Every one of them. And those who were standing and being machine-gunned down included my own brother. Right in front of us. Right in front of me. And I had no more desire even to breathe. Forget about anything else, because anything else I couldn't do.

The SS guard left, and within half an hour—I don't think it was more than half an hour—suddenly tanks rolled in. Tanks rolled in and [it was] the first time I have seen a white star on a tank. No idea. The first reaction was, maybe the Russians ran out of red paint. I mean we didn't know what the insignia meant. And not one but many tanks, trucks came in. And the hatches opened up, and the people coming out of the tanks, they were black. I would say that 70-75 percent of that force was black. And for the first time in my lifetime [I] saw a black human being—physically. I mean I'd seen them in movies, American movies, as a kid, but I never saw a black person [in real life]… So automatically the first we knew was that they are Americans. They couldn't be French, they couldn't be English, they couldn't be Russian. What I know now, I didn't know it then, that this was the second camp what they liberated in two days. The previous day they liberated another camp…

Here are guys, taking off their clothes, their shoes [to give to the liberated prisoners], handing out packages. Handing out cans, handing out whatever they had. Trying to do for their other humans. And if they would have known… By the goodness of these people, if they had a sandwich [and fed it to one of the prison-ers], that sandwich killed that person that they liberated. The [malnourished] body could not take the calories. I was lying on top of three packs of what they call K rations. K rations—I understand today exist in the American army—is a box which has 6-7,000 calories of food in it, which is wrapped in brown paper, I know it today by heart… I didn't have the strength to do anything else but really lay on top of it. And that's the reason why I am alive.

These guys left after ten minutes… I know that I had a pair of shoes and a pair of pants from one of these guys. Suddenly the next group came in, and the next group looked to me like men from the Mars or men from somewhere out in space. We realized that they are Americans because they are wearing a similar uni-form and they had an armband with a red cross on it. These guys had rubber boots, you know like a fisherman has it all the way to the hip, and rubber gloves all the way to the shoulder, and mask, and God knows what. Suddenly they came with a pump, and they started to spray something on us. My thinking was at that time that these guys have seen the movie, but they don't know what real life is because I don't need baby powder. But within seconds I realized what they did. We didn't know what it was, but within seconds I had no more lice. Before that we were infected by millions of those lice. Later I found out what they sprayed. It was DDT. I mean thank goodness today's world doesn't use DDT, but DDT in seconds killed all the lice.

I was taken by these Red Cross people on a stretcher. I was put on a stretcher. I was taken into a school building—right there—which became ... a shelter... According to records I was 32 kilos. 32 kilos is roughly 70 pounds. Sometime in June, July, they taught me how to walk, how to stand up and walk.

Source: Gottlieb, George. Videotaped interview conducted by Joan Karen Benbasat, September 24, 1996. Survivors of the Shoah Visual History Foundation, Testimony 20035.

14.2
Striving to Survive Until Liberation – 1945
Excerpt from an Interview with Holocaust Survivor Henry Oertelt

Henry Oertelt was imprisoned at Auschwitz along with his brother and survived the death march to Germany in January of 1945. They were then transferred between several different camps during the closing months of the war. Their existence became a race against time, as they struggled to avoid death until they could be liberated by one of the Allied armies.

We were loaded up again, and we were taken to a camp called Flossenbürg, which is located in northeast Bavaria. Flossenbürg was a camp designed to hold 5,000 prisoners. When we arrived there, there were about 140,000 there. At that time though, we were not assigned to any working place anymore. We would be kept busy in head counts from morning to evening. Prisoners just dropped on the spot. It was an automatic thing that the prisoners next to them would have to carry them away, putting them on big body piles, who then eventually would be thrown onto some trucks and would be taken to the crematorium and burned.

Nothing else happened there. That's the way it was. Except, I developed something very, very miserable. I developed a growth under my left arm here that started to grow and grow, and eventually developed into the size of an orange, a big orange, grapefruit almost... I was fairly helpless. My brother was constantly with

Henry Oertelt, Videotaped interview conducted by Solomon Awend, 21 November 1995. Survivors of the Shoah Visual History Foundation, Beverly Hills, CA, USA.

me there. And suddenly an order was given that they were looking for one thousand men that would be able to be mustered out for a work command to be taken out of the camp, not too far away, where they intended to build an airstrip. So we went by the doctors, and I tried to hide this thing, but the doctors noticed, and they sent my brother this way [to the work detail] and kept me on the side of being kept in the camp. And this was the way I was there until we finally were ordered out of the camp.

We were put into the column. We were now moving out. And we were marching now between the American lines, back and forth. The American lines tried to encircle the German contingent. And it was like maybe three, four, five miles from one side to another. We came there, the shooting got closer, we turned around, marched back. And so, nothing to eat at all we received. We actually pulled grass out of the ground—old, dried-up grass. Now it is April 20th of 1945. The new grass hadn't grown yet. And so, we are marching and marching...

Now you got to imagine the group of marchers there. Most of them are literally skeletons. Skeletons with bones and skin pulled over who tried to drag themselves along according to the speed as the guards on our sides provided. And this was not like a Sunday afternoon stroll, I can assure you. And of course these weak, wretched souls would stumble over the slightest pebble on the road that we marched on and would fall to the ground. At which moment, the guard came and would shoot them in the head. At the end of the column was a truck. The bodies were picked up and thrown onto the truck.

I weighed eighty-two pounds, and with that I was not the skinniest guy on the block by any means. There were guys, really, that couldn't have weighed more than sixty, sixty-five pounds. You couldn't believe that these guys were still moving along—trying, knowing that liberation is near, trying to hold themselves up as much as possible. Didn't have a chance. Didn't have the strength. They just succumbed.

And so therefore I was trying to fight my hallucinations—I started to hallucinate. And I knew when somebody hallucinated, they usually soon lost their control and would fall and then the shot would come. And so I started to hallucinate, and I tried to talk to myself, "hey, don't let it happen."

And as it turned out, some guy behind me yelled, "hey guys, look, turn around." And I turned around, and I saw what I still consider the most beautiful sight of my life: a contingent of American armored vehicles coming down the hillside with their American insignia on it. And our guards, of course, at that moment took off in all directions.

And then we stopped. We stopped. And saw at that moment the commander of the American outfit stop in front of us and directed us back to the one road where there was an American Red Cross contingent. He says, "it's just a quarter of a mile up that one road. They are there, they are waiting for you there already. Sorry we couldn't come any sooner to you," he said. And he made a remark that sounded to us utterly ridiculous. He says, "now anyone that wants to walk that quarter mile, just go that way, not this or that." And so we said, "my gosh, walking?" He said, "otherwise there will be trucks and jeeps to pick you up, don't worry about it."

Anyway, while these vehicles were coming by, they were shooting out of their turrets. They were actually a fighting contingent, fighting the Germans. They're shooting, but while they were riding by and shooting, they opened the hatches and threw out all kinds of ration boxes, the military ration boxes.

All of a sudden, we had eaten something, and I said, "you know something, this man said we don't have to walk." Now it starts to occur to me, now that I had something in my stomach, that I'm a free man... "How do you feel about walking? You know something, we now can walk at the speed that *we* want to walk. You know, if we make a few steps and we want to sit down, we sit down. Can't we do that now?" Just like little children that learned to walk. All of a sudden it occurred to us that that is possible.

And so we decided to walk, ... and it took us nearly four hours, I believe, or more, to walk that quarter mile. In the mean time the jeeps came up and down that road. I think we were the last ones in.

And finally we made it... There was a tall Red Cross guy in front of me, American Red Cross uniformed man. And he wanted to have my food box. That was the moment I lost it, you know? "No," [I said], "this was the first possession. You'll never get your hands on that. No way!" Then it all came in focus. And then that's when I actually collapsed... I was on my back for about a week. And they fed us, actually, with broth and light things. Very, very much controlled.

And then after a week [the Red Cross man] said "here's your box back."

> *"I turned around, and I saw what I still consider the most beautiful sight of my life: a contingent of American armored vehicles coming down the hillside with their American insignia on it."*

Source: Oertelt, Henry. Videotaped interview conducted by Solomon Awend, 21 November 1995. Survivors of the Shoah Visual History Foundation, Testimony 7069.

14.3
A Final Spasm of Hatred – 1945
The Last Political Testament of Adolf Hitler

As the Russian Army closed in on Berlin in the spring of 1945, German Chancellor Adolf Hitler wrote this document, his final statement, on April

29, 1945. His closing words express no regret for his actions, which brought ruin upon Germany and set in motion the most awful and widespread campaign of genocide in human history. Instead, he once more lays all blame for the war upon the Jews. In addition, his statement angrily accuses Nazi officials Heinrich Himmler and Hermann Göring of betraying the Third Reich. Just prior to writing this letter, Hitler had learned that Himmler had attempted to enter into secret negotiations with the Allies to bring about Germany's surrender. Hitler also had come to believe that Göring was trying to seize leadership of Germany.

Hitler committed suicide on April 30, 1945, a day after writing this letter. Germany surrendered to the Allied powers just over a week later, on May 7, 1945.

More than 30 years have now passed since I in 1914 made my modest contribution as a volunteer in the first world-war that was forced upon the Reich.

In these three decades I have been actuated solely by love and loyalty to my people in all my thoughts, acts, and life. They gave me the strength to make the most difficult decisions which have ever confronted to mortal man. I have spent my time, my working strength, and my health in these three decades.

It is untrue that I or anyone else in Germany wanted the war in 1939. It was desired and instigated exclusively by those international statesmen who were either of Jewish descent or worked for Jewish interests. I have made too many offers for the control and limitation of armaments, which posterity will not for all time be able to disregard for the responsibility for the outbreak of this war to be laid on me. I have further never wished that after the first fatal world war a second against England, or even against America, should break out. Centuries will pass away, but out of the ruins of our towns and monuments the hatred against those finally responsible whom we have to thank for everything, international Jewry and its helpers, will grow.

Three days before the outbreak of the German-Polish war I again proposed to the British ambassador in Berlin a solution to the German-Polish problem—similar to that in the case of the Saar district, under international control. This offer also cannot be denied. It was only rejected because the leading circles in English politics wanted the war, partly on account of the business hoped for and partly under influence of propaganda organized by international Jewry.

I also made it quite plain that, if the nations of Europe are again to be regarded as mere shares to be bought and sold by these international conspirators in money and finance, then that race, Jewry, which is the real criminal of this murderous struggle, will be saddled with the responsibility. I further left no one in doubt that this time not only would millions of children of Europe's Aryan peoples die of hunger, not only would millions of grown men suffer death, and not only hundreds of thousands of women and children be burnt and bombed to death in the towns, without the real criminal having to atone for this guilt, even if by more humane means.

After six years of war, which in spite of all set-backs, will go down one day in history as the most glorious and valiant demonstration of a nation's life purpose, I cannot forsake the city which is the capital of this Reich. As the forces are too small to make any further stand against the enemy attack at this place and our resistance is gradually being weakened by men who are as deluded as they are lacking in initiative, I should like, by remaining in this town, to share my fate with those, the millions of others, who have also taken upon themselves to do so. Moreover I do not wish to fall into the hands of an enemy who requires a new spectacle organized by the Jews for the amusement of their hysterical masses.

I have decided therefore to remain in Berlin and there of my own free will to choose death at the moment when I believe the position of the Fuehrer and Chancellor itself can no longer be held.

I die with a happy heart, aware of the immeasurable deeds and achievements of our soldiers at the front, our women at home, the achievements of our farmers and workers and the work, unique in history, of our youth who bear my name.

That from the bottom of my heart I express my thanks to you all, is just as self-evident as my wish that you should, because of that, on no account give up the struggle, but rather continue it against the enemies of the Fatherland, no matter where, true to the creed of a great Clausewitz. From the sacrifice of our soldiers and from my own unity with them unto death, will in any case spring up in the history of Germany, the seed of a radiant renaissance of the National-Socialist movement and thus of the realization of a true community of nations.

Many of the most courageous men and women have decided to unite their lives with mine until the very last. I have begged and finally ordered them not to do this, but to take part in the further battle of the Nation. I beg the heads of the Armies, the Navy and the Air Force to strengthen by all possible means the spirit of resistance of our soldiers in the National-Socialist sense, with special reference to the fact that also I myself, as founder and creator of this movement, have preferred death to cowardly abdication or even capitulation.

May it, at some future time, become part of the code of honour of the German officer—as is already the case in our Navy—that the surrender of a district or of a town is impossible, and that above all the leaders here must march ahead as shining examples, faithfully fulfilling their duty unto death.

———

Second Part of the Political Testament

Before my death I expel the former Reichsmarschall Hermann Goering from the party and deprive him of all rights which he may enjoy by virtue of the decree of June 29th, 1941, and also by virtue of my statement in the Reichstag on September 1st, 1939, I appoint in his place Grossadmiral Doenitz, President of the Reich and Supreme Commander of the Armed Forces.

Before my death I expel the former Reichsfuehrer-SS and Minister of the Interior, Heinrich Himmler, from the party and from all offices of the State. In his stead I appoint Gauleiter Karl Hanke as Reichfuehrer-SS and Chief of the German Police, and Gauleiter Paul Giesler as Reich Minister of the Interior.

Goering and Himmler, quite apart from their disloyalty to my person, have done immeasurable harm to the country and the whole nation by secret negotiations with the enemy, which they conducted without my knowledge and against my wishes, and by illegally attempting to seize power in the State for themselves.

In order to give the German people a government composed of honourable men—a government which will fulfill its pledge to continue the war by every means—I appoint the following members of the new Cabinet as leaders of the nation:

> President of the Reich: Doenitz.
> Chancellor of the Reich: Dr. Goebbels.
> Party Minister: Bormann.
> Foreign Minister: Seyss-Inquart.
> Minister of the Interior: Gauleiter Giesler.
> Minister for War: Doenitz.
> C-in-C of the Army: Schoerner.
> C-in-C of the Navy: Doenitz.
> C-in-C of the Air Force: Greim.
> Reichsfuehrer-SS and Chief of the German Police: Gauleiter Hanke.
> Economics: Funk.
> Agriculture: Backe.
> Justice: Thierack.
> Education and Public Worship: Dr. Scheel.
> Propaganda: Dr. Naumann.
> Finance: Schwerin-Grossigk.
> Labour: Dr. Hupfauer.
> Munitions: Saur.
> Leader of the German Labour Front and Member of the Reich Cabinet: Reich Minister Dr. Ley.

Although a number of these men, such as Martin Bormann, Dr. Goebbels etc., together with their wives, have joined me of their own free will and did not wish to leave the capital of the Reich under any circumstances, but were willing to perish with me here, I must nevertheless ask them to obey my request, and in this case set the interests of the nation above their own feelings. By their work and loyalty as comrades they will be just as close to me after death, as I hope that my spirit will linger among them and always go with them. Let them be hard, but never unjust, above all let them never allow fear to influence their actions, and set the honour of the nation above everything in the world. Finally, let them be conscious of the fact that our task, that of continuing the building of a National Socialist State, represents the work of the coming centuries, which places every single person under an obligation always to serve the common interest and to subordinate his own advantage to this end. I demand of all Germans, all National Socialists, men, women and all the men of the Armed Forces, that they be faithful and obedient unto death to the new government and its President.

Above all I charge the leaders of the nation and those under them to scrupulous observance of the laws of race and to merciless opposition to the universal poisoner of all peoples, international Jewry.

Given in Berlin, this 29th day of April 1945.   4:00 a.m.
                                                          Adolf Hitler.

Witnessed by
Dr. Josef Fuhr.   Wilhelm Buergdorf.
Martin Bormann.   Hans Krebs.

Source: Hitler, Adolf. Final Political Testament, April 29, 1945. Reprinted as Document 3569-PS in *Nazi Conspiracy and Aggression*. Vol. 6. Washington, DC: United States Government Printing Office, 1946.

14.4
Liberation from Theresienstadt – 1945
Excerpt from the Testimony of Shmuel Krakowski

The Soviet Army liberated a large number of concentration camps, including some of the notorious extermination camps in Poland and other territories previously controlled by the Nazis. In the following account, Shmuel Krakowski, a native of Łodź, Poland, tells of his experiences at Theresienstadt (now the town of Terezin in the Czech Republic), which was captured by the Soviets in the closing days of the war. As he indicates, his joy at gaining his freedom was quickly tempered by a dawning realization of the magnitude of the Holocaust.

I woke up that day, just as on the day before, and all the previous days—very, very hungry.

We lay on the bare floor, prisoners closed in a prison within a larger prison.

Reprinted with permission from Yad Vashem Archives.

We had arrived here a fortnight earlier with the death march from Rehmsdorf, a subcamp of Buchenwald. We were more than 4,000 Jewish concentration camp prisoners when they took us out of Rehmsdorf in the early days of April. Only 500 of us reached the Czech town of Terezin, which had been transformed by the Nazis into a Jewish ghetto, known by the German name Theresienstadt. All the others were killed or died on the way. Among those who perished were some of my closest friends from our underground youth organization in the Lodz ghetto: Rysiek Podlaski, Abramek Kociolek and Sruled Krajkowski.

They locked us into the huge building called Hamburger Kaserne. Those outside the gate, the resident prisoners of Theresienstadt, were more lucky. They at least had some freedom to move through the few streets of the ghetto. We knew the Third Reich had collapsed, and that our liberation was a matter of days or even hours. Unfortunately, for people exhausted after the suffering of the death march and years of starvation, those hours of waiting for the liberators to come seemed very long. Each hour stretched to eternity. Many of us were in agony, as was one of my best friends Lutek Nachtstern. There was no longer any doubt that for these people the liberation would come too late. For the rest of us it was a tragic race; which would happen first—the liberation or death from starvation?

I don't remember who was the first that morning to look out of the window. I well remember his cry of joy: "Boys, the Russians are here." Thus, we were liberated.

With many others, I decided to run out immediately and welcome the liberators. Many of us were not able to do so. They were too weak to move, but had no choice but to lie and wait for the liberators to come and bring them food, and to arrange medical treatment.

The gate of the Hamburger Kaserne was still closed. A Czech policeman stood outside and tried to persuade us to remain within, because, as he said, we were an epidemic danger for those outside. It sounded like nonsense to remain imprisoned after the liberation had finally come. We refused to obey and stormed the gate. The Czech policeman gave up and disappeared. We soon found ourselves on the road outside the ghetto. There we saw several Red Army tanks, a military supply truck and a few Russian soldiers on bicycles escorting a huge column of German prisoners of war. Germany was defeated and we saw it now with our own eyes. This was the day we had been waiting for.

We were very hungry, so the first thing we did was to ask the Russians to give us something to eat. The soldiers were extremely friendly to us but didn't have much to offer. The only thing they had in their supply truck was sugar, a lot of sugar, and salted pork. I preferred to satisfy my hunger with sugar. I remembered how a few days earlier a doctor in the Hamburger Kaserne, who was also a prisoner, warned us to be very careful of what we ate when the day of liberation came, because we had suffered prolonged starvation. I decided that the pork would be too fat for my starved stomach.

I ate the sugar. I remembered that in normal times sugar was used only for tea and cakes. Now I ate spoonfuls of sugar. This strengthened me, and maybe even save my life. It was a wonderful feeling which I hadn't experienced for almost five years. I could now eat as much as I liked. I knew I would never be hungry again.

We were told that German soldiers were in hiding in the vicinity. They tried to remain hidden until nightfall and then escaped under the cover of darkness. We were asked to help the Russians comb the area and find the Germans. This we were more than happy to do. We were supposed to move in a scattered line into a wooded area with which we were not familiar. We had no idea whether it was a large forest or just a few acres of trees.

I soon lost sight of my friends on the left and right and felt quite lonely in these unfamiliar surroundings. Suddenly, from behind the trees a tall, fat German soldier appeared. I was terribly frightened. I had no arms. What if he decides to shoot me? Shall I die a few hours after being liberated? Fortunately, the German raised his hands and I saw that he was more frightened than I was. His whole body trembled, and he screamed like a madman:

"Hitler kaput. Ich was kein Nazi! Hitler kaput. Ich war kein Nazi" [Hitler is finished. I am not a Nazi].

Encouraged by his behavior, I took him to the road. Some of my fellow ex-prisoners appeared with "their" Germans. All of them tried to convince us very loudly and very nervously that they had never been Nazis. They had always hated Hitler.

"Look, none of them was a Nazi. How, then, was it that the Nazi regime succeeded in holding out to this very day?" said one of my friends.

Those captured Nazi soldiers seemed to be more frightened of us than of the Russians. I thought I knew the reason. The Nazis knew that those who survived would tell the world the story of their barbarity.

By afternoon I felt very tired and decided to go back to Theresienstadt, to the Hamburger Kaserne. I had no other place to go, and I also wanted to see how my friends who had remained there were feeling.

As I walked along the road two uniformed men on bicycles came up to me. At first I didn't recognize them. They were not wearing those German uniforms which unhappily we had gotten so familiar with during the past sad six years of war. Neither were they the uniforms of the Red Army soldiers of whom we now saw so many around us. It took me a few minutes to remember. These were the uniforms of the Polish Army which I hadn't seen since that tragic September in 1939.

"Polish Army?" I asked the men.

"Yes" was the answer.

The two men introduced themselves. They were Jews, officers of the Polish Armored Corps, which had been fighting until the day before some 30 kilometers distant from this place. They had been told that there was a large concentration camp of Jewish prisoners in the vicinity and they were eager to see their liberated brothers. I told them I was one of them and volunteered to be their guide.

We reached Theresienstadt and entered the first barrack. Here were women, mostly from Poland and Hungary, who, like myself, had come with the death marches from other concentration camps. They received the officers with indescribable joy.

"Our brothers! Jewish officers! At last, at last, you are with us!"

They shook hands, kissed each other and cried with joy. The officers asked many questions. They were eager to know where the women came from and all the details of their suffering in the ghettos and camps. One after the other, the women told their story of their unbelievable experiences under the Nazis. The stories were interrupted with expressions of great happiness: to be able to sit here, secure, with Jewish officers, to tell them their stories, knowing that Nazi Germany had come to an end and would never rise again.

Suddenly, one of the women asked the officers, to tell their story in turn, the story of soldiers at war. And then almost immediately, the mood of all of us changed. The joyful atmosphere disappeared, giving way to grief and sorrow. The lieutenant told his story. He was from Vilna. He had been mobilized into the Red Army. He had fought in many battles and was wounded at Stalingrad. After recovering he was transferred to the newly-created Polish Army. Times changed for the better. They defeated the Germans and continually moved westward. To their great sorrow, in all the liberated places they found no Jews. The Germans had murdered an entire nation—our nation. After entering Poland, the lieutenant asked for a few days leave to visit his native Vilna. "There I found only my stones, the familiar buildings and streets with none of the people who used to live there before," the officer told us.

In liberated Lublin the only Jews were the soldiers in the Red and Polish armies, as well as some Jewish partisans who came out of the forest. On the long march through Poland, in the hundreds of towns and villages through which they passed, there were no more Jews. Everywhere there were only extermination sites and mass graves. Theresienstadt was the first place they had met so many Jews, thousands of Jews who had survived the Nazi rule.

Thus, we learned that our fate was much worse than we had expected. Although we had seen a lot and experienced the worst, we still had hoped, still had dreamed. All those days we had struggled to survive, hour after hour, day after day, there had been no time to grasp the enormity of our tragedy. Now everything became clear. No longer were our families waiting for us; no homes to go back to. For us, the victory had come too late, much too late.

Source: *The Anguish of Liberation—Testimonies from 1945*, edited by Y. Kleiman and N. Springer-Aharoni. Jerusalem: Yad Vashem, 1995.

15

REFLECTION
AND REMEMBRANCE

Rabbi of Kiev Moshe Aysman and Israeli officers stand at attention during a Holocaust commemoration ceremony at Menorah monument in Babiy Yar in Kiev, September 5, 2005. Nazi soldiers killed more than 200,000 Jewish people here during World War II.

INTRODUCTION

Reading the death toll of the Holocaust can have a numbing effect—the raw numbers can make the human suffering seem distant and abstract. But to achieve a full understanding of the scope of the crime, a few stark numbers must be kept in mind. According to most estimates, between five million and six million Jews were killed (a definitive number is impossible, given the lack of precise records and the chaotic conditions that existed when many of the murders took place). In *A History of the Holocaust,* scholar Yehuda Bauer settles on 5.8 million, which is close to the total listed in several other well-respected studies. Bauer estimates this to be one third of all the Jewish people on the planet at that time.

The Holocaust created enormous social, political, and spiritual ripples throughout the world. In fact, the Holocaust was one of two issues that emerged from World War II (the other being the prospect of nuclear annihilation) that raised immense questions about human morality and the fabric of modern society. Was the attempted extermination of a targeted ethnic group a one-time event, or did it suggest that humankind was entering a new phase where the murder of innocent civilians could become a common matter of state policy? If similar scenarios threatened to become a reality, what was the responsibility of other nations to intervene? Perhaps even more troubling were the questions of personal responsibility among the citizens of Germany and other countries that were allied with the Nazi government. Why did so many citizens agree to support—or fail to oppose—actions that violated the most basic notions of human decency and morality? The struggle to answer these questions continues to the present day, even as recent world history has been darkened by other campaigns of genocide or "ethnic cleansing" in places like Cambodia (in the 1970s), the former Yugoslavia (in the early 1990s), Rwanda (in 1994), and Sudan (in the mid-2000s).

The Holocaust also reshaped Jewish settlement patterns. Many of the European Jews who survived the Holocaust no longer wanted to remain in Europe. After all, their former communities had been obliterated, and remaining in Europe conjured up painful memories and fears of further persecution. The latter fears were not unfounded. In fact, anti-Jewish violence continued in parts of Europe even after the war, with a particularly deadly pogrom erupting in Kielce, Poland, in 1946.

In choosing a new home, large numbers of European Jews were attracted to the Middle Eastern area then known as Palestine, where a Zionist movement had been growing since the turn of the twentieth century. Having suffered so terribly under European governments, many of these people reasoned that the only hope for security was to establish a Jewish state. Displaced Jews from Europe began to arrive in Palestine in increasing numbers in the years immediately following the war, and they were instrumental in the founding of Israel in 1948. Jews also emigrated to other lands in large numbers.

Bringing Nazi Criminals to Justice

The judgment and punishment of some of those who carried out the Holocaust began even before the war ended. The Nuremberg war crimes trials that took place between 1946 and 1948 were the best known of these proceedings, in large measure because they focused on some of the most senior Nazi officials. Twelve were sentenced to death, including Hermann Göring (who committed suicide before being executed), Hans Frank (head of the Government General in Poland), Alfred Rosenberg (an architect of the Nazi philosophy), and Julius Streicher (editor of *Der Stürmer*). Seven others received prison terms, including Albert Speer, who served as the German minister of armaments and war production. He was one of the few Nazis to express regret for the Holocaust, though he also claimed to have no direct knowledge of the killings. Auschwitz commander Rudolf Höss was sentenced and hanged in Poland in 1947 in a separate legal proceeding.

Several of the Nazis believed to have taken a large role in the Holocaust died without ever facing trial. Reinhard Heydrich was assassinated by Czechoslovakian rebels during the war. Adolf Hitler and Joseph Goebbels committed suicide shortly before Germany surrendered; Heinrich Himmler did the same after being captured by the Allies. While the trials that immediately followed the war focused attention on Nazi atrocities, Allied prosecutors did not attempt to punish everyone involved in the immense genocidal system created by the Nazis. Only a small percentage of those involved in the Holocaust murders were brought to trial.

The search for those responsible for the Holocaust extended through the end of the twentieth century, spearheaded by the so-called Nazi hunters who pursued their own independent investigations. The most famous of these figures was Simon Wiesenthal, a concentration camp survivor, who tracked down hundreds of former Nazis who fled Germany during the last days of the Third Reich. Among his other accomplishments, Wiesenthal played a role in the capture of Adolf Eichmann, one of the key figures in charge of the Final Solution. Eichmann had managed to escape arrest immediately after the war but was captured in Argentina in 1960. Brought to trial in Israel, he was found guilty and executed in 1962. Wiesenthal also discovered the whereabouts of Karl Silberbauer, the Gestapo agent who arrested Anne Frank and her family in 1944.

Retribution brought a measure of satisfaction to some Holocaust survivors, but most still spent decades struggling with the psychological implications of what they had endured. Guilt was a common emotion—caused by the fact that an individual had survived while so many others perished. In certain cases these feelings were made worse because the survivors had been forced to abandon fellow victims—even members of their own families—in order to improve their chances of survival. Recurring nightmares that returned the victim to the overwhelming fear of their Holocaust experience was another common aftereffect.

The trauma of the genocide was severe enough that it even extended to succeeding generations. Children of Holocaust survivors often grappled with their own feelings of guilt because they didn't directly experience the hardships of their parents. In addition, some Holocaust survivors were overly protective of their offspring or placed unrealistic expectations on them, which sometimes triggered emotional and behavioral problems for the children. On the other hand, it would be deeply unfair to suggest that all Holocaust survivors lived stunted lives because of their awful experiences. Many became contented and productive members of society, and numerous individuals distinguished themselves as professional, political, and community leaders in Europe, the United States, and elsewhere.

Just as personal reactions to the Holocaust have been diverse, so too has the global response varied according to place and time. To speak in very general terms, the Holocaust received rather limited attention until the 1960s. Once the major war-crimes trials wrapped up, the majority of people who had lived through the Nazi era tried to put it behind them. Few Holocaust survivors became prominent spokespeople during this era, and some of them remained silent by choice—sharing the common view that the painful events of the 1930s and 1940s were better left alone.

Bearing Witness

Roughly fifteen years after the war ended, however, the veil of silence began to lift. Some of the great voices of Holocaust literature—Elie Wiesel and Primo Levi, for instance—began to publish their accounts, and the trial of Adolf Eichmann gave Jewish victims a prominent public forum to recount their experiences. The 1960s also saw the children of those who had lived through the war years come of age, and this generation demanded a fuller accounting of the events that had cast such a grim shadow over their family histories.

In the United States, interest in the subject became especially strong in the 1990s. It was spurred by the Holocaust film *Schindler's List,* by the opening of Holocaust museums and memorials all across the country, and by the founding of several organizations dedicated to recording the experiences of those survivors who were still living.

At the same time that the public became more willing to confront the reality of the Holocaust, a small group of extremists have championed an opposing view: they claim that the Holocaust never occurred. Known as deniers or revisionists, they argue that the story of Jewish genocide has been fabricated by the Jews themselves in order to win sympathy—once again perpetuating the myth that the Jewish people are carrying out a vast conspiracy against the rest of humankind. A typical tactic of the deniers is to attack small inconsistencies in Holocaust histories and testimonies (for instance, the number of people who were placed in a gas chamber at one time) and then suggest that such flaws make the entire account of the Holocaust suspect. But anyone who doubts the reality of the Holocaust has to ignore an overwhelming body of evidence that proves that the genocide did indeed take place. In most cases, the deniers are less interested in engaging in an honest discussion of history than they are in advancing their anti-Semitic agenda.

The rhetoric of these extremists has inspired many Holocaust survivors to become more vocal about their experiences. This determination to bear witness has become increasingly important as the number of living survivors of the Holocaust grows smaller with each passing year. Fortunately, the activities of remembrance organizations such as Yad Vashem and the USC Shoah Foundation Institute for Visual History and Education have preserved the testimony of thousands of people who experienced the terror of the Holocaust. These accounts, combined with the official documentary evidence regarding Nazi activities, bear witness to one of the most monstrous campaigns carried out in human history. And their stories provide a powerful reminder to present and future generations that when malice, ignorance, and prejudice stalk the land, tragedies of awful scope often ensue.

15.1
The Long Reach of the Holocaust – 1986
Excerpt from Maus II: And Here My Troubles Began *by Art Spiegelman*

The son of Holocaust survivors, Art Spiegelman drew on his parents' experiences to create the two-volume graphic novel Maus, *for which he was awarded the Pulitzer Prize in 1992. (The title comes from the German word for "mouse," and the comic-book style illustrations in the novel depict the Jews as mice and the Nazis as cats.)* Maus *is partly a recounting of the horrific events that Vladek Spiegelman, Art's father, went through in Poland in World War II and partly a chronicle of the long-term effects that the Holocaust had on the entire family.*

Indeed, Spiegelman is unflinching in describing how memories of the Holocaust haunted his family. He relates how the Holocaust negatively affected his relationship with his father, and he discusses how it contributed to his mother's suicide in 1968. "It's only when I left home that I got some sense that not everybody had parents who woke up screaming in the night," commented Spiegelman in one interview.

Maus also explores how the Holocaust experiences of his parents triggered Holocaust fantasies during the author's childhood. In one scene, for example, the character of Art tells his wife how "I did have nightmares about S.S. men coming into my class and taking all us Jewish kids away. Don't get me wrong. I wasn't obsessed with this stuff. . . . It's just that sometimes I'd fantasize Zyklon B gas coming out of our shower instead of water. I know this is insane, but I somehow wish I had been in Auschwitz with my parents so I could really know what they lived through!... I guess it's some kind of guilt about having had an easier life than they did.... I feel so inadequate trying to reconstruct a reality that was worse than my darkest dreams."

In the following excerpts, Art Spiegelman's autobiographical character discusses the difficulties of being the son of Holocaust survivors. The passages also touch on the ongoing emotional problems experienced by Vladek Spiegelman.

I WONDER IF RICHIEU AND I WOULD GET ALONG IF HE WAS STILL ALIVE.

YOUR BROTHER?

MY *GHOST*-BROTHER, SINCE HE GOT KILLED BEFORE I WAS BORN. HE WAS ONLY FIVE OR SIX.

AFTER THE WAR MY PARENTS TRACED DOWN THE VAGUEST RUMORS, AND WENT TO ORPHANAGES ALL OVER EUROPE. THEY COULDN'T BELIEVE HE WAS DEAD.

I DIDN'T THINK ABOUT HIM MUCH WHEN I WAS GROWING UP... HE WAS MAINLY A LARGE, BLURRY PHOTOGRAPH HANGING IN MY PARENTS' BEDROOM.

UH-HUH. I THOUGHT THAT WAS A PICTURE OF YOU, THOUGH IT DIDN'T *LOOK* LIKE YOU.

THAT'S THE POINT. THEY DIDN'T *NEED* PHOTOS OF ME IN THEIR ROOM... I WAS ALIVE!...

THE PHOTO NEVER THREW TANTRUMS OR GOT IN ANY KIND OF TROUBLE... IT WAS AN IDEAL KID, AND I WAS A PAIN IN THE ASS. I COULDN'T COMPETE.

THEY DIDN'T *TALK* ABOUT RICHIEU, BUT THAT PHOTO WAS A KIND OF REPROACH. HE'D HAVE BECOME A *DOCTOR*, AND MARRIED A WEALTHY JEWISH GIRL...THE CREEP.

BUT AT LEAST WE COULD'VE MADE *HIM* GO DEAL WITH VLADEK. ...IT'S *SPOOKY*, HAVING SIBLING RIVALRY WITH A SNAPSHOT!

347

Source: Spiegelman, Art. *Maus II: And Here My Troubles Began.* New York: Pantheon, 1991.

15.2
Bearing Witness – 1996
Excerpt from an Interview with Holocaust Survivor David Mandel

In the following commentary, Holocaust survivor David Mandel recalls his family's experiences after the Holocaust. He touches on several reactions that were common among Holocaust survivors. His father, for example, struggled with a great deal of guilt because he had been unable to save the lives of five family members during those nightmarish years. Mandel himself coped with his horrible memories by building a new life for himself in the United States. As time passed, he also began to speak out about his wartime experiences, vowing to bear witness to the Holocaust so that such events might be avoided in the future. As he explains, part of his inspiration for speaking out came from a desire to refute the so-called Holocaust deniers—anti-Semitic extremists who say that the Holocaust never took place.

It was a rough life for my dad, especially, having lost most of his family. I remember I noticed it more than ever—started to notice it in the D.P. [displaced persons] camp—how in the middle of the night he would cry out. He took on the responsibility that it was his fault. See, my sister, who was five years old, there was a gentile family who loved her very much, and they begged my father to have her stay with them [before the Mandels were deported to Auschwitz-Birkenau]. And at the time my father thought about it, but he came to the decision, you know, that families have to stick together. No normal person would have thought at the time that in the twentieth century they would kill men, women, and even little children. [The sister died in a gas chamber along with her mother and three brothers.] Also, the fact that [upon arrival at the concentration camp] he sent my younger brother back to the mother—trying to help out my mother and his younger children, and [as a result] he sent him to his death. My father lived for thirty years after having survived the Nazi death camps…

We were lucky to have come to the United States. On July 15, 1946, we arrived in New York… Then after that we came to Pittsburgh, and we lived with our aunt. My father got a job as a carpenter. I got a job, and I went to night school to learn English. My brother went to continue on as a dental technician. And we started a new life. My father was matched up with a lady in Detroit whose husband passed on, and so we eventually moved to Detroit. My father remarried to a wonderful lady who comes from the same part of the world as we do, but she lived here

David Mandel, Videotaped Interview conducted by Elissa Schosheim, 1 February 1996. Survivors of the Shoah Visual History Foundation, Beverly Hills, CA, USA.

for some thirty-odd years before [and therefore wasn't in Europe when the Holocaust took place]. She had her own children and also comes from a very religious home, and my father was religious. He was a God-fearing, very pious man....

And somehow I never married. And I moved eventually to Grand Rapids, Michigan. I went to work for a man in a men's store, I remember, [in] 1948 for $25 a week. Eventually became his partner, and then I bought him out. And I enjoyed working. I kept busy. I kept my mind occupied. I took up golf. And I keep busy. I'm a very hyper person—I gotta keep going all the time. And I'm retired now to Florida....

For the first thirty-five years I didn't speak about the Holocaust, but I'm committed [now] to bear witness to what happened for all those who died. And the fact that there are people—deniers, revisionists—who claim that the whole thing is a hoax, and they're doing it while survivors are still alive, I have to speak up. Even though every time I speak, it pains me.

And I've made up my mind to speak to the youth, the future generations. They want to know. They are our future historians. They are our future voters. They are our future leaders. It's important that they have to know about the Holocaust, that they have to study the Holocaust. The Holocaust is part of history. It's important to mankind to know what took place. God forbid that it should ever happen again. Maybe by [my] being a witness, [others] can become witnesses to avert a Holocaust like this from ever happening again.

Source: Mandel, David. Videotaped interview conducted by Elissa Schosheim, 1 February 1996. Survivors of the Shoah Visual History Foundation, Testimony 11722.

15.3
"I Don't Know the Answer" – 1995
Excerpt from an Interview with Holocaust Survivor Peter Hersch

Peter Hersch was born Pinchas Herskovics in 1930 in Loza, a town that was then in Czechoslovakia and later was annexed by Hungary. In 1944, when he was thirteen years old, his family was deported to Auschwitz-Birkenau, where his mother and three younger siblings were killed. His father also likely died in Auschwitz. Hersch and his older sister were the only members of the family to survive the Holocaust. In the following passage from an oral interview conducted by the Shoah Visual History Foundation, Hersch recounts how a chance encounter delivered him from the Nazi gas chambers soon after his arrival at Auschwitz. This fateful event helped shape the atti-

Peter Hersch, Videotaped Interview conducted by Ruta Osborne, 2 July 1995. Survivors of the Shoah Visual History Foundation Testimony 3658.

tude that Hersch has developed toward the Holocaust—a mix of wonder at the fact that he survived and incomprehension that people were capable of willfully wreaking so much death and misery on other people.

I was with my father ... and I don't know, somebody was watching over me. This woman walked up to me. And she asked me, "how old are you?" I said, "I'm thirteen." And she said quickly, she said "don't say you're thirteen. Say you're seventeen." And she was with the S.S. there, walking around, you know?

So I said to my father, "you know, she told me to say I'm seventeen." And he said, "say you're seventeen, if she told you." And that saved my life, you know, in a way, because they were walking around, the S.S., and asking "how old are you?" .... Everybody they were asking, you know? And they came to me, too. So of course I didn't look seventeen. I'm short, and I was with those clothes ... the [oversized] striped uniform. So I said I was seventeen. He looked me up and down and up and down, and he left me there, left me with my father.

So that was unbelievable. I mean, it was just luck that she walked over to me... She wasn't dressed in a uniform. She was walking around with these S.S. Whether she was [one of the soldier's] girlfriends—I don't know what it was....

What the Germans did to us, I can't forget. I cannot forget. And I still can't, for the life of me, understand how it could have happened. I cannot understand, and I—I don't know. I just don't know. Yet, I can't blame all the Germans. In the young generation, how can I say that it's their fault, too? I can't. But I've never been back to Germany since then, since I left.

I do want to, before I die, I do want to go back one day. And my sister wants to go back to Auschwitz to say Kaddish [the Jewish prayer for the dead] for my parents and my brothers and sisters because that's where they died.

I tried to survive—number one. I tried. I didn't give in. I never gave in for one minute. And I'm also lucky that I wasn't shot.... That I had this girl in Auschwitz coming to me and telling me to say that I'm older. Why would she say something like that to me?

So it's a miracle, anyway. I mean it's—I mean I don't know the answer. I don't know the answer. But I survived.

Source: Hersch, Peter. Videotaped interview conducted by Ruta Osborne, 2 July 1995. Survivors of the Shoah Visual History Foundation, Beverly Hills, CA, USA.

15.4
"I Have Tried to Fight Those Who Would Forget" – 1986
Text of Elie Wiesel's "Hope, Despair and Memory" Nobel Peace Prize Acceptance Speech

Author and humanitarian Elie Wiesel is perhaps the most famous survivor of the Holocaust. He was born in 1928 in Sighet, Transylvania, which is now part of Romania. At age fifteen, he and his family were deported by the Nazis to Auschwitz-Birkenau. Wiesel and his two older sisters survived, but both his mother and his younger sister were murdered at Auschwitz. Wiesel and his father were later transported to the Buchenwald death camp, where his father perished shortly before the camp was liberated by Allied forces in April 1945.

After the war, Wiesel wrote an internationally acclaimed memoir about the Holocaust, La Nuit or Night, which was eventually translated into more than thirty languages, and more than forty other books of fiction and non-fiction. He also served as Chairman of the President's Commission on the Holocaust, Founding Chairman of the United States Holocaust Memorial Council, and co-founder (with his wife, Marion) of the Elie Wiesel Foundation for Humanity. Over the years, he has also been a tireless human rights advocate for repressed and disenfranchised peoples around the world.

In 1986 Wiesel's decades of human rights work—and his determined efforts to keep the world from ever experiencing another Holocaust—were formally recognized by the Norwegian Nobel Committee, which awarded him the Nobel Peace Prize in Oslo, Norway, on December 10. "[Wiesel has] become a witness for truth and justice," declared the Committee. "From the abyss of the death camps he has come as a messenger to mankind—not with a message of hate and revenge, but with one of brotherhood and atonement. He has become a powerful spokesman for the view of mankind and the unlimited humanity which is, at all times, the basis of a lasting peace.... Elie Wiesel's standpoint is not characterized by a passive obsession with a tragic history; rather it is a reconstructed belief in God, humanity, and the future." Following is the text of "Hope, Despair and Memory," Wiesel's Nobel acceptance speech.

Your Majesty, Your Royal Highnesses, Your Excellencies, Chairman [Egil] Aarvik, members of the Nobel Committee, ladies and gentlemen:

Words of gratitude. First to our common Creator. This is what the Jewish tradition commands us to do. At special occasions, one is duty-bound to recite the following prayer: "Barukh shehekhyanu vekiymanu vehigianu lazman haze"— "Blessed be Thou for having sustained us until this day."

Then—thank you, Chairman Aarvik, for the depth of your eloquence. And for the generosity of your gesture. Thank you for building bridges between people and generations. Thank you, above all, for helping humankind make peace its most urgent and noble aspiration.

I am moved, deeply moved by your words, Chairman Aarvik. And it is with a profound sense of humility that I accept the honor—the highest there is—that you have chosen to bestow upon me. I know your choice transcends my person.

Do I have the right to represent the multitudes who have perished? Do I have the right to accept this great honor on their behalf? I do not. No one may speak for the dead, no one may interpret their mutilated dreams and visions. And yet, I sense their presence. I always do—and at this moment more than ever. The presence of my parents, that of my little sister. The presence of my teachers, my friends, my companions...

This honor belongs to all the survivors and their children and, through us to the Jewish people with whose destiny I have always identified.

I remember: it happened yesterday, or eternities ago. A young Jewish boy discovered the Kingdom of Night. I remember his bewilderment, I remember his anguish. It all happened so fast. The ghetto. The deportation. The sealed cattle car. The fiery altar upon which the history of our people and the future of mankind were meant to be sacrificed.

I remember he asked his father: "Can this be true? This is the twentieth century, not the Middle Ages. Who would allow such crimes to be committed? How could the world remain silent?"

And now the boy is turning to me. "Tell me," he asks, "what have you done with my future, what have you done with your life?" And I tell him that I have tried. That I have tried to keep memory alive, that I have tried to fight those who would forget. Because if we forget, we are guilty, we are accomplices.

And then I explain to him how naïve we were, that the world did know and remained silent. And that is why I swore never to be silent whenever [and] wherever human beings endure suffering and humiliation. We must take sides. Neutrality helps the oppressor, never the victim. Silence encourages the tormentor, never the tormented. Sometimes we must interfere. When human lives are endangered, when human dignity is in jeopardy, national borders and sensitivities become irrelevant. Wherever men and women are persecuted because of their race, religion, or political views, that place must—at that moment—become the center of the universe.

Of course, since I am a Jew profoundly rooted in my people's memory and tradition, my first response is to Jewish fears, Jewish needs, Jewish crises. For I belong to a traumatized generation, one that experienced the abandonment and solitude of our people. It would be unnatural for me not to make Jewish priorities my own: Israel, Soviet Jewry, Jews in Arab land... But others are important to me.

Apartheid is, in my view, as abhorrent as anti-Semitism. To me, Andrei Sakharov's isolation is as much a disgrace as Joseph Begun's imprisonment and Ida Nudel's exile. As is the denial of solidarity and its leader Lech Walesa's right to dissent. And Nelson Mandela's interminable imprisonment.

There is so much injustice and suffering crying out for our attention: victims of hunger, of racism and political persecution—in Chile, for instance, or in Ethiopia—writers and poets, prisoners in so many lands governed by the Left and by the Right.

Human rights are being violated on every continent. More people are oppressed than free. How can one not be sensitive to their plight? Human suffering anywhere concerns men and women everywhere. That applies also to Palestinians to whose plight I am sensitive but whose methods I deplore when they lead to violence. Violence is not the answer. Terrorism is the most dangerous of answers. They are frustrated, that is understandable, something must be done. The refugees and their misery. The children and their fear. The uprooted and their hopelessness. Something must be done about their situation. Both the Jewish people and the Palestinian people have lost too many sons and daughters and have shed too much blood. This must stop, and all attempts to stop it must be encouraged. Israel will cooperate, I am sure of that. I trust Israel for I have faith in the Jewish people. Let Israel be given a chance, let hatred and danger be removed from their horizons, and there will be peace in and around the Holy Land. Please understand my deep and total commitment to Israel: if you could remember what I remember, you would understand. Israel is the only nation in the world whose existence is threatened. Should Israel lose but one war, it would mean her end and ours as well. But I have faith. Faith in the God of Abraham, Isaac, and Jacob, and even in His creation. Without it no action would be possible. And action is the only remedy to indifference, the most insidious danger of all. Isn't that the meaning of Alfred Nobel's legacy? Wasn't his fear of war a shield against war?

> *"I swore never to be silent whenever [and] wherever human beings endure suffering and humiliation. We must take sides. Neutrality helps the oppressor, never the victim. Silence encourages the tormentor, never the tormented."*

There is so much to be done, there is so much that can be done. One person —a Raoul Wallenberg, an Albert Schweitzer, Martin Luther King, Jr.—one person of integrity, can make a difference, a difference of life and death. As long as one dissident is in prison, our freedom will not be true. As long as one child is hungry, our life will be filled with anguish and shame. What all these victims need above all is to know that they are not alone; that we are not forgetting them, that when their voices are stifled we shall lend them ours, that while their freedom depends on ours, the quality of our freedom depends on theirs.

This is what I say to the young Jewish boy wondering what I have done with his years. It is in his name that I speak to you and that I express to you my deepest gratitude as one who has emerged from the Kingdom of Night. We know that every moment is a moment of grace, every hour an offering; not to share them would mean to betray them.

Our lives no longer belong to us alone; they belong to all those who need us desperately.

Thank you, Chairman Aarvik. Thank you, members of the Nobel Committee. Thank you, people of Norway, for declaring on this singular occasion that our survival has meaning for mankind.

Source: Wiesel, Elie. "Hope, Despair and Memory" (Nobel Lecture, December 11, 1986). In *Nobel Lectures, Peace 1981-1990*, edited by Irwin Adams. Singapore: World Scientific Publishing Co., 1997.

15.5
Commemorating the Holocaust – 2005
Text of the European Parliament's "Resolution on Remembrance of the Holocaust, Anti-Semitism, and Racism"

The legacy of the Holocaust continues to have an enormous impact on political events in Europe. The prospect of additional mass killings of civilians has haunted the continent ever since World War II, and the "ethnic cleansing" that took place in the 1990s in the territories that once made up Yugoslavia showed that the danger was still very real. In addition, sporadic anti-Semitic incidents and other forms of racial, ethnic, and religious discrimination have continued to raise concerns in recent decades. The creation and growth of the European Union (EU), which began in the 1990s, has held out some hope that the increased cooperation among European nations will lead to more effective measures to combat such incidents. In January 2005 the European Parliament, the legislative body of the EU, adopted the following resolution, which encourages official commemoration of the Holocaust and urges member nations to condemn racism, anti-Semitism, and the persecution of minorities.

The European Parliament,

– having regard to Articles 2, 6, 7 and 29 of the Treaty on European Union and Article 13 of the EC Treaty, which commit the Member States to upholding the highest standards of human rights and non-discrimination, and to the European Charter of Fundamental Rights,

– having regard to its previous resolutions on racism, xenophobia and anti-semitism of 27 October 1994, 27 April 1995, 26 October 1995, 30 January 1997 and 16 March 2000, to the report of its Committee of Inquiry into Racism and Xenophobia of 1990 and its Written Declaration of 7 July 2000 on remembrance of the Holocaust,

– having regard to Council Regulation (EC) No 1035/97 of 2 June 1997 establishing a European Monitoring Centre on Racism and Xenophobia (EUMC) and to the EUMC's various reports on racism in the EU, including "Manifestations of Anti-Semitism in the EU 2002-2003" and "Perceptions of Anti-Semitism in the European Union", both published in March 2004,

– having regard to the Berlin Declaration of the second OSCE Conference on Anti-Semitism, held in Berlin on 28-29 April 2004, and to the recent appointment by the OSCE of the Personal Representative on Combating Anti-Semitism,

– having regard to the Declaration of the Stockholm International Forum on the Holocaust held on 26-28 January 2000, which called for increased education on the Holocaust,

– having regard to the establishment of 27 January 2005 as Holocaust Memorial Day in several EU Member States,

– having regard to Rule 108(5) of its Rules of Procedure,

A. whereas 27 January 2005, the sixtieth anniversary of the liberation of Nazi Germany's death camp at Auschwitz-Birkenau, where a combined total of up to 1.5 million Jews, Roma, Poles, Russians and prisoners of various other nationalities, and homosexuals, were murdered, is not only a major occasion for European citizens to remember and condemn the enormous horror and tragedy of the Holocaust, but also for addressing the disturbing rise in anti-semitism, and especially anti-semitic incidents, in Europe, and for learning anew the wider lessons about the dangers of victimising people on the basis of race, ethnic origin, religion, social classification, politics or sexual orientation,

B. whereas Europe must not forget its own history: the concentration and extermination camps built by the Nazis are among the most shameful and painful pages of the history of our continent; whereas the crimes committed at Auschwitz must live on in the memory of future generations, as a warning against genocide of this kind, rooted in contempt for other human beings, hatred, anti-semitism, racism and totalitarianism,

C. whereas discrimination on religious and ethnic grounds continues to be practised at various levels, notwithstanding the important measures adopted by the European Union in application of Article 13 of the EC Treaty,

D. whereas Jews in Europe are experiencing a heightened sense of insecurity as a result of anti-semitism disseminated on the Internet, manifested in the desecration of synagogues, cemeteries and other religious sites, attacks on Jewish schools and cultural centres, and attacks on Jewish people in Europe, causing numerous injuries,

E. whereas the Holocaust has been seared on the consciousness of Europe, especially for its murderous hatred of Jews and Roma on the basis of their racial or religious identity, despite which anti-semitism and racial and religious prejudice continue to pose a very serious threat to their victims and to European and international values of democracy, human rights and the rule of law, and therefore to overall European and global security,

F. whereas there needs to be an ongoing dialogue with the media about the way their reporting and commentary can contribute both positively and negatively to the perception and understanding of religious, ethnic and racial issues, and to the presentation of historical truth,

1. Pays homage to all the victims of the Nazis and is convinced that lasting peace in Europe must be based on remembrance of its history; rejects and condemns revisionist views and denial of the Holocaust as shameful and contrary to historical truth, and expresses concern over the rise of extremist and xenophobic parties and growing public acceptance of their views;

2. Calls on the institutions of the European Union, the Member States and all European democratic political parties to:

   – condemn all acts of intolerance and incitement to racial hatred, as well as all acts of harassment or racist violence,

   – condemn in particular and without reservation all acts and expressions of anti-semitism of whatever kind,

   – condemn in particular all acts of violence motivated by religious or racial hatred or intolerance, including attacks on religious places, sites and shrines belonging to Jewish, Muslim or other faiths, as well as against minorities such as the Roma;

3. Urges the Council and the Commission, as well as the various levels of local, regional and national government in the Member States, to coordinate their measures to combat anti-semitism and attacks on minority groups including Roma and third-country nationals in the Member States, in order to uphold the principles of tolerance and non-discrimination and to promote social, economic and political integration;

4. Is convinced that these efforts should also include the promotion of dialogue and cooperation between the different segments of society at the local and national levels, including dialogue and cooperation between different cultural, ethnic and religious communities;

5. Reaffirms its conviction that remembrance and education are vital components of the effort to make intolerance, discrimination and racism a thing of the past, and urges the Council, Commission and Member States to strengthen the fight against anti-semitism and racism through promoting awareness, especially among young people, of the history and lessons of the Holocaust by:

– encouraging Holocaust remembrance, including making 27 January European Holocaust Memorial Day across the whole of the EU,

– reinforcing Holocaust education through the use of all the Holocaust memorial institutions, especially the Auschwitz-Birkenau Museum (Państwowe Muzeum Auschwitz-Birkenau w Oświęcimiu) and the Berlin Holocaust Information Centre (Stiftung Denkmal für die ermordeten Juden Europas) as European resources, making Holocaust education and European citizenship standard elements in school curricula throughout the EU, and setting the current fight against racism, xenophobia and anti-semitism against the background of the Shoah (Holocaust),

– ensuring that school programmes in the 25 EU countries address the teaching of the Second World War with the utmost historical rigour and by taking advantage of Parliament's insertion in the 2005 budget of provision for schools throughout the EU to adopt war graves and monuments;

6. Welcomes the declared intention of the Luxembourg Presidency to restart the stalled discussions on the proposal for a Council Framework Decision on combating Racism and Xenophobia, and urges the Council to reach agreement on a ban on incitement to racial and religious hatred throughout the EU while preserving legitimate free speech;

7. Invites the Commission to start a review of the application of the Racial Equality Directive 2000/43/EC aimed at strengthening European Union anti-discrimination measures and to organise a major conference involving all the actors concerned, in particular political representatives, public institutions at a national, regional and local level, and NGOs and associations active in this field;

8. Instructs its President to forward this resolution to the Council, the Commission and the governments and parliaments of the Member States and candidate countries.

Source: "European Parliament Resolution on Remembrance of the Holocaust, Anti-semitism and Racism." January 27, 2005, European Parliament. Available online at http://www.europarl.eu.int/omk/sipade 3?PUBREF=-//EP//TEXT+TA+P6-TA-2005-0018+0+DOC+XML+V0//EN&L=EN&LEVEL=2&NAV= S&LSTDOC=Y&LSTDOC=N.

GLOSSARY

Leading Figures of the Holocaust

Anilewicz, Mordecai (1919-1943) – Leader of the Jewish resistance movement in the Warsaw Ghetto.

Chamberlain, Charles Stewart (1855-1927) – English author who praised Germanic peoples as genetically superior and characterized Jews as a drag on the advance of civilization; described by Adolf Hitler as the "prophet of the Third Reich."

Eichmann, Adolf (1906-1962) – Nazi official with the paramilitary SS (*Schutzstaffel*) who played a leading role in implementing and executing the "Final Solution"—the Third Reich plan to exterminate all Jews in Europe.

Frank, Anne (1929-1945) – Jewish teenager who wrote *The Diary of a Girl*, a famous Holocaust memoir detailing her family's desperate efforts to avoid capture by the Nazis.

Frank, Hans (1900-1946) – Nazi official who was head of the Government General in occupied Poland; his actions contributed to the murder of millions of Polish Jews and Poles during World War II.

Gobineau, Joseph Arthur Comte de (1816-1882) – French writer who promoted the idea of Aryan genetic superiority.

Goebbels, Joseph (1897-1945) – Deeply anti-Semitic Nazi leader who served as propaganda minister for the Third Reich.

Göring, Hermann (1893-1946) – Leading Nazi official who founded the Gestapo—Nazi's Germany's secret police—which played a major role in identifying Jews and other "enemies of the Third Reich" for forced deportation and murder.

Heydrich, Reinhard (1904-1942) – Head of the intelligence unit of the SS (*Schutzstaffel*), the paramilitary arm of the Nazi Party, and a major architect of the Holocaust.

Himmler, Heinrich (1900-1945) – Commander of the SS (*Schutzstaffel*), the paramilitary arm of the Nazi Party, and one of the leading organizers of the Holocaust; he was the chief architect and administrator of the Nazi extermination camp system in Poland, where more than half of all Holocaust victims were murdered.

Hitler, Adolf (1889-1945) – Leader of the Nazi Party in Germany and Chancellor of Germany from 1933 to 1945; his deep convictions about Aryan supremacy and virulent anti-Semitism were important factors in the Holocaust.

Höss, Rudolf (1900-1947) – Commandant of the Auschwitz death camp, where more European Jews were killed than in any other camp during the Holocaust.

Levi, Primo (1919-1987) – Italian Jew who survived a year at Auschwitz to become a leading writer on the Holocaust.

Rosenberg, Alfred (1893-1946) – An early shaper and architect of Nazi philosophy who served in a variety of important government posts for the Third Reich.

Stalin, Joseph (1878-1953) – Tyrannical leader of the Union of Soviet Socialist Republics (USSR) from the mid-1920s until his sudden death in 1953.

Streicher, Julius (1885-1946) – Nazi publisher who edited *Der Stürmer,* one of Germany's most deeply anti-Semitic newspapers, and published numerous virulently anti-Jewish children's books.

Vom Rath, Ernst (1909-1938) – German diplomat whose November 1938 assassination at the hands of a German Jew became the pretext for Nazi officials to launch Kristallnacht.

Wallenberg, Raoul (1912–?) Swedish diplomat who saved thousands of Hungarian Jews from death at the hands of the Nazis during World War II.

Wiesel, Elie (1928-) — Jewish death camp survivor who became a renowned political activist, humanitarian, and writer after World War II; in 1986 he was awarded the Nobel Peace Prize.

Wiesenthal, Simon (1908-2005) – Jewish Holocaust survivor who became a famed "Nazi hunter" after World War II, tracking Nazi war criminals all around the world.

Holocaust Terms and Phrases

Allies – During World War II, the group of nations led by the United States, Great Britain, and the Soviet Union that joined in war against Germany and other Axis powers.

Anschluss – German term for the forced annexation of Austria by Germany in March 1938.

Anti-Semitism – Opposition to and discrimination against people of Jewish faith or ethnic background.

Aryan – In Nazi racial theory, a term for people of pure—and thus superior—Germanic (Nordic and Caucasian) blood.

Axis Powers – During World War II, the nations of Germany, Italy, and Japan, who fought together against the Allied powers; the Axis alliance eventually came to include Bulgaria, Croatia, Hungary, Romania, and Slovakia as well.

Brown Shirts – *See* SA.

Concentration Camp – Prison camps constructed by Nazi Germany to hold "enemies of the Third Reich," including Jews, political prisoners, homosexuals, Gypsies, and Polish citizens. Types of concentration camps included prison camps, labor camps, and death camps.

Death Camp – Nazi concentration camps devoted to the extermination of their inmate populations; some of these camps (like Auschwitz-Birkenau) used gas chambers to carry out mass executions of Jews and other targeted peoples, while others (such as Dachau) were not equipped with gas chambers but still killed thousands by starvation, disease, and murder.

Death March – Forced marches of prisoners over long distances under horrible conditions; these marches were launched by the Nazis late in World War II in reaction to mounting fears that approaching Allies might be able to liberate camp inmates.

Deportation – Forced removal of people from their residence and mandated relocation elsewhere.

Einsatzgruppen – SS death squads that operated in Nazi-occupied territories during World War II; they carried out mass executions of more than one million civilians during the war.

Final Solution – Nazi euphemism for the extermination of all Jews in Europe.

Genocide – The deliberate, systematic destruction of a racial, cultural, or political group.

Gestapo – Nazi Germany's Secret Police.

Ghetto – Originally a Yiddish word that referred to the segregated sections of cities where Jews were forced to live during the Middle Ages, the word and concept were revived by the Nazis, who sealed Jews into poor sections of cities as part of their Final Solution scheme.

International Military Tribunal – An international court chartered by the governments of the United States, Great Britain, the Union of Soviet Socialist Republics, and France to prosecute Nazi war criminals.

Judenrat – Jewish community authority, appointed by the Nazis to administrate affairs within Jewish ghettos and other occupied areas.

Kristallnacht – Also known as The Night of Broken Glass; this Nazi-led pogrom against Jewish families, businesses, and synagogues throughout Germany and Austria took place on November 9, 1938.

Nazi – Member of the National Socialist German Workers' Party, the right-wing and virulently antisemitic political organization led by Adolf Hitler from 1921 to 1945.

Pogrom – Russian word for "devastation," and the term used to describe organized violence against Jews, usually with the tacit approval of state authorities.

SA – *Sturmabteilung* or Storm Troopers, also known as "Brown Shirts"; an armed organization within the Nazi Party that carried out various terrorist and intimidation activities in Germany during Hitler's rise to power.

SD – *Sicherheitsdienst*; the primary security and intelligence arm of the SS in the Third Reich.

Shoah – Hebrew word often used by Jews for the Holocaust.

SS – *Schutzstaffel*; originally formed in 1925 as Hitler's personal guard, it gradually grew into the overseer of all Nazi police and security systems and the primary organization responsible for carrying out the "Final Solution" in concentration camps and occupied territories.

Sudetenland – A mainly German-speaking region of Czechoslovakia that was annexed by Germany in October 1938.

Third Reich – The Nazi designation of Germany from 1933 to 1945.

Wannsee – A Nazi conference held on January 20, 1942, beside Lake Wannsee in Berlin, where Nazi officials decided to make total annihilation of European Jews an explicit policy objective.

Wehrmacht – Combined armed forces of Germany from 1935 to 1945.

Weimar Republic – Term for Germany's national government from 1919 to 1933, when it was a parliamentary democracy.

CHRONOLOGY

Note: This Chronology of Holocaust events includes a see reference feature. Under this arrangement, many events listed in the chronology include page references to relevant primary documents featured in the book.

1871

The independent states of Germany are unified into the German Empire.

1889

April 20   Adolf Hitler is born in Braunau, Austria.

1914

August 2   The German army invades Luxembourg, beginning World War I.

1918

November 11   The Armistice is declared, ending the fighting in World War I.

1919

January   Germany's first postwar election is held. The results lead to formation of the Weimar Republic.

June 23   The German National Assembly accepts the terms of the Treaty of Versailles. It requires Germany to accept responsibility for World War I, give up European territory and foreign colonies, reduce its military, and pay reparations to other nations. *See p. 37.*

September   Adolf Hitler joins the German Workers' Party, soon to become the National Socialist German Workers' Party (NSDAP) or Nazi Party. *See p. 43.*

1923

November 8-9   The Nazis stage a failed revolt against the German government. Hitler is arrested and convicted of treason but serves only eight months in prison. *See p. 51.*

1925

July 18   Adolf Hitler's political manifesto *Mein Kampf* is published. *See p. 53.*

1929

November   The worldwide economic downturn known as the Great Depression begins.

1930

September 14   Election victories give the Nazis 107 seats in the German Parliament, making them the second largest political party in the country.

1932

July 31   Election victories make the Nazis the most powerful party in the German Parliament with 230 seats.

1933

January 30   Hitler is named Chancellor of Germany.

February 27   A fire at the Reichstag (German Parliament building) is used by Hitler and the Nazis to issue an emergency order that suspends many of the civil-rights statutes in the German constitution. A crackdown on political groups and newspapers opposed to the Nazis follows.

March 5   Parliamentary elections strengthen the Nazi hold on the German legislature.

March 20   The Nazis establish their first concentration camp, at Dachau.

March 24   The Law to Remove the Distress of People and State (also known as the Enabling Law) is passed, giving Hitler the power to rule by decree and transform the country into a dictatorship. *See p. 63.*

April 1   The Nazi Party institutes a nationwide boycott of Jewish shops and businesses.

April 7   The Law for the Reestablishment of the Professional Civil Service, the first German law to discriminate against "non-Aryans," is passed. *See p. 69.*

April 26   The Gestapo is created in the German state of Prussia by Hermann Göring.

September 29   Nazis prohibit Jews from owning land.

November 24   The Law against Habitual and Dangerous Criminals is passed, giving Nazis the legal authority to send beggars, alcoholics, unemployed people and other "undesirables" to concentration camps.

1934

June 30 "The Knight of the Long Knives," in which Hitler conducted a deadly purge of the SA leadership to further consolidate power.

August 2 Hitler becomes *Führer* (leader) of Germany and Commander-in-Chief of Germany's armed forces.

1935

May 21 The Third Reich bans Jews from serving in the German military.

September 15 The Nuremberg Laws, which declare that Jews are not German citizens, are enacted. *See p. 75; p. 78.*

1936

March The SS "Death's Head" Division is established to staff concentration camps.

August The Summer Olympic Games are held in Berlin.

1937

July The Buchenwald concentration camp opens.

1938

March 13 Germany annexes Austria, and a few days later, the SS is placed in charge of Jewish affairs in Austria.

April 26 The Third Reich passes laws requiring Jews to register all their wealth and property with the state.

July 25 Nazis prohibit Jewish doctors from practicing medicine.

September 29 The Munich Agreement between Germany, Italy, Great Britain, and France is signed; this agreement allows Nazi Germany to annex the "Sudetenland," a portion of western Czechoslovakia. By the following year Hitler's government controls the entire country.

October 27-28 Jews of Polish nationality residing in Germany are deported.

November 9-10 The Nazi government orchestrates *Kristallnacht*—the "Night of Broken Glass"—a wave of violence that targets Jews all across Germany. A series of severe anti-Jewish measures follow soon after. *See p. 113; p. 115; p. 116*

November 12 Germany fines Jews for damages related to Kristallnacht. *See p. 122.*

November 15 Jewish students are expelled from all non-Jewish schools in Germany.

1939

January 30   Adolf Hitler warns in a speech that, should a second world war take place, it would result in "the annihilation of the Jewish race in Europe." *See p. 179.*

March 15   Germany occupies Czechoslovakia.

August 23   Germany and the Soviet Union conclude a nonaggression pact.

September 1   Germany invades Poland, beginning World War II. *See p. 145.*

September 3   Great Britain and France declare war on Germany in retaliation for its invasion of Poland.

October   Nazis launch euthanasia program against sick and disabled citizens in Germany. *See p. 176.*

November 23   Regulations are issued required all Polish Jews over age ten to wear yellow Stars of David.

1940

February 12   First deportation of German Jews into occupied Poland. *See p. 161.*

April-June   The German army conquers much of western Europe, including Denmark, Norway, Belgium, the Netherlands, and France.

June   Nazis establish the Auschwitz concentration camp.

September   Germany begins a sustained and intensive bombing campaign against London, England.

October   Jews are deported from southwestern Germany and sent to concentration camps in southern France.

November 15   The Warsaw Ghetto is sealed off by Nazi forces from the outside world.

1941

April   Germany invades Yugoslavia and Greece.

June 22   Germany attacks the Soviet Union. Special units of the German SS, the *Einsatzgruppen*, begin the systematic murder of Jews, usually by gunfire, in areas of eastern Europe captured by the advancing German Army. *See p. 191; p. 194; p. 206.*

July 31   Nazi leader Hermann Göring authorizes Reinhard Heydrich, the head of the SS intelligence unit, to make preparations for a "total solution" to the "Jewish problem." *See p. 182.*

August 5-7   More than 10,000 Jews are murdered by the Nazis at Pinsk, Poland.

September   Nazi commanders begin conducting their first gassing experiments at Auschwitz.

September 1   German Jews ordered to wear yellow Stars of David. *See p. 83.*

September 17   The Nazis commence general deportation of German Jews.

September 19   5,000 Jews are murdered by Nazi forces at Zhitomir, Ukraine.

September 29-30   More than 33,000 Jews are murdered by members of the *Einsatzgruppen* at Kiev, Ukraine.

October 23   Jews are prohibited from emigrating from all German-controlled areas of Europe.

October 29   Approximately 10,000 Jews are killed in the "Great Action" at Kovno, Lithuania. *See p. 217; p. 225.*

December 7   The Japanese attack the U.S. fleet at Pearl Harbor in Hawaii; the United States responds by declaring war against both Japan and its allies Germany and Italy.

December 8   The first extermination camp killings begin at Chelmno, Poland.

1942

January 2   Nazi officials hold the Wannsee Conference outside Berlin to discuss methods for carrying out the so-called Final Solution.

March   Mass killings begin at the Belzec extermination camp in Poland.

April   Mass killings begin at the Auschwitz-Birkenau extermination camp in Poland. *See p. 253.*

May   Mass killings begin at the Sobibór extermination camp in Poland.

June 29   At a press conference in London, the World Jewish Congress estimates that the Nazis have already killed over one million European Jews.

July   Mass killings begin at the Treblinka extermination camp in Poland; the majority of the victims are from the Warsaw ghetto. *See p. 227.*

July   Nazis begin deporting Jews from Amsterdam and France to concentration camps in Poland.

October   Himmler orders all Jews in concentration camps on German soil to be sent to the Auschwitz and Majdanek death camps.

December   The United Nations Information Office in New York releases a report that confirms and authenticates proliferating accounts that the Nazis are trying to exterminate all Jews in Europe.

1943

February 2   After months of fighting, German forces at Stalingrad, Russia, surrender. This defeat begins the German retreat westward from Russia.

April 19-May 16   The remaining Jewish residents of the Warsaw ghetto rise up against the Nazis, killing many German troops before the resistance is finally crushed. *See p. 289; p. 291; p. 292, p. 294.*

May   Dr. Josef Mengele arrives at Auschwitz and begins conducting "medical" experiments on prisoners.

June 11   Himmler orders the liquidation of all Jewish ghettos in occupied Poland.

September 3   Italy secretly signs an armistice with the Allies, six weeks after Mussolini is toppled from power.

September-October   A mass rescue operation carried out by Danish citizens allows 7,000 Jews to escape to safety in Sweden.

October 14   A massive prison break of Jewish inmates and Soviet prisoners of war takes place at Sobibor; most are caught and executed, but fifty prisoners escape.

1944

January 3   Red Army troops reach the eastern border of Poland.

March 19   Nazis occupy Hungary.

May 15   Nazis begin deporting Hungarian Jews to Auschwitz. *See p. 258.*

June 6   Allied forces land at Normandy in the pivotal D-Day invasion of France.

July   Swedish diplomat Raoul Wallenberg arrives in Budapest; over the next several months he uses his office to save an estimated 33,000 Jews in Nazi custody.

August 4   Anne Frank and her family are arrested by the Gestapo in Amsterdam.

October   Members of the *Sonderkommando* prisoner brigade at Auschwitz-Birkenau stage an uprising that damages one of the crematoriums.

November   The gassings at Auschwitz-Birkenau come to an end as SS Chief Himmler orders the destruction of gas chambers and crematoria.

1945

January	The Nazis begin death marches of camp prisoners out of Poland and into Germany; these death marches ultimately claim an estimated 250,000 Jewish lives. *See p. 313*
January	Soviet troops liberate Budapest and Warsaw.
January 27	Soviet forces capture Auschwitz.
April 10	Allied troops liberate the Buchenwald death camp.
April 15	British troops liberate the Bergen-Belsen concentration camp. Prisoners in other German camps are likewise freed by Allied forces in the closing weeks of the war.
April 23	Soviet troops arrive at the outskirts of Berlin.
April 30	Adolf Hitler commits suicide in Berlin. *See p. 331.*
May 7	Nazi Germany surrenders, ending World War II in Europe.
May 9	Göring is captured by American forces.
May 23	Himmler commits suicide after being captured by Allied soldiers.
November 20	The first of the Nuremberg War Crimes Trials begins.

1946

October	The first and most important Nuremberg War Crimes Trial concludes, with many Nazi defendants sentenced to death.
October 16	Göring commits suicide two hours before his scheduled execution.
December	The second Nuremberg War Crimes Trials begin, targeting Nazi doctors and scientists who committed atrocities during the war.

1948

May 14	The State of Israel is proclaimed.
October	The last of the Nuremburg trials ends.

1952

September 10	The Federal Republic of Germany (West Germany) agrees to pay restitution to victims of the Holocaust.
November	A memorial to the victims of the Bergen-Belsen concentration camp is dedicated in Germany. Other memorials are also established at the Dachau and Sachsenhausen camps.

1961

April-June   Adolf Eichmann is tried in Israel after his capture in Argentina a year earlier. He is convicted in December and executed the following year.

1986

December 10   Holocaust survivor Elie Wiesel receives the Nobel Peace Prize for his literary and humanitarian works.

1992

A memorial to the victims of the Holocaust opens at Wannsee, Germany, where in 1942 Nazi leaders drew up plans related to the Holocaust.

1993

April 22   The United States Holocaust Memorial Museum opens in Washington, D.C.

2004

December 15   A national memorial to Holocaust victims opens in Berlin.

2005

January 27   The European Parliament officially commemorates the Holocaust with its "Resolution on Remembrance of the Holocaust, Anti-Semitism, and Racism." *See p. 355.*

November 5   The United Nations General Assembly passes a resolution designating January 27 as an annual Holocaust memorial day.

PHOTO CREDITS

FURTHER READING

General/Overview

Arad, Yitzhak, Yisrael Gutman, and Abraham Margaliot, eds. *Documents on the Holocaust: Selected Sources on the Destruction of the Jews of Germany and Austria, Poland and the Soviet Union*. Jerusalem: Yad Vashem, 1981.

Bauer, Yehuda. *A History of the Holocaust*. Rev. ed. New York: Franklin Watts, 2000.

Dawidowicz, Lucy S., ed. *A Holocaust Reader*. New York: Behrman House, 1976.

———. *The War against the Jews, 1933-1945*. New York: Bantam, 1986.

Dwork, Debórah, and Robert Jan van Pelt. *Holocaust: A History*. New York: Norton, 2002.

Gilbert, Martin. *The Holocaust: A History of the Jews in Europe during the Second World War*. New York: Henry Holt, 1986.

———. *Never Again: A History of the Holocaust*. New York: Universe, 2000.

Hilberg, Raul. *The Destruction of the European Jews*. 3 vols. New York: Holmes & Meier, 1985.

Holocaust Education Foundation "Holocaust Teacher Resource Center." http://www.holocaust-trc.org.

Kershaw, Ian. *Hitler 1889-1936: Hubris*. New York: Norton, 1999.

———. *Hitler 1936-1945: Nemesis*. New York: Norton, 2000.

Lewy, Guenter. *The Nazi Persecution of the Gypsies*. New York: Oxford University Press, 2000.

Meltzer, Milton. *Never to Forget: The Jews of the Holocaust*. New York: Harper, 1976.

Nazi Conspiracy and Aggression. 10 vols. Washington, DC: United States Government Printing Office, 1946.

Noakes, J., and G. Pridham. *Nazism 1919-1945: A Documentary Reader*. 3 vols. Exeter, UK: University of Exeter Press, 1997.

Ofer, Dalia, and Leonore J. Weitzman, eds. *Women in the Holocaust*. New Haven: Yale University Press, 1998.

Shirer, William. *The Rise and Fall of the Third Reich: A History of Nazi Germany*. New York: Simon & Schuster, 1960.

Stackelberg, Roderick, and Sally A. Winkle, eds. *Nazi Germany Sourcebook*. London: Routledge, 2002.

Survivors of the Shoah Visual History Foundation. "Surviving Auschwitz: Five Personal Journies." http://www.vhf.org/survivingauschwitz

Trial of the Major War Criminals before the International Military Tribunal, Nuremberg, 14 November 1945-1 October 1946. 42 vols. Nuremberg, Germany: International Military Tribunal, 1947.

United States Holocaust Memorial Museum. http://www.ushmm.org.

Yad Vashem: The Holocaust Martyrs' and Heroes' Remembrance Authority. http://www.yadvashem.org.

Yahil, Leni. *The Holocaust: The Fate of European Jewry, 1932-1945.* New York: Oxford University Press, 1990.

The Roots of Anti-Semitism

Cohn-Sherbok, Dan. *Atlas of Jewish History.* New York: Routledge, 1994.

Flannery, Edward H. *The Anguish of the Jews: Twenty-three Centuries of Anti-Semitism.* New York: Macmillan, 1965.

Patterson, Charles. *Anti-Semitism: The Road to the Holocaust and Beyond.* New York: Walker and Company, 1988.

Segel, Binjamin W. *A Lie and a Libel: The History of the Protocols of the Elders of Zion.* Edited and translated by Richard S. Levy. Lincoln, NE: University of Nebraska Press, 1995.

Sherman, Franklin. Introduction to "On Jews and Their Lies." In *Luther's Works,* Vol. 47, *The Christian in Society IV,* by Martin Luther. Edited by Franklin Sherman. Translated by Martin H. Bertram. Philadelphia: Fortress Press, 1971.

World War I and the Rise of the Nazi Party

Allen, William S. *The Nazi Seizure of Power: The Experience of a Single German Town, 1922-1945.* Rev. ed. New York: Franklin Watts, 1984.

Evans, Richard J. *The Coming of the Third Reich: A History.* New York: Penguin, 2005.

Gordon, Sarah. *Hitler, Germans, and the "Jewish Question."* Princeton, NJ: Princeton University Press, 1984.

Lindeman, Albert S. "A Decade of War and Revolution (1914-1924)" and "The Fascist Era: Europe between the Wars." In *Esau's Tears: Modern Anti-Semitism and the Rise of the Jews.* Cambridge, UK: Cambridge University Press, 1997.

Oertelt, Henry. Videotaped interview conducted by Solomon Awend, 21 November 1995. Testimony 7069. Survivors of the Shoah Visual History Foundation, Beverly Hills, CA.

Persecution by Law

Johnson, Eric A. *Nazi Terror: The Gestapo, Jews, and Ordinary Germans.* New York: Basic Books, 1999.

Mendelsohn, John, ed. *The Holocaust.* Vol. 1, *Legalizing the Holocaust: The Early Phase, 1933-1939.* New York: Garland: 1982.

Miller, Richard Lawrence. *Nazi Justiz: Law of the Holocaust.* Westport, CT: Praeger, 1995.

Pressure and Propaganda

Burleigh, Michael, and Wolfgang Wipperman. *The Racial State: Germany 1933-1945.* New York: Cambridge University Press, 1991.

Langer, Walter C. *A Psychological Analysis of Adolph Hitler: His Life and Legend.* Washington, D.C.: Office of Strategic Services, n.d. Reprinted online by the Nizkor Project. http://www.nizkor.org.

The Yellow Spot: The Outlawing of Half a Million Human Beings. London: Victor Gollancz, 1936.

Kristallnacht

Oertelt, Henry. Videotaped interview conducted by Solomon Awend, 21 November 1995. Testimony 7069. Survivors of the Shoah Visual History Foundation, Beverly Hills, CA.

Read, Anthony, and David Fisher. *Kristallnacht: The Tragedy of the Nazi Night of Terror.* New York: Random House, 1989.

Thalman, Rita, and Emmanuel Feinermann. *Crystal Night: 9-10 November 1938.* London: Thames and Hudson, 1974.

Voluntary Emigration before the War

Drucker, Olga Levy. *Kindertransport.* New York: Holt, 1992.

Mendelsohn, John. *Jewish Emigration: The S.S. Saint Louis Affair and Other Cases.* London: Taylor and Francis, 1982.

War and Forced Resettlement

Lukas, Richard C. *The Forgotten Holocaust: The Poles under German Occupation, 1939-1944.* Lexington, KY: University Press of Kentucky, 1986.

Arriving at the "Final Solution"

Browning, Christopher R. *The Origins of the Final Solution: The Evolution of Nazi Jewish Policy, September 1939-March 1942.* Lincoln, NE: University of Nebraska Press and Yad Vashem, 2004.

Evans, Richard J. *The Third Reich in Power: 1933-1939.* New York: Penguin, 2005.

Atrocities in the War Zones

Langerbein, Helmut. *Hitler's Death Squads: The Logic of Mass Murder.* College Station, TX: Texas A&M University Press, 2004.

Life and Death in the Ghetto

Adelson, Alan, and Robert Lapides, eds. *Lodz Ghetto: Inside a Community under Siege.* New York: Viking Penguin, 1991.

Dawidowicz, Lucy S. Introduction to *A Holocaust Reader.* Edited by Lucy S. Dawidowicz. New York: Behrman House, 1976.

Landau, Elaine. *The Warsaw Ghetto Uprising.* New York: Macmillan, 1992.

Spies, Marcia Ceitlin. Videotaped interview conducted by Joyce Tapper, 31 July 1995. Testimony 4963. Survivors of the Shoah Visual History Foundation, Beverly Hills, CA.

Murder in the Concentration Camps

Arendt, Hannah. *Eichmann in Jerusalem: A Report on the Banality of Evil.* New York: Penguin, 1994.

Feig, Konnilyn G. *Hitler's Death Camps: The Sanity of Madness.* New York: Holmes & Meier, 1979.

Gottlieb, George. Videotaped interview conducted by Joan Karen Benbasat, 24 September 1996. Testimony 20035. Survivors of the Shoah Visual History Foundation, Beverly Hills, CA.

Mandel, David. Videotaped interview conducted by Elissa Schosheim, 1 February 1996. Testimony 11722. Survivors of the Shoah Visual History Foundation, Beverly Hills, CA.

Rees, Laurence. "Rudolf Höss—Commandant of Auschwitz." BBC International Online: Wars and Conflict: Genocide under the Nazis. http://www.bbc.co.uk/history/war/genocide/hoss_commandant_auschwitz_01.shtml.

Survivors of the Shoah Visual History Foundation. "Surviving Auschwitz: Five Personal Journeys." http://www.vhf.org/survivingauschwitz.

Resistance

Gutman, Yisrael. *Fighters among the Ruins: The Story of Jewish Heroism during World War II.* Washington, DC: B'nai B'rith Books, 1988.

Scholl, Inge. *The White Rose: Munich, 1942-43.* Middletown, CT: Wesleyan University Press, 1983.

Stadtler, Bea. *The Holocaust: A History of Courage and Resistance.* West Orange, NJ: Behrman House, 1994.

Hiding and Escape

Anolik, Erna Roth. Videotaped interview conducted by Suzie Eisenstock, 10 November 1996. Testimony 22586. Survivors of the Shoah Visual History Foundation, Beverly Hills, CA.

Bierman, John. *Righteous Gentile: The Story of Raoul Wallenberg, Missing Hero of the Holocaust.* New York: Anti-Defamation League, 1981.

Block, Gay, and Malka Drucker. *Rescuers: Portraits of Moral Courage in the Holocaust.* New York: Holmes and Meier, 1992.

Bluglass, Kerry. *Hidden from the Holocaust: Stories of Resilient Children Who Survived and Thrived.* Westport, CT: Praeger, 2003.

Flender, Harold. *Rescue in Denmark.* New York: Anti-Defamation League, 1963.

Fogelman, Eva. *Conscience & Courage: Rescuers of Jews during the Holocaust.* New York: Anchor Books, 1994.

Gies, Miep, and Alison L. Gold. *Anne Frank Remembered: The Story of the Woman Who Helped Hide the Frank Family.* New York: Simon and Schuster, 1988.

Gilbert, Martin. *The Righteous: The Unsung Heroes of the Holocaust.* London: Doubleday, 2002.

Keneally, Thomas. *Schindler's List.* New York: Simon and Schuster, 1992.

Mandel, David. Videotaped interview conducted by Elissa Schosheim, 1 February 1996. Testimony 11722. Survivors of the Shoah Visual History Foundation, Beverly Hills, CA.

Meltzer, Milton. *Rescue: The Story of How Gentiles Saved Jews in the Holocaust*. New York: HarperCollins Children's Books, 1991.

Tenboom, Corrie. *The Hiding Place*. New York: Bantam, 1971.

Liberation

Goebbels, Joseph. *Final Entries, 1945: The Diaries of Joseph Goebbels*. Edited by Hugh Trevor-Roper. Translated from the German by Richard Barry. New York: Putnam, 1978.

Gottlieb, George. Videotaped interview conducted by Joan Karen Benbasat, 24 September 1996. Testimony 20035. Survivors of the Shoah Visual History Foundation, Beverly Hills, CA.

Oertelt, Henry. Videotaped interview conducted by Solomon Awend, 21 November 1995. Testimony 7069. Survivors of the Shoah Visual History Foundation, Beverly Hills, CA.

Reflection

Berger, Alan L., and Naomi Berger, eds. *Second Generation Voices: Reflections by Children of Holocaust Survivors and Perpetrators*. Syracuse, NY: Syracuse University Press, 2001.

"The Cambodian Genocide Program." Yale Center for International and Area Studies, Genocide Studies Program. http://www.yale.edu/cgp/.

Conot, Robert E. *Justice at Nuremburg*. New York: Carroll and Graf, 1984.

Epstein, Helen. *Children of the Holocaust: Conversations with Sons and Daughters of Survivors*. New York: Putnam, 1979.

Hersch, Peter. Videotaped interview conducted by Ruta Osborne, 2 July 1995. Testimony 3658. Survivors of the Shoah Visual History Foundation, Beverly Hills, CA.

Lipstadt, Deborah E. *Denying the Holocaust: The Growing Assault on Truth and Memory*. New York: The Free Press, 1993.

Mandel, David. Videotaped interview conducted by Elissa Schosheim, 1 February 1996. Testimony 11722. Survivors of the Shoah Visual History Foundation, Beverly Hills, CA.

Wiesenthal, Simon. *The Murderers among Us: The Simon Wiesenthal Memoirs*. New York: McGraw-Hill, 1967.

Bibliographies

Edelheit, Abraham J., and Hershel Edelheit. *Bibliography on Holocaust Literature*. Boulder, CO: Westview Press, 1986.

Stephens, Elaine C., Jean E, Brown, and Janet E. Rubin. *Learning about the Holocaust: Literature and Other Resources for Young People*. North Haven, CT: Library Professional Publications, 1995.

Teaching about the Holocaust: A Resource Book for Educators. Washington, DC: United States Holocaust Memorial Museum, 2001.

INDEX

I

J

M

N